Carmen

A GYPSY GEOGRAPHY

Ninotchka Devorah Bennahum

Carmen

A GYPSY GEOGRAPHY

Wesleyan University Press Middletown, Connecticut

Wesleyan University Press

Middletown CT 06459

www.wesleyan.edu/wespress

© 2013 Ninotchka Devorah Bennahum

All rights reserved

Manufactured in the United States of America

Designed by Mindy Basinger Hill

Typeset in Centaur MT Pro

Library of Congress Cataloging-in-Publication Data

Bennahum, Ninotchka.

Carmen, a gypsy geography / Ninotchka Devorah Bennahum.

    pages   cm

Includes bibliographical references and index.

ISBN 978-0-8195-7353-7 (cloth : alk. paper) —

ISBN 978-0-8195-7354-4 (ebook)

1. Carmen (Fictitious character)—Historiography.

2. Romanies—Material culture.

3. Romanies—Social life and customs.

4. Romanies—Mediterranean Region.

5. Romanies—Spain. 6. Flamenco—Spain.

7. Flamenco—Social aspects—Spain. I. Title.

PN57.C33B46 2013

700'.451—dc23   2012050033

5   4   3   2   1

For my father, David Alexander Bennahum,
physician, poet, historian, who introduced me
to the notion of a feminist consciousness
many years ago and who helped me to imagine
a connection between the ancient goddess
and Carmen

For Rebecca Wright (1947–2006), ballerina
and colleague, who believed in and taught the
academic rigor of classical ballet

Contents

Illustrations

Preface

Regardless of the words, it seems the melodic contour of the song
describes the nature of the land over which the song passes . . .
Music is a memory bank for finding one's way about the world.

Bruce Chatwin, *The Songlines*

Carmen, a Gypsy Geography began as I finished the final chapter on the life of the
great Spanish dancer Antonia Mercé, *La Argentina*. Both women were dancers, one
real, the other a mirage of history, geography, and imagination.

Along with the many provincial women *La Argentina* brought to life on the
stages of Europe and America, she also danced *Carmen*, fusing the two Gypsy
dances — the *Seguidilla* (Act II) and the *Habanera* (Act IV) — into modern expressions of her Spanish nationalism. As *La Argentina* was well educated on the subject
of Gypsy *baile*, she understood their historical importance as mirrors of Spanish
history. The *Seguidilla*, descendent from the Moorish *Fandango* and *Zambra*, originated in the Mozarabic world. By the eighteenth century, it had been transformed
into the *Seguidillas Sevillanas* in Seville and the *Seguidillas Manchegas* in New Castile.
(*Manchegas*, short for La Mancha, came from the Arabic "Al Mansha," meaning
the dry land or wilderness between Madrid and Andalusia.)

The *habanera* also came from pre-Inquisition Spain. But rather than developing
as a multiethnic dance form inside of Spain, the *habanera* was imported from the
Spanish Caribbean. As Seville was the largest slave port in Europe in the fifteenth
century, the African and Caribbean rhythmic influence on the evolution of Gypsy
flamenco and the Spanish court influence on dances circulating throughout the
Afro-Caribbean were significant. *La Argentina* had learned the original *habanera* in
1915, on tour in Havana. She transposed it into a Gypsy *baile*, adding two layers
of rhythm — footwork sequences and castanets — to the original choreography.
She understood that the choreographic folklore housed in *Carmen* was, in fact, a

looking glass from which she could continue her archeological study of Spanish dance history.

During a first research trip to the Parisian libraries of spectacle—the Arsenal, Richelieu and the Paris Opéra—I studied Georges Bizet's stage notes written into the corners of his original score for the premiere production of *Carmen* on 3 March 1875. Bizet notated substantial choreographic stage directions, drawing attention to the physicality of the singer's body in relation to the score.[1] I subsequently studied hundreds of productions of *Carmen*, from its 1875 failure in Paris to its Viennese success later that year and throughout the world thereafter. I hoped that by tracing the choreography for the second and fourth acts of the opera, I might be able to explore the evolution of flamenco as danced throughout the world inside of Bizet's orientalist, romantic staging of Prosper Mérimée's *novella*. But this was not the story that I wanted to tell.[2]

Upon returning from Europe, I bought a ticket in New York to see Salvador Tavora's *Carmen*, a dance-theatre, Gypsy flamenco production on tour from Seville. I had seen Tavora's magical realism in 1991 in 'Al Hama de Granada, a village abandoned by its former Arab inhabitants and located forty-five kilometers from Granada, where celebrated baños (hot springs) have drawn Andalusians in search of medicinal healing since before the Hispano-Arab conquest of Spain in the eighth century. It was a fantasy tale told through flamenco *compás* (rhythm). The *cante* carried the story, the singer seated on a makeshift, raised wooden platform inside the patio of an old convent—*el patio del Carmen*. Tavora's *Carmen* was scheduled to open in New York on 11 September 2001. Two days later, on 13 September, by order of the mayor, City Center became the sole theater in New York City to be open, an historical first. The show was free to anyone who went—and everyone went.

New Yorkers stood through long portions of *Carmen*, shoulder to shoulder. It was as if they needed, finally, to touch each other, to know that they were alive, safe, still breathing. *Carmen* began with the traditional Spanish brass: thirty-two cornets used both in the opening procession of the bullfight and to great effect by Bizet in Act I of *Carmen*, to signal the fate that Carmen personifies. As used by the Falange in the Spanish Civil War, the cornets resounded loudly, penetrating in their call, a brassy *llamada* that signaled the start of the tale.

Tavora's *Carmen* was by no means brilliant. It did not compare to Rafael Aguilar's robust portrayal of *Carmen*, also told through flamenco, Gypsy choreography, and dramaturgical direction. (I had seen Aguilar's in Paris, a welcome destination for Gypsy artists dancing full-length Flamenco-theater works.) But I shall never forget that show: Carmen murdered by Don José, her crime, a desire to be free. She is sacrificed to a man's will.[3]

I began chasing Carmen in an almost obsessive manner. I read close to two thousand press reviews from around the world from 1875 to the present. I began to understand her cult-like following in opera houses, movie theatres, and on concert stages throughout the world. Why, I kept asking myself, should this beautiful piece of music be the most performed opera in history? Carmen, in her emotional intensity, albeit mythic, and her bold desire to be free, to drink the riches of life, seem to me to be the true underpinnings of the opera's worldwide success.

Two years later, I joined the History Department at the University of Colorado at Boulder as a visiting professor. The chair, Thomas Zeiler, a baseball and diplomatic historian, asked me to teach a class in the history of the Middle East, as my specialty was Gypsy history and culture and diasporic performance arts. I discovered a wonderful collection of Muslim theology and of Middle Eastern history in the university's library and read in translation the medieval Muslim, Sephardic, and Christian scholars of Islamic Spain. Particularly interesting were the works of Muslim geographers and Sephardic translation scholars who traveled between Muslim Spain, North Africa, and the Middle East, working in various courts and port cities along the way. In their poetic writings and descriptive analyses, the culturally rich worldview of the Mozarabic Renaissance was revealed.

I also absorbed the histories of Americo Castro, Henri Pirenne, and Bernard Lewis. Here, among theology, philosophy, and history, I began to weave connections between flamenco and the Gypsy presence in Spain as a receptacle for the rich cultures and peoples expelled formally by the Spanish in 1492 (the Jews) and 1508 (the Muslims). In my classroom at CU-Boulder and in the library, I found Carmen.

She became a symbol of all women, not just of nineteenth-century orientalist opera, but also of the women of the medieval and ancient Middle East and Maghreb regions. Carmen first appeared in a romanticized novella that sets up a character study of a woman, Carmen, and a man, Don José, in the midst of the geography and history of Andalusia. This was the hot, dry land where the Gypsies hid and, finally, settled between the early Middle Ages and the twenty-first century.

Carmen appears to Mérimée through a puff of smoke; he is smoking the very tobacco she rolls when he catches a glimpse of her. The reader is left with the poetic impression that it is not he who sees her first, who invents her, but rather she who sees him, who invents him. In Carmen, Mérimée, who spent fifteen years shaping her character, unearthed himself.

Carmen's role links her to earlier cultures and their images of women. Through

Carmen I explore how the ancient Middle East, Islamic Spain, and nineteenth-century France viewed and treated women. It is no accident that Carmen is born in a time of the frenzied regulation of middle- and upper-class women's lives and bodies. Her resonance as a libertine spirit inside this conservative, bourgeois milieu made her all the more seductive a character, and all the more annoying to the French audience whose rejection of the opera became historic.

Overnight, thanks to the French critics, Carmen became famous, the embodiment in popular consciousness of the anti-heroine, the "bad girl." While the novella seemed tame enough as she did not appear in the flesh (in fact, it met with immense popular success, published as a serial in *La Revue des Deux Mondes*), the opera and its real-life *femme* did not fare as well. A "real" Carmen brought to life on stage led to a barrage of criticism that literally ritualized her, sacrificing even Bizet's complex, thematic melodies in favor of middle-class morality. Until she was surely dead and gone, the critics continued to publish articles linking her singing voice to "evil." Herein began a complex historiography of prejudice against the ideal Gypsy woman whose crime was to be free.

Most academic studies of Carmen, whether literary, operatic, filmic or theatrical, center upon her as a Gypsy *femme fatale*, at times earthy and sensual, at others lascivious, aggressive, uncontrollable. While some late twentieth-century writers like Winton Dean, Mina Kirstein Curtiss, Evelyn Gould, Susan McClary, Carolyn Abbate, Catherine Clément, and Lou Charnon-Deutsch have written excellent books that expand the symbolism of Carmen and her musical and literary character, none focus on the dance history that represents her status in the novella, in film, and on the operatic stage.[4] They may discuss her musical identity, as does Abbate, but none discuss choreographic history and analysis as central to an investigation of her character and public representation. Furthermore, they do not explain her cultural significance earlier than the nineteenth century. We will find that, for Bizet, Carmen's power, her resonance as a woman, is in the way she moves across the stage. Influenced by Delsarte, Bizet understood the power of corporeality expressed both in the voice and in the movement of the body as she crosses the stage. To ignore this is to ignore Bizet.

While these authors, to whom I am indebted, helped me capture the landscape of criticism to date, I was left wondering how the very essence of Carmen — a Gypsy living in Spain — came to life in the European mind. So I began here: Carmen remained a product of the European Romantic imagination as she emerged from Prosper Mérimée's ethnographic study of Gypsy culture inside of Spain in 1830, as well as from his close reading of Gypsyologist George Henry Borrow's books.

Gypsy Woman Dancing, photograph by Gaston Paris, n.d.
Gaston Paris / Roger-Viollet Archives, Paris, France

To explore what Carmen means, I have constructed a narrative that moves through geography, mythography, ethnography, and history, centering on the mythical, musical, dance, and poetic cultures that produced Gypsy flamenco. The most profound sources remain the novel and the libretto, and from them I take my lead.

The Theoretical Introduction lays out the theories surrounding my analysis of *Carmen* and demonstrates how the historical, literary, and theoretical ideas fuse into single chapters. It begins with the theory of myth; through the characterizations of Carmen on stage, in literature, and on screen, I attempt to draw for the reader a history of Gypsy women. In so doing, I invoke the writings of Gaston Bachelard and Walter Benjamin, as well as the multidisciplined writings of historians such as Henri Pirenne (*Mohammad and Charlemagne*), Americo Castro (*The Structure of Spanish History*), Fernand Braudel (*Memory and the Mediterranean* and *A History of Civilizations*), William McNeill (*The Rise of the West*), Gerda Lerner (*The Creation of Patriarchy* and *The Creation of Feminist Consciousness*), and Bernard Lewis (*The Muslim Discovery of Europe*; *The Arabs in History*; *The Middle East*). I add to social history the philosophical writing of Henri Bergson, the phenomenological writings of Gaston Bachelard, Islamic art and architectural history, flamencology, border theory, travel writers, nineteenth-, twentieth-, and twenty-first century Gypsy ethnologists and musicologists and, finally, the philosophy of Gilles Deleuze.

French theorists and Mérimée scholars, as well as *Carmenistas* (Carmen scholars), have been seminal in unraveling intellectual views of *Carmen* since the 1960s. But it is the literary work of Prosper Mérimée and the score and its changes by Georges Bizet that leave the most important footprints for anyone interested in the history of Carmen. I am grateful to these tracings. I think of them as road maps, methodology that helps me advance a theory of Carmen and of *Carmen*.

Chapters 1 and 2 follow the men who imagined these many Gypsy figures in the character of Carmen. Both chapters are biographical studies of *Carmen, la novella* and of the opera *Carmen*, as well as of Prosper Mérimée and Georges Bizet. Chapter 1 begins with a bio-historical sketch of Mérimée, who imagined Carmen, giving birth to an idea that reached the status of myth in mid-nineteenth-century Europe. Chapter 2 explores how music, stage design, literary tale, and history fuse to draw out multiple images of a woman who lives in many cultures and geographies at once. Interestingly, Mérimée and Bizet sketched Carmen many times over many years. She occupied their consciousness in previous works before becoming the character she elicits in both the novella and the opera.

Chapter 3 offers the idea that Carmen represents an atavistic link to previous cultures. I study her ritual importance to ancient culture as depicted on cave walls and pottery, as well as the symbolism of the female body and her spiritual and social meaning in ancient Mesopotamian agricultural communities. I propose the notion that, on a narrative level, Carmen is the symbolic representation of the fertility goddess of the ancient Mediterranean world whose image endures to this day. She continues to fascinate artists and audiences alike, her essence resonating with good and evil, sacred and demonic. Mérimée's Gypsy dancer and Bizet's character reflect the mythic embodiment of a *gitana*, whose morphology in

Spanish and European cultural memory recalls the female principle embodied in the great goddess and her relationship to the moon. It is here at the pre-historical level that we unearth the key iconography of Carmen: the male/female fusion of moon and bull, symbolism that will dominate Picasso's interpretation of Carmen.

Chapter 4 traces the migration of the Gypsy from India to Spain, moving along the port cities that hug the Mediterranean coastline. I describe the evolution of flamenco *cante*, *baile*, and *toque* and discuss the rich cultural tradition of Mozarabs, Hispano-Arabs, and Sephardim in Andalusia, into which the Gypsies entered and settled just prior to the Spanish Inquisition that began in 1478.

Gypsies came to Rome from India in 1422 and to Barcelona from Rome in 1423. By the sixteenth century, they had migrated along the southern and western Iberian coast, traveling north across the Pyrénées and into southern French villages and towns, lands once occupied by the Moors — Toulouse, Narbonne, Poitiers. I narrate their rejection as outsiders in each place that they settled in Europe.

The chapter continues by introducing the Gypsy migrant into the Renaissance culture of Andalusia, the tri-cultural traditions — Mozarabic, Sephardic, and Christian — that enriched its musical, literary, and architectural worlds. I trace a connection between the physical environment into which the Gypsy walked in the fifteenth century and the birth of flamenco. Flamenco is the dance form that embodies and communicates Gypsy culture. This chapter, theoretical at base, muses upon the relationship between flamenco and public, secular, and religious Islamic architectural spaces. I examine how space, flamenco, and chant meet inside alcazars and mosques, and argue how these architectural shapes that surround the body with dozens of dizzying columns and sublime light helped the Gypsy dancer embody choreography, song, and movement — a mobile historical document, mapping identities now long gone from Andalusia. I posit the following questions: Is it mere coincidence that flamenco has the same number of movements as Arab music? Is the centering and re-centering of the flamenco *bailaora* in the deep song *soleá* a mapping of identity reflective of the contemplative portals and pathways in the Andalusian mosque and garden, seen as routes of spiritual passage? Furthermore, I look into the way Arab music and flamenco are related and speculate about links between Gypsy art and medieval and Renaissance Spanish history.

Chapter 5 traces another space in the nomadic geography of the Gypsy dancer as she emerges, as if out of the sand, to appear in the cafés of the Northern African coastline. It is there that she becomes a dancer in the male-populated cafés of the Middle East, tourist destination of European Romanticism.

Chapter 6 completes this study of *Carmen* through the work of the modern Spanish master Pablo Picasso. Picasso's interest in Carmen originated in 1896 when he first drew her image, a portrait. The representation and character of Carmen moved through his life in Barcelona where, as a young, impoverished art student and painter, he lived next door to the Gypsies. The chapter then studies Picasso's use of Carmen to translate his own exploration of masculinity and femininity through his Minotaur series and his drawings of bullfights. Through his images of the man-beast and the death ring, Carmen's libertine spirit, physicality, eroticism, and sexuality emerge as central themes in his painting, sculpture, and drawing. Like Carmen, Picasso emerged from the shores of Andalusia; a Gypsy and a Spaniard in search of identity.

Chapter 7 studies several excellent early and late historiographic approaches to the notion of contact between Arabs and Christians in the eighth century. It continues, investigating the arguments of Henri Pirenne, Americo Castro, and Bernard Lewis and developing an image of Islamic Spain as it comes into being, architecturally and socially, between the ninth and fifteenth centuries. This is the world the Gypsy entered in the fifteenth century. On linguistic, architectural, religious, and socioeconomic levels, Islamic-Mozarabic Spain, situated in 'Al Andalus, was extraordinary in its triptych of cultures. Complex, wealthy, and literate, it boasted rich court and street cultures that, I argue, affected the birth of a modern art form, flamenco. I argue that the Gypsy becomes a receptacle for the popular cultures and histories through which she passes.

Chapter 8, the culmination of this archeological study of Carmen, houses five close readings of seminal performances of *Carmen* and the Carmenian *Siguiríya*. Finally, I add the coda, a close reading of a particular dance performance that aims to illuminate a final image concept from throughout the book. I analyze significant historical moments in the choreography, identifying, in Deleuzian terms, theoretical points in the dance.

Acknowledgments

I have been chasing Carmen most of my life or, perhaps, she's been chasing me. In theaters, archives, *tablaos*, flamenco studios, and on concert stages, I have searched for her. This book articulates the spiritual, geographic map of that experience and hunt.

Writing a book is a labor of love and many people contribute to its final shape. First I must thank my editor, the Editor-in-Chief of Wesleyan University Press, Suzanna Tamminen, for her belief in what she termed a "poetic history" of flamenco and in the idea that the female body — that of the Gypsy dancer — could house history and hold it in the bounds of human form, allowing it to flow forth into present-day consciousness as she moves across the stages of the Islamic Mediterranean world. I would also like to thank the staff of Wesleyan University Press, in particular Leslie Starr, and the University Press of New England, Amanda Dupuis and Rosemary Williams, as well as seminal dance editor/writer Elizabeth Zimmer for her excellent editorial eye.

Secondly, I am indebted to my good friend Daniel Potter, literary theorist and information designer, who taught me through generous and painstaking analysis to understand and articulate the theoretical space of the body in historical and literary analysis. Had it not been for these discussions and endless editing, this work would not have come to be.

While enrolled in Professor Robert DuPlessis' History seminar, *Women and Social Change*, my father gave me several books of female poets from the ancient Middle East, including Lerner's *The Majority Finds Its Past: Placing Women in History*. *Carmen, a Gypsy Geography* originated in DuPlessis' seminar and in the idea that women drive history and contribute to its shape, flow, and historical articulation.

I am forever lucky that my mother is Professor Emerita Judith Chazin-Benna-hum. In her many published works and our numerous coffee-talks, she communicated to me her commitment to the steps of a dance as constructing a language worthy of close study; a vocabulary of movement that drives historical experience. I am also grateful to Professor Lynn Garafola, whose ability to see clearly the shape of history, and dance's place in it, always seems magical. I feel indebted to Professors Michelle Heffner-Hayes and Sharon Friedler who believed in each *escobílla*—entrance and exit of Carmen, the ultimate Gypsy flamenco *bailaora*—and helped it come to be. Their feminist interpretations of dancers' movements have long inspired me. For new, Africanist perspectives on Flamenco and Gypsy cultural history, I welcome the inspiring new scholarship of Dr. Meira Goldberg and Dr. Katita Milazzo. And thank you to Susan Glazer, Director of the School of Dance at the University of the Arts, who gave me the courage to really teach from my gut.

I would also like to thank my friend and colleague, the Editor-in-Chief of *Dance Magazine*, Wendy Perron, with whom I've hung out many a night after the theater discussing the notion of female choreographic embodiment and the global explosion of female dance artists. I am forever grateful to my great friend, choreographic new media artist and composer, Kim Arrow, who has always thrown lightning bolts of creative inspiration my way.

I am indebted to the staff of the Bibliothèque Nationale de l'Opéra, especially chief music librarian, Romain Feist, and archivist, Valerie Gressel, who over the course of many visits helped me to unearth archives ranging from Bizet's scores to bullfighting; the staff of the New York Public Library for the Performing Arts; and the librarians at L'Institut du Monde Arabe. I thank especially curator and matador Patrick Simeon of the Musée des Cultures Taurines in Nîmes for educating me on the subject of the French bullfight. I am also grateful to Tanisha Jones, Director of the Moving Image Archive of the Special Research Collections of the New York Public Library for the Performing Arts at Lincoln Center, as well as the head of Photographic Archives, Alice Standin, and the wonderful curators Barbara Cohenstratyner and Jan Schmidt. I would like in addition to express my gratitude to the staff at the Roger-Viollet Archives, who helped me to place photographs in this book, and to Christine Pinault of the Musée Picasso.

For her many lessons on the twin subjects of feminist archiving and desert peoples, I thank Roselyne Chenu for the courage with which she lives. I am grateful to Antoine Malmoud for his help with the Musée Picasso in Paris and Kate Butler for her curatorial advice on the subjects of Picasso and Surrealism. And I am indebted to seminal Mérimée scholar from the Centre National du Recherche, Antonia Fonyi, and Jean-Marie and Gemmia LeClézio for their discussion on the subject of the desert and notions of Romantic escape.

And I would like to thank the wonderful faculty and staff and dancers at

American Ballet Theater, some of whom I have had the honor of working with and learning from since 1996: Kevin McKenzie, Rachel Moore, Mary Jo Ziesel, Christine Spizzo, and Raymond Serrano (1950–2010), Susan Jaffe, Melissa Bowman, Heidi Gunter, Molly Schnyder, Raymond Lukens, and Leslie Browne. I am grateful for each day that I can stand outside a dance studio and watch you work. Teaching dance history to generations of dancers from around the world and bearing witness to a veritable creative explosion in ballet performance continues to be an honor and a pleasure. The groundbreaking theoretical ballet technique and training by ballet masters, Franco da Vita and Raymond Lukens, in particular, has taught me a great deal about the intellectualism and rigor of ballet. Each step performed daily renews the place of the body in history.

I thank my teachers: Bob Wolfe (Piano), Lucy Hayden (Ballet), T. Kaori Kitao (Art History and Aesthetics), Selma-Jeanne Cohen (Dance History), Robert DuPlessis (Women's History and Social Change); Marjorie Murphy (American History), Cynthia Novack (Cultural Anthropology of Dance), Brooks McNamara (Popular Culture), Richard Schechner (Performance Studies), Deborah Jowitt (Dance Criticism), Mark Franko (Performance Theory), Peggy Phelan (Feminist Theory), all of whom taught me to see. I thank wholeheartedly Vice-President for Academic Affairs, Long Island University, Dr. Jeffrey Kane.

For their infinite love and wisdom, I thank sincerely my friends and colleagues: William Burgos, Stuart Fishelson, Linda Tomko, Marcellus Blount, Janice Ng, Elisso Tarassachvili, Roz Gershell, Brett Fortier, Megan Duke, Eric Saunders, Jan Rosenberg and Fred Siegel, Eric Foner, and Scott and Christine Sunquist who let me live in their little flat in Paris, affording me endless research time in Paris; Annie Maïllis, bullfighting and Picasso aficionado, whose insight into southern Arab-French culture has greatly inspired this text; Ellen Crane and Ron Fried, the late Mitch Goldbaum, Sophia Fatouros, Weedy Paige Abrams and Scottie Fliegel, David Thornquist and Jane Potter, Andrea and Phil Gordon; the loving staff at Beit Ha Yeladim Preschool and Rabbi Steve Cohen; and my colleagues at the University of California, Santa Barbara: Dean David Marshall; Director of the University Art Museum and American art historian Bruce Robertson; creative installer and artist, Rollin Fortier; art historian Anne Birmingham and Interdisciplinary Humanities Center administrator Emily Zinn; artist/scholar Kim Yasuda; graphic artist Alejandro Casazi and race historian Bianca Brigadi; race sociologist Emiko Saldivar and cultural anthropologist Casey Walsh; classicists Francis Dunn and Dorota Dutsch; and wonderful colleagues and staff in the Department of Dance and Theater: Suk-Young Kim, Christina McMahon, Eric

Mills, Linda Flegal, Irwin Appel, Nancy Colahan, Valerie Houston, Christina McCarthy, Delila Moseley, Jerry Pearson, Mira Kingsley, Christopher Pilafian, Leo Cabranes-Grant, Davies King, Carlos Morton, Annie Torsiglieri, Risa Brainin, Michael Morgan, Tom Withaker, Ellen Anderson, Susan MacMillan, Renita Davenport, Mary Tench, Debi Vance; dear friends: Howard and Joanne Chase, Dr. Suki John, Dean Jim Linnell and Jennifer Predock-Linnell, María Benitez, Martin Santangelo and Soledad Barrio, impresaria and friend Carlota Santana, Marilyn Tyler for her insight into the score of *Carmen*, which she has sung many times; seminal flamenco artists, Eva Enciñas-Sandoval, Marisol and Joaquin Enciñas. And thank you to my daughter's father, Carlos René Siverio, IT engineer par excellence and loyal friend who thankfully never tires of walking around the City.

And to my beloved family: my grandmother, Midge Bennahum (1913–1991), whom I still miss daily—always a bit of a Gypsy herself; my great aunt Stella Fischbach (1909–2012) for her infinite strength of character and clarity of mind; my grandfather Maurice Chazin (1905–1992), who himself left behind files and books that reveal his own exploration into the rich cultures of the Islamic Mediterranean and Andalusian worlds; my cousins David Solomon Bennahum, Hillary Raphael, James and Therese Lack, and Samantha Bennahum; my uncle, Rabbi Joel Chazin; my stepchildren, Sarah and Kevin Black, and parents-in-law emeritus, Marge and Stan Black; my cousin, the fine poet Judy Berke; my insightful, magical sister, Rachel Sarah Bennahum, and her beautiful family; my brother Aaron Daniel Bennahum and sister-in-law, Elizabeth Aikens, artists in their own right; and, finally, to my beautiful daughter, Mariana Lucia Bennahum, now four years old, who has brought infinite light to my life.

Carmen

A GYPSY GEOGRAPHY

A Theoretical Introduction

Spain is a bundle of local units tied together by a rope of sand.

Richard Ford, *Hand-book for Travellers in Spain and Readers at Home, Describing the Country and Cities*[1]

[Spain] is a collection of small, mutually hostile or indifferent republics held together in a loose federation. At certain great periods (the Caliphate, the *Reconquista*, the *Siglo de Oro*), these small centers have been infected by a common feeling or idea and have moved in unison and then disbanded into political fragmentation.

Gerald Brenan, *The Spanish Labyrinth: An Account of the Social and Political Background of the Civil War*[2]

History deals with connections and with arbitrarily elaborated casual chains. But since history affords an idea of the fundamental citability of its object, this object must present itself, in its ultimate form, as a moment of humanity. In this moment, time must be brought to a standstill.

Walter Benjamin, *Theses on the Philosophy of History*[3]

Historians have written hundreds of histories of Spain. Their work explores political, religious, social, and economic change over time. Some writers, like Raymond Carr and Bernard Lewis, have produced seminal texts that constitute a history of things Spanish. Lewis, in particular, is a pleasure to read because of his extraordinarily rich, multilingual investigation of Muslim, Sephardic, and Christian Spain. Carr echoes Lewis's attempt to transport the reader to a past time, producing populist histories that credit the peasant and the unnamed manual laborer, creating an Andalusian identity that extends to modern Spain. In asking, for example, why "neither the Christian kings, nor the Moors triumphed over the forces of centripetal localism" that govern Spain to this day, Carr points to the difficult nature of excavating the Spanish past.[4] Still, to Carr and Lewis, the finest of them all, Spanish history is revealed through conquest and political will. Their histories are translations of events past, derived from detailed and interesting documents.[5]

It is ironic that Gypsy artists, who not only transported eastern musical and dance forms into Spain but fused them with Mozarabic and Sephardic influences, should be so marginalized in Spanish history. If the Gypsy, illiterate and itinerant, is barely noted by historians studying Spain, how is his/her contribution to time and Andalusian identity recorded? I would argue that flamenco—the cultural currency of the Gypsy and the most important element in Andalusian, Carmenian, Gypsy identity—provides the key. Gypsy history lives in the *baile* (the dance) and the *cante* (the song). In these explosive, self-positioning acts of communication and expressivity is to be found the history of Carmen and of the Gypsy, the nomadic outsider on European soil. The *cante jondo*, the guttural deep song and wailing prayer of the beat poet narrator of every Gypsy dance, is a historiographic act of retrieval, the uninscribed past pulled by the *cantaor* into the present. Their narrative, individual interpretations of collective memory unfold before the audience.

"We need history," Walter Benjamin tells us, quoting Friedrich Nietzsche, "but our need for it differs from that of the jaded idlers in the garden of knowledge."[6] While historians remind us that the Iberians, Carthaginians, Phoenicians, Greeks, Romans, Visigoths, Moors, Jews, and Christians left something behind for us to know them by, I wonder how the presence of history—its immanence—might not be the artifact for which they search to unearth a meaning of things in sequential rather than poetic order. Can historians' interpretations of the past change through studying the dancing body, the Gypsy *flamenca*? Could the notion of artifact be expanded?

I believe the figure of Carmen, in essence a figure of the presence of the past on stage at any given moment in time, is the "document" for which we search. Her fingers, hands, arms, and feet inscribe a map of the world—an intensely personal geography—that traces her conscious memory of the present moving back into the past and returning to center again at the end of a long *Soleá*.

> Momentary whims begin, given a certain accumulation, to sketch an itinerary,
> to map the imaginary land that stretches out inside of us.[7]

The second reason I question the value of histories that attempt to reach into the past to interpret the present and see into the future is that the Gypsy, to his/her mind, has no history. Yet she, like Carmen, lives. Politically, religiously, and economically peripheral to the natural order of things Spanish, the Gypsy has lost her place in conscious memory or in what Walter Benjamin reminds us is a group of people, the redeemed of humankind who are "granted fullness of [their] past."[8]

Arriving at a Gypsy history, at their contribution to the spirit of Spain, is very difficult, in part because they recycle a mystique about themselves and their long journey from India and Egypt to Spain. After centuries of abuse by local authorities, they tend to fabricate and obfuscate both identity and history in order to protect themselves. Gypsy history, as any fine *cantaor* will tell you, happens in the present. As Henri Bergson argues, history is in the *durée*, the time between the singer's wail and the dancer's quicksilver call back to him. The Gypsy's history is a lived one. It can only be read from the stage where, in the most precious space of liberty, the dancer and singer bear witness to the moment as past and present fuse inextricably as one. Like a Tibetan sand painting, Gypsy history cannot be held or owned or archived; it must be experienced in the moment of its execution. This aesthetic anarchism — mocking traditional forms of rendering meaning and memorializing them — is uncannily present in the figure and movement of Carmen.

I turn to Walter Benjamin and Henri Bergson for entrance into the notion of immanence as historical time. In his seminal 1940 essay, "On the Concept of History," Benjamin writes:

> The past carries with it a secret index by which it is referred to redemption. Doesn't a breath of the air that pervaded earlier days caress us as well? In the voices we hear, isn't there an echo of now silent ones? . . . If so, then there is a secret agreement between past generations and the present one. Then our coming was expected on earth. Then, like every generation that preceded us, we have been endowed with a *weak* messianic power, a power on which the past has a claim. Such a claim cannot be settled cheaply. The historical materialist is aware of this.[9]

Perhaps El Greco (1541–1614) in his *View of Toledo* (1596–1600) best captures the religious and moral angst of post-Inquisition Spain. His distillation of the tragedy is channeled through images of wrapped space and jagged hillside physiognomy that look as if someone has twisted the land until it cracked. El Greco demonstrates in pigment and hue — in the violence and emotionalism of his grays, blues, whites, and blacks — the existential loss to Spain of the Jews and the Arabs at the hands of the Holy See. This painting asks us to remember that, for the impoverished heirs of *El Siglo del Oro*, the sound of Arabic is missing in the streets.[10] A man of El Greco's sensitivity was able to translate this loss into pigment.

The Theoretical Ideas That Surround This Gypsy Geography

> If we could enter into an image, if we could sympathize with it, we
> would sense ourselves caught between one idea and another and thus
> we would sense pieces of the idea or the image as we reside there. The
> intuition of duration is the intuition of what is other.
>
> Henri Bergson, *The Creative Mind*[11]

The seminal French philosopher and theorist Henri Bergson (1859–1941) aids us in deciphering the historical riddles placed before the audience as the dancers move through time and space. Bergson, the first Jew to be elected to the Académie Française, reveals in *The Creative Mind* (*La Pensée et le mouvant, essais et conferences*, 1934) that to allow an historical idea — a work of art — to be meaningful, to acquire historical mobility, the viewer must develop intuition — that is to say, sympathy or even empathy. To do so, one must enter art, rather than approach it, as historians tend to do, from the outside. For Bergson, to enter into a work in a given moment in time or, in the case of dance or fiction, to become one with its being — its temporality, its tempo — is to seize ourselves from within, to "install oneself within the *durée*" — the duration or time signature — of the experience in order to feel a "certain well-defined tension whose very determinateness seems like a choice between an infinity of possible durations," or possible historical interpretations.

> In the durée, one can speak of the experience of freedom. Freedom is mobility.
> Duration is memory: the prolongation of the past into the present.[12]

Freedom is the essence of the Gypsy experience and is at the heart of Carmen; to be free, to live free, to die free. To unpack the past-presentness of the character of Carmen, we must be able to resonate with — to experience — her longing for freedom as temporally present and prescient. She turns her people's misfortune into fortune, her historical elision into presence. If we can enter into the work of art — into the *Soleá* — what then can we glean from Gypsy history, Gypsy experience, Gypsy geography? Here is where Benjamin and Bergson become relevant. In both philosophers' discussions of *immanence*, we glimpse the ability of the viewer to physically and psychically enter into the work of art, into the moment of performance and elided history. This notion of immanence, to my mind, becomes almost Kabbalistic. The person entering the work moves into the light and dark spaces of the performative event, living, embodying, and understanding on a psychic level how the shards of history become whole.

Bergson believed that to enter the work of art was to "sense ourselves caught" in the moment.[13] I sat once in the Albaicín, the Gypsy quarter of Granada, listening to a flamenco singer and guitarist and staring up at the massive stonewalls of the Alhambra palace. As I heard the Arabic and Sephardic-sounding rhythms and intonations I felt transported at once into the palace itself, back in time. It was as if the present-ness of the *cante* at that moment and the past-ness of the Gypsy's complex relationship to Spanish history had fused in the bounds of sound. Experiencing or analyzing duration, or *la durée*, Bergson continues, becomes a means of integrating one's experience with infinity of durations.[14] Intuition is thus an "integral experience" made up of an infinite series of acts that correspond to degrees of durées. While *la durée* certainly does not explain the entire experience, the experience is still an integral one in the specific sense of integrating an infinity of durations. We cannot know all durations. The durée is that to which everything is related. Intuition is memory. This gives one the ability to enter into the moment of history itself, to not only sympathize with it but to have an "integral experience" of it, to understand it from within.

And then there is the idea of the image as less a thing, an object of perception, and more of a representation—the outline of the thing, its suggestive qualities, its historicity. Bergson introduces the idea of the internal order of things. In its Hispano-Arab and Sephardic cross-culturalism expressed through its singer's quasi-religious chanting and its dancer's mapping of an unsettled, nomadic identity on stage, flamenco explodes with anger and control at various moments in time. It is as if the dancer is tracing the painful history of the Gypsy, negotiating his/her peripheral status in Europe as itinerant musician (or as *archivist*), carrying from stage right to stage left a prescient consciousness of things past and things to come. The dancer finishes each *esobillo*—or danced passage—exhausted; the weight of the truth presses down too heavily, pushing her back into the earth from which she comes.

The richness in Bergson is the notion that if we can enter into an image—a moment in performative time—we can empathize with it and, therefore, come to know or sense the idea or image in which we reside. Our intuition of its duration—of *la durée*—metamorphoses into an understanding of what is other—other than us, and thereby something we in turn become, if only fleetingly.

Marcel Proust, Bergson's maternal cousin, created an epic personal narrative, *À la recherche du temps perdu*, out of the notion of capturing lost moments.[15] At each juncture of my research, I have landed at an undocumented moment of the Gypsy. This predicament has led me to crystallize images of a Proustian nature to try to explain the past-present geography of Carmen. In this narrative, Proust teaches us the notion of a sudden surge of memory that enters into us, without warning, through sensorial gateways. The experience of recall insists on the presence of the past with an emotional force perhaps stronger than any document. If each moment in a performance fuses into a genealogy of time, then the logical purpose of performance, in this case flamenco, would be to endow the spectator with historical memory as sudden, ecstatic recollection.

In an attempt to analyze the dance itself—the *baile* as artifact, as evidence of historical consciousness—I turn to the seminal German-Jewish literary philosopher Walter Benjamin (1892–1940). Gypsy identity—Carmen's fictional and onstage identity—is contained in movement and sung verse. Each performance, each *Soleá* or *Siguiríya*—dances from the deep song flamenco canon—represents an individually expressive interpretation of Gypsy history. The unfolding of hands, the circling of the stage (discussed in Chapters 7 and 8) give individual voice to the meaning, the cultural currency, the memory and historical consciousness of each member of a Gypsy clan. To most traditional historians, these dances are not seen as evidence of historical time—as events—or even as historical truths. Rather, they are simply songs and dances. But to a Gypsy, the *baile* and the *cante* resonate Gypsy experience in time and place. This is where the Bergsonian theory (reflective of Gaston Bachelard's notion) of *élan vital*, or impulse, comes into play. I interpret vitality as animist, a force of nature: producing and releasing a historically stored-up energy to the spectator through movement and sound.

Henri Bergson's notion of "integral experience" becomes relevant here. In *The Creative Mind*, he lays out the notion of experience as an "indefinite series of acts which correspond" to one another as degrees of duration, or *la durée*. The interrelationship between *les durées*, their *intertextuality*, I take to mean as their dialectical discourse (or dialogue)—the temporal relationship of flamenco movements to the musical notes. The tenor of each note, ranging from *melismata* elongation to percussive stops, lends emotional resonance to the piece and affects how the dancer emerges on stage as woman and artist. If it is understood that each movement, each note, and the tempo with which they are delivered can be considered artifacts of the Gypsy experience, then her body's generation of movements at various speeds may in fact bear witness to her historical consciousness. This experience can never be static, as flamenco is built on improvisation. If the *esobíllo*, or flamenco passage—utterance—is self-determined, at the will of the performer, then each performer will generate reflections upon past experience each time she dances or sings on stage.

Young Gypsy Dancer, Sacromonte, Granada, photographer and date unknown.
Roger-Viollet Archives, Paris, France

Further, Bergson in *Matter and Memory* discusses his theory of consciousness as "matter resolve[d] into numberless vibrations, all linked together in uninterrupted continuity, all bound up with each other and traveling in every direction like shivers."[16] If these mindful vibrations could be considered flamenco motions, then the choreographic invention of the Gypsy artist might also be considered a conscious and successive attempt to reproduce one's view of history *ad infinitum* on stage.

Finally, in several performance readings of Gypsy flamenco *Carmens*, I turn to the French Philosopher Gilles Deleuze (1925–1995) and his notion of the "plane of immanence," important to his work on Spinoza and most fully developed in 1995 in his co-authored book with Félix Guattari *What is Philosophy?* I apply Deleuze's notion of "*a pure plane of embeddedness, an unqualified immersion,* an infinite smooth space," to the concept of Carmen as nomadic historian.[17] In the case of flamenco, Carmen dances on a plane of immanence. The opera's performance history itself is seen here as a series of becomings without *telos*.

Bernard Lewis has provided me the most insight into Muslim Spain. Lewis creates a portrait in words by describing the keys from a Jewish home in Andalusia that now hang on the wall of a Moroccan house, offering evidence of the range of artifacts useful in interpreting historical events and the notion of memory.[18] But the philosophical approach to history offered by Bergson, Benjamin, Bachelard, and Proust has given me the courage to consider the flamenco *baile* as a living historical document, its shreds of evidence ever-changing, radiating unwritten and unwritable history in the present moment of appearance.

The Gypsy, in this case Carmen, has no home. In the third act of the opera, she and her Gypsy smuggler colleagues walk up the steep slopes of the Sierra Morenos, Bizet's sonorous translation of their homelessness and displacement. Like the tribe out of which she steps onto the stage, Carmen occupies no fixed point in space. Her restless motion, a metaphor for nomadism and defiant identity, fatigues anyone who would attempt to arrest and hold her as object. Carmen is, at her genealogical root, both a lamentation and a redemption of the paradoxical notion of a Gypsy geography.

Carmen's body provides a map of Gypsy history. Through her mythic status as a creation figure, we better understand the Gypsy history of Spain. In fact, only when perceived and received on this level does the power of the story and the opera make sense. Similarly, only through myth and body in motion and expression can we catch a fleeting glimpse of the fullness of Gypsy history and Gypsy geography, subjects that remain largely uninscribed.

CHAPTER ONE

Inventing *Carmen*

PROSPER MÉRIMÉE AND THE GYPSY
PRESENCE IN WESTERN EUROPE

As historian and archaeologist, [Mérimée] is a man of erudition turned artist.
Walter Pater[1]

Figures of the body whose texture forms musical signifying . . . these figures
of the body I do not always manage to name.
Roland Barthes[2]

Carmen and the pre-history she traces when she moves or sings is not only the
title of the novella or an opera, but also a concept developed in different spaces
throughout this book. *Carmen* in Spanish means villa or country house, a residence
that stands between town and country, between culture and nature, between civic
and savage existence.[3] Ultimately, Carmen dies for having trespassed, for having
crossed over to happiness with a Spaniard: Escamillo, the toreador. But she also
dies for daring to be free.

In this chapter I examine the writings of Prosper Mérimée and his lifelong,
archeological relationship to the figure of Carmen, whom he develops into myriad fictional shapes throughout his literary career. Mérimée's historical interest
in Carmen parallels the French Romantic obsession with *the foreigner*, in this case
the Gypsy — *la gitana* — within European borders.[4] The confidant of the Empress
Eugénie, and a senator and member of the inner circle of Emperor Napoleon
III, Mérimée develops literary themes that speak to his own conservative politics
and political ambition; perhaps this is proof of his desire to situate himself both
in French history and within the French literary imagination.[5] I begin with a
bio-historical sketch of Mérimée, *homme de plume* of the latter half of the Resto-

ration (1814–1830), July Monarchy (1830–1848), Second Republic (1848–1852) and Second Empire (1852–1870). I consider Mérimée's literary development of the Gypsy between 1830, when he first learns of her story, and 1845 when he publishes *Carmen, la novella*.[6]

Prosper Mérimée

Archeologist, philologist, traveler, art critic, historian, and writer of eighteen novels, Prosper Mérimée was born at Broglie on 18 September 1803 to Jean-François Léonor Mérimée and Anne-Louise Moreau.[7] A man of regal demeanour and Jeffersonian stature, Mérimée inherited his family's travel-lust. His maternal great-grandmother, Marie Leprince de Beaumont (1711–1780), was a prolific writer who fled an unhappy marriage. The author of more than seventy volumes of children's stories, her many journeys, like those of her great-grandson's, would inform much of her writing.[8]

Mérimée's paternal grandfather, of Norman lineage, was a wealthy lawyer and a steward to the Maréchal de Broglie. His father, Léonor Mérimée (1757–1836), "a man of the world and a respected artist,"[9] was a painter of "competent mediocrity," as well as an art historian and a permanent secretary of the École des Beaux Arts.[10] Léonor spent his life tracking down technical methods of pre-modern painting, a precursor to his son's expeditions. Having sent Prosper to the Lycée Napoleon, Mérimée *père* pushed his son to study law at the University of Paris. A *boulevardier*, Mérimée instead frequented Parisian literary salons, where he met Henry Beyle (Stendhal), the two becoming lifelong friends.[11]

Mérimée *fils* was not interested in law but rather in writing, becoming one of France's finest writers of short story fiction in the early to mid-nineteenth century.[12] His gift as a short story writer was his descriptive ability, his economy of language, and his psychological interest in narration. Oftentimes, he placed himself as narrator in oddly self-reflexive ways inside his text, realizing a relationship between fictional characters and self heretofore unknown. Early in his career, he wrote under a woman's pseudonym, Clara Gazul, a Spanish actress whom the author had invented. Mérimée also began publishing articles on Spanish theater as early as 1825 (he was then only twenty-two years of age) in *Le Globe*. The core of his early attempts at short story prose was published in Parisian journals and as a collection of early writings in 1833 in a book entitled *Mosaïque*.

Mérimée was a confirmed bachelor. He never married but was known, like

Jean-Jacques Rousseau, as a confidant and friend to numerous wealthy, political, and highly educated Salon women. His love affairs were numerous and helped to enhance his popularity in Parisian consciousness. Among his lovers were the author George Sand (1804–1876), the lyric actress Josephine Céline Cayot, and his real love, Valentine Delessert (1806–1894), who was the wife of the Paris Préfet de Police.[13] He also boasted friendships with Sir Anthony Panizzi (1797–1879), Director of the British Museum; the painter Eugène Delacroix (1798–1863); the Romantic writers Victor Hugo (1802–1885) and Charles Nodier (1780–1844); Eugène Viollet-le-Duc (1814–1879), the architect and champion of French neo-Gothicism; the Russian novelist Ivan Turgenev (1818–1883), who taught him about Russian literature; and his most famous friendship, Empress Eugénie (1826–1920), wife of Napoleon III (1808–1873). Through his close, lifelong ties to the Empress and her mother, as well as his own work in government, Mérimée became a cherished and influential member of the Emperor's inner circle.

The research for his books came from his work in government. Mérimée entered public service in 1834 and rose to the position of Inspector General of Historic Monuments and Antiquities, a post he held until 1853. Like his great-grandmother, he was consumed by a love of foreign languages and places, traveling extensively through France, southern Europe (especially Spain) and the Near East in the 1830s and 1840s. He investigated and classified ancient Roman architectural ruins, acquiring classical knowledge that he transformed into both historical and mythic settings in his stories.[14] In May of 1831, Mérimée was named chevalier of the Légion d'Honneur.

Mérimée had a peculiar character that, to a certain extent, illuminates his writing. A man "capable of affection and almost incapable of passion," he could be grim with a "predilection for tragic and terrible subjects." He was sarcastic, indifferent, and skeptical, but was also a warm man who boasted many close friendships wherever he traveled, fascinated as he was by the lives and customs of the peoples he visited and the civilizations he studied. His closest friendships were with educated women, some of whom he bedded. With others, however, he cherished lifelong friendships. Born in Napoleonic times, just after the Emperor "sealed the tomb" on the French Revolution and the French Enlightenment, Mérimée was a child of the Romantic era; he took a lifelong interest in mysticism, the supernatural, *l'éxotique*, and the newly discovered "anthropological" notion of *les couleurs locales*, or local color.[15] These spiritual interests gave him the insight needed to paint the figure of Carmen.

In Search of Mérimée's Carmen

Critics contend that Mérimée began his life as a serious writer in 1825 with *Une Femme est un diable* (*A Woman Is a Devil*), which he introduced by reading it aloud to a private audience. The work signals the start of his interest in two lifelong themes: Carmenian women and faraway lands. Expanded into a larger theatrical work, *Le Théâtre de Clara Gazul*, it was performed in 1898 at the Parisian Odéon Théâtre.[16] The action takes place during the Spanish Inquisition. Three clerics judge the fate of a young woman named Mariquita, who has been accused of witchcraft. Fray Antonio, the youngest cleric, is tormented by the memory of a woman from the countryside he once had seen. From Antonio's description, we hear an early sketch of Carmen: "I see her everywhere . . . her huge dark eyes . . . resembling those of a cat." Mérimée's description presages the character of Carmen:

> When Mariquita appears before the Inquisitional court, Fray Antonio closes his eyes to push out of his mind another woman who might cause him to forget his vows. This scene must be a sketch for the moment when Don José in a quick second chooses to forsake his career and let her go free. Mariquita is then asked what her profession is. She replies, "I sing, I dance, I play castanets . . ." Antonio, upon looking straight into Mariquita's eyes, cannot push her from his mind. He begins to obsess over her, just as Don José will do. Antonio betrays his holy vows saying: "I am damned Mariquita! I only think of you. . . . I will sacrifice my eternal salvation for a woman!" He runs to Mariquita's jail cell and begs her to marry him. Mariquita convinces him to run away. Antonio turns to another priest in the jail and says: "Marry us or I will kill you." They fight and Antonio stabs him. By the end of the play, Antonio says: "In one hour, I [became] a fornicator, a liar, and a murderer." Mariquita replies: "I think you would agree . . . Woman is a Devil."[17]

A "born archeologist," Mérimée wrote stories and essays that bear witness to his acute and passionate appreciation for the sensual in other cultures.[18] Mérimée's fiction showed him to have other gifts: a romantic imagination and a remarkable ability to tell a gripping love story. With these tools and a proclivity to use violence in his stories, he took Paris by storm.

Mérimée published *Le Théâtre de Clara Gazul* anonymously in 1825. A collection of six short plays supposedly translated from the fiction of the Spanish actress Clara Gazul, the book caused a stir in Paris. The cover of the book was a fake portrait of the author cross-dressed as Gazul, wearing a *mantilla*. It was a huge popular success, leading Mérimée to publish, four years later, his first novel. Mérimée described locales and people with geographic, narrative, and historic detail that resembles the twentieth-century ethnography of Claude Lévi-Strauss. This scholarly approach to writing fiction, essays, and plays won a large Parisian following; Mérimée was published for two decades in the popular Parisian journals *La Revue de Paris* and *La Revue des Deux Mondes*, where many of his stories were serialized and devoured by a French society that awaited each subsequent installment.

In *Chronique du Regne de Charles IX* (1829), perhaps his finest work of writing, the author demonstrated a talent for evoking historical moments with easy, comprehensible language to which the public could relate. Using a compositional style that reappears in *Carmen*, *Chronique* ends with a Protestant, Bernard de Mergy, who—madly in love with a Catholic, Diane de Turgis, during the Religious Wars of the sixteenth century—kills a Catholic soldier for her. Also in 1829, Mérimée began to use his own name. The first collection of stories published under his name was *Mosaïque* (1833). It contained the stories *Mateo Falcone* and *La Vase Étrusque*.[19] Here Mérimée evolved his deepening interest in antiquity and in Spain, capturing local color through vivid description with an economy of means, humor, and sensationalism.[20]

In 1837, he wrote a fantasy tale, *La Vénus d'île* (*The Venus of the Island*). It combined Mérimée's two lifelong passions: archeology and women. The narrator explains:

> There are two meanings. One could translate it as "Beware of whomever loves you, beware of lovers." . . . But seeing the diabolical expression on the statue's face, I would sooner believe that the artist wanted to warn the viewer to protect himself from this awful beauty. So I would translate it as: "Be careful if she loves you [Prends garde à toi si elle t'aime]."[21]

The earlier narrative intrusion serves as a prelude to Carmen's infamous warning to Don José: *Et si je t'aime, prends garde à toi* (If I love you, watch out, protect yourself!). This tale also marks the beginning of what one might call Mérimée's physicalization of the text. That is to say, Mérimée's intensely descriptive passages citing the physiognomy of his fictive *Gitanas* foreground a heightened sensoriality, a documentary aspect of his writing. It was as if he were taking photographs of them in their natural surroundings.

By 1840, Mérimée had begun to outline Carmen in the character of Columba, another supernatural female character who appears in *La Revue des Deux Mondes*, also published in serial form. Taking his inspiration from the island of Corsica, Mérimée brings to life Carmen's precursor: "Columba's eyes shone with malevolent joy . . . This tall, strong woman, fanatical about her ideas of barbarous honor, arrogance in her eyes, her lips curling in a sardonic smile."

Five years later, in 1845, Mérimée assigned to Carmen's body the physiognomic detail of an archeological investigation:

> Her skin, though perfectly smooth, was almost of a copper hue. Her eyes were set obliquely in her head, but they were magnificent and large. Her lips, a little full, but beautifully shaped, revealed a set of teeth as white as newly skinned almonds. Her hair—a trifle coarse, perhaps (African)—was black, with blue lights on it like a raven's wing, long and glossy . . . There was something strange and wild about her beauty. Her face astonished you, at first sight, but nobody could forget it. Her eyes, especially, had an expression of a mingled sensuality and fierceness that I had never seen in any other human glance.[22]

Mérimée's quest to develop the prototype for Carmen gestated throughout the 1830s, fed by his research travels to study classical ruins in France and Spain. In his new post of Inspector General of Historic Monuments "in which capacity he became one of the first French scholars to argue for the need to preserve old architecture and classify it scientifically," he conducted long architectural surveys and subsequent reports. *Voyage dans le Midi de France* and *Histoire de Don Pedro I, Roi de Castille* represent two such volumes.[23] Part travel diary, part scientific data, part anthropological assessment in literary form, these and other writings, like the previous work of George Borrow on Gypsies (which Mérimée had read), began a new literary style of writing for his job. Available to the nineteenth-century French public hungry for "l'éxotique," this "official" work encouraged Mérimée's growing popularity.

Mérimée left for Spain during the July Revolution of 1830. There he met Don Cipriano de Montijo, Count of Teba. A wonderful conversationalist, Mérimée charmed Montijo who, as the story went, invited him home to meet his wife, the Scottish countess Doña Mañuela (née Kirkpatrick). "Don Cipriano could have rendered his wife and Eugénie [their daughter] no greater or more enduring service: Mérimée became their friend for life."[24] And, in exchange, the Countess recounted to her new friend what would become the story of Carmen. Fifteen years later, in 1845, Mérimée wrote *Carmen*.

Doña Mañuela had read in a Madrileño newspaper the tale of a *jacquerie* from Malaga who had murdered his mistress — a Gypsy — for having "devoted herself to the public" and having refused to be in his company exclusively.[25] Mérimée altered Montijo's populist story, conceived as an intimate study of an Andalusian *gitana* rather than as a passionate love affair that ends in violent murder, and transformed it into a character study.

In 1853, Eugénie de Montijo (1826–1920) married the Emperor of France, Napoleon III.[26] This solidified Mérimée's socio-political status in France; he became her lifelong adviser, as he had been her tutor in Spain, as well as an *"ami de maison"* who frequently visited the Palais Royal, Biarritz, and Compiègne, and (reluctantly) even gave the Emperor himself literary lessons.[27] His friendship and tutorial relationship to the Empress gained him the post of Senator in 1853, a position he held until his death. The literary result of these diplomacies and friendships was committed to many *lettres* written by Mérimée between the mid-1830s and his death in Cannes on 23 September 1870, five years before *Carmen* came to the Parisian stage. These erudite correspondences have been described as Rabelaisian in their bold cynicism and Swiftian in their humor, with keen insights into the state of Europe in the mid-nineteenth century.[28]

Carmen owes her origins to Mérimée's 1830 trip to Spain and to his lifelong acquaintance with the Countess of Montijo.[29] But Carmen also owes her birth to the author's visionary ability to believe in and develop a good story. The theme of the newspaper story, as recounted to him by the Countess, centered on a passionate love affair.[30] In his hands it became a more focused, ethnographic character study of a Gypsy Carmen and her itinerant world. "I have just spent eight days isolated in order to write, not only the doings and fiery gestures of Don Pedro but a story that you told me fifteen years ago, and that I am afraid I have spoiled."[31]

In 1846, Mérimée completed the fourth section of *Carmen*, and it is this section of the novella that bears witness to his devotion to this Gypsy study. In it, he writes an essay on Caló, the Gypsy language. This bears the unusual mark of an

Gypsy Festival, Sacromonte, Granada, photographer and date unknown.
Roger-Viollet Archives, Paris, France

archeological mind rather than a straight fiction writer, or *romancier*. Could this be one of the clues to the story's endurance?

Carmen, like most juicy tales, was serialized. Mérimée broke the story into four long parts that were published in the Parisian paper *La Revue des Deux Mondes*, allowing the public to build up an increasing appetite for the next installment. Don José narrates the story of *Carmen*, recounting it to the author from prison at the end of his life. Mérimée's use of the first person for these long descriptive passages at times almost conflates the author with the murderer. This self-reflexive device seduces the reader, who wanders into Don José's jail cell with the author, and it acts to join the reader to Don José. We feel as responsible for Don José's fate in the novella as we feel connected to the stage persona of Carmen in the opera.

In Search of Don José

As Mérimée's own persona figures so prominently in this quasi-travel diary novel, using a documentary approach to description and character development, we must also discuss the history of the creation of another male lead, Don José.[32] As he did for Carmen, Mérimée wrote numerous sketches of the protagonist who would become Don José. Perhaps the closest study is to be found in *L'Histoire de Rondino* (*The Story of Rondino*), a character who, like Don José, becomes a soldier and who, like Carmen, is fated to die.

From law-abiding soldier-citizen to murderous cultural hero of the peasantry, Rondino fights against injustice, killing anyone who tries to stop him. As will happen with Don José, Rondino seeks to return home, a place Mérimée describes as far away. For Spain, this could mean any one of forty-nine provinces and, thus, an exotic locale within one's home country.[33] It is a literary device that serves to distance the character from the reader and gives us the option of not sympathizing with him. "I want to go home," says lance corporal Rondino to his colonel. After committing murder, Rondino flees, taking refuge on a small farm in the mountains. Don José escapes with Carmen and her band of smugglers into the Sierras. There are numerous similarities between the two leading male characters as well: Rondino is chased by the carabinieri and kills one of them; Don José also runs his sword through an officer who comes to see Carmen in her Triana haunt; Rondino becomes a fugitive, running from the law, skipping from farm to farm, a cultural hero with the peasantry for challenging the police; Don José too wins acceptance for having committed murder. Here, Mérimée reveals the anti-establishment—anti-monarchical, anti-clerical—spirit within Spain (and France).[34]

Finally, Mérimée also experiments with first-person narration early on in *Rondino*. He writes of a wealthy landowner "who I knew," and immediately we are drawn in, as we are with Don José's final words, as if we are listening to someone's confession, because in the moment visualized by Mérimée along a dusty Andalusian road, he encounters a man whom he comes to understand is a fugitive, a murderer. The slow, detailed way in which Mérimée reveals the outcast's true nature seduces the reader into reading on, and taking an empathetic and suspicious view of the bandit. While both plots are simple, the ethnographic detail is titillating and narratively successful. Like Don José, Rondino is also descended upon by a band of thieves who demand his help in exchange for a "share of the loot." Unafraid and unthreatened (unlike the more developed character study of Don José),

Lucien Muratore as Don José in Carmen, *Act IV,* painting by
Léon Canniccioni. Musée des Beaux-Arts, Marseilles, France
Neurdein / Roger-Viollet Archives, Paris, France

Rondino replies, "I am an honest outcast, not a thief. Don't ask me to do anything
like that again or you will be sorry," as if to say, "murder is gentlemanly; to steal is
common."

Rondino also prepares the way for the cultural exclusion of Don José, something Carmen uncannily points out in pretending to speak his native tongue. A
Navarese, Don José does not belong in Andalusia, even as a regimental soldier.
Nor does Rondino, who marks himself as a foreigner, belong either: "I could
not live," he declares, "anywhere but in my own land." Here the author's ability
to insert geographical memory — psychic space — into his narrative is profound.
Rondino, Don José, and Carmen all come from somewhere else, beyond the edges
of the page. Carmen, like Rondino, travels within Spain with a kind of restless
anxiety. Consciously, Mérimée lends nuance to the larger story of the peripheral
relationship of the Gypsy to a European society that is obsessed throughout industrialization with ownership of land and control of increasing wealth. Lastly,
like Don José and Carmen, Rondino foretells his future: "I will try to avoid being
hung as long as possible."

The Archeology of Carmen

Mérimée's *Carmen* derives from three sources. The first, previously discussed, was the newspaper story recounted to him by the Countess of Montijo, of the Kirkpatrick family of Scotland, descended from exiled Jacobites. The second important source was his extensive 1830 journey through Spain. The author, a bachelor of twenty-seven, had plenty of time to explore the land at will. He hired a bodyguard who served as a guide (much like the character of Antonio in the first scene of *Carmen*) and two horses and rode frequently on the dusty, empty roads of Andalusia. With Mérimée's appetite for local color and his linguistic ability, these explorations gave him a sense of the topography of the land and the diverse cultures living within Spain. On one of his trips, he came upon a *venta*, a small inn, where he stopped for some cold gazpacho. A young woman named Carmencita, who his guide later told him was a witch—at the time a code word for *gitana*—serves him. Clearly taken with her, he drew a sketch of this young lady in his notebook, enough to remind him of her physical features.

The third research source was Gypsy lore with which most European literati were familiar. Several years before Mérimée sat down to write *Carmen*, the English travel writer George Borrow had published a number of studies and travel guides regarding Gypsies. The first two, *Lavengro* and *The Romany Rye*, dealt specifically with the British Gypsy population. Following Borrow's interest in the Gypsies and their language, Romani, the Gypsy Lore Society was founded in England in 1888. Its founders dedicated the journal's publications and conferences to the philological, cultural, and linguistic history of the Gypsy people, whom they believed to have migrated from India to Europe in the fifteenth century.

From 1835 to 1839 Borrow worked for the British Bible Society, distributing bibles as a *colporteur* in Spain and Portugal. This migratory work led to his unique perspective on the Gypsies of southern and northern Spain and to the publication of two studies: *Zincali: An Account of the Gypsies of Spain* (1841) and *The Bible in Spain* (1843). Borrow's literature created a wave of popular interest in the Gypsy people, whom he characterized as exotic and far removed culturally and socially from Western European society. To a certain extent, he tried to proceed within a realistic documentary approach, describing their "ways." Even though he did not speak Caló, he wrote about their language and customs, romanticizing them as an Eastern people living in a Western land. Since Borrow had no formal training in linguistics and had no knowledge of *Romani*, the evidence for his ideas was sorely lacking. What he did accomplish was twofold. First, he added to the European

Romantic imagination, already somewhat shaped by the Romantic ballet stage (*La Gipsy* had premiered in 1839 and *La Gitana* in 1845). Gypsies were exactly the socially peripheral individuals who made sense in any ethnographer's search for *la couleur locale*. Second, Borrow accumulated a set of visual descriptions. This gave Mérimée ample written background information for his novel. With the 1845 publication of *Carmen, la novella* in three installments in the journal *La Revue des Deux Mondes*, receptive, romanticized French readers were already on the edge of their seats, waiting for such a tale with enthusiasm. *Carmen*, as a literary idea and persona, could not fail.[35]

A stream of French writers created, on the ballet and music stage at the Paris Opéra, a Romanticized, orientalist fantasy world that existed only in their imaginations. Eugène Delacroix's immense canvases of Sabine rape and jihad warriors riding across the sun-beaten Sahara to conquer and convert other tribes also helped to prepare the French public. Christian soldiers fought Muslim warriors whose armies waited at the gates of European civilization. The ability of the average French person to escape from *la vie quotidienne* and into the richly colored oriental world of silk clothing, hanging gardens, waterfalls, and innocent, helpless women hidden behind screens and patios was enriched by the color and texture of these literary sources.[36] The East pushing on the West, as the Ottomans did and as 'al Tariq had also done nine centuries earlier, is reflected in these ballets and storylines.[37] This steamy, sexualized, erotic atmosphere enabled Mérimée to present Carmen to a receptive public.

Professor Antonia Fonyi, seminal Mérimée scholar and literary critic at the Centre National de Recherche Scientifique in Paris, has theorized *Carmen*'s beginnings. Fonyi argues in a series of critical works that Mérimée's phenomenological approach to the character of Carmen—conceiving of her through rings of smoke—enabled the author to inhabit her body and her character. The reverse of this relationship is that Carmen becomes the author, writing her own narrative and, in this light, seeing—as does the artist—her fate before anyone else does. It is, Fonyi states, Mérimée's life as an archeologist-author, not just as a writer, that enables him to meditate on the character of Carmen.[38]

Synopsis of *Carmen*: Mérimée's Novella

Mérimée's Carmen differs from the opera libretto in many ways. His story is told in fragments by an English gentleman and archeologist who travels through Spain conducting research. The novella begins in the first person: "I have always suspected the geographers of not knowing what they were talking about when they place the battlefield of Munda within the country of Bastuli-Poeni, near the modern Monda, a few leagues north of Marbella."[39] With his self-reflexive tone, Mérimée's narrator admits that he was able to locate the site in the book of an "anonymous author" whose *Bellum Hispaniense* he had found in the Duke of Osuna's library.[40] Citing both the *Bellum Hispaniense* and the Duke of Osuna in the first line of the book brings a scholarly and archeological feeling of research and discovery to his novel.[41] Mérimée is introducing himself, albeit subtly and with great care.

Fonyi offers enlightening commentary on the beginning of the novel, establishing for us the importance of the narrator's later meetings with Carmen and Don José. She introduces the notion of *arché* in her analysis of *Carmen* and Mérimée.[42] *Arché*, Fonyi argues, is an "invisible inscription."[43] (I imagine it as resembling the signature of a great painter in code on a painting or letters chiseled into stone on a statue by its sculptor.) In Fonyi's writings, *arché* appears as a metaphysical concept. It means origin, genesis, beginning, something that is incomplete, unknowable, an intermediary between ideas. *Arché* in *Carmen, la novella* transforms into an archeological concept, a ruin, the idea of the past rather than the past itself. Mérimée, we know, commences his novel with a narrator who is a historian, also claiming to be an archeologist. In search of the battlefield of Munda where Julius Caesar conquered the armies of the sons of Pompey, Mérimée takes the reader into the past through a geographical setting, asking us to visit with him what Fonyi describes as a "locale of the present." In other words — if one listens to the signifiers — the story opens with the quest of the *antique world* that has become so foreign to the *modern world* that the memory of its very location has been wiped out.[44] History to Fonyi's mind laces the first few pages of the book, as if to say that the present cannot exist without Carmen; her story begins only after this detailed introduction. History becomes the author's pathway to his fiction.

Carmen commences with no less a character than a hero's hero, the emperor Julius Caesar. While we may know something of Caesar's imperial exploits on behalf of Rome, what we remember best is his love affair with Cleopatra, Queen of Egypt. So in love was Caesar with Cleopatra that he gambled the stability of the Roman Empire on his obsessive passion for her. In connection with Caesar, who was also, like himself, an archeologist-geographer, Mérimée consciously unfolds his love story in the footsteps of one of the most celebrated love affairs in history.

Cleopatra embodies the final, relevant connection — inscription — that Mérimée reveals to his reader. Gypsies, Mérimée learned in Borrow's books, were thought to have emigrated from Egypt, their nickname becoming "Egypcianos," or Egyptians. If Carmen came from Cleopatra's land, then Don José, a soldier and officer, must historically have come from Caesar's. Because desire is a human trait, an obsessive, dangerous play by a Roman emperor for an African queen, and the same desire by a Spanish soldier for a Gypsy, become overlaid; station in life and passion do not have to be commensurate with one another. Ultimately, an emperor and a common soldier sacrifice their careers for the women they love.

After pronouncing himself present in his book, Mérimée returns to his literary narrative. Along a dusty road, he and his guide Antonio come upon a bandit, Don José Lizzarrabengoa, a Basque from the northern provinces. In conversation with this man, who the guide suspects is the famous *bandido* Don José de Navarre, the story of Carmen begins.

It is a tremendous composition. "Finding myself in Andalusia about the beginning of 1830," the author writes, "I made a rather lengthy excursion."[45] Mérimée plays himself in the character of the narrator, an English archeologist. Antonio, the guide, who will disappear after the first scenes, represents the moral voice of society. In exchange for a reward, he will reveal Don José's whereabouts. And then there is the figure and character of Carmen, whom Mérimée outlines for us, slowly and deliberately. His descriptions give her a shape, contour, and personality that, once described, will come to overwhelm both her creator — Mérimée — and us.

The story continues. The Englishman and the bandit part company, and our narrator travels from Murvieda, site of an ancient Roman battle he had been researching between Caesar and Pompey, to the city of Cordova, locus of the first Muslim kingdom in Europe. In Cordova, he will visit the Dominican library where "I expected to find some interesting information concerning the ancient Munda."[46]

The geographical configuration of the narrative is interesting. It allows the Englishman to study Carmen as he would a *tel* (archeological site hidden in the earth) or a classical monument; she is an ornament of the East, a seductress, like a harem girl.

> I was smoking, leaning upon the parapet of the quay, when a woman ascended the steps that led down to the river and seated herself close to me. She had in her hair a large bunch of jasmine that emitted a strong perfume. She was simply, perhaps poorly, clad in black. As she approached me the bather let fall on her shoulders the mantilla with which she had covered her head and, in the starlight, I could perceive that she was pretty, young, well-made, and that she had very large eyes. I quickly threw away my cigar. She at once appreciated this attention — a politeness entirely French — and hastened to inform me that she liked the smell of tobacco-smoke very

much, and that even she herself smoked when she could get very mild cigarettes. She condescended to take one, and lighted it at the burning end of a cork that a child brought us for a halfpenny. Smoking together we conversed so long—the pretty bather and I—that we found ourselves alone upon the quay. I did not consider that there was anything indiscreet in suggesting that we should go and have some ices at a neveria.[47]

Seated at a small, candle-lit table at the *neveria*, the Englishman becomes curious about her origins. "You are at least Andalusian?" he asks. "You must be Moorish?" I stopped, not liking to say 'a Jewess.'"[48] Carmen replied, "you see quite well that I am a Gypsy. Do you wish me to tell you *la baji* (your fortune)? Have you ever heard of La Carmencita? I am she!"[49] Telling his reader that he had studied the occult sciences at university, he excuses his desire to let her read his fortune and then goes on to describe her physical features. "My Bohemian," he writes, conflating her Gypsy ethnicity with that of an Eastern European Romany, "could not pretend to the necessary perfection."

> Her skin, though quite smooth, approached somewhat to the coppery tinge. Her eyes were obliquely set, but large and full; her lips rather thick, but well cut, and permitted the teeth—white as blanched almonds—to be seen. Her hair was perhaps a trifle coarse, but had a blue sheen running through it, like that one sees in a raven's wings, and was long and luxuriant. Not to weary you with a detailed description, I will merely say that with each fault, she united a good point . . . She was of a strange and savage beauty—a face which at first surprises you, but it was one you could never forget. Her eyes especially had an expression at once voluptuous and fierce, which I have never since noticed in any human eyes.[50]

The use of the words "strange" and "savage" are used to describe animals. In his anthropomorphization of her, he relegates her to sub-human, noble savage status. Animals that must be caged are considered "fierce," too dangerous to be allowed to roam freely.

The Englishman offers to escort her home to have his fortune told. Carmencita leads him across the river to her hovel. They enter and sit down and she begins to read his palm when Don José bursts into the room, furious that Carmen has brought home another man. He sees the Englishman and turns toward Carmencita. She, to avoid his wrath, runs her "hand under her chin," to signal him to kill their guest. Remembering the Englishman, Don José refuses and escorts him outside where our narrator discovers he is left without his watch.

Several months later, the Englishman travels to Cordova again. The authorities contact him to say they have found his watch and that the thief is about to be executed for murder. He goes to see the thief at the jail and discovers Don José, sitting in his cell. The Englishman sits down to chat with him and Don José proceeds to tell him the story of how he met Carmen.

Don José Lizzarrabengoa was a corporal in the army. He fled the North having killed a man in a brawl. But he defends himself: "When we Navarros play tennis we forget all else. One day when I had won a match, a youth of Alava picked a quarrel with me. We fought with maquilas, and still I had the advantage, but I was obliged to fly the country. I fell in with some dragoons and enlisted in the Almanza regiment of cavalry. I quickly became a corporal . . . a fair way to become quarter-master when, to my misfortune, I was put on guard on the tobacco manufactory of Seville."[51]

Having joined an Andalusian regiment, Don José describes the tobacco factory as "that great building outside the ramparts near the Guadalquivir," with four or five hundred women who work rolling cigars.[52] "A free Navarro," Don José explains, "I was always accustomed" to keeping busy. Busy weaving a chain of brass wire to sustain his priming-needle, he heard the women shout, "Look, the *gitanilla!*"

> I looked up and . . . I saw that Carmen, whom you know of, at whose house I found you some months ago. She wore a red skirt, very short, which exposed to view her white silk stockings, with many a hole in them, and tiny shoes of morocco leather, tied with scarlet ribbons. She had thrown back her mantilla so as to display her shoulders, and an immense bunch of acacia blossoms, which was stuck in her chemise. She also carried a flower in her mouth, and she walked with a movement of a thoroughbred filly from the Cordova stud. In my country a woman in such a costume would have made people cross themselves. At Seville every one paid some gay compliment to the girl on her appearance. She replied to them looking sideways as she went along, with her hand on her hip, as bold as the true gypsy she was.

Again, she is described as part-animal, part-woman, dangerous and to be feared.

Carmen stops in front of Don José and asks in an Andalusian dialect, "Gossip, will you give me your chain to hang the key of my strong box on?" He replies, "It is to hang my priming-needle on." Carmen replies, "Ah, the señor makes lace, then; he requires needles . . . Well my hearty," she continues, "make me seven ells of black lace for a mantilla, thou primer of my soul."[53]

Then taking the flower from between her lips, she flipped it at me with a movement of her thumb, and struck me between the eyes. Sir, I felt as if I had received a bullet in the forehead . . . When she had entered the factory I perceived the flower, which had fallen at my feet. I do not know what possessed me, but I picked it up when my comrades were not looking, and put it carefully in my vest.[54]

After Carmen enters the factory, a riot breaks out. Carmen has slashed another worker's face with a knife. Don José, the guard in charge, must arrest her. He enters the factory with several men and discovers a woman "sprawling on the floor drenched in blood, with a cross, an X cut on her face with a knife. Opposite the wounded woman . . . I perceived Carmen, restrained by five or six of her associates."[55]

Don José escorts Carmen to the guardhouse where the quartermaster tells him her crime is serious and that she must go to prison. "We started for the city," Don José tells the Englishman. "At first the Gypsy maintained a strict silence, but in Serpent street . . . she began her maneuvers by letting her *mantilla* fall upon her shoulders so as to enable me to see her winning face, and, turning, towards me as far as she could, she said,

"My officer, whither are you taking me?"

"To prison, my poor child . . ."

"Alas . . . Let me escape. I will give you a piece of *bar lachi* [a lodestone—a charm] which will make you beloved by all the women."

Carmen then had no difficulty in discovering that I came from the Provinces. You know, sir, that the gypsies having no definite country of their own, are always wandering hither and thither, speaking all languages, and the majority of them are as much at home in Portugal as in France, or in the Provinces, or Catalonia; even amongst the Moors and the English they can make themselves understood. Carmen, then, knew the Basque dialect pretty well.[56]

Mérimée's fantastical treatment of the Gypsy nomads emerges, as previously stated, from his reading of George Borrow's *The Zincali*. Following Borrow, Mérimée presents them and Carmen as without country, without home, without identity. They exist because they exist, but with no root planted in any ground—with no historical consciousness either of their past or future. This classist view stands in sharp contrast to the regionalist histories housed in the *cante* by the Gypsy flamenco singer who sees Triana, the Gypsy *barrio* of Seville, as sufficient identification: to belong to a particular place in a particular moment in time.

Don José continues his story:

> "Friend of my soul," Carmen added. "Are you from the country?"
>
> "I am from Elizondo," I replied in Basque, very much moved at hearing my native tongue.

Lying convincingly about her true identity, Carmen remarks:

> "And I am from Etchalar," she said. "I was brought to Seville by the gypsies.[57] I have been working in the factory to take me back to Navarre again to my dear mother, whose only support I am, and the little *barreteca* [garden]. Ah, if I were only there again, near the white mountains! They have insulted me because I do not belong to this country of pick-pockets, merchants of rotten oranges; and these low women are all against me because I declared that their 'jacks' of Seville, with their knives, would not frighten one fellow from our part of the country, with only his blue *beret* and his *maquilla*."[58]

Don José confesses:

> She spoke in broken Basque, and I believed she came from Navarre. Her eyes, mouth and complexion stamped her a gypsy. I was befooled—mad—and no longer paid attention to anything. I thought that if the two Spaniards with me had said anything in disparagement of the country I would have slashed them across the face just as she had treated her comrade. In fact I was like a man intoxicated.[59]

Speaking to the Englishman, Don José admits that, against orders, he let Carmen escape. Upon being discovered, Don José's rank is reduced to private, he is disgraced and sent to prison for one month.

After being released, Don José sees Carmen again when she comes to dance at an officers' party outside of which he is standing guard. She whispers to him, "If you want good fried fish, come to Lillas Pastia's in Triana." When his tour of duty finishes for the evening, Don José goes to the Gypsy's restaurant, where he meets Carmen who tries to convince him to desert his regiment—give up his upstanding life—and join her. That night, back on duty, Carmen approaches Don José with her band of smugglers and asks him to allow them to pass. He yields.

Some time later, Don José returns to Lillas Pastia's seeking Carmen and discovers her in the arms of one of his officers. He attacks the officer and kills him. Afraid, he flees the city with Carmen and her criminal associates, becoming a fugitive. They leave the city—the safe, civilized space—and flee into the Sierra Morenos, the mountain range north of Seville. This murder secures him a place among the Gypsy smugglers. Together, they hide out between the rocky crevices of lookout points, waiting for wagon trains to rob.

Carmen suggests they flee elsewhere. Don José replies, "If I keep with you in the mountains, I shall always be sure of you . . . There will be no lieutenants to share with me."[60] A deserter and a murderer seeking refuge from the law in the mountains of Andalusia, Don José wanders the Sierras with Carmen, who entices wagon trains passing through to stop; then Don José and his company rob them. One day, he learns that Carmen is married to a one-eyed Gypsy murderer named Garcia whose release from the galleys she has arranged. I reproduce a longer passage here so that the grain of Mérimée's voice, the texture of his text, come alive. "I soon met Garcia the one-eyed; he was one of the most repulsive villains whom Bohemia ever reared, a dark skin and a still blacker soul. He was the most unmitigated ruffian that ever I met in my life."[61]

When Garcia arrives, he kills him in a knife-fight and Carmen, seemingly indifferent about Garcia's death, agrees to marry Don José.

> For many months I was happy with Carmen; she continued to be useful to us in our operations and gave us notice of the good things we could "bring off." She stayed sometimes at Malaga, sometimes at Cordova, sometimes at Granada; but at a word from me she would leave any place and come and meet me in an isolated inn, or even in the camp.
>
> "Do you know," Carmen says, "that since you have really become my *rom*, I care less for you than when you were my fancy man . . . What I wish is to be free and to do as I please. Take care — do not push me too far. If you trouble me too much I will find some fellow who will serve you as you served Garcia."

After being shot in a surprise attack by Spanish soldiers, Don José escapes, finding shelter in a nearby forest. A fellow smuggler carries him the rest of the way to a cave and then goes to find Carmen, who returns at once.

> For fifteen days she never quitted me for a moment . . . As soon as I could stand up again she carried me off to Granada in secrecy. The gypsies everywhere found us safe lodging, and I passed more than six weeks in a house two doors from the official who was searching for me.

While Don José hid in Granada, there was a *corrida* attended by Carmen. There she met a picador, Lucas Inaito. Don José's comrade told him of Lucas and, having confronted Carmen about him, she replied, "He is a man with whom we can do some business."[62]

Fortunately the picador left for Malaga . . . I forgot Lucas; perhaps she also forgot him, for the time at any rate. It was about that time sir that I met you, first near Montilla, then afterwards at Cordova. I will not say anything about our last interview. You perhaps know more about it than I. Carmen robbed you of your watch; she also wanted your money and particularly the ring you wear on your finger, which she said is a magic ring, which she was very anxious to possess. We had a violent quarrel; I struck her.

"There is a fiesta at Cordova," Carmen said; "I am going to see it. Then I shall find out who has money, and will tell you."

"Carmencita," I asked. "Is it true that you no longer love me?" . . .

"I will follow you to death, yes; but I will not live with you any longer!"

"You are going to kill me, I see that quite well," she said. "It is fated; but you will never make me yield . . . José, you ask me to do what is impossible. I no longer love you; you love me still; and, for that reason you want to kill me. I could very easily lie to you, but do not care to take the trouble. All is over between us. As my *rom* you have the right to kill your *romi*, but Carmen will always be free. Calli she was born, and Calli she will die!"

"You love Lucas?" I said. "Yes, I have loved him, like you, for a while; perhaps less than you. At present, I love no one, and I hate myself for having loved you."

I threw myself at her feet; I took her hands in mine . . . I offered her all . . . She took possession of me—I drew my knife; I wished she had displayed some fear and pleaded for mercy, but the woman was a demon . . . I stabbed her twice. It was Garcia's knife . . . She fell at the second thrust without a cry. I can still see her splendid black eyes regarding me steadily; then they became troubled and closed. I remained insensible beside the body for a good hour. Then I remembered that Carmen had often said that she would like to be buried in a wood . . . I excavated a grave with my knife, and placed her in it. Then I mounted my horse, and galloped to Cordova, and at the first guard-house I made myself known. I said I had killed Carmen . . . It is the Calli who are to blame for having made her what she was.[63]

Don José's final sentence in his long narrative confession brings the entire scene full circle. He is ultimately hanged for her murder, even though she is a Gypsy woman; he blames the Gypsies for his vengeful action since they produced progeny such as Carmen, so full of lust, sex, "dark" beauty, and seduction as to lead him into the labyrinth of destiny. Sophoclean in tone and feel, Don José's steps toward death, like those of Oedipus, actually occur at the very beginning of the novel. Each fated step brings him closer to a predetermined ending; one to which he seems to have been inextricably intertwined by a force greater than humanity.

Mérimée's story is compelling for many reasons. First, Mérimée's descriptions of places, peoples, and characters' motivations are both passionate and succinct. For example, in just one sentence he describes multiple events that lead to Don José's murder of Carmen. A peasant tells him that there will be a bullfight in Cordoba; he travels there. The reader already imagines Don José waiting for Carmen outside the *corrida*, his blood "boiling" as he enters into a psychotic break with reality. The seminal British art historian Walter Pater recognizes Mérimée's ability to turn tales of "violent death with visual exactness," in a "cold-blooded, impersonal" style that carries no pain and no pity for the reader.[64]

Nineteenth-century readers were indeed held captive by each scene in his novella, originally published scene-by-scene. They waited for the next moment in the story to be revealed. The characteristic nineteenth-century French woman was shy, chaste, innocent, pure, religious, and maternal. Carmen appears violent, murderous, free, unafraid, wild, cruel, boundary-less; she is Dionysian. But Don José, a member of "good" society, is also savage. He gives up everything for his pathological love of her. But this is only a surface reading. Most significant is Mérimée's ethnographic, Romantic approach to her.

Walter Pater harshly criticized Mérimée's desire to animalize the Spanish, the Oriental, and the African, pointing out the author's predilection for drawing characters "as alien as the animals."[65] Pater explains Mérimée's animalizing of the foreigner as stemming from a fatal motive: a Romantic desire to attach "wild power," raw sub-human power—"the very genius of nature itself"—as motivation for actions and events.[66] In a powerful critique of Romanticism's non-empirical folly and vampiric quest for the evil within the foreigner, Pater takes aim at Mérimée and at the French Romantic literary movement. "It is as if there were nothing to tell of in this world," Pater argues, "but various forms of hatred and love that is like lunacy."[67] Crediting his "brief composition [and] faculty of design," Pater still condemns Mérimée as being "the unconscious parent" of a gothic effect in French literature, one unworthy of his writing ability.[68]

But it is just this effect—its storytelling and sculpturesque quality of design—that endows Mérimée with the ability to keep the nineteenth-century reader on the edge of his/her *chaise longue*. For in his stylistic approach to character development, Mérimée holds mastery over his subject, in this case Carmen, as if he were a player in the political realm. This is perhaps why Pater finds Mérimée to have failed himself and his art as he finds in him a superficiality that he cannot resolve.

The Thieving Magpie, painting by Carlos Vázquez, Salon of 1912.
Neurdein / Roger-Viollet Archives, Paris, France

But should Mérimée be faulted for trying to set the French literary imagination on fire? There is no question that Mérimée was not Victor Hugo, nor Charles Baudelaire. His desire to perfect his writing is trumped by the tremendous amount of time he spends at court. And being a friend of the Empire, his state position as classifier of national monuments — as one who decides how France will remember and consecrate the past as critical to an understanding of the present — Mérimée wields the power to define not only architectural memory (particularly Roman), but also how the French literary imagination will or will not be accepted by the regime.

With the political exiles of both Victor Hugo and Charles Baudelaire and the trial of Gustave Flaubert, one might argue that Mérimée triumphed into eternity for setting something loose that he could not ultimately control. He gave Bizet a gift: Carmen. She lives on forever in popular consciousness. This gift went against the grain of Mérimée's predisposition to control his material; he could manipulate Carmen only as far as an archeologist might control any *tel* excavated. Memory must be unearthed, framed, and ultimately handed over to the future.

Prosper Mérimée lived only sixty-seven years; he died several decades before his contemporaries Victor Hugo and Stendhal. By the age of sixty, he was already quite ill with emphysema and rheumatic heart disease, and he longed for the sun and the warmer climate of southern France. Completing his final work in Cannes, he died there on 23 September 1870.

Mérimée wrote the story of *Carmen* between the French revolution of 1830 and the Paris Commune of 1870. Georges Bizet wrote the music for his opera of the same name just after the Prussian invasion of Paris, which was followed by an economic depression in 1871. Mérimée died five years before *Carmen* premiered on 3 March 1875 on the stage of the Théâtre de l'Opéra-Comique. He and Bizet never met.

CHAPTER TWO

Georges Bizet and the Genealogy of *Carmen*

Human creations are situated essences.

Americo Castro, *The Structure of Spanish History*[1]

Just as Mérimée could not have predicted *Carmen* transformed into Bizet's opera, so Bizet could not have known the enormity of the future of his creation. Bizet left behind a gift to operatic and French history: the extraordinary transformation of literary characters into musical form. It was a gesture that the great Spanish historian Americo Castro considers a "magico-human projection" of the literary into a performative act.[2] Bizet transliterated Mérimée's "storied characters," giving them musical dimension and expressive human capacity. In this way, perhaps unknowingly, in creating *Carmen*, the most performed opera in history, he forged an artistic and historiographic relationship between Mérimée and the figures of Carmen and Don José.

Through the story of *Carmen* (*cuento*), her singing (*cante*) and corporeal presence (*baile*), Carmen, the Hispano-Gypsy, reemerges onto the stages of Europe, becoming what Castro refers to as an "immanent element"—a creative force that emanates both from Mérimée and Bizet.[3] Within the powerful expression that bursts forth from Carmen's body, the history of the Gypsy in Europe is renewed and reinforced. What Bizet ultimately achieves is not only the art of song but, perhaps more importantly, the art of memory. He reconfigures Mérimée's understanding of what is most essential in Carmen and Don José: freedom and pathos. Bizet, like Mérimée, creates a form of art—the opera *Carmen*—into which the characters of Carmen and Don José extend their *élan vital* (vital aliveness) so necessary for evoking the rich history of Mozarabic Spain that will concern us throughout this text. Each man bequeathed history a gift.

Georges Bizet

Alexander César Léopold Bizet was born at Bougival, outside Paris, on 25 October 1838, his parents' only child.[4] Bizet, a *bonhomme* who called himself "Georges," was a private man who sought solitude as often as he attended soirées where he played the piano for his friends. He became a respected pianist and, had he not loved composing more, might have pursued a concert career. Blessed with a remarkable memory for music, he could recall entire scores with ease. He read widely and was known to speak his mind. Bizet was enthusiastic about other people's musical ideas, absorbing distinct genres of music into his own musical inventions. In music he found his spiritual and philosophical center.[5]

His father, Adolphe Armand Bizet (1810–1886), was from Rouen and had worked in Paris as a wigmaker and hairdresser before becoming a singing teacher who coached opera singers. Georges Bizet's mother, Aimée Joséphine Delsarte (1815–1861), a very fine pianist, came from Cambrai in northern France. Originally from a religious Catholic family of musicians, Aimée moved to Paris to be near her brother, François, the celebrated singing teacher and musical reformer. Adolphe and Aimée married and went to live in northern Paris, near the six Delsarte cousins with whom Georges spent his childhood. It is thought that Aimée, not Adolphe, taught Georges to read music and play the piano. Following in his mother's footsteps, Georges also became interested in his uncle François's ideas. At eight years old, Georges could sing a song having only heard it once before and without looking at the music.

François Delsarte's (1811–1871) reformist musical principles, to which Bizet was exposed at a young age, arguably influenced his scores and the way in which he integrated stage directions, choreography, and musical notation, particularly into the orchestral score of *Carmen*.[6] Delsarte, a St.-Simonian and a teacher of rhetorical gesture, "devised an elaborate system linking life (vitality, emotions), mind and soul in a triune scheme that was applied to the parts of the body, the way the body parts combine in movement and the directions movements proceed in space."[7] Delsarte espoused the notion that all parts of the body were musical and, therefore, expressive.[8]

In France, one had to attend the Paris Conservatoire to become a professional musician. It was the center of training where young performers and composers made the necessary connections that would launch their professional career. Bizet was only nine years old when his father enrolled him on 9 October 1848.[9] Ten years later, Bizet graduated from the Conservatoire a virtuoso pianist and entered the professional compositional arena.

A bibliophile, Bizet attracted the attention of the finest teachers. He was already an exceptional pianist, with perfect pitch and at ease with harmony and counterpoint, when he auditioned for the Conservatoire. Piano was his anchor, and he began his music studies in Marmontel's class and won a *premier prix* for *solfège* within six months.[10] He won a *deuxième prix* in 1851 and a *premier prix* in 1852.[11] That same year, Bizet signed up for Benoist's organ class. Two years later, he won *deuxième prix* for organ and fugue and, in 1855, a *premier prix* for both. It is important to note that a number of Bizet's teachers at the Conservatoire composed ballet music with Gypsy themes. Benoist collaborated on the score for *La Gypsy* in 1839 and Auber, the Director of the Conservatoire, composed a similarly titled ballet, *La Gitana*, performed at the end of 1839.

Bizet supplemented his keyboard studies with counterpoint, which he studied with Piërre Zimmerman (1785–1853) and Charles Gounod (1818–1893), who substituted for Zimmerman when he became ill.[12] Gounod had a formative influence on Bizet, who once said to him, "You were the beginning of my life as an artist. I spring from you."[13] He then began to study composition with the distinguished artist Jacques François Fromental Halévy (1799–1862), who had written the popular opera *La Juive*.[14] Halévy composed a great deal both in lyric and grand opera, working at the Paris Opéra and the Opéra-Comique. In 1854, Halévy was appointed Permanent Secretary of the Institute, a respected and prestigious position.

The year 1854 was a prolific one for Bizet.[15] He composed a series of works for piano and his father published three of his songs, along with a few piano pieces. By 1855, he had written his first opera, *La Maison du Docteur*. It was as an arranger of Gounod's *First Symphony* that he learned the techniques that would emerge in his first opera: orchestration, melodic invention, and thematic handling.[16]

Bizet also distinguished himself under the tutelage of Halévy, winning prizes for fugue and organ. An early work from the Conservatoire, *Symphony in C* (1855), not performed until 1935, identified him as a talented prodigy. Bizet entered the Prix de Rome in 1856 at the age of fourteen and took second place, a prize that provided him free entrance into the lyric theaters of Paris. One year later Bizet, like his mentor Halévy, and also for a cantata, earned the coveted Grand Prix de Rome.[17] For this, he was awarded the Cross of the Legion of Honor. The prize took him away from home for three years (1857–1860), giving him the educational opportunity of a lifetime, including exposure to Roman, Renaissance and Baroque art and architecture.

In 1856, Bizet entered an operetta competition offered by composer Jacques Offenbach, the manager of the Théâtre des Bouffes. Parisians Ludovic Halévy (who would write the libretto for *Carmen*) and his peer, Léon Battu, wrote the one-act libretto for an *opéra bouffe à l'Italien*, *Le Doctor Miracle*, for which competitors had to write music. Bizet and fellow composer Charles Lecocq entered and tied for first prize. They split the reward of twelve hundred francs. Both men's compositions were performed eleven times.[18]

Bizet left for Rome in December of 1857.[19] The Prix de Rome recipients resided at the luxurious Villa Medici, Napoleon Bonaparte's site for the French Academy in Rome. Bizet also journeyed into southern France through northern Italy. He and his fellow *pensionnaires* sailed from Genoa to Livorno, visiting Pisa, Florence, Siena, and later Anzio, Naples, Pompeii, Perugia, Assisi, Bologna, and Venice.[20] He enjoyed women and profited from a Mediterranean climate with its bright, sunny days. In the villa, Bizet was known as a convivial Frenchman who, in Rome, seemed to make friends more easily than in Paris. Greatly admired for his nightly piano-playing, Bizet was invited often to the homes of friends. In 1860, another French composer, Ernest Guiraud, arrived at the Villa Medici. This coincidence was profitable for Bizet as, in Italy, the two became lifelong friends. Guiraud came to know Bizet's tastes and talent, living in such close proximity to him that when Bizet died prematurely, Guiraud felt he had the close knowledge of Bizet required to dare to transform his composition. This friendship became significant after Bizet's death because it was Guiraud who would edit the score for *Carmen*, removing the spoken dialogue and replacing it with sung verse. Responding to the French public and critics' dislike for the opera during its first thirty-six Parisian performances, Guiraud tightened the score.

It is also important to note in this study of the compositional context surrounding *Carmen* that exotic geographies and characters had interested and inspired Bizet for some time. Italy provided a plethora of Romantic images for the impressionable Bizet. At various moments, he considered Spanish subjects—pre-Carmens. He considered operatic scores on "oriental" themes: Victor Hugo's *La Esmeralda* as well as Cervantes' *Don Quixote*. Bizet was drawn to a musical transliteration of Hugo's Romantic Orient as "Arab, even Spanish, because Spain is still the Orient; Spain is half African, Africa is half Asiatic."[21]

At the end of 1858 Bizet was to have submitted to the Académie des Beaux Arts in Paris, according to the rules of the Prix, a mass, a cantata, or some other form of religious music. One musicologist argued that he "hesitated" because he disliked liturgical music, being a man who did not believe in God.[22] Bizet instead chose to submit an opera, as this was where his interests lay and, being in Rome, he had heard and seen many operatic productions. However, he did not submit a traditional opera; rather, he taunted the committee by submitting an *opera bouffa*, instead of a mass, for his first-year qualification. In a second-hand bookshop, he had come upon *Don Procopio*, a libretto by Carlo Cambiaggio first performed in 1844, set by the younger Fioravanti. With this libretto, Bizet submitted his composition and received correspondence from the committee, praising his new work's "easy and brilliant touch."[23]

While living at the Villa Medici, Bizet managed to persuade a French poet living in Rome, Louis Delâtre, to write a series of verses for an "ode-symphonie."[24] Bizet's goal was an opera in six movements for soloists, chorus, and orchestra whose model was the popular, exotic work by Félicien David, *Le Désert*.[25] Bizet thought that the work, entitled *Vasco de Gama* after the famous Portuguese ship captain who first sailed around the Horn of Africa, displayed the "harmonic style and rich orchestration" toward which he was working. In 1859, this cantata was accepted by the committee and performed in Paris upon his return in 1863. Bizet had petitioned the Académie to allow him to stay in Italy one more year rather than go for the required year to Germany, and their subsequent acceptance enabled him to travel throughout Italy in the company of Guiraud.

The final work required of the Prix was a symphony, and Bizet remained in Italy finishing this final composition.[26] His was an original idea: symphonic themes inspired by Italian cities where he had been, in essence an ethnographic approach to his art. Here one may trace the root of his understanding of the musical character of Carmen: she is from Andalusia, a musical environment, and her ethnicity — *gitana* — must be reflected in the tenor of the sounds. Her physiognomy and geographical movement throughout the libretto must sound as if they are in story form. While Bizet never traveled to Spain, his experiences in Italy clearly prepared him to translate Mérimée's imagination into music.

In July of 1860, Bizet and Guiraud left for Paris. Bizet traveled slowly, visiting towns and ruins on his way north. While a previous prize given by French composer Jacques Offenbach, for Bizet's first stage work, as well as the Conservatoire's *premier prix*, had helped to launch Bizet's musical career, his Italian sojourn and the cultural and musical experiences he had absorbed contributed to both storyline and sound for the next fourteen years. Still, he had to earn a living, so he taught piano to children, wrote transcriptions of operas, orchestrated other composers' work and wrote operas on commission. Moving in the Parisian musical world, he made as many connections as he could. Bizet left Paris only twice thereafter. In 1862, he traveled to Baden-Baden with Berlioz, Gounod, and Ernest Reyer; a second sojourn was to Belgium,[27] but he would spend the rest of his short life mostly in Paris, working. He composed four grand operas in fifteen years, but died before his musical significance was accepted. Most musicologists agree that Bizet was handicapped by the French public's exclusively operatic tastes in music. Jouvin denounced *The Pearl Fishers* in *Le Figaro* as a "systematic orgy of noise."[28] Deeply injured by these remarks, Bizet understood that he could not cater to critical or public taste, and, yet, he suffered it.

Perhaps most important with regard to Bizet's early compositional career were the "catastrophic performances of *Tannhäuser*" at the Paris Opéra in 1861.[29] The public booed noisily. Mérimée, who was also in the audience, wrote that it was "a colossal bore . . . It seems to me I could write something like it tomorrow, inspired by my cat walking over the keyboard of the piano."[30] Bizet had returned to a Paris whose music critics' narrow-minded dismissal of Wagner perhaps opened the doors, albeit slowly, for experimentation in new French musical composition. Upon hearing Wagner, Bizet began what musicologist Susan McClary defines as a "complex relationship with German music."[31] Bizet's generation of Conservatoire peers had been encouraged by Gounod "to study the Germans as models."[32] Even Bizet had said early in his career, "next year I shall write something tragic and purely German . . . I am German by conviction, heart and soul."[33]

Bizet, just twenty-three years old, recognized in *Tannhäuser* its spiritualism—the same tenor of spirituality he had discovered in *La Juive*—and was reported by Jouvin to have called Wagner a "Verdi with style."[34] While he would have to absorb the French press's pejorative Wagnerian labeling of his work for the rest of his life, Bizet continued to approach each new work of composition as if it were his first, with a demi-spiritual quest for the truth and his perfection of it. Even Nietzsche, who would later become an ardent supporter of Bizet's, believed *The Pearl Fishers* to have been influenced by Wagner's *Lohengrin*, an opera with which the young French composer was not acquainted until 1869 when he began to study its score. But it was the seminal Romantic critic Théophile Gautier (1811–1872) who justified Bizet's aesthetic debt to Wagner. Gautier writes, "M. Bizet belongs to the new school of music and has broken away from made-to-order arias . . . and all the old formulae. He follows the dramatic action from one end of a situation to the other and doesn't cut it up into little motifs . . . Richard Wagner must be his favorite master and we congratulate him on it."[35]

Often in the company of musicians, Bizet was known to attend Friday evening musical salons at the home of his teacher, Fromental Halévy. One night, Bizet happened to display his extraordinary sight-reading capacity, playing for none other than Franz Liszt and Hector Berlioz, the latter holding Bizet's virtuoso technique in the highest regard: "His talent as a pianist is also great enough that no technical difficulty can stop him in his transcriptions of orchestral music, which he can do at sight . . . He must be recognized as a composer in spite of his rare talents as a sight-reader."[36]

On 8 September 1861, his ailing mother died at the age of only forty-five. Bizet consoled himself with his parents' maid, Marie Reitner, who gave birth to their son, Jean, in June of 1862.[37] Three months previously, his beloved teacher Halévy had died and, as Georges had never got on with his own father, Halévy's death proved to be a tremendous loss.

In 1862, Bizet rejected a prestigious teaching position at the Conservatoire, choosing instead to complete his obligation to the Prix de Rome. He composed a one-act comic opera, *La Guzla de l'émir*, with a libretto by Jules Barbier and Michel Carré. The work was criticized for its "over-instrumentation," but accepted as his final submission to the Académie. It was rehearsed at the Opéra-Comique but withdrawn by Bizet when the director of the Théâtre-Lyrique (who had been offered 100,000 francs per year to produce a Prix de Rome winner's work) invited him to compose a new work. With this incentive, the manager of the Théâtre-Lyrique, Léon Carvalho, an impresario in his own right, was able to take chances on lesser, even unknown, composers. However, the final condition of the academic Prix de Rome was that no opera given to the committee for review be performed in a commercial venue. The Prix was to be preserved as a tutorial experience, not a professional one. Bizet thus withdrew *La Guzla*. Instead, Caravalho suggested another theme: *Les Pêcheurs de Perles* with a libretto by Eugène Cormon and Michel Carré.[38] Between 1862 and 1863, Bizet worked tirelessly on the music, his first professionally-commissioned score. Caravalho moved the location of the piece, originally set in Mexico, to what is now Sri Lanka but was then British-occupied Ceylon, as he was searching to produce something à la mode, an orientalist-themed work likely to please the bourgeois French appetite for the exotic.[39]

On 23 September 1863, *Les Pêcheurs de Perles* opened at the Théâtre-Lyrique. Absorbing into the opera unfinished pieces of music, among them Bizet's opera *Ivan IV*, *Pêcheurs* resounded as an accumulation of all of Bizet's previous work. The music critics harshly criticized the libretto "as absurd and the score as noisy and offensive." Some were shocked by the impudence of Bizet, at the age of twenty-four, appearing on stage at the end to take a bow.[40] Jouvin wrote in *Le Figaro* that there are, "neither fishermen in the libretto nor pearls in the music."[41] And the music critic of *Le Ménestrel Universel*, Gustave Bertrand, referred to it as a "weak imitation of the funeral march in *La Juive*, with the shocking, violent effects of the latest Italian school—and much too much screaming."[42] But the composer Hector Berlioz praised the work: "[The music is] quite successful. It contains many beautiful, expressive pieces, full of fire and color . . . M. Bizet . . . took the journey to Rome, he has come back without having forgotten what music is. Since his return to Paris, he has rapidly acquired the unusual reputation of an incomparable score reader."[43]

Berlioz and Lizst believed that Bizet could certainly have pursued a career as a pianist. Berlioz's remark translates less as a criticism of his composition and more as a recognition of his maturing artistry. Despite its lack of appeal to some nineteenth-century critics, the score must have had merit if, from the late nineteenth to the early twentieth centuries, both Emma Calvé, who sang the role of Carmen 1,389 times, and Enrico Caruso, who premiered the role of Don José in America, agreed to sing the opera.[44]

Les Pêcheurs was unsuccessful at the box office even though its critical reception was significant. Berlioz commented in a final review for the *Journal des Débats* that "the score of *Les Pêcheurs de Perles* does M. Bizet the greatest honor."[45] Bizet's continued interest in ode-like melodies as a sonorous means of evoking the Romantic idea of the "East," some of which were echoed in the score for the fourth act of *Carmen* a decade later, were beyond anything the French public had heard or understood. Some critics hailed Bizet as the "leader of the new French school" of composition.[46] Others condemned him. Bizet's use of impressionistic musical themes to describe landscape and provoke an emotional response fell on deaf ears. This was the beginning of his trouble with the press and an emerging middle-class French audience. A silly story was acceptable to their bourgeois social mores, but a modernist sound was unfamiliar and misunderstood. The work was performed only eighteen times, from September to November, and was taken off the stage until 1886, eleven years after Bizet's death.

Between 1864 and 1866 Bizet supported himself as an arranger for Gounod, whose compositions influenced him to such an extent that Bizet's work from this period bears some resemblance to Gounod's. Bizet arranged a version of *Ave Maria* by Bach and Gounod as a piano solo, as well as six choruses for piano solo and an arrangement of Handel's *Harmonious Blacksmith Variations*. He also managed to publish a song, *Vieille Chanson*, and several piano pieces called *Vénise*. By the end of 1866, *La Jolie Fille de Perth* was finished (one can hear the influence of J. S. Bach in the repetitive, ode-like quality of moments) and, in the same year, Bizet published another song for piano, *Adieux de l'Hôtesse Arabe*. Bizet, however, remained poor. Unable to make enough money to survive, he moved out of Paris to a suburb called Le Vésinet, where his father had purchased an acre of land and built two cottages on it, one of which he offered Bizet. A railroad ran out to this land, allowing Paris and work to remain accessible still to the composer.

Bizet struggled financially for the duration of the 1860s, but succeeded in eking out a modest living, taking whatever work came his way. Gounod, his patron and his friend, helped him when he could and Bizet gave piano performances at Parisian society salon evenings, including a royal evening at the Louvre. "I am the victim," Bizet believed, "of a persecution, of a conspiracy against me," referring to French public taste and the end of Louis-Napoleon's reign. He did not live long enough to see his own success realized as a transformational art that would change opinion about French opera and open the public's ears to new sounds. *Carmen* would become one of the most performed operas in musical history, grossing millions of francs over time.[47]

With the birth of his beloved theater at Bayreuth, Richard Wagner's operatic style was to have a profound effect throughout the 1860s on how French music critics reviewed Bizet. Every new operatic composition by Bizet was to some degree compared negatively to Wagner. In reviewing *Les Pêcheurs*, Jouvin accused Bizet of Wagnerism, writing his "little opera with his eyes humbly fixed on the tyrannical Wagner, who had completely dominated him."[48] This infuriated Bizet. Reacting emotionally to the dogmatism of yet another influential music critic, the reactionary and influential Scudo, who wrote for *La Revue des Deux Mondes*, Bizet challenged him to a duel.

"Wagnerism," declared the 1911 *Encyclopaedia Britannica*, "was a sort of spectre that haunted the imagination of many leading members of the musical press. It sufficed for a work to be at all out of the common for the epithet 'Wagnerian' to be applied to it. The term, it may be said, was intended to be condemnatory and it was applied with little understanding of its real meaning."[49] This Wagnerian label paradoxically contributed to the French public's negative reception and understanding of *Carmen* and to the Viennese, Belgian, and German audiences' acceptance of the work as a masterpiece. "Wagnerian" remained an insult in French musical criticism of the 1850s, 1860s, and 1870s, whereupon it metamorphosed into a compliment.

In 1866, the enterprising Caravalho of the Théâtre-Lyrique offered Bizet another commission: an opera based on Sir Walter Scott's *Fair Maid of Perth*. Working tirelessly, Bizet premiered his second opera on 26 December 1867, calling it *La Jolie Fille de Perth*. In the opera, the protagonist, a Gypsy named Mab, pre-figured the character of Carmen and *La Jolie Fille*'s "danse bohémienne" was integrated into the fourth act of *Carmen*. Unfortunately, the opera was, like *Les Pêcheurs*, not a success, playing only eighteen performances.

On 3 June 1869, Bizet married Geneviève Halévy (1849–1926), the second daughter of his former professor, Fromental Halévy. They had a civil ceremony, as Georges was neither religious nor Jewish, much to the dismay of the Halévy family.[50] Bizet had known Geneviève most of her life and it is thought that by 1867 they were in love. Over time, Bizet's lack of complete success and intense mood swings, as well as Geneviève's own emotional intensity, made their marriage grueling.[51] The two became deeply unhappy and, eventually, incompatible. Geneviève was used to salon evenings; her husband, a more private person, was less inclined to these social engagements. By the time their son Jacques was born, their marriage was already in serious trouble.

At the end of 1868, nearing the outbreak of the Franco-Prussian War, France fell into economic recession. The Théâtre-Lyrique went bankrupt, as did Bizet's sponsor, Caravalho. On 19 July 1870, France declared war on Prussia. On 2 September, at the Battle of Sedan, Napoleon III was captured and the Prussians won the war almost instantaneously. Profoundly troubled by the Prussian occupation of the city, Bizet, along with Camille Saint-Saëns and Jules Massenet, joined the National Guard. Paris declared herself an independent republic and, within two weeks, the Prussian army surrounded, attacked, and then entered Paris. Meeting little resistance from the French population—already exhausted from two civil wars already fought that century, the revolutions of 1830 and 1848—the Prussians were able to seize the city quickly.

The Prussian siege of Paris forced theaters to close, putting many artists out of work. The Garnier opera house, still under construction, was used as a hospital and a food warehouse. Fleeing the subsequent Commune and civil killings, Bizet and Geneviève moved outside the city to Le Vésinet. Once the Prussians left Paris with the armistice of 26 January 1871, theaters reopened their doors and Bizet had work. "The restoration of peace in June brought with it the prospect of reinvigorating French music from within."[52] Tastes had changed, though. Jacques Offenbach's dominance at the Théâtre-Lyrique and in French popular consciousness was finished and people sought a new sound. The directors of the Opéra-Comique, Camille du Locle and Adolphe de Leuven, looked to Bizet, a promising thirty-four-year-old composer, to create something refreshing. The result was a one-act comic opera, *Djamileh*, based upon an orientalist harem fantasy, *Namouna*, written by poet Alfred de Musset in 1832.

In *Djamileh*, his third opera, Bizet finally realized one of his musical and dramaturgical goals: to create through music a landscape of exotic flavor and romantic escape — to be in touch with the Romantic school. *Djamileh* premiered on 22 May 1872 and, like *La Jolie Fille*, was not a success at the box office. However, it was a musical success, praised for the music's ability to evoke a faraway landscape, as if it were a painting or a photograph. Bizet commented: "It is not a success, [but] I am still extremely satisfied with the results. The press has been very interesting; never before has a one-act comic opera been taken so seriously and I may add, so passionately argued . . . Reyer, Weber, Guillermot of the *Journal de Paris* . . . that is to say more than half of the daily press — have been very warm. De Saint Victor, Jouvin, etc. have been favorable in the sense of conceding me talent and inspiration — all corrupted by Wagner."[53]

Because the work demonstrated Bizet's original, maturing voice as a composer, Du Locle and De Leuven offered him a third operatic commission. They invited him to compose a three-act opera for the Opéra-Comique with a libretto by Ludovic Halévy, his wife's cousin, and Henri Meilhac. This experiment became *Carmen*.

Preceding *Carmen* was another exotic work, *L'Arlésienne*. Commissioned by Léon Carvalho, now the artistic director of the Théâtre du Vaudeville and staunchly committed to new French composition, *L'Arlésienne* shared *Djamileh*'s attempt at local color with its intimate, Provençal impressionism.[54] As in most comic operas of the day, Bizet wrote music for sung dialogue, a prelude to *Carmen*.

Bizet transformed Alphonse Daudet's play *L'Arlésienne* into a successful score, a translation of narrative and emotion into sound. He broke up the sung dialogue into suites of speech-like dialogue, or recitatives, thus achieving a harmonious balance between poetic verse and music. The arrangement of musical sections united sung poetry with dramaturgy. The opera premiered on 1 October 1872, but it was a failure. Performed a mere twenty-one times, *L'Arlésienne* was too experimental for a conservative French audience. Its story is rather odd: a young man becomes infatuated with a young lady from Arles (never seen on stage). She falls in love with someone else and he commits suicide, ruined by his love for her. Bizet wrote twenty-seven musical pieces that were played between scenes of spoken dialogue in the opera, but as his music was atmospheric and narrative, this arrangement between words and notes was ineffective, serving to construct a rupture between the two media.

Mmes. Deschamps-Jehin, Galli-Marié, de Nuovina, Ch. Wyns, "Escamillo," Schmumann-Heink, Calvé, Delna, Marié de l'Isla in the role of Carmen; photographer and date unknown. Roger-Viollet Archives, Paris, France

Gounod, like many artists, fled Paris during the siege and did not return for some time. This left Bizet free, immediately after the siege, to concentrate solely on his own work. This new composition would become *Carmen*.[55] However, Bizet placed it to one side, in search of paying assignments, and was offered an opportunity he could not refuse. The Paris Opéra asked him to compose an opera based upon the Spanish hero, El Cid, with a libretto by Louis Gallet. Working quickly, Bizet finished this new opera, *Don Rodrigue*, by October. But bad luck struck again: the Opéra on the rue Le Péletier burned down on 28 October that same year—the fourth opéra house to burn to the ground.[56] While *Don Rodrigue* was never performed, Bizet absorbed its final act into an opera overture, *Patrie*, performed in February of 1874.

By December of 1873, Bizet had approached the mezzo-soprano Célestine Galli-Marié, an established star of the Opéra-Comique, to sing the title role of Carmen.[57] The ultra-conservative director De Leuven postponed rehearsals many times, citing decency problems with the libretto. Du Locle turned to Ludovic Halévy for help in persuading De Leuven, saying "perhaps you can convince him."[58] Halévy writes in 1905, on the occasion of the one-thousandth performance of

Carmen, that he "had not finished [his] first sentence when De Leuven interrupted: "Carmen! The Carmen of Mérimée? Wasn't she murdered by her lover? And the underworld of thieves, Gypsies, cigarette girls—at the Opéra-Comique, the theater of families, of wedding parties? You would put the public to flight. No, no, impossible!"[59] Halévy finally convinced the reluctant De Leuven to accept at least the story of *Carmen*, De Leuven warned, "But I pray you, try not to have her die."[60] Eventually, De Leuven became so appalled that he resigned from the theater in 1874, selling his part in the Opéra-Comique to Du Locle and leaving the theater for good.[61] Du Locle subsequently stepped into the role of sole director of the Opéra-Comique and the opera proceeded.

Carmen was orchestrated at Bougival in the summer of 1874.[62] Bizet worked tirelessly on the piano score, playing the piano for rehearsals and changing the score as he played. He encountered difficulty in rehearsals with both the orchestra and singers. He sought to resolve one of his goals: realism. He asked the singers to sing in a candid, direct style and to be convincing as people. The female chorus, for example, was directed to smoke and fight simultaneously, to which they vociferously objected, unused to such a request. Bizet, having chosen Galli-Marié to play Carmen and Lhérie to play Don José, was firmly supported in his efforts by his stars, which helped somewhat to mollify the chorus.

Bizet's remarkable ability to write music that evoked people, landscape, and culture through melody and counterpoint reached its greatest height in *Carmen*, whose many character drawings—Carmen, Don José, Escamillo, and Lillas Pastia— necessitated such a strategy. Bizet discovered in Mérimée's *novella* the sense of exotic, historic locales he yearned to translate musically—an expressive freedom to orchestrate far away geographical places and characters that his previous works prefigure. Character study in Bizet's hand metamorphosed into geography and place, aided by nuanced hints of Hispano-Arab melody. Bizet single-handedly rewrote portions of the libretto between 1874 and 1875, choosing a musical cadence for the words that Halévy and Meilhac failed to provide. The Metropolitan Opera Association printed the following: "The libretto which Meilhac and Halévy constructed from Prosper Mérimée's conte was not by any standards perfect and probably seems more unforgivable now than in 1875. It was greatly abused at the time, it is true, but on grounds of moral depravity; while we find fault with its moral offensiveness, an act of treachery to Mérimée."[63] In De Leuven's opinion, Bizet's inclusion of Gypsies, murderers, thieves, and loose women was seen as a moral and, thus, commercial disaster for the likes of a middle-class family theater.

In trying to understand why the opera failed, the Metropolitan Opera Association Press Department wrote the following:

> It was not impossible to put Mérimée's Carmen on the 19th century stage: she was by all accepted standards a *fille de Satan*, an unrepentant thief, liar and tart, unwashed and dressed in dirty and tawdry rags. As it was, the comparatively drawing-room figure drawn by Meilhac and Halévy was considered extremely improper and Carmen was regarded as a most sophisticated and advanced entertainment to which not all men would take their wives and no man would take his daughters.[64]

It is interesting to note that while Bizet never traveled to Spain, he possessed an uncannily intimate knowledge of the country's musical history, including the popular seventeenth-century Spanish *zarzuela*. Like the *zarzuela*, *Carmen* contains sung and spoken dialogue woven together through musical interludes. Within the *zarzuela* performance could be found (in the sheet music), *seguidillas, habaneras, boleras,* and even the Moorish *fandango* whence the *seguidillas* derived.[65] The use of these forms in *Carmen* reveals Bizet's scholarly, ethnomusicological approach to his compositional work.

Plot Summary

Prosper Mérimée's 1845 novella was the kernel for Georges Bizet's 1875 opera. *Carmen, la novella* drew a wide Parisian audience as her story had become a part of popular lore: libertine Gypsy woman killed by vengeful, jealous Spanish lover. Bizet, like many Parisians, read *Carmen* first in *La Revue*. It was exotic, sexy, and entertaining. Staging a risqué story, keeping the passion and sensuality alive throughout a four-act opera, would have been difficult had Bizet not relied upon himself to rework the libretto given to him by Henri Meilhac and Ludovic Halévy. Bizet — like his first Carmen, Célestine Galli-Marié — understood the original *femme fatale* character described by Mérimée. Both the tenor and hue of his musical composition fit perfectly the geography and stereotypical character studies outlined by Mérimée.[66]

Mérimée's descriptive powers were amply demonstrated in the precision of his writing and the intimacy, for example, of his character studies. Not only do we begin to form an idea of their identity (however foundational the image), but also we are able to sketch in our mind how they walk, talk, and even react to the world.

Lyric Artist in the Role of Carmen, photographer and date unknown.
Albert Harlinque / Roger-Viollet Archives, Paris, France

Carmen premiered on the stage of the Opéra-Comique on 3 March 1875. It ran for forty-five performances that year and three more in 1876. Twelve years later, the Opéra-Comique caught fire. As most of the theater was built with wood, a great deal was lost in the maelstrom of flames, including archival program and scene design and costume records. Thus, the history of *Carmen*'s premiere can be reconstructed only from materials that escaped the fire. These exist in the form of newspaper reviews; the Choudens publications of libretto, staging manual, and score; and the opera's famous poster of Carmen at the entrance to the bullring in the fourth act, caught in the arms of Don José who has just killed her. The music criticism, in particular from *L'Illustration* of 13 March 1875 contained illustrations of the full production scenes.[67]

The opera's libretto departs in many ways from Mérimée's original storyline. The author, who is played by an Englishman, is the narrator in the novel but not in the libretto. Mérimée has Carmen travel extensively and frequently throughout Andalusia, from Cordova to Gibraltar and back on her smuggling trips and lover's liaisons. In the opera, the audience does not experience many landscapes. The character of Micaëla does not appear in the book, whereas she is the pivotal good girl in the opera. Escamillo from the opera is Lucas in the novel. Awaiting execution, Don José recounts to the Englishman the details of his life of crime. This is a powerful narrative device; we begin to empathize with Don José as he becomes more familiar to us through our narrator. Don José receives no such softening in the opera; he comes to Seville a murderer and there he will die. The opera's character studies are so tightly bound they become caricatures; only the music is nuanced. The novel's characters, on the other hand, become more singular as the story is told by Don José or by the English archeologist. Further, the archeological explorations and historical musings of our writer enrich the geographical descriptions and scenes between Carmen and everyone else in the book. The opera is dependent upon scenery, scene changes, and the audience's prior knowledge of Spanish towns and arenas as well as the musical intonation that casts a rich spell.

The 1875 program notes tell us that the opera takes place in the 1820s in and around Seville.[68] (The novel's locales were in Cordova, Gibraltar, and outlying Andalusian areas.) While the original designs for the opera are lost, seminal graphic artist Émile Bertin (1898–1957) re-imagined them, drawing details of the earlier version from gravures printed in journals. In Act I, the curtain rises on a scene thus re-imagined by Bertin who has painted a typically Andalusian space: a large, open sun-soaked earthen plaza surrounded by two- and three-story apartments.[69]

Pink, yellow, brown, lavender, sky-blue, and deep red color the buildings' facades. Rounded archways make up most first stories and passageways. Narrow steps lead up to what looks to be the entrance to a large building: in the distance looms the famous Sevillian Giralda, a syncretic architectural fusion of Moorish and Spanish design. Using the Giralda as a piece of the first act's skyline serves to identify our protagonist, Carmen, with Moorish and Spanish roots—the minaret was erected in the early twelfth century by a fundamentalist Berber/Arab dynasty known as the Almohads for their capital city mosque and was later transformed into the bell tower for the Cathedral of Seville.[70] While the Giralda seems an obvious decorative choice for a Sevillian scene, its austere geometric design shooting up like a pre-modern skyscraper into the air beyond softer, more intimate structures was clearly an ethnographic design choice by Bertin.

In the middle of the frame, Bertin situates narrow, sand-colored stairs that lead up to the famous tobacco factory, symbol of Europe's new industrialization and a mercantile rise to capitalism.[71] The factory, known in Spanish as La Cortuja, was erected between 1728 and 1771.[72] Situated beside the Guadalquivir River, the only navigable river in Spain and home to ships arriving with tobacco from Haiti, Cuba, and the Dominican Republic, the Real Fabrica de Tabacos (Royal Tobacco Factory) employed some three thousand *cigarenas*, female cigar makers. Three-quarters of Europe's cigars were rolled there between the late eighteenth and late nineteenth centuries.

The tobacco factory, situated on the calle San Fernando, when in operation, contained 21 courtyards, 21 fountains, 10 wells for cleaning the factory, 116 grinding mills, 40 reviewing mills, and 87 pens and stables to contain 400 animals used for the milling work. Constructed in the shape of a citadel, it also had a chapel, sentry boxes, drawbridges, and a moat.

In 1950, the tobacco factory was converted into the rectorate of the University of Seville and the factory work was transferred to the Remedios neighborhood. When it was finally closed in 2003, its 233 workers, mostly women, claiming to be the "rightful heirs" of Carmen, protested the closure of a practice that had been an institution in Spain for four hundred years, "We're not like the seductive, folkloric Carmen the world knows," said Concepcíon Gomez, a thirty-two-year employee whose grandmother and great-grandmother worked in the former factory. "We're referring to the hard-working women who earned a salary, who dared to smoke in public and who were pioneers in the feminist fight."[73] "If the factory closes," said Josefa Modrena, "we'll lose a tradition that has been passed down from mother to daughter since the nineteenth century." The first women were hired in 1812 while their men were fighting Napoleon's troops. Spain has a dismal record for working women and the factory planned to lay off its female workers first. When Mérimée wrote *Carmen*, the factory had 3,000 workers. By 1875, when the opera opened, it boasted 6,500 women. Soul-sisters of Carmen, the women revolted three times in the 1800s as they earned only one peseta for every 1,000 cigars rolled.[74] Many revolts followed, intensifying in the 1930s when "the women dunked the factory director in a fountain because he had criticized their work too harshly."[75]

Naturally affected by popular lore, Bertin imagined Carmen, at the beginning of the opera, standing alone outside the factory in a long, yellow dress with a red flower pinned to her white mantilla, a high comb holding her scarf on top of her head *à la éspagnole*.[76] She wears clothing the color of Rajasthani Gypsy women's saris. A sharp mustard-colored skirt cascades in flounces down to the ground. Her shirt, a deep-red jacket in the style of a matador, is tied above the waist so that some skin shows between the two pieces of clothing. Carmen stares off into space, waiting her turn.

Outside the factory where only women (Gypsy and *payo*, Spanish) work rolling cigars, Spanish soldiers stand guard. The traditionally blond-haired, blue-eyed Micaëla, dressed in Basque peasant costume with a long blue skirt, arrives in search of Don José. She carries a message from his ailing mother. Morales is the only guard she encounters. His gruff and sexually aggressive manner frightens the ingénue and she departs.[77] Soon after, Lieutenant Zuniga and Corporal Don José relieve Morales. After lunch, the factory whistle sounds and hundreds of young women begin to pour into the square facing the factory, as they make their way back to work after their break.[78] The scenery visualizes a tightly controlled social arena, akin to a bullring: an amphitheater with young women who work under guard inside a place of industry; go home to their mothers for lunch; and return at the call of their foreman. The women have little freedom, following the rules of time and work; the men, who sit outside hoping to catch a peek of a skirt or shoulder, have the ability to enter the factory in order to keep the peace. To complete this fantasy scene, Meihac and Halévy have the young ladies flirting with the Spanish soldiers as they reenter the factory.

Carmen appears with a cassia flower between her teeth. Soldiers try to engage her in conversation but her gaze continues to circle the scene until she discovers Don José, the only soldier to pay her no notice. She fixes her attention on him "in the fashion of women and cats that come only to those who pay no attention to them." Carmen walks over to Don José, swaying her hips back and forth "like a filly from the finest Cordoban stables." The descriptive treatment of Carmen by the librettists portrays her, as did Mérimée, as an animal or an artwork, outside the realm of the human.

Don José, feeling her presence, looks up, catches Carmen's glance and nervously returns to his work of fixing a little chain. Carmen is undeterred by his reaction. Instead, she throws her flower at him like a dart, hitting him in the chest. Startled, he jumps up at the moment that the factory bell sounds and the soldiers return to the guardhouse, leaving him the sole soldier on duty.

Sitting quietly outside the factory, Don José (we are told by the program notes) contemplates the idea that in Navarre, his home state, Carmen would have been burned as a witch. Before the first moment of dialogue, we are clear that Carmen's character is demonic, dangerous—the antithesis of Micaëla, who returns at that moment. Micaëla gives Don José a kiss and a letter from his mother urging him to marry Micaëla. Don José decides to follow his mother's advice and marry her. Suddenly, he hears shouts coming from the factory. Zuniga rushes into the factory, ordering Don José to follow him into the mob of women, all of whom are barely dressed and shouting at one another. Making his way toward the center of the crowd, he discovers Carmen, whom Zuniga reports has knifed Mañuelita, carving designs into her cheeks. Zuniga attempts to question Carmen, who replies, singing in Caló. Carmen then breaks away and he orders, much to his chagrin, that a "good-looking girl" be tied up. Zuniga tells Don José that he must arrest Carmen. He ties her hands and then escorts her out of the factory. Outside, Carmen tells him that he should release her. "Why?" he asks. Carmen lies, telling him that she loves him. She asks Don José to loosen the rope that binds her hands, promising him that she will meet with him later. As they walk toward the jail, Carmen breaks free and runs away. Zuniga arrives to discover Carmen gone. He leads Don José to jail, his punishment for allowing her to escape.

The curtain rises for Act II on the Gypsy Lillas Pastia's tavern on Seville's rampart.[79] It is one month later and Don José is to be released from prison.[80] The scene begins in a room decorated with colored frescoes. The walls are *azul*—the light Mediterranean blue typical of Andalusia—with red flowerpots decorating the balustrade and walls. Red doors stand in the back, giving the scene an inviting feel. Pastia's restaurant-bar is a two-tiered patio with a large space left empty in front of little wooden café tables, stools, and chairs. The café's upper balcony is decorated with earth-colored curtains and has small brown doors leading to rooms the audience never visits. A black-and-white poster of a bull's head whose sharp horns reach upward decorates the left-hand wall near the staircase that rises to the typically Spanish second story. Carmen sings, "Close to the wall of Seville, I know a certain old tavern. Together we'll dance the 'seguidilla,' And we'll drink Manzanilla!"[81]

Reduced to the rank of private, Don José readies himself to leave the jailhouse (we read of this; we do not see it) while Gypsies gather upstairs for a party of prostitutes, alcohol, and dancing. Gypsy girls dance to entertain the dragoons. Carmen announces the *Seguidillas*:

> The stillness at the end of day is broken by a lazy jingle. The sleepy air begins to tingle. The Gypsy dance is under way! And soon the tambourines of Spain and strumming guitars competing, continue on and on, repeating the same old song, the same old strain, the same old song, the same refrain . . . The Gypsy men play on with fire! Their tambourines loudly whirring! The pulsing rhythm fiercely stirring, enflames the Gypsy girls' desire. Their passion carries them away, their agile bodies turn and sway in burning frenzy and abandon. On and on they dance, madly driven like a whirlwind no force can stay![82]

As the soldiers make advances on the *gitanas bailandas*, Zuniga flirts with Carmen, hoping she has forgiven him for having her arrested. Zuniga informs her that Don José is free. As the soldiers with Zuniga begin to depart, Escamillo, a bullfighter, arrives, cheered on in a parade by everyone for having won his fight that day. The soldiers, devotees of the *corrida*, stay to invite him for a drink and he joins them, noticing Carmen, Frasquita, and Mercedes seated at a nearby table as he sits down. To Carmen, Escamillo sings "Señorita, one word. I'd like to know your name. And when I fight again, it shall be on my lips!" Carmen responds, "My name? It's Carmen. Or else Carmencita." Escamillo: "And if I say I love you?" Carmen: "Then I would say you are wasting your time."

Escamillo and the soldiers finally leave Pastia's tavern as El Dancaïro, leader of the Gypsies, arrives with El Remendado, with whom he has been plotting a smuggling job. Their plan: to smuggle textiles from Gibraltar inland to sell. El Dancaïro wants Carmen, Frasquita, and Mercedes' assistance in their plan in case they need help. But Carmen refuses to leave, singing, "I'm in love as never before!" Seeing Don José approach the bar, El Dancaïro sings, "Men like that we need to have on our side!" To induce him to join the *contrabandistas*, Carmen dances for Don José, singing, "Now that you're here, I'll dance for you, for you alone, señor. And even more than that, I'll sing and play my music. You sit right here, Don José." Carmen dances with castanets until bugles are heard in the distance, recalling soldiers to their barracks. Carmen accuses him of not loving her. Don José, believing her, tries to persuade Carmen of his undying love and devotion to her, "drawing from the vest of his uniform the flower which Carmen threw at him." "Carmen," he professes, "I love you!" In an attempt to inveigle him into the smuggling profession, she tells him, "People in love belong together. They cannot bear to be apart. Carry me off and far away, over the highest hills and deepest valleys. I would know that you love me then! Carry me across the mountains"—the Sierra Morena into which they will escape from the law with their stolen merchandise.

As Don José gets ready to return to his camp, there is a knock at the door. Zuniga enters. Upon seeing the private, he says "Oh, shame, my lovely Carmen, your taste is rather poor! When there's an officer who offers so much more, it's a private you prefer!" Zuniga then commands Don José to leave. Suddenly El Remendado and El Dancaïro appear and seize Zuniga as their prisoner until the Gypsies have had time to escape, unseen by the law. Having hit Zuniga, his superior, Don José has no choice but to join the Gypsy band. The curtain descends upon the Gypsy chorus singing to Don José, "Come follow us into the mountains, be one of us, be our companion, come with us and you will see what life can be, once you are totally free . . . Happy to roam the open spaces, all the world for a home, we obey our will alone. Best of all, a priceless possession, our life is free!"[83]

Act III is set in the Sierra Morena, the mountain range above Seville. Bizet's sublime, sonorous composition accompanies Carmen and her Gypsy band of smugglers as they make their escape from the law. Loaded down with stolen goods they hope to sell for "gold and riches," the smugglers climb the steep path ahead. Don José is now a fugitive.

Bertin's designs for Act III balance the music's sense of expansive natural space with meditative calm. Using a dark blue for the mountainsides, blue-white for the snowy mountain peaks in the distance, and earthy (yellow and brown) tones for nearby rocks and boulders, Bertin sketched a sublime, almost dreamy scene whose steep dimensions harmonized perfectly with the rocky plateau where the Gypsy thieves would finally rest, reading fortunes, speaking with one another, and singing. The music is beautiful: an intermezzo finds a solo flute sounding a simple melody, joined by a harp, a clarinet, and finally by the strings. The sound of these few instruments brings an existential feel to the earthy geography and makes one wonder what lies ahead for everyone; a sense of foreboding and tragedy is slowly woven into the score.

Exhausted, the Gypsies rest at the top of a hill. Frasquita and Mercedes sit down and, using a rock as a table-top, take out a deck of cards—a sign that the nineteenth-century French audience read as Gypsyesque. They accompany their own fortune-telling with a light melody. "Contrasted to this delicate music is Carmen's entry with discordant figures, somberness and slow melody."[84] Carmen reads her fate in the cards and reacts musically by singing a *queíjo* from the *cante jondo* lamentation. Her vocalization set against her fellow *gitanas'* singing isolates her voice, focusing our attention on her. She is announcing, as only a Gypsy can (channeled in the music of Bizet), that she will die.

Don José and Carmen begin to fight. Carmen tires of his obsession and he continues to threaten that he will kill her if she leaves him. Having read the cards, Carmen accepts her fate as El Dancaïro and El Remendado return to camp to report that the *gitanas* must distract the customs officers who guard the city wall. El Dancaïro orders Don José to remain at camp to cover their rear while everyone else travels to the city to try to move the merchandise.

Don José climbs up upon a high cliff, the perfect lookout place. In another part of the mountains, Micaëla, searching for Don José, moves closer to the Gypsy encampment. Lost and scared, she thinks she spots him and shouts, but he does not hear her. As she approaches him she discovers that he is, indeed, not her beloved. Rather, she has come by accident upon Escamillo, who has been purchasing bulls nearby. Having heard a rumor that Carmen was in the area, he has come looking for her. Escamillo and Micaëla find Don José. When Escamillo arrives, Don José asks his identity. He replies, "I am Escamillo, toreador of Granada." "Escamillo . . . You were foolish to take such a great risk!" Don José replies threateningly. Unthwarted, Escamillo answers blithely, "Yes, there you may be right. But you see, I'm in love, my friend. And love takes chances . . . Who would not risk his life pursuing his romances?"[85]

Searching to understand whom he loves, Don José presses him and Escamillo responds that he loves "a most exciting Gypsy girl," named Carmen. "She loved another man," he explains, "a soldier who deserted his brigade to please her." But, he continues, "the loves of a Carmen do not last six months." "You don't mind," Don José says facetiously. "I love her, yes, I do. I love her, my friend, I love her madly!" Beginning his intimidation tactic, Don José moves slowly toward Escamillo saying, "But when anyone takes a Gypsy from her people, you know, of course, he has to pay . . . The price is to be paid with knives to the finish!" Jokingly and totally nonplussed, Escamillo, replies, "Oh, what a treat, my boy. I'm overcome with joy. Now I know where I stand." As they begin to duel, Escamillo slips and falls. Just as Don José is about to plunge his knife into him, Carmen enters and grabs his arm. Carmen brings Escamillo good rather than bad fortune. "I am a lucky man to owe my life to Carmen!" he says, thanking her. Just then, the smugglers return. The *gitanos*, who know and respect Escamillo, allow him to escape the vengeful behavior of Don José, and Escamillo departs, inviting them and Carmen to his next *corrida*. The toreador theme can be heard in the music along with the foreboding shrill of flute and horns announcing the tragedy ahead.

As the Gypsies get ready to depart, El Remandado spots Micaëla, who has been hiding behind a rock this whole time. Micaëla urges Don José to return to his ailing mother and both Carmen and the Gypsies encourage him to do so. Don José, paranoid, threatens Carmen, "So you want me to leave you so that you can quickly run off into Escamillo's arms! I swear, I won't leave you ever . . . You and I belong together, till the end for good or ill! I won't leave until the day I die! . . . You are mine and mine you stay. You are mine and I'll never let you go! I will force you to obey, our destiny willed it so." Taking a few steps toward Carmen he completes his speech, "We shall meet again!" Finally, he departs with Micaëla as the curtain comes down.[86]

Act IV opens to an extraordinary image by Bertin, surely inspired by the Roman arenas in Arles and Nîmes. The program note tells us that it is a plaza in Seville whose ancient walls fill the upstage space. Immense and dizzying red- and white-striped arches like those found in the mosque in Cordova decorate the upper reaches of the stage. A black bull's head hangs between two arches in front of the entrance to the arena, its sharp horns reaching upward like crescent moons.

Bizet introduces the crowd, lacing the processional march with choral cries that announce the beginning of the fight. The music then bespeaks the entrance of the toreador Escamillo and his fellow matadors who will fight that day. Carmen is dressed in red, white, and black, the colors of the Cordovan alcazar. Her Gypsy *bata de cola* (a cascading, serpentine dress with a long train worn by female flamenco dancers) cascades downward and her left hand holds up a fan as her body casts a dark shadow on the red gates leading to the bullring. In the distance, the light stone-colored inner arches can be seen.[87] They are reminiscent of the ruined bullring in Arles that dominates the center of an ancient village. A few people sit poised in the upper balcony of the stands, watching intently the death-dance beneath.

Crowds of people enter the bullring, readying themselves for the bullfight. The crowd shouts Escamillo's name and the toreador enters with Carmen on his arm. Bizet has studied the music of the opening *cuadrilla*, using French horns to sound like the typical Spanish cornet and bugle that announce the start of the *corrida* to those watching in the stands. Escamillo tells Carmen, "If you love me, Carmen, then, today, of all days, you will be proud of me, if you love me, if you love me."

Carmen responds publicly, "I am yours, Escamillo . . . I never loved a man with such passion before!"[88]

Here a double narrative emerges as we share the role of spectator with the people inside the frame of the stage. As we listen to the bass sounds—brushed cymbals—that announce the ritual circling of the bullring by the *cuadrilla*, an oboe "introduces a sweet, tragic theme" into the seemingly normal Sunday afternoon.[89] Bizet's score weaves processional musical with a fatalistic leitmotif that announces danger, a return to the call of the cards that Carmen, standing still as Don José approaches like a panther, has embraced.[90]

Having spotted Don José outside, Frasquita advises Carmen to leave the area. Mercedes tells Carmen that Don José is hiding in the crowd waiting for her. Carmen confirms that she sees him, saying, "I am not afraid of a soul in the world. I will stay and I'll wait for him here." The "Toreador Song" is heard in the distance, with cellos added. A hushed chorus accompanies Frasquita's and Mercedes' forewarnings. The processional sounds recommence and the crowd enters the bullring. Carmen and Don José are the only people left outside the arena.

Don José emerges to Carmen's right. Bertin imagines his presence, menacingly, as he hides between archways that lead out to the street. He is clothed in a red cape, tall boots, and the typical Gypsy scarf tied around his head like a *bandido*. Don José moves toward Carmen, in the direction of the bullring. Bertin follows the design for the previous three acts, leaving plenty of open space in the center and downstage portion of the frame. This large pool of pink, red, and earth-colored floor serves to isolate Carmen, pushing her up against the red door in her bright white dress. While the portal leads ultimately to the bullring where she would have been safe, Carmen does not turn to open it. Rather, she faces her fate, Don José, whose long black shadow shows him moving slowly toward his victim. The beautiful, almost liltingly yellow light that Bertin uses to offset the deep red hue of the arches can be read as hope that Carmen will turn toward the red doors and run inside to safety, hope that Don José will be arrested and carried away. Yellow replaces red as Carmen's fate is sealed in the triangular space formed by the two upstage archways. The audience watches the unfolding scene of vengeance; specks of black and blue are seen in the red stands above Carmen.

"So you came back?" taunts Carmen. Don José: "I do not mean you harm, I beg you, I implore you . . . we'll start life anew. It will be a new existence, far away." Sardonically, Carmen replies, "You are talking like a dreamer. I won't live, I won't pretend! What was between us is over; once and for all this is the end! You know, I never lie, once and for all, this is good-bye!" Hearing cheers inside the bullring, Carmen turns to enter the ring, but Don José, desperate and obsessed, steps in

Caroline "La Belle" Otero and Frank, photographer and date unknown.
Roger-Viollet Archives, Paris, France

front of her to stop her. "I love him!" Carmen exclaims. "And even in the face of death, with my dying breath, I shall love him!" She turns to try to open the gates to the amphitheater when Don José grabs her, saying, "By God, then die!" He stabs her. Carmen falls lifeless in his arms. The orchestra responds to her death with a reprise of Don José's last, sung notes. And the curtain falls.[91]

A Composer's Composer

I should write better music.

Georges Bizet, 1866[92]

Unlike Prosper Mérimée, whose *Carmen, la novella,* was enjoyed and lauded throughout his lifetime, Bizet remained a composer's composer, perhaps too intellectual for his time. Bizet set himself the same high standards he admired in others: the intellectualism of Mozart, Robert Schumann, Félix Mendelssohn, and Carl Maria von Weber; the mystical melodies of Gounod; the passion of Giuseppe Verdi; the sheer power of Wagner; and the complex, oriental landscapes illustrated by Meyerbeer. "As an artist and a man, I am purifying myself and becoming better . . . I want to do nothing chic. I want to have ideas before beginning a piece."[93] Breaking with the French school of "*flonflons,* trills and false chords," Bizet suffered ostracism by critics and audiences alike.[94] This, along with chain-smoking and sixteen-hour workdays, may have contributed to his fatal heart attack three months after the premiere of *Carmen.*

Today he is remembered as "the most naturally gifted and original of French composers of the mid-nineteenth century and universally remembered for his opera *Carmen.*"[95] But this was not the case during his life, a fact he profoundly understood and which caused him great suffering: Bizet began many operas that he left incomplete; his moody, restless spirit led him into quarrels, even with friends, and revealed a deep insecurity that, even without the trivial bourgeois prejudices, might still have left him with an inner struggle. While Bizet was never at peace with himself and his artistic life in the public milieu, several great minds expressed sincere admiration for the composer. The most famous was Friedrich Nietzsche (1844–1900), who discovered in Bizet a wealth of tonal melodies and an honest realism that he respected, twin antidotes to his own countryman Richard Wagner's "teutonic tone."[96]

Well-versed at the end of his Roman sojourn in the two styles that came to dominate his melodic approach to composition, the Viennese classical style and

French melody and counterpoint, Bizet seemed to live a lonely life as a composer in France. Had he lived in Germany, despite Wagner's jealousy of his genius, Bizet and Wagner might have become friends; while separated by countries, both shared a similar desire to unearth in melody a new religion of contemporary sound, overwhelming in its repetitive, ritualistic song cycles. No composer since Bach had composed in this manner. What distinguished Bizet, however, was that he used his thematic melodic invention as a means of inventing atmospheres, locales, and cultures, musical bridges to another world, one where the audience could imagine and wander free, like Carmen herself.

And here Bizet's Romanticism began. Had he been a photographer on a sojourn to Egypt, or a novelist, he surely would have suffered less. His music, much like the spirit of *Carmen* in its open-ended spiritualism, frightened a confined and judgmental French public. Bizet spoke about music in terms of faith and vision. Composition engendered a spiritual quest, a search perhaps for the inner peace and balance he sought. Carmen possessed the freedom that Bizet was missing. In her, perhaps, he discovered something he lacked in himself: pride born of self-determination and skillful autonomy. Like Mérimée, Bizet also invented the perfect alter ego. Using Gypsy guitar rhythms for the *seguidilla* and *habanera*, Bizet experienced the explosive, untamed, and simultaneously highly truthful rhythmic nature of flamenco, an African, Arab and Hindu-inspired form of music so complex that even he might have struggled with its *compás* (flamenco polyrhythm) and *letras* (sung verses).[97]

A History of *Carmen*'s *Seguidillas*

Referred to as the national dance of Spain, the *seguidillas* (meaning small successions) originated as a regional folk dance in the eighteenth century.[98] Danced by aristocrats and peasants alike, in courts and in villages, the dance was performed in a circle, usually by two couples that faced one another. Each dancer executed an endless series of steps in 3/4 or 3/8 time with tremendous energy. Traditionally accompanied by lute and guitar, a tambourine and dulzaina (reed wind instrument) and self-accompanied with castanets, the dance is also accompanied by trite love songs that are illustrated by dancing couples changing partners. Its lilting melodies, almost angst-filled, are both infectious and saddening. The *seguidillas*' eighteenth-century court form was captured by Francísco José de Goya y Lucientes (1746–1828) in his famous painting *Dancing on the Banks of the Manzanares*. Dance historians and musicologists trace the *seguidillas* to Castilla de la Mancha, the region surrounding Castilla la Nueva (the new Christian capital at Madrid), while others give it an Andalusian origin and place its dancing near the Sierra Morena, the mountain range outside Sevilla. (*Mancha*, from whence *Manchegas* derives, is from the Arabic 'al Mansha, meaning dry land or wilderness.)

Spanish dance historian and performer Matteo refers to the *seguidillas* as a "joyous, bucolic dance with . . . breathless rhythm which seems almost nonstop . . . [t]he matrix from which all other dances such as the *sevillanas* and the *bolero*" emerged in the late eighteenth to early nineteenth centuries.[99] These were not only privately danced forms but choreographies seen in the *café cantantes* of industrializing European cities. The eighteenth century saw the emergence of the *seguidillas voleras*, or *boleras*: the *seguidillas sevillanas*, performed only in Seville; and the *seguidillas manchegas*, deriving from the Moorish *fandango* and *zambra*. Most likely the *seguidillas* has persisted because of its improvisational steps that enable couples and individual dancers to dance beside and in reaction to the musical accompaniment.

The dance begins with an *entrée*, or entrance, during which time the musicians play a musical introduction as the dancers walk in measured step around the room, *con grazia* (with grace), toward each other and into place. Abrupt endings, known as *bien parados*, complete each dance phrase or *copla*, a stylistic flair that made its way into other forms of Spanish and Gypsy dance. The sequence of steps in the *seguidillas* is as follows: Introduction, *salida*, *estribillo*, *copla*, *estribillo*, *copla*, *estribillo*, *copla*, *bien parado*. Castanets are played by the performers using the "ta tarara tarara ta" metric phrase. Gypsy dancers performing in nineteenth-century *cafés cantantes* throughout Spain transformed the *seguidillas* into the *siguiríyas*, a twelve-count phrase. The *cante jondo* narrative of the singer, which opened the choreography to solo improvisational performance, intensified the dance's traditionally happy tone.

Most important are the many kinds of *seguidillas*. Traditional dance historians and fierce Spanish nationalists writing at the beginning of the twentieth century, in an attempt to advocate for a pure Hispanic cultural expression, argued that the *seguidillas* was immune to outside cultural influences. "The *seguidillas*," argued seminal Spanish dance scholar Marina Grut, "is intrinsically Spanish with no foreign influence."[100] While one can argue that it is "intrinsically Spanish," it is quite impossible to prove no foreign influence. Where does the Gypsy transformation of the *siguiríyas* into the *cante jondo* emerge if not in the East? Spain, it can be shown, has had a great deal of foreign influence. Since the time of the Iberians, the country has been invaded by Greeks, Phoenicians, Romans, Gothic tribes, and Arab-Berber tribes from North Africa and the Middle East who remained within its borders for eight hundred years. Dance and music are beautifully positioned to absorb the myths and expressions of new immigrant cultures, open to influence in ways that more restricted parts of the socio-political landscape are not.

While these dance historians are correct in arguing that the form originated inside Spain, others are just now exploring the influence of economy on the form itself. The *seguidillas* is thought to have had its most populous expression in Seville, whence the *seguidillas sevillanas* derives. Slave ships from the Afro-Caribbean world arrived in Seville. West African rhythms were absorbed into field work songs and dances by Spaniards and Gypsies who worked beside them in the fields and the area itself, 'al Andaluz, retained its Hispano-Arab and Sephardic origins with rich musical traditions that over centuries were also absorbed by Gypsies and Spaniards into flamenco *letras* and *compás*. The *seguidillas*' complex layering of steps and rhythm, an infusion of ideas from the African diaspora and Gypsy traditions, maps an international identity for this dance whose origins remain a point of conjecture for musicologists, ethnologists, and dance historians interested in the history of Spanish dance practice.

Criticizing *Carmen*

> I won't mince words. Your *Carmen* is a flop, a disaster! It will never play
> more than twenty times. The music goes on and on. It never stops. There's
> not even time to applaud. That's not music! And your play—that's not a
> play! A man meets a woman. He finds her pretty. That's the first act. He
> loves her, she loves him. That's the second act. She doesn't love him anymore.
> That's the third act. He kills her. That's the fourth! And you call that
> a play? It's a crime, do you hear me? A crime!
>
> Jean Henri Dupin to Ludovic Halévy, 1875[101]

> Monsieur Bizet, as is known, belongs to that new sect who believe in
> vaporizing musical ideas instead of enclosing them within definite bounds.
> Melody [for him] is old-fashioned, the song overpowered by the orchestra,
> leaving only an echo. [But] melody is the design of music. If one takes
> that away, there is left only educated noise.
>
> Paul de Saint-Victor, *Le Moniteur*, 3 March 1875

> After a second hearing, after becoming more accustomed to the style
> of the score, I saw the real qualities of the work, qualities that
> become apparent only when one listens for them. Read at the piano,
> this work may be more appreciated than hearing it for the first
> time on stage.
>
> Benoît Jouvin, *Le Figaro*, 1875

After its forty-eighth performance, *Carmen* was taken off the stage at the Opéra-Comique. *Carmen* was not performed again in France until 1883. The opinions of Monsieurs Dupin and Saint-Victor, along with many other writers' harsh criticism of *Carmen* as Wagnerian melodrama, may indeed have led to Bizet's sense that he was being persecuted, dismissed by critics—the public face of the bourgeoisie whom he saw as totally misunderstanding his art form. Whether the French public's outrage at the story and score of *Carmen* precipitated Bizet's heart attack so soon after the premiere is hard to say. He was, after all, a young man, just thirty-seven years old. Interestingly, Monsieur Saint-Victor's condemnation of Bizet's score deeply penetrates its sonic radicalism. Saint-Victor accuses Bizet of "vaporizing musical ideas instead of enclosing them within definite bounds." If one replaces the word "vaporizing" with "spiritualizing" and "elongating" the musical phrase, one might just unlock the secret to Bizet's compositional genius. Further and perhaps more significant from the benefit of hindsight seems to be Monsieur Jouvin's writing in *Le Figaro*, a prefiguring to the words of Nietzsche in his spiritual attachment to Bizet's musical philosophy.

The day before his death, Bizet signed a contract for *Carmen* to be performed at the Imperial Opera House in Vienna in the fall of 1875. The opera received rave reviews both in Vienna and, later, at the Théâtre de la Monnaie in Brussels. Three years later, *Carmen* "swept victoriously across Germany" achieving "the most complete and universal of all operatic triumphs."[102] German composer Johannes Brahms "regarded *Carmen* as 'the greatest opera produced in Europe since the Franco-Prussian war' and attended no fewer than twenty performances."[103] Eventually the French audience grew to accept *Carmen*, a success Bizet would never enjoy.[104] But the work did not succeed in its original form: Act II was only finally performed at the Paris Opéra Garnier Théâtre on 11 November 1900, and *Carmen* was performed in full for the first time only on 21 December 1907.

Bizet, Wagner, and Nietzsche

Surprisingly, it was the German reformer, philologist, and philosopher Friedrich Nietzsche who came to Bizet's rescue. He argued that Bizet's score for *Carmen* had, indeed, nothing to do with Wagner—that the two composers stood at a clear distance from one another and that he preferred Bizet to Wagner. Of

Carmen, he remarked, "This music seems to me to be perfect. It comes forward with lightness, suppleness . . . light-footed are the Gods . . . It is cruel, exquisite, full of fatalism and yet it remains popular . . . It is rich, precise. It constructs, it organizes, it is finished . . . I repeat, this music has made a better man of me. Music must be Mediterraneanized . . . !"[105] Wagner was outraged at Nietzsche's embrace of Bizet's composition over his own. But he too was moved by *Carmen*. Its melodious passages echoed the ritualistic effect of his lengthy song cycles from *Tristan und Isolde* (1857). This affection of Wagner for the music of the scenes between Micaëla and Don José is further attested by a statement once made by the French composer Paul Vidal, who had known Wagner's friend, the pianist Joseph Rubinstein, in Rome a year after Wagner's death. According to Vidal, Rubinstein declared that "the composer of *Tristan* repeatedly obliged him to play *Carmen* on the piano. The phrase, 'ma mère, je la vois,' especially delighted him. He saw in its naïve freshness 'the point of departure for a renewal of French dramatic music, invigorated by melody of this genuinely popular type.'"[106]

Wagner recognized in *Carmen* the lyric tragedy he sought in his own sounds, a kind of spiritual theater connecting audience to performer in a ritualistic *pas de deux*. It was not Bizet who failed at the 3 March 1875 premiere of the work but, rather, the bourgeois French public that did not understand what they had just heard, interpreting it literally rather than philosophically, as both Wagner and Nietzsche had done.

In terms of tonality, many music critics of the nineteenth century drew comparisons between Don José's outburst in Act IV of *Carmen* and Wagner's *Tristan*. In 1888, thirteen years after the creation of *Carmen* and six years after the premiere of *Parsifal*, Nietzsche published a long essay dedicated to "The Case of Wagner" (*Der Fall Wagner*) that he used to support his theories concerning Bizet's compositional and historic accomplishment.

> Yesterday I heard . . . *Bizet's* masterpiece for the twentieth time. Again I stayed there with tender devotion, again I did not run away. This triumph over my impatience surprises me. How such a work makes one perfect! One becomes a "masterpiece" oneself.—And really, every time I heard *Carmen* I seemed to myself more of a philosopher, a better philosopher, than I generally consider myself: so patient do I become, so happy, so Indian, so *settled* . . . To sit five hours: the first stage of holiness!—May I say that the tone of Bizet's orchestra is almost the only one I can still endure? That other orchestral tone which is now fashion, the Wagnerian, brutal, artificial and "innocent" at the same time and thus it speaks all at once to the three senses of the modern soul,—how detrimental to me is this Wagnerian orchestral

tone! I call it *scirocco*. I break out into a disagreeable sweat. *My* good weather is gone.

And once more: I become a better human being when this Bizet speaks to me. Also a better musician, a better *listener*. Is it even possible to listen better?—I actually bury my ears *under* this music to hear its causes. It seems to me I experience its genesis—I tremble before dangers that accompany some risk, I am delighted by strokes of good fortune of which Bizet is innocent.—And how odd! deep down I don't think of it, or don't *know* how much I think about it. For entirely different thoughts are meanwhile running through my head . . . Has it been noticed that music *liberates* the spirit? gives wings to thought? that one becomes more of a philosopher the more one becomes a musician?—The gray sky of abstraction rent as if by lightning; the light strong enough for the filigree of things; the great problems near enough to grasp; the world surveyed as from a mountain.—I have just defined the pathos of philosophy.—And unexpectedly *answers* drop into my lap, a little hail of ice and wisdom, of *solved* problems . . . Where am I?—Bizet makes me fertile. Whatever is good makes me fertile. I have no other gratitude, nor do I have any other *proof* for what is good.

This work, too, redeems; Wagner is not the only "redeemer." With this work one takes leave of the *damp* north, of all the steam of the Wagnerian ideal. Even the plot spells redemption from that. From Mérimée it still has the logic in passion, the shortest line, the harsh necessity; above all, it has what goes with the torrid zone, the dryness of the air, the *limpidezza* in the air. Here, in every respect, the climate is changed. Another sensuality, another sensibility speaks here, another cheerfulness. This music is cheerful; but not from a French or German cheerfulness. Its cheerfulness is African; fate hangs over it, its happiness is brief, sudden, without pardon. I envy Bizet for having had the courage for this sensibility which had hitherto had no language in the cultivated music of Europe, for this more southern, browner, more burnt sensibility . . . How the yellow afternoons of its happiness do us good! During it, we look into the distance: did we ever find the sea smoother? And how soothingly the Moorish dance speaks to us! How even our insatiability for once gets to know satiety in this lascivious melancholy! Finally love, love translated back into *nature*! *Not* the love of a "higher virgin"! No Senta-sentimentality! But love as fatum, as *fatality*, cynical, innocent, cruel and precisely in this *a piece of nature*! That love which is war in its means and at bottom the *deadly hatred* of the sexes! I know no case where the tragic joke that constitutes the essence of love is expressed so strictly, turned into so terrifying a formula, as in Don José's last cry, which concludes the work:

"Yes! *I* have killed her,
I—my adored Carmen!"

Nietzsche was the first important critic and philosopher to have understood and credited Bizet's translation of Mérimée and of the French Romantic literary tradition into musical form. His personal love of *Carmen* as a work of artistic release is infectious. Having listened to the opera twenty times, Nietzsche says, "one becomes a 'masterpiece' oneself." Every time he encounters the music, he returns to center, like a flamenco dancer circling herself. Each performance of *Carmen* became a metaphysical experience for Nietzsche; the score turned him into a better philosopher, closer to the grain of truth. He also says that he becomes a better *listener*, entering into the work of art with facility.

Nietzsche's emotional prose points to the idea that the music carries an inherently ritualistic pulse; that it transforms the listener, pulling him into the score — onto the stage — slowly, subtly, causing Nietzsche to "experience its genesis." Nietzsche is evoking the compulsive, hypnotic impulse in the score — its *élan vital* — and reacting metaphysically to it. For Nietzsche, *Carmen's* ode-like melodies mark the beginning and end of Bizet's imagination — the genealogy of his Spanish, Mediterranean ideas that spill forth from the stage and into Nietzsche's body.

Nietzsche says that he "did not run away" despite the length; the music's archaic and primal layers had an internal, meditative effect on him, like Carmen herself. Moment by moment, a layer of self is peeled back, creating a profound internal effect. Nietzsche's evocation is awe-inspiring because it enacts a mode of empathetic reception: the music takes on psycho-physical-metaphysical dimensionality, shape, and form for Nietzsche; it allows him to escape from the book, from the claustrophobia of northern Europe, and from the thrall of Wagner. It leads him inside a labyrinth to his most central core of being where he discovers himself to be "fertile" — alive.

Nietzsche goes on to recognize and hold in the bounds of literary form the sensuality of the music. He seems to be translating Mérimée sonically here by breaking Europe into two sensibilities: north and south, cold, damp, and dark versus hot, dry, filled with abundant "African cheerfulness." Nietzsche has also unearthed a reverse ethnography that we will explore further in Chapter 3. He sees and feels himself transformed from a man living endlessly within the dark, wintery skies of northern European and transported instantly to the warm, inviting climate of the South. The harshness of the burnt sun expressed in Carmen's trill runs and "Moorish dances" (Nietzsche has clearly read Mérimée)[107] and long solos stands in sharp contrast to the overwhelmingly Romantic idealism of master teacher Richard Wagner. Bizet, to Nietzsche's mind, is ushering in a vitalist turning point in music history. Wagner, his older teacher, remains rooted in Romanticism, an era from which Nietzsche is now ejecting himself in his typical "untimely" manner, entering the presence of the work and simultaneously the future of art. Wagner's self-styled superiority represents in Nietzsche's mind the European moralistic superiority against anything new. Bizet, whose lack of ego is unearthed by Nietzsche in his meditation on the score of *Carmen*, becomes the philosopher's preferred source for musicality within philosophy.

For Nietzsche, the genius of Bizet's score was its Dionysian quality achieved through plot and sound. He loved the raw, sensual power of Carmen herself and the way in which she reveals her Gypsy character through song and dance. Here, one might point to Roland Barthes's notion of the "grain of the voice"—it is the idea that the voice is the narration. For Bizet and his written stage directions to *Carmen*, this meant the corporeality of the sound of music itself lives in the physicality of Carmen's singing.

Nietzsche also saw the raw power in *Carmen* as expressive of the Greek notion of fate—*moira*. Carmen's Otherness and destiny are communicated musically to the audience as Bizet craftily melts major key shifts into minor ones. This major–minor sonic shift—the resolving of one key shift into the other within a symphony—opened French lyric opera to a ritualistic choral tenor in the third act. These compositional breakthroughs resonate with the Greek ideals that preoccupied *The Birth of Tragedy*. Like Medea, Carmen is an uncontrollable being, larger than life, epic and timeless. Her singing—her sonic phrases—becomes her body and the body of opera.[108]

Nietzsche was drawn also to the chromaticism achieved through Bizet's complex layering of melodic and contrapuntal sound. *Carmen*, like Wagner's *Tristan und Isolde*, contained the hyper-pronunciation of consonants and syllables, the passionate symphonic ode-like quality in the "Toreador Song," for example, and the Dionysiac "love-death," sexuality, and lust tonality of sound sung by Carmen in the *habanera* and *seguidillas* songs. Bizet developed the Mediterranean quality of these major–minor key shifts to identify the Gypsy—the foreign—in Carmen's character. In the chromaticism and shifting melodic harmonies, Nietzsche discovered the restlessness in Don José's and Carmen's souls: their pre-destined crossing of paths, violent mood swings, and premature deaths foreseen by the very tarot cards she throws.

Just as Wagner hoped to subsume and recycle the notion of a Christian ideal—the cosmos carried by voice and staging—in the *Gesamtkunstwerk* (total work of art) in his operas, Bizet unknowingly had, in Nietzsche's eyes and ears, achieved a similar texture in sound and character study: a sonic universe to choreograph the senses rather than a mere musical event.[109] *Carmen*, for Nietzsche, had achieved in character study alone what Wagner, to Nietzsche's mind, had not achieved as success after success occurred, the "Dionysiac belief in eternal rapture."[110] For Nietzsche, Bizet's music was not only transcendent, it was vitalist.

To the feminist musicologist Carolyn Abbate, the genius of Bizet is his use of a musical plot that liberates Carmen's voice from the very plot she engenders. To Abbate's mind, the voice itself carries a secondary plot that serves to redefine the female—Carmen's—role on stage in time. Could this be the quality recognized by Nietzsche in describing the music for *Carmen*? So complex and textured are these sounds that they delineate an entirely new character: a Gypsy freed by the composer from traditional operatic plots and even from Mérimée's ethnographic narration. If the voice, as Abbate argues, is a "series of isolated and rare gestures in music," Carmen's voice moves outside the score, as if separating itself from the orchestra. Bizet's invention of melodious, ritualistic sound embodies the sheer physical power of sound to become its own narrative. Carmen's voice becomes a "source of sonority; [her] presence resonates intelligence."[111]

Perhaps most importantly, Nietzsche recognized in *Carmen* the Gypsy geography: her ancientness translated through sound into tragic philosophy. With *Carmen*, Bizet, like Wagner, abandoned the two-dimensionality of the Other, the foreign, *l'éxotique*, which Romanticism and French lyric and grand opera laid out before the bourgeois French public like an assembly line of sitcoms that they consumed with hunger and ignorance.[112] Like the Gypsy whose *élan vital*—in this case, the tragic impulse to surge forward toward her death—he imagines, Bizet's success is to break the history of opera into two. *Carmen*'s naturalism and realism, achieved through Bizet's intrusive marking of the score with Gypsy polyrhythm and inescapable melodies, force the audience to witness her essence—her presence—and open the sonic border to opera's future. *Carmen*'s *vérité dramatique*, its truth-telling, is achieved with "almost brutal force and naturalness," forcing the listener into a tête-à-tête with her as she awaits an untimely death.[113] *Carmen* becomes the first folk drama, Nietzsche's hope for the resuscitation of society. For Nietzsche, Bizet has absorbed Wagner's revolution: "the elucidation of an idea in a symbolized dramatic form."

Carmen and Carmen "signal a border-crossing," from nineteenth- to twentieth-century opera, from romantic to realist music, from stable to unstable sexual norms in that a cigarette-smoking woman "audaciously takes control."[114] For this monumental alterity, this female act of treason against France, Carmen, like Eve, must die, erased from the stage. Her musical presence shatters into a series of fragments in the audience's mind and her dangerous musical energy is "contained by her death."[115] Crushed by the very plot she sings, Carmen of the nineteenth century is no more. However, she endures. We will find her again in the mythic past, along the Islamic Mediterranean coast and moving inside Europe in the twentieth and twenty-first centuries.

CHAPTER THREE

Mythic Space and Ancient Carmen

> Mythology has the merit to preserve for us very old ideas about the impenetrable
> secrets of this world . . . In fact, I find that the ancient Greeks did as we do. . . .
> Note the singular conformity of all religions to leave the idea of the divinity of
> the demiurge in the background and to give him intermediaries that are either
> half human or totally human.
>
> F. de Rougement, 1855[1]

The evolution of Carmen's mythic status recapitulates the origins of the female
archetype that emerged as a goddess figure in the world of the ancient Middle
East. The semiotic relationship between the bull, the goddess, and Carmen resonates with more remote times and spaces than either Bizet or Mérimée may
have consciously evoked. Methodologically, the unearthing of these times and
spaces requires a departure from Romantic and Orientalist critical approaches in
order to excavate a more archaic layer of the figural geography of Carmen — the
mythic space of *Carmen* as it is illuminated by the iconic representation of the
mother goddess throughout history. Carmen's nineteenth-century stage persona
lives in the past and present, her spiritual being, we may imagine, having flowed
through the Paleolithic and Neolithic periods.[2] She reflects the complex set of
forces deployed by one who is both creator and destroyer.

Looking closely at Mérimée's Carmen and her musical transmutation in Bizet, we discovered that Carmen inhabits a liminal space. Across a small gulf of
time, we imagined a conversation between Mérimée and Bizet that invokes in
the Romantic era a creation myth.[3] Carmen is a woman of mythological status:
she lives with one foot in life and the other in death. Her body, the landscape
of orientalist cartography, possesses magical powers that further remove her

from any human or chronological dimension, dislocating her to the world of ancient myth.

A myth provides psychological space, at times spiritual. Mythic power rests not on intellectual consciousness but rather on the dissolution of the subject/object divide — the ability to inhabit both seen and unseen worlds. As we trace the contours of this space, we approach the possibility of the impossible: a Gypsy geography. Ultimately, the Gypsy — Carmen — is stripped of physical geography and left only with exile and the space of displacement.[4] From one perspective, this is impoverishment, from another empowerment. Gypsies retain a mythic core or infrastructure somehow resistant to "history."

As we watch her on stage, Carmen's power to embody a paradoxical geography emerges from the idea that, while she is without a center, she nevertheless returns us to our own center. This will also appear in flamenco *soleá* and *cante jondo*: the repeated centering and re-centering of the dancer, mapping her identity in space until she reaches a perfect, life-centered place, a virtual performative geography.[5]

While most analyses of Carmen are rooted in nineteenth- and twentieth-century Romantic and Orientalist literary texts, I wish to return to the world of the ancient Mediterranean. I unearth in this period an archeology of Carmen's power. I trace the development of a consciousness lying at the heart of a society that would see Carmen's power as wicked rather than good, a human being whose modern symbolism resonates with and calls into question our relationship to our ancient past.

Studying the transference of mythological and societal power from the mother goddess to the male warrior gods in the ancient Middle East and throughout the emerging city states of Asia Minor and Europe helps us to trace a reversal in the mythology of women. The advent of patriarchal mythologies commences in the third millennium BCE with the evolution of agriculture, land ownership, and inheritance.[6]

Ancient Carmen

The worship of the female principle began with celebrations of spring, fertility, birth, and rebirth after the long winter of Ice Age Europe.[7] It can be seen in the worship of the moon goddess Astarte and in the worship of Isis, goddess of the Nile, whose great flood each year irrigates and fertilizes the land. Worship of the moon and the lunar cycle reflects the twenty-eight-day menstrual cycle. The new or quarter moon is the sign of the rebirth of the moon; therefore the symbol of the female goddess Astarte is one of the bull's horns that resemble the quarter moon. Astarte, wearing the curved horns of the moon above her head, embodies a fusion of the male and female, the matriarchal and patriarchal, as agricultural society with its property and land ownership supersedes the hunter-gatherer culture of the pre-agricultural epoch.

From roughly 30,000 BCE in the Paleolithic and Chalcolithic periods, archeological data such as clay, marble, bone, copper, and gold from over three thousand sites in southeastern Europe (the site of the Romantic birth of Carmen) testify to a "communal worship of the Mother Goddess."[8] Seminal historian Gerda Lerner describes an earth mother figure who mediates between the human and supernatural worlds; multiple symbols of the navel, the vulva, the squatting position in childbirth, the moon, and pregnant woman decorate archeological shards as evidence of the fertility cult and the power given women in daily life. "The fertility cult," writes Lerner, "became firmly established in the religion of the Ancient Near East with the rise of agriculture in the Neolithic civilization in and after the fifth millennium BCE."[9] The figurines' heads and bodies are decorated with bulls' horns and heads, symbols of male virility, procreativity, and the lunar cycle. They have been discovered in Russia, Iraq, Anatolia, Nineveh, Jericho, and southern Mesopotamia.[10]

Images of female goddesses, as well as those of trees, snakes, birds, and eggs, on pottery and walls are evidence of the idea that an earth mother was worshiped by ancient humans. Belief in the mother goddess is a tradition that has continued to the present day. The great goddess embodied a unity of earth, stars, humans, and nature.[11] In Sumer she was called Ninhursag; in Babylon, Inanna; Kubab and Ishtar in Phoenicia; Astarte in Canaan; Anath in Greece; and Hekate-Artemis in Rome. Early on, her sexuality was considered sacred. Guardian of life and death, night and day, light and darkness, the female force was transcendent and omnipotent.[12]

For thousands of years, priestesses as messengers of the gods were endowed with certain powers through their female sexuality. When divine worship of the female was displaced by the rise of agriculture and urban civilization, proto-patriarchal forces began an active repression of matriarchal culture. What had previously endowed women with sacredness—the ability to bear children—was now used to confine them to the home. Gerda Lerner refers to this disempowerment as the "declassing of goddesses." After the third millennium BCE, although encoded in legal statutes, male dominance could never fully sweep away the power of the female principle.

In my attempt to distill the power of Carmen from her stereotype, I turn to a history of female archetypes whose imagery and representation deepened my conviction that the Carmen myth expresses key aspects of these historical phenomena. As we see below, the idea of Carmen emerges in the demotion of the mother-goddess figure and the "ascendance and later dominance of her male consort/son. In some Mediterranean societies, she merges with a storm-god to become a male creator god who heads the pantheon of gods and goddesses. Wherever such changes occur, the power of creation and of fertility is transferred from the goddess to the god."[13]

The goddess of the moon and of the female principle, Astarte (4000–3000 BCE), descends from the fertility goddesses of Ice Age Europe. The Ice Age goddesses are pregnant; their swollen bellies reveal them as procreators, pregnant like mother earth. Worship of her roundness implies exaltation of fertility and procreation. Held in the hand of one famous goddess, the Venus of Laussel from southern France (25,000–20,000 BCE), is the half-crescent moon, symbol of ancient human worship of the female principle: the twenty-eight-day lunar cycle that governed the seasons, the days and nights, the hunting and gathering of Ice Age people. Worship of her body as moon also represents worship of the lunar cycle. The half-crescent moon is also the shape of the horns of a bull, in this case of a bison. Later in the historical record, Astarte or Venus cups in her hand the moon-as-bull, a powerful image of the female goddess merging the symbol of male virility with her own body. Her body was given a vase-like embodiment in the Mesolithic Age (8000–5500 BCE), her arms shaped in clay into the handles of jugs that one grasped when carrying seeds for planting. Her limbs were transformed into crescent moons, symbol of the female. During the Ice Age (25,000 BCE–10,000 BCE), the Mother was referred to as Astarte. In the Neolithic and Bronze Ages, her nomenclature changes moved in tandem with history, Astarte becoming Isis, Ishtar, and Inanna. The symbolism of woman was widespread; her swollen belly came to be seen as the embodiment in figurine form of the goddess who feeds mortals. Considered healers and procreators, women held powerful roles in agrarian society. They were seen as the living embodiment of the Great Earth Mother who gave life.

Limestone images of the Venus of Willendorf date from 25,000 BCE. She sits on a throne, her belly swollen with child, her head raised, her heels planted on the ground. She seems to be bearing down, pushing her child out of her body and into the world. Paleolithic artists carved this childbirth image in ivory or bone or drew it on cave walls in southern and northern Europe. What this distinct Ice Age art shares is female imagery: breasts, vulva, hips, and swollen stomach. But the images are also diverse. One can see young girls, adolescent, pregnant and non-pregnant women considered to be Venus. The Venus figurines unearthed in Italy, France, Austria, and Siberia bear witness to the importance of female fertility and procreativity in Ice Age homo sapiens' lives.[14] The Venus figures show traces of red paint or red earth, symbolizing women's menstrual cycle as connected to the primal nature of red earth.

Relevant to our argument that the image of Carmen is connected to the history of the image of women in Middle Eastern and southern European culture is the interweaving by cave artists of animal imagery with birthing imagery associated with the moon's cycles.

Ancient worship of a woman who holds a moon-shaped drum with five smaller moon-shaped metal cymbals—indicating that she heals the sick and protects alehouses and prostitutes—metamorphoses in the Babylonian and Greco-Roman worlds into subjugation. The woman who plays the moon-shaped drum in the Neolithic Age is now seen as a prostitute since she plays music, holding onto the very shape that once defined her.

Frame drums held by bulls or various animals seem to connect human and non-human imagery and show the playing of music as part of ritual existence, possibly trance-induced states. Animals holding or playing frame drums and birds flying through the air as if the embodiment of humans in ecstatic stances are found throughout the Lascaux caves, signaling the idea of religious ritual in daily life; a spirit world now seems to intervene in human life.

With the melting of the ice, oceans rose and rivers flooded, irrigating large portions of land. Over thousands of years of climate change, between 10,000 and 5000 BCE, plants and trees evolved and women's work went from foraging and gathering on forest floors to sowing and harvesting. Between 8000 and 5000 BCE, female laborers tended the new crops while men continued to hunt and herd.[15]

Images of women and men dancing to the beat of a drum, all surrounding a great bull with long, pointed horns, date from 6000 BCE, discovered in ancient Anatolia (present-day Turkey) in the Catal Huyuk. Archeologists have argued that dancing images such as this one are symbolic of religious rites, signaling that a tribe with enough to eat can permit the emergence of ceremonial culture. Neolithic women grew and harvested grain, making pottery in their spare time—vessels in which to store their food supplies. William McNeill posits the idea that grain contained spirits and that "propitiation of that spirit" might benefit a pious harvester who left part of the grain—the seeds—behind, thus aiding an increased crop in the following year.[16] As men slowly turned from hunting to trading in grain, we see a revival of Venus figurines during the seventh century BCE. As grain supplies increased with fertile land, larger spaces to store the grain became necessary and men built them along the banks of the Tigris and Euphrates rivers, the Nile, and the great rivers of India and China. These became the first cities.

Images of Neolithic Musicians and Planters

As European and Middle Eastern — Mesopotamian — societies moved out of the Ice Age into the Neolithic Age (8000–4000 BCE), pottery with images of women playing or carrying frame drums appears. This percussive instrument with its five tiny, moon-like diadems and its circular face reappears in the hands of early Iberians, Gaditanes or dancing girls, and Gypsies throughout history. Alongside Neolithic women carrying drums are cave-paintings of men who appear to be flying through the air or floating in space, a metaphor for a trance-like, ecstatic state that certain plant products induce when molded, fermented, or smoked.

With the rise of the first civilizations in ancient Mesopotamia between the Tigris and Euphrates rivers, as well as along the Nile and Indus river valleys (3500–2500 BCE), worship of the Great Earth Mother and of the female principle begins to decline. Iconography and pottery shards reveal that women are shown in their magical and biologically procreative roles as healers, seers, and deities — human representations of the power of the female principle. In ancient culture, these values governed society, but in time, this power declines with the establishment of a priestly class. As agrarian society develops, small huts and whole villages come to protect and till the rich soil along the riverbanks. Tools like the wheel, plow, and hoe are invented — these are more efficient than a woman who bends down to drop seeds into the soil to be tilled by hand. Ploughs drawn by oxen, however, are heavy and require a man's physique to manipulate them through a field.

Both frame drums and grain sieves found in early agrarian burial grounds were shaped in circles like the full moon. It is thought that the origin of the frame drum (which became the tambourine) is the grain sieve. This would indicate that women were musicians in these early agrarian societies.[17] In ancient Sumer, the word for *grain sieve* is synonymous with *drum*. Archeologists argue that the frame drum was also used by women as a sacred container for food. The feminist metaphor of food grown by women and stored in ceramic vases made by women is potent, as is the ritual role of dance invocation.

Music and religious ritual were intimately connected to planting crops. Seed-bearing grasses such as wheat, barley, and millet evolved from ancestral grasses eight or nine thousand years ago in Anatolia and the Zagros Mountains, leading Neolithic farmers to believe in the spirit of the grain. As the grains were planted and harvested by women, these women became linked with the concept that to propitiate the spirit in the grain helped grow more crops.[18] Excavations in Catal Huyuk reveal pregnant mother-goddess figures seated on thrones dating from 5000 BCE. The west-facing slopes of the Zagros range near Mesopotamia and the "wide southern border of Anatolia, Syria, Palestine and Lebanon" remain well-watered areas, hence the concept of the "fertile crescent."[19] As Fernand Braudel further notes, "The fertility is the result of the relief which halts and captures the rains of the winter depressions as the mountains turn into a series of water-towers for the regions down below. The streams pouring down from the hills explain the presence, so near the Syrian desert, of the woodland and vegetation" that provided Neolithic cultures with plants for cultivation.[20]

Excavated in Turkey at Catal Huyuk, relevant to our search for Carmen, was the huge female goddess discovered on the top of a doorway in a house, her legs spread wide open, her arms stretched out to the sides, her pubic region opened to give birth to a bull's head, his horns used as a ladder to an upper terrace. The fertility goddess, the essential divinity of Neolithic cults, appears here in many versions: as a young girl, as a pregnant woman, reminiscent of the Paleolithic Venuses, or sometimes giving birth to a bull. The bull is the male god, generally represented by a bull's head alone, or by rows of horses, only rarely in anthropomorphic shape.

In the Paleolithic religion, mural frescoes and friezes represented animals — bulls, cattle, deer, boar, leopards — that were the goddess's sacred beasts, found in the cave art of France and Spain. These murals cover entire walls. Women were discovered buried under the "principal platform in the house, in the place of honor, a sign that this was a society where mothers, priestesses and goddesses reigned."[21]

Bull-Goddess Imagery

Returning to our search for the progenitors of Carmen, we observe the Paleolithic image of the moon goddess holding a bull's horns. Agrarian goddesses are also shown associated with masculinity and the phallus. One of the most interesting ancient goddesses, the vulture goddess Hathor who ruled Upper Egypt, was the primary goddess of the Nile River Valley. She wears a vulture headdress and plays a frame drum. A female symbol of death and resurrection, unlike her namesake, she does not kill her prey. When they are already dead, she consumes them, transmuting their souls to life in the form of an egg, symbol of fertility, regeneration, and new birth. Twice-born, as the god Dionysus himself will be, Hathor's second birth is thought to enable the vulture to soar higher into the divine realm, freed from earth as a bird goddess.[22] A female goddess body with breasts and face is chiseled into stone on an Egyptian wall, wearing a headdress with the bull's horns that fly off to the sides like winged creatures, inside of which is the sacral egg. The only goddess to move freely through the stratosphere—able to feel rain and sun, wind and thunder—the bird goddess knows what lies outside the human realm, flying through the upper reaches of the sky.

Carmen's song embodies an ancient practice: the connection through music sung by women to the sacred world. Women's bodies were considered holy because they had musical ability, giving birth to song—their spirit world—and to children—incarnational (ecstasy)—to new life.[23] But Carmen's song in the nineteenth century does not show a woman worshiped for her musical qualities. On the contrary, she is a libertine and it removes her one step further from the ideal of the chaste, noble, Christian woman.

Bizet's libertine song for Carmen allows her lips to articulate the words "free bird." Breaking with societal rules, she reveals through her own instrument—her singing voice—her destiny, presaging a premature death. Carmen also sings about personal liberty, something most women could not experience in the nineteenth century. The ancient Egyptian and Anatolian vulture goddess, whose feminine powers let her fly into the sky after procreation, presages Carmen's declaration that she too will be free in resurrection. A Gypsy clairvoyant like the goddess Kali, she sees freedom in the death that awaits her.

Another interesting historical legacy, perhaps absorbed into Mesopotamian urban cultures and retained throughout the history of the ancient Middle East, is the idea that a goddess, in this case the bird goddess, possessed prophetic powers. In playing the frame drum, she was thought to have been able to enter a trance state in which the power to see into the future came to her. The ritual worship of prophecy through musical trance is found in Greece centuries later among oracles and virgin priestesses, and in Mediterranean Gypsy culture. Carmen, the mythic Gypsy, possesses the power to see into her own future. Prophecy, also known as fortune-telling, was lauded and considered a mark of great wisdom in Asia Minor and Mesopotamia.[24]

Myths once transmitted orally by Mesopotamian village women and priestesses are by 3500 BCE recorded in stone cuneiform writing by priests "to serve political ends."[25] Namu, the Mother Goddess, once the creator of the universe and mother of all gods, is dropped from the priestly list, her powers possibly transferred to her son, Enki, "in an apparent attempt to justify this bit of priestly piracy."[26]

Until the third millennium, iconography reveals the mother goddess as the most revered deity, holding the highest position.[27] By 1100 BCE, in the Sumerian text *Enuma Elish*, an entirely new creation story is recorded.

In *Enuma Elish*, the beginning of time is represented by chaos in the universe. Tiamat, another mother goddess, "is confronted by rebellious primitive gods who wish to create order. A terrible battle ensues in which a young god who then physically destroys Tiamat and creates out of her carcass the earth and the heavens, leads the rebellious gods. The gods now also slay Tiamat's husband and, from his blood, mixed with soil, they create humankind."[28] Marduk, the Babylonian god of war, kills Tiamat's husband, absorbing the power of the female goddess to maintain harmony in the world. Fertility worship and care for mother earth is transmuted into glorification of war, justified by a need to keep peace among the heavenly gods. "It is not surprising," writes Lerner, that the mother goddess "not only loses her supremacy but generally becomes domesticated and transformed into the supreme god's wife. Yet, at the same time, in some mysterious way, she separates off and acquires a new life and new identity in a variety of forms, which continue to have force in popular religion." The king from here on out, beginning with Hammurabi, absorbs the female deity's divine and earthly powers, "the flow of power, sacredness and energy between god and king" stolen from that of earthly women.[29] This then sets earth women against a system that becomes a means of controlling, manipulating, and subordinating them to channel/circumscribe/appropriate the very procreative powers that previously accorded them a divine role in the cosmos.

From the second millennium BCE, we see recorded the dethroning of the mother goddess. Her vitality comes under suspicion, a procreative spirit that forces women to assume a less public role. The life-giving mother goddess becomes the faithful wife, her divine powers stripped away and given to the male warrior gods. It is a stunning political move on the part of ancient Mesopotamian priests and kings, inventing a new religious and cultural system and reinventing the image and symbolism of women, to hide and subjugate them.

Creating Myths about Women

Linking Genesis to *Enuma Elish* and other Mesopotamian creation stories is the birth of the goddess Nin-ti, whom the creator mother Ninhursag causes to be born out of Enki's rib, hence Nin-ti's name, "Lady of the Rib." Just as Nin-ti was born of Enki's rib, so Eve was created from the thirteenth rib on Adam's right side (Genesis 2:21). As in *Enuma Elish* in which gods may have many partners, in Genesis, Eve represents Adam's second wife, his first being Lilith who lived close to the earth, at the base of the trunk of the Tree of Knowledge. She is considered to have left him.[30]

While ancient wisdom and mother goddess symbolism is retained in the body of Eve, so is the creation story itself. Like the Sumerian creation myth *Enuma Elish*, the Garden of Eden is also a space bordered by four rivers.[31] As Sumerian civilization was dependent upon its water systems, with trade going up and down the Tigris and Euphrates rivers, it is no wonder that the Sumerian worldview is surrounded by water. In *Enuna Elish*, gods are granted authority with Inanna, goddess of the City of Uruk. While a sense of the sacred is humanized, ancient wisdom and thought is feminized and given over to women who hold history in their sacred bodies.[32]

In the Sumerian creation myth written in the Babylonian era (roughly 1100 BCE), we discover the root of the Hebrew book of Genesis.[33] In the Myth of Enki and Ninhursag, written roughly four hundred years before Genesis, we read chiseled into stone the creation of the Mesopotamian world in which a female goddess, Ninhursag, is the creating god defining through her acts the final shape of the world.[34] This is a particularly interesting myth as, on a literary level, its prose unites and involves images of goddess women from multiple eras. As her divine powers change, we, as spectators of the ancient world, are given a mirror into shifting images of women's sacred power in the early civilizations of the Fertile Crescent.

Ninhursag, queen of the mountain, who may have represented an earlier Mesopotamian goddess Ki, and is later reformed in myth and renamed Enki, creates the earth. But in the story, we see the transition from worship of an omnipotent female deity to the slow encroachment of a male god in the process of creation and destruction of the world. The great Sumerologist Samuel Noah Kramer argues that previous to her written incarnation in myth as Ninhursag, her name was Namu, the great mother goddess who was the creator of the universe and mother of all gods.[35]

In the myth of Enki and Ninhursag, Ninhursag creates the world. She allows eight plants to grow in the garden and forbids the gods to eat from them. Enki, the water-god, does eat though and Ninhursag condemns him to death. Subsequently, Enki becomes deathly ill. The god Fox intervenes on Enki's behalf, asking Ninhursag — a divine woman with ancient powers — to commute his death sentence. She invents a healing deity for each of his plagued organs. For the rib, she says: "To the goddess Ninti I have given birth for you." *Ninti*, according to Gerda

Lerner, means "female ruler of the rib," and of life.³⁶ In Hebrew, *Hawwa*, or Eve, means "she who creates life," suggesting a fusion between the Sumerian Ninti and the biblical Eve. As in the Bible, Eve is born of Adam's rib. But in her name resides an earlier history; *Hawwa* in Aramaic means "serpent." From Paleolithic to Mesolithic cultures, only women could communicate with snakes, messengers of the underworld. Priestesses could transmit the serpent's message from one world to the next and to humans, thus connecting spiritual dimensions.

Where woman was originally thought to be the divine creator of all living and inanimate things, Yahweh — a male god — replaces her. Ninhursag and various fertility goddesses before her were divine mothers. In prayers to Ishtar, the goddess was thought to have "opened the wombs of women." Yet in the book of Genesis, it is God who creates: "And the Lord saw that Leah was hated, and he opened her womb . . . And God remembered Rachel . . . and opened her womb."³⁷ "Pro-creativity," argues Lerner, is clearly defined as emanating from God."³⁸

The Fourth Act of *Carmen*, Thresholds, Crossing from One Spirit World to the Next

Earth mother, seen in the goddess of Sumer in the early agrarian planting cultures of the Indus Valley, is called Inanna, mother goddess of all things whose divine energy was thought to keep people alive. Genesis and the myth of Inanna's descent to the nether world — a world we imagine outside of our consciousness, located in a distant, unreachable psycho-geographical space beneath the earth — share in anthropological terminology the notion of threshold. There exists a resonance between aspects of the story of Genesis and the death of Carmen, knifed by the anti-hero Don José underneath the Mozarabic arches of the *corrida*. Inanna and Eve live peacefully, powerfully, and happily in a unified spirit world. For Inanna, this means an earthly spiritual dimension and for Eve the earthly, magical Garden of Eden. For Carmen, her alive-time, or time before a death-threshold, occurs during the first three acts of the opera. Both the opera — the music and text — and our experience of Carmen terminate in her death.

Inanna presents one of the greatest early myths of a trans-world being who lives on the precipice of both our consciousness and spiritual metamorphosis, perhaps the reason she carried such powerful weight in ancient Sumer and has been recycled throughout the ages. Many Christian female saints bear traces of Inanna's passage from one dimension to the next. In fact, the Byzantine mosaics of Constantinople, in which the Virgin Mary's feet touch hell while her body extends into heaven, represent an earthly and otherworld body that stretches from one space into the next simultaneously. Inanna's passage through the gates of the present down into the underworld was recorded in stone. Assyriologist Samuel Noah Kramer in his seminal 1944 text *Sumerian Mythology* provides a translation of the goddess' descent:

> From the "great above" she set her mind toward the "great below,"
> . . . .
>   To the nether world she descended,
> Abandoned lordship, abandoned ladyship,
> . . . .
> Upon entering the first gate,
> The shugurra, the "crown of the plain" of her head, was removed.
> . . . .
> Upon her entering the seventh gate,
> All the garments of ladyship of her body were removed.
> "What pray, is this?"
> "Extraordinarily, O Inanna, have the decrees of the nether world been perfected,
> O Inanna, do not question the rites of the nether world."
> . . . .
> At their word, the word which tortures the spirit,
> The sick woman was turned into a corpse,
> The corpse was hung from a stake.

Inanna is killed.

This myth resonates with the story of Carmen in a number of ways. Inanna, like Carmen, is both heroine and anti-heroine; ultimately, she dies a violent death. Inanna is one of two sisters, Ereshkigal being the other. Inanna and Ereshkigal represent light and darkness, like Odette and Odile or even Carmen in love with Don José and Carmen no longer in love with Don José. The light and dark in each woman illuminate and fade respectively; they are pieces of being and dying that, together, compose a whole being.

Inanna, in death, becomes a goddess with two parts that confront one another, epitomizing or symbolizing "the whole sense" of the road of being.[39] "The hero," observes mythologist Joseph Campbell, "whether God or Goddess, man or woman, the figure in a myth or the dreamer of a dream, discovers and assimilates his opposite (his own unsuspected self) either by swallowing it or by being swallowed," self-annihilated or killed by someone else for lack of self-knowledge. "One by one the resistances are broken. He must put aside his pride, his virtue, beauty, and life and bow or submit to the absolutely intolerable. Then he finds that he and his opposite are not of differing species but one flesh. Or, as James Joyce has phrased it, "equals of opposites, evolved by a one-same power of nature or of spirit, as the sole condition and means of its 'himundher' manifestation and polarized for reunion by the symphysis of their antipathies."[40] It is not the antipathy between Carmen and Don José or between Inanna and Ereshkigal that fascinates us but, rather, the struggle within Carmen that she ultimately loses. She is self-sacrificing rather than sacrificed by Don José.

According to Lerner, in the Old Babylonian period "the daughters of kings and rulers were appointed as high priestesses of the Moon God or of the goddess Ishtar. The *en* or *entu* priestesses were the counterparts of the male high priest."[41] The foundation for the ritual of a mortal woman impersonating a fertility goddess who marries a god came from Uruk in Sumeria. Dating from 3000 BCE, Inanna, patron goddess of the city, is seen as participating in a Sacred Marriage.

"The Sacred Marriage" Lerner tells us, "was performed in the temples of various fertility-goddesses for nearly two thousand years." Interestingly, it is the goddess who, in sleeping with a male god who is considered to have died previous to their union (Marduk, Baal, or Osiris, for example), brings him back to life and who "could make him alive, who could make him king and who could empower him to make the land fertile." Up until the first millennium, fertility as sexual imagery "permeated poetry and myth and found expression in statuary and sculpture."[42] This worship of women's procreative ability to heal, resurrect, and bless community through union with men continues underneath or alongside the formation of laws regarding women's enforced legal status and code of social etiquette. Repression forms the basis of a potent mythology surrounding the myth of Carmen.

By the time of Hammurabi (1792–1750 BCE) and the legal Code that he left behind in the City of Babylon, fertility priestesses who lived and worked in temples reenacting the Sacred Marriage rite were forbidden from real marriage and child-bearing. Their powers before what William McNeill terms "the rise of civilization" were considered so potent as to be necessary to everyday survival, but their "sacred service" was not separated out from the rest of the community.[43] That is to say, the goddesses' significance was not mythic before Sumeria but, rather, knit into the social fabric of everyday life. After the rise of temple culture in early urban civilization, the priest class extracts the goddess, moving her out of daily, agrarian life and solely into a marginal realm of the priest-controlled sacred function. Yet, the Code of Hammurabi drew a clear "distinction between respectable and non-respectable women."[44]

With increased urban wealth, female slaves bought or captured in battle were brought into wealthy homes. Gerda Lerner argues that economic growth in cities like Sumer and Akkad enabled the wealthy to purchase female slaves—the spoils of war—to work in domestic servitude. It further enabled middle- and upper-class families to have more children and, as they practiced polygamy, multiple wives. Dwellings became like haciendas with multiple apartments where various families could live in enclosed, secluded spaces. One must mention the influence of the Indo-Aryan cities of Mohenjo Daro and Harappa, whence the Aryan notion of purity infiltrated Mesopotamian society. Rules for moral and social conduct emerged under the Assyrians, and by the time of the Babylonians, women's purity—their chastity—was enforced by legal code. The acquisition of female slaves freed upper-class women from domestic duties, but they still were secluded. This signaled the beginning of what would be called a *harem*, a formal gathering of women, named during the Abbasid dynasty in the sixth and seventh centuries CE. With roots in ancient Mesopotamian society, *harems* took their name from the architectural design that enforced women's seclusion and separation from public life. The word *harem* means "forbidden place," an inner room where only the men of the house could visit. Beginning with the Assyrians, this meant wealthy, upper-class men who could afford to build homes with multiple, enclosed apartments where polygamous home life was possible.[45]

With agriculture and land ownership women were subordinated and veiled, the male principle dominating the female. It is precisely against this ancient repression that Carmen and all landless Gypsies rebel. The replacement of the great goddess by male gods removed women from positions of spiritual and political power. Mérimée's creation of a character like Carmen at a point in history when political and social revolutions swept Europe, indicating great societal tension in moving from pre-industrial to modern capitalist societies, is no coincidence. His extraordinary character creation was prescient. Like the majority of Mérimée's other artistic creations—the preservation of national historic monuments and the memorializing of classical spaces in France and Western Europe—*Carmen* memorializes a history of women.

Insight into the origins of the passive, all-suffering Micaëla and her antithesis, Carmen, can be found in societies of the ancient Middle East that excluded women from public space. Veiling did not distinguish free from enslaved or indentured, nor upper class from lower. Distinction between women was based on sexual activities. "Harlots and unmarried sacred prostitutes may be free women, yet they are grouped with slaves. A slave concubine [could have been] veiled, if accompanied by her mistress, but even a freeborn concubine may not be veiled if she walks out alone."[46] Women who served one man, what Lerner refers to as domestic women under the protection of a husband or father, were considered respectable women who had to be veiled. Women not under one man's protection and sexual control were classed as "public women" and forbidden to wear a veil.[47]

> [H]e who has seen a harlot veiled must arrest her, produce witnesses (and) bring her to the palace tribunal; they shall not take her jewelry away (but) the one who arrested her may take her clothing; they shall flog her fifty (times) with staves (and) pour pitch on her head.[48]

As women's independence in society was reduced to a minimum, so was their contact with men. Three millennia before Islam, Sumerian court ladies were forced to veil. As prostitution and slavery were sanctioned by ancient Mesopotamia, rules for married and unmarried, free and enslaved women emerged. A sign of marital status, the veil, or as it is called in Arabic, the *hejab*, was a material reminder of social status, drawing a sexist, hierarchical border between the respectable — married and wealthy women — and the disreputable — prostitutes, slaves, and poor women. Carmen is never veiled until the end of the opera when she is about to die. (In death is redemption for one's sins, says the Christian world.) The veil symbolized chastity, not property.

Covering the head, neck, shoulders, and, in some cases, the face, separated upper-from lower-class women. The material covering of wealthier women was met by their architectural seclusion as they were forced to remain inside courtyards. There was thus an architectural veiling of body and being.

Classifying respectable versus non-respectable women became an affair of the state, regulated by a court of law with witnesses and prosecutors and public trials for offenders.[49] State intervention in a very public manner into the private lives and morality of ancient Mesopotamians became, under the Assyrians, a matter of legal record that would endure until the twentieth century. Later, under the Babylonians, the Code of Hammurabi marked "the beginning of the institutionalization of the patriarchal family as an aspect of state power."[50] Lerner cites the year 1250 BCE as the moment that a legal code gave power to the state to regulate people's sexual lives. Veiling, birth control, abortion, and women's sexuality were from here on out regulated by what became a patriarchal state that used these social controls to substantiate its omnipotence. "The sexual regulation of women," argues Lerner, "underlies the formation of classes and is one of the foundations upon which the state rests."[51] It is also the reason that Don José believes he is allowed to, and must, kill Carmen at the end of the opera and the novel. The state would fall to anarchy if she lived as a "free bird."

Shifting Images of Women through Urbanization

The shift in worship away from an auspicious mother goddess who protects prostitutes and all peoples began what Lerner argues was a several-thousand-year-old "Creation of Patriarchy." It is my argument that this process began an imaging of woman and of the female principle that changed from a healthy and holy worship of Earth Mother and the mother goddesses to the creation by the priest class of iconographic materials and written, cuneiform, publicly displayed tablets of law that imaged archetypes of "good" women. This mythic sanctioning of the virtuous, law-abiding wife and mother was contrasted with the bad or evil woman. At this point Assyrian, Babylonian, and later Islamic law began to punish women who diverged from a given sociocultural role. This is where the body of Carmen begins: in the third millennium.

In the *Law of Eshnunna*, veiling was encoded. By the second millennium in Assyria, rules for women's public and private lives were dictated.[52] The Assyrian kings of the fourteenth to the eleventh centuries BCE developed extensive rules regulating life within the household. Women of the Achamenid dynasty (559–331 BCE) were completely secluded. By the seventh century BCE, respectable Byzantine and Sasnian women were also secluded and veiled in public. While upper-class women were free from domestic duties, they spent their lives inside unless performing charitable work, the only public work allowed them. (Let us not forget the Hindu custom of *sati*, or widow-burning.)

Veiling, harems, and seclusion represented the slow removal of women from the public sphere in Mesopotamia. In numerous written codes of moral conduct, women were rendered subordinate to men. Men could sleep with slaves. Women could only have sexual relations with their husbands. Thus a sanctioned treatment of women emerged, governing sexuality and social life. The idea of female purity and chastity superseded the ancient idea of procreative woman as powerful and wise. For women, purity became bondage.

Bodies That Sin

The transition from polytheism to monotheism, according to Mesopotamian historians Thorgild Jakobsen, Samuel Noah Kramer, Gerda Lerner, William McNeill, and Jonathan Kirsch took several thousand years. The Hebrew Bible was written down circa 250 BCE. Both the Bible and the *Qu'ran* contain traces of earlier religious practice consisting of worship of the fertility goddess, a polytheistic pantheon of male deities, and animism. Spiritual beliefs such as animism are active to this day, particularly among nomadic desert and rural populations in the Fertile Crescent. These more complex rituals, the above historians argue, were absorbed over centuries into new religious traditions in the daily life of a living spiritual tradition, but continued to be practiced for centuries after the birth of the People of the Book. (Again, one sees writing's role in the recording of history.) This said, the most powerful argument against the fertility goddess, the removal of her living powers, came from two sources: Mesopotamian (Babylonian and Assyrian) laws that legalized a code of female conduct and Judaism's fiercely patriarchal legal system.

Motherhood was reduced to the bearing of children. Matrilineal descent was replaced by patrilineal descent. Gerda Lerner believes that procreation itself became symbolically a male act that legitimized a patriarchal line of kinship, inheritance, and survival.[53] Rather than women being remembered, men were cited as markers of tribal ties and time passage. For example, Isaac is called "the son of Abraham," not the son of Abraham and Sarai. The "generations of the sons of Noah" are "sons of their fathers."[54] Women are written out of history.

To begin with, Adam renames Woman, calling her Eve. The act of a man naming a woman is patriarchal for in a name resides her identity; he is giving it to her rather than she taking it for and onto herself. Eve is now interpreted as a temptress — the first Carmen. Eve does not rename Adam as only he can name himself. Lerner, quoting John Calvin, writes that Adam was "taught to recognize himself in his wife; as in a mirror, and Eve, in her turn, to submit herself willingly to her husband, as being taken out of him, out of one of his 'lower parts' of his rib."[55] The primal idea that in Woman's body resides Man endows her with a complex and rich iconography that continues to trace a history of monotheism, absorbing aspects of more ancient traditions. Spiritually, she becomes one with Adam, not as his inferior but as part of his soul.

Inside of her body, Adam will reside; inside of his, Eve will be. As Woman was born of Adam's side, near his heart, ultimately she shared his consciousness, his immortality, writes Sarah Grimké.[56] Eve and Adam are one; they share an identity as first people, complete with, in and of each other. Together, they must survive their Expulsion, a metaphor for Jewish history. The people's memory is dependent upon men and women together.

In Sumerian, and later in Greek, mythology, the Tree of Life is drawn by artists and poets as a totem, a vertical passageway between spirit worlds that reaches into the earth and the sky simultaneously.[57] Spirits of the dead in ancient Mesopotamia were thought to move from the earth into the tree's roots—from the underworld—to the heavens through its branches and leaves. Mesopotamians believed that at the root of the tree lived a goddess—Lilith—with the power to regenerate life through the honey-like sap that flows out of the bark of the tree and drops onto the ground.[58] The symbolism of the Tree of Life, described in the Bible centuries later around 250 BCE by rabbinic scholars, excludes any mention of an earth goddess who lives in the tree. In fact, the power of a goddess to offer rebirth is eliminated altogether from monotheistic tradition.

A second early Sumerian great goddess in Mesopotamian mythology inhabits a tree, known as the Huluppu Tree. Memorialized in a poem from the second millennium BCE called *Inanna's Descent*, the great goddess is said to have come across the Tree of Creation that has been uprooted and swept away by the strong current of the Euphrates River. Inanna, in an effort to preserve the tree, saves it by planting it in her sacred garden in her holy city of Uruk. Inanna, it is thought, is going to use the great tree's wood to make herself a bed and a throne. Unknowingly, Inanna introduces this uncontrollable natural world into the capital city when she carries the tree to Uruk. Like Eve after her, Inanna's sexual powers are located inside a secret garden.

Inanna asks Gilgamesh, the warrior-king, for help in an attempt to calm her secret garden. Gilgamesh kills the snake, causing another woman whose name is Lilith, and a ferocious bird, Imdugud, to flee, and severing Inanna's connection to the heavens. From the tree, Gilgamesh fashions a bed and a throne for Inanna. She, in return, carves for him a drum and stick to summon his soldiers to war. So much death follows that Inanna descends to the underworld where the branches of the tree reside. As Inanna descends, her body fuses with the roots of the tree inside the earth.

Lilith

> To banish his loneliness, Lilith was first given to Adam as wife. Like him she had been created out of the dust of the ground. But she remained with him only a short time, because she insisted upon enjoying full equality with her husband. She derived her rights from their identical origin. With the help of the Ineffable Name, which she pronounced, Lilith flew away from Adam, and vanished in the air. Adam complained before God that the wife He had given him had deserted him, and God sent forth three angels to capture her. They found her in the Red Sea, and they sought to make her go back with the threat that, unless she went, she would lose a hundred of her demon children daily by death . . .
>
> The woman destined to become the true companion of man was taken from Adam's body, for "only when like is joined unto like the union is indissoluble." The creation of woman from man was possible because Adam originally had two faces, which were separated at the birth of Eve.
>
> Louis Ginzberg, *Legends of the Jews* (1909)

In the book of Genesis, we meet Eve. Her name in Aramaic, a patois fusion of Greek and Hebrew, is *Hawwa* (הַוָּן) meaning "she who creates life." She is the second wife of Adam. Lilith, his first wife, according to Jewish legend, lives at the base of a tree.[59] Hidden in the tree are wild creatures. A snake lives at the roots of the tree, suggesting Inanna's connection to the underworld. A wild woman and a windspirit, Lilith has chosen the lower branches of the tree for her home.

Lilith is considered a wise creature, living in physical proximity to the female deity. In this place, she can absorb the sacred wisdom of the snake that, in shedding its skin, is itself reborn every year. Interestingly, Mesopotamians used the snakeskin for the head of a frame drum. (In Greek mythology, a goddess's power enters her body through her navel, or *omphalos*, a symbol of her connection to the center of the earth.)

While Inanna descends into the earth, biblical Lilith emerges out of the earth. But she does not travel far, living just above the surface. This metaphor of the feminine taken from power by the male God and finding a new home inside of the earth is telling. Rather than remaining the metaphysical embodiment of dirt and water, flowers and seeds, the female goddess plunges into or out of mother earth. Is this a hiding place?

Lilith represents the divine feminine, the primordial, untamed aspects of the female principle that no man can control. She also represents the transition from Mesopotamian animism to Judaic monotheism where the woman is transfigured into mortality. No longer can she attain sacred status.

Carmen embodies Lilith and, like the goddess before her, will be forced from earth; she is an uncontrollable creature above ground. There is no room for her. In the biblical Garden of Eden, written in the *Torah*, Lilith reappears as the untamable part of Eve that must be exorcised, punished, and removed.[60]

Lilith is considered to have become so domineering that Adam leaves her; Lilith subsequently transforms into a demon, invading men's dreams and sending the snake to tempt Eve into eating the apple. In the poem *The Huluppu Tree*, the wild divine must be ritually sacrificed in the service of the warrior-king.

In *Inanna's Descent*, orally transmitted for centuries, beginning hundreds of years before the book of Genesis was written down, the goddess asks her priestess Lilith to help her return from the underworld. The priestess knows the way out of the underworld and leads Inanna out of danger, as Gilgamesh will lead his men into battle, by playing a drum. The rhythm of the drumbeat, like a primal heartbeat, illuminates the path to earth. The drum, used by shamans to heal and balance, symbolizes the ritual road between spirit worlds. Its rhythmic timbre reveals the totemic route up and down.

In the later *The Huluppu Tree*, Inanna turns not to her priestess-seer but to her omnipotent king, Gilgamesh, who uses the ancient drumbeat to begin a war to rid the tree of wild creatures (the wildness in woman). In a departure from the earlier poem that preserves great goddess powers, *The Huluppu Tree* allows Gilgamesh to protect and house Inanna; her spiritual powers are symbolically usurped forever by his paternal actions. Inanna is left with the power to construct a drum, an instrument used to communicate with the spirit world. As she descends, the drum's powers are lost; the drum itself is turned into a destructive tool that sweeps away the very source of the goddess's powers as Gilgamesh proceeds to lose the drum. Inanna symbolically becomes passive; it is Gilgamesh who gives her powers rather than she who uses what is already in her possession.

Inanna, who represented life and death as equally potent forces, becomes the goddess of war, uniting her procreative and destructive powers. (In ancient Greece, Inanna would be called Artemis and, in ancient Rome, Diana. These divine women, while still non-mortals, were seen as hunters, gaining strength only from their destructive iconography.) With a shifting mythology, there is no record, oral or written, of the power once attained by women. By the time of Abraham the prophet and the later writing of the Bible, the mother goddess's potency was diminished. She lived as a distant memory in agrarian communities who worshiped the earth for the fruit of her crops. Both the symbolism and iconography of the great goddess as driving our life force were extinguished. At the end of the myth, Gilgamesh and other kings after him now dance for war as does even Inanna in "the dance of Inanna."[61]

One further recycling of the Inanna myth is in the story of the Biblical prophetess and judge Deborah, who is described as sitting under a palm tree. Inanna was considered the goddess of the date palm, the Tree of Life that grows only in the Fertile Crescent and not in the Western world.

Traces of the Sumerian myth of Inanna and her sister Ereshkigal, two halves of one person, can also be found in the story of Adam and Eve. Eve is born of Adam's body and, according to biblical legend, leads him to sin; he is born of her. He gains knowledge of himself through contact with the serpent and the Tree of Knowledge thanks to Eve. Her curiosity and independent thought leads to his self-knowledge: that he is indeed a man living in paradise and must now leave; further, that there will be defined a righteous path and a sinful road. But, more importantly, it is his physical connection to Eve — their being of one flesh and bone — and his coming into knowing that they are the same human being that leads both to be exiled or rather, to be self-exiled — to leave the self in the other in order to become something new, someone with even deeper self-knowledge.

The archetypes of Carmen before Carmen are myriad. Carmen, like the great goddess Inanna, inhabits multiple spheres. Carmen, who deals her own death card, will ultimately enter the land of the dead. Inanna must save herself from perishing at the hands of her own sister goddess, Ereshkigal. To do so, she tells her messenger Ninshubur to "cry for her in the assembly hall of the Gods." While traveling through the nether world "she should have failed to return."[62] Like Carmen who passes through the gates of the arena on her way to death, Inanna comes to a threshold, a temple gate made of lapis lazuli. As Carmen is met by a gatekeeper, Don José, so is Inanna. The chief gatekeeper Neti asks Inanna who she is and why she has come. *I am the queen of heaven*, she replies. *The place where the sun rises*. The chief gatekeeper, Neti, has been instructed by Inanna's sister to give her access to all seven gates but to "remove at each portal a part of her clothing."[63] By the seventh gate, Inanna stands naked before her sister's throne. "She bowed low. The seven judges of the nether world, the Anunnaki, sat before the throne of Ereshkigal and they fastened their eyes upon Inanna — the eyes of death."[64]

Crete, Meaning Strong or Ruling Goddess

The Grecian goddesses Cybele, Aphrodite, Demeter, and Persephone represented the divine mother goddess cult transported to Greece from Mesopotamia. On Crete, the Grecian goddess was called Rhea and Ariadne. A sea-trading empire with close economic and cultural ties to her East, Cretan culture also worshiped the female principle. "Of all the ancient civilizations, the Cretan goddess ruled the longest as a goddess who was One in Herself, without losing all or part of her power to a divine husband."[65] Unlike Mesopotamia, there was never a male deity here as omnipotent as the Cretan goddess.

During Greek times, one final mother goddess cult emerged, symbolic of the power accorded women in the agricultural worldview.[66] Minoan civilization died out, probably as a result of earthquakes in the late second millennium BCE. By roughly 1500 BCE, Mycenaean warriors who ruled the Greek mainland absorbed some of the mother goddess worship of Crete. (The island's name means "strong or ruling goddess.") For the next several centuries, until 1200 BCE, Greece experienced one invasion after another by Aryan hordes. While Greeks built a fiercely militaristic culture to fight off these invasions, Greco-Cretan religious ritual nevertheless remained intensely matriarchal. Worship of a Cretan goddess endured without her losing power to her divine husband.[67] Celebration of Cybele, goddess of the mountain, absorbed in Greek invasions of Anatolia, was transformed into Artemis, goddess of the hunt. The Greeks painted Artemis in the image of a virgin child and built temples in her name. Worshiped in ecstatic dancing circles by men and women, Artemis became associated with the eighth-century BCE Dionysian spring festivals of dithyrambic celebration.[68]

Unlike Carmen, whose statue was built in Seville after her premiere as a stage figure, the Grecian love for Artemis was symbolized in the construction of one of its most beautiful temples at Ephesus, to which pilgrims began to journey in homage to her. Music played on the frame drum, flute, and song in the form of an early Grecian chorus, as well as circle dances, were elements in her celebration. By the time of Aristotle in the fifth century BCE, Cybele/Artemis's Phrygian cult was accepted in an increasingly patriarchal Athenian society. Her temple was shared with the law archives and a sanctuary to her was constructed at the port of Piraeus, from which all ships came and left for trade in the Mediterranean. Seated beside Athena Nike, Aphrodite was also considered an Olympian goddess, her frame drum and wild beasts accompanying her.

The Mythic Art of Joseph Campbell

Renowned mythologist Joseph Campbell revealed in his distinguished book, *The Hero with a Thousand Faces*, the psychological and cultural meaning of mythic figures found on cave walls, pottery shards, in poems, and chiseled into stone figurines.[69] These mythic figures' sacred and profane shapes communicated to Campbell an essence, specifically the notion of a threshold guardian: a mythic goddess figure or creature whose "preliminary embodiment is the dangerous aspect of . . . presence." While Campbell is speaking about worship of sacred temple creatures such as winged bulls, lions, and dragons, one could extend his argument to include Carmen, whose body and character are absorbed into popular symbolic consciousness in a lasting and profound manner. "No creature," wrote the great Indian anthropologist Ananda K. Coomaraswamy in 1940, "can attain a higher grade of nature without ceasing to exist."[70] The cosmic power to self-annihilate belongs to Carmen and to the ancient world of goddesses to which she belongs. The allegory of the fall of the goddess belongs to history.

Campbell, in his discussion of the universal aspects of mythological female figures, refers to J. C. Flugel.[71] Investigating the idea that the woman's body is able to profess spirituality, Campbell agrees with Flugel that it is the physicality of the female form—its materiality—that engages the senses. Carmen's body, as described or witnessed by Prosper Mérimée, is that of a Gypsy woman. Her body is not caged inside the stiff European corset that confines the movements of torso and hips. Rather, Carmen, her clothing that of a poor woman, loosens her poet's shirt and, at times, layers her skirt with a flamenco shawl, adding color and v-shaped lines to her costume.

The imagery in *Carmen* reminds us of the imagery of the Cretan great goddess. Like Inanna and Ishtar, the Minoan goddesses Rhea and Ariadne were celebrated in the bullring with bull-jumping and an early dithyrambic circle dance.[72] As in earlier Mesopotamian culture, Minoan temple frescoes and pottery housed a narrative of goddess worship through wall paintings that spoke to the myth of Rhea who sat in a sacred cave. She played a drum to call people's attention to the oracles. Cretan association of Rhea with the cave recalled the Paleolithic and Neolithic use of the dark, womb-like cave as symbolic of female procreativity and as sacred shelter for documenting on walls the meaning and symbolism of daily life.[73]

As millennia pass, each newly invented goddess absorbs the ancient powers of her predecessors. Ariadne, meaning "holy" in Greek, provides an early example of the ancient seductive powers ascribed to women that Carmen will later absorb.

Daughter of the moon goddess Pasiphae, meaning "the all-illuminating" one, Ariadne is willful, intelligent, and determined to escape the labyrinth in which she is forced to live as a prisoner of war.

An architectural extension of the cave, Ariadne's dwelling place is a spiral—a labyrinth—symbol of self-discovery and initiation, as is the meditative quiet of an isolated cave. Ariadne is a beautiful goddess with flowing golden hair and pale skin, trapped at the very center of the labyrinth constructed by her father to hide his bastard son, the Minotaur, half-man, half-beast, the product of his wife's unfaithful liaison with the bull from the sea. Caught inside this man-made cave, Ariadne hopes to escape but cannot pass the dangerous Minotaur (her half-brother), who eats young maidens. Theseus, the son of the King of Athens, pursues her. In his quest to save her from the Minotaur, he discovers himself.

Ariadne rolls out a ball of string to Theseus so that he can find his way to her and, of course, to his manhood, as he will inherit the throne from his father. Theseus rescues her, marries her, and loses her to the god of wine, Dionysus, who becomes her lover.

Perhaps most interesting about the myth of Theseus and Ariadne is the notion of the labyrinthine cave, symbolic of the earlier Paleolithic cave-temple. Carmen, too, repeats this myth of the safety provided by the dark, labyrinthian cave. There are several instances in the opera and the novella in which Carmen moves into or escapes from caves that shelter her alongside her dangerous, minotaur-like Gypsy bandits.

Unlike Don José in *Carmen* who destroys himself in his obsessive love for her, Theseus is able to walk into the cave, into himself, circling his own consciousness as he picks up the string that leads him to his love and her inner realm. Don José, we are told by Mérimée, never comes to know himself. Moments before he is to be executed for killing Carmen, he blames her and not himself for his murderous actions. Don José's mythic lack of self-knowledge stands in sharp contrast to Carmen, who faces her truths early on in both the novel and the opera, having dealt herself the death card.

The demoting of the female goddess and replacement of her primary impor-tance with a male god led to the idea of the good and the bad woman: the evil, sinful woman—Eve who becomes Carmen—and the righteous Virgin Mary. This transition was possible because ancient Mesopotamians held a primal view of gods and goddesses as dwelling in sacred spaces and within certain peoples: priestesses and, later, priests. With deep roots in ancient Babylonia, the idea of the dwelling place of a god or goddess is moved from an animist tradition in which a god or goddess might live in water, trees, earth, or inside caves, into the temple where the priest, and several priestesses, worked to care for the gods, leaving them food, votive images, and other offerings.[74]

Like Artemis, Carmen absorbed the attention of entire villages and cities.[75] Unlike Artemis, and more like Ariadne, Carmen's mythology remains traceless; it resides in the minds of Europeans and, at times, in the *cante jondo* dance and song — prayer — of flamenco. That is to say, she is remembered as a modern goddess — part heroine part anti-heroine — but not accepted to the point of architectural construction in her name.

CHAPTER FOUR

The Gypsy Inside
and Outside of History

The Peninsula acts as a sounding board for Oriental races who usually give
their richest sounds in it: the Arab, the Jews, and the Gypsy. It was in Spain
that Arab civilization rose to its highest brilliancy; Spanish Jews were the
greatest luminaries of Hebrew civilization since Biblical times; and as for the
Gypsy, the superiority of the Spanish type over any other is not to be proved
by books, but by the observation of the living specimens that may be
found in Andalusia.

Salvador de Madriaga[1]

The other peoples of this group who have not cultivated the sciences are
more like beasts than like men. For those of them who live farthest to the
north, between the last of the seven climates and the limits of the inhabited
world, the excessive distance of the sun in relation to the zenith line makes
the air cold and the sky cloudy. Their temperaments are therefore frigid,
their humors raw, their bellies gross, their color pale, their hair long and lank.
Thus they lack keenness of understanding and clarity of intelligence and are
overcome by ignorance and apathy, lack of discernment and stupidity.

Sa'id ibn Ahmad al-Andalusi, *Northerners, Seen from Andalusia* (1068)[2]

Gypsy Geography, a Cartography of Exile

If you are left off the map, do you exist? Can a people without a homeland, exiled
from every country they enter, have an identity, a sense of themselves drawn from
geography and cultural tradition? Is it possible that, if the center keeps shifting, a
people can stay alive, cognizant of history in the present? If you travel into exile
without return, does your identity disintegrate? What if your people are gone

for years or even centuries? What, ultimately, becomes the ground of memory and consciousness? Is it possible to hold in the bounds of human form the past, present, and future, to carry historical memory on your back as you walk or dance through space and time? What if someone else shapes your memory for you, imposing from without what is remembered and what is forgotten? If the center of the world is geographically constructed, a provisional mapping that informs identity—true both of the Arabs and the Europeans—is the value of cartography not called into question?[3]

To work towards answers, however provisional, and to raise questions, this chapter addresses in detail the paradoxical conceptual contours of a Gypsy geography. The twentieth-century French historian Jean-Paul Clébert summarizes the singularity of Gypsy geography: "The Gypsies represent . . . the unique example of an ethnic whole perfectly defined which, through space and time for more than one thousand years and beyond the frontiers of Europe, has achieved success in a gigantic migration—without ever having consented to any alteration as regards the originality and singleness of their race."[4]

What are the components, the traces, erased or alive in, at times, uninscribed formats of this singularity? We are not seeking origins but rather something more like signposts, relays, and in this searching encounter the distortions of Europeans' attempts to codify Gypsy history and identity. If you ask a Gypsy *cantaor* where he comes from, he will tell you *I am from Lebrija* or *I am from Murcia* or, the most famous of them all, *I am from Triana*, the Gypsy *barrio* of Seville and the space of Carmen's origin. If you ask him if he ever considers India or Egypt points of origin, he will laugh. In an interview conducted with the Gypsy musician Pedro Cortés, I received the following response: "My people are regionalists. They think of themselves as coming from their hometown; they don't even consider themselves Spanish. Gypsies live only in the present moment, never in the past or in the future. They have endured so much oppression, they can't be sure of what's next."[5] Spatially, Gypsies are regional. Temporally, they live in the *now*. They are always only Gypsy. Their identity relates only to their family clan and the pueblo in which they live today. If you ask if they once came from the Punjab, they'll shake their heads *no*. They might have visited the Gypsies of India and even conversed in Caló with them, and they understand on a profound level that their people once emerged from the same geographical place. But that was long ago, before

Eastern European Gypsy Musicians and Dancers, photographer and date unknown.
Roger-Viollet Archives, Paris, France

their present state of being — the only place a Gypsy lives because that is all that he or she can count on.[6] This spatial–temporal dynamic of identity is consistent with the Gypsy experience in Spain and Europe.

The Question of Origins

Carmen's geography can be traced as far east as India and Mesopotamia, and as far west as the Maghreb. To the medieval Arab geographer, the Maghreb was considered the far western portion of the world. Meaning "Spain," or far northwest Africa, the Maghreb was imagined as a frontier outpost, a place with little light compared to the great civilization already built centuries earlier by Arab architects, thinkers, poets, and scientists. An easterner living in the western mind, Carmen stands at a geographic crossroad, revealing the relativity of the notion of

Algerian Gypsy Woman, Blida, Algeria, photographer unknown, circa 1890.
Neurdein / Roger-Viollet Archives, Paris, France

geography itself. Passing through the peripheries of the Arab world, the Gypsies crossed into the "barbarian" lands of Western Europe.

Our purpose here, however, is not to reify the categories of East versus West so crucial to Orientalism (and its critique), but rather to perceive the relativity of cartography as it maps personal, tribal, religious, and national agency. Carmen is a problematic figure who escapes this dualism, both as a woman and a Gypsy. She stands outside the border, her dancing delineating its own frontier.

The Arabist geographic vision of the world serves as a map, a reverse ethnography of how the first Arab historians — geographers — viewed Europe.[7] Like Carmen, they too came from the East and entered Europe with learned and worldly eyes. Mérimée and the nineteenth-century Romantic literary school observed the Gypsy as the foreign element within Europe; Carmen remained an accidental act of itinerant tourism. The Gypsy, even today, continues to be judged harshly by European governments as less than equal, a dark figure who does not belong.

In Arabic writings, we see a reversal of that ethnography. The Arab geographers 'Al Mas'du and Ahmad al'Andalusi, like Carmen, came from the East, from cities — Baghdad, Damascus, and Kabul — whose rulers patronized a literary and artistic Renaissance, a retrieval of Greek classical culture. Self-conscious about their enlightenment, these geographers compare France to winter: "cold, damp," and dark. "The power of the sun," meaning illumination, "is weak among them."[8] 'Al Mas'udi even goes so far as to criticize their personalities, stating that "warm humor is lacking among them."[9]

The Gypsies may have entered Spain just as Hispano-Arab (Nasrid) rule crumbled, bringing to an end eight hundred years of Mozarabic cultural expression. From this Middle Eastern root-source, Mérimée indicates, derives Carmen.

Gypsyologists have long argued that Gypsies' wandered into Spain in multiple migrations.[10] Most late nineteenth- and early twentieth-century Gypsyologists agree that the Gypsies wandered into Spain from Italy, France, and England throughout the fifteenth century. The eighteenth- and early nineteenth-century Gypsyologists are less concerned with the Gypsies' fifteenth-century appearance in Spain and more interested in the possibility of tracing their origin from two professions: first, their metalworking and blacksmithing, which took them inside Persian, Roman, and North African armies from the third century BCE until the Spanish Inquisition; and, secondly, their singing and dancing, which also led to their being hired by the Persian rulers.

The most significant migrational and linguistic history written on Gypsies who toiled at metalworking from India to the Middle East can be attributed to the following writers: Heinrich Grellman (1792), Jules Bataillard (1844), J. A. Vaillant (1868), Franz de Ville (1956), and Jules Bloch (1956). The importance of their arguments lies in their significant attempts to unearth a connection between the Gypsy metalworkers of Persia and the Gypsy metalworkers of Europe. Subsequently, twentieth-century flamencologists used the prior Gypsyologists' migrational and philological studies to analyze the Andalusian Gypsy songs and the rhythmic structures of relay work at the forge: blacksmithing and metalworking. The percussive theme of the *martinete*, the *cante jondo* Gypsy male solo, brings the sound of metal-on-metal.[11] One might even compose a more specific image, that of the hammer on the horseshoe. The *cantaor* times his singing and the dancer his *baile* to the metallic sounds of these instruments.

Most significant is the notion of multiple earlier migrations into Spain with the Arabs and their Berber allies seeking to conquer Spain and France — what Arab geographers referred to as "the dark North" — in the armies of Charlemagne.[12] In his attempt to understand the origin of the Gypsies, Jean-Paul Clébert writes that the "'Egyptians,' known in the West before the fifteenth century" may have been the "famished-looking hordes that followed Charlemagne's armies."[13] Clébert goes on to situate the Gypsies in the Sassanid dynasty (226 BCE–641 CE) citing the *Shah Nameh*, or Persian *Book of Kings* written by the poet Firdusi (c. 1000 CE). Firdusi, writes Clébert,

informs us that about the year 420 B.C.E., a wise and beneficent prince realized that his poor subjects were pining away for lack of amusements. He sought a means of reviving their spirits . . . he sent a diplomatic mission to the Maharajah of India and begged him to choose among his subjects and send to him in Persia persons capable by their talents of alleviating the burden of existence and able to spread a charm over the monotony of work. Behram Gour soon assembled twelve thousand itinerant minstrels, men and women, assigned lands to them, supplying them with corn and livestock in order that they should have the wherewithal to live in certain areas which he would designate; and so be able to amuse his people at no cost. At the end of the first year these people had neglected agriculture, consumed the corn seed and found themselves without resources. Behram was angry and commanded that their asses and musical instruments should be taken away and that they should roam the country and earn their livelihood by singing. As a consequence these men, the *Luri*, roamed the world to find who would employ them . . . thieving night and day on their way.[14]

"In the year 940 CE," Clébert continues, "the Arab historian Hamza confirms this account. It remained for writers on the subject to relate the *Luri* to the Gypsies."[15] What is significant about these accounts is the firm locating of the Gypsies outside of India.

While the migration inside Persia is thinly documented, the Gypsy migration inside Europe is no more robust historically. But with the notion that they may have worked in the armies of Charlemagne, it seems logical that they might also have taken another route from Persia, through Egypt to Spain by way of the Atlas Mountains of North Africa in the armies of Arabs and Berbers. Gypsy nomads are thought to have taken work in armies that paid them for their metalworking skills.

The Gypsy migration to Spain (or travel by Gypsy men in Arab armies at the very least) in the early eighth century explains the much more documentable fact of the deep absorption into flamenco of Arab, Mozarabic, and Sephardic culture. If this hypothesis is correct and Gypsies did indeed travel in Arab armies that eventually settled first in Cordoba and then spread throughout the Iberian Peninsula, then the Arabic cultural and artistic influences on Gypsies are more easily drawn. This chapter considers those Gypsies who settled in "Al Andaluz"—the blue lands—and theorizes a connection between Muslim culture and the art form known as flamenco.

We must imagine a world of nomadic Gypsies when we read the travelogues' attempts at a Gypsy migrational history. This history is clouded by racist accounts of a heathen tribe of "idolaters, or atheists totally neglectful of worship of any kind" who are frequently compared to the Israelites by some European "historians."[16] A slimly documented history of a global migration has unfortunately fallen into the hands of writers and obfuscated their own perspectives on when, why, and by what means the Gypsies reached Spain. The gravity of this inaccuracy becomes all the more apparent when one attempts to trace the evolution of the character Carmen in the European mind and of her art form, flamenco. I begin with the writer with the greatest influence on Prosper Mérimée, George Borrow. Borrow profoundly shaped the cultural, religious, social, and economic image of Gypsies as pejorative in nineteenth-century European imagination. For these reasons, we will take an in-depth look at his book *The Zincali*, which becomes the first *textbook* of Gypsy life in Europe.

Borrow (1803–1881), the leading Gypsyologist of the Romantic era, was commissioned by the British Bible Society (subsidized by the Earl of Clarendon, to whom he dedicates his 1841 travel book, *The Zincali: An Account of the Gypsies in Spain*) to distribute the Protestant Christian Bible in Spain. In so doing, he came upon the largest group of people living in Europe yet to be completely converted: the Gypsies. While Borrow's book provides a colorful documentary approach to his subjects, his diary-style prose reveals his shock at the idea that they might be sworn "atheists," or worse, animists.[17]

Most pertinent to an understanding of the figure of Carmen, the question of what she represented to Europeans in the mid- to late nineteenth century may well be answered in Borrow's book. Joining a stream of writers from the eighteenth to the nineteenth century attempting to trace the origin of the Gypsy tribes and their migrational path into Spain, Borrow continues an orientalist, Romantic account of their origins in India. He paints them, as did most European writers, living in a static culture whose "primitive habits and customs" have remained "the same as they were four hundred years ago." While Borrow confirms numerous times the notion that the "Romas of Hindustan" wandered first into eastern Europe and then into Spain, he refers to them as a "thievish wandering sect . . . without history or traditions, and unable to look back for a period of eighty years."[18] This may explain, despite the hyperbole, why writing a thorough Gypsy history has been so difficult for many twentieth- and twenty-first-century writers.

While he succumbs to the notion that the Gypsies originally emerged from India, Borrow has trouble proving it, as he can find no trace of an Indian deity or ritual being that they observed. Thus he concludes:

> Though cloudy ideas of the Indian deities might be occasionally floating
> in their minds, these ideas passed away when they ceased to behold the
> pagodas and temples of Indian worship, and were no longer in contact with
> the enthusiastic adorers of the idols of the East; . . . for should it please
> the Almighty to reconduct the Romas to Indian climes, who can doubt
> that within half a century they would entirely forget all connected with the
> religion of the West! Any poor shreds of that faith which they bore with
> them they would drop by degrees as they would relinquish their European
> garments when they became old, and as they relinquished their Asiatic ones
> to adopt those of Europe; no particular dress makes a part of the things
> essential to the sect of Roma, so likewise no particular God and no particular
> religion . . . But what is evident is that they arrived at the confines of Europe
> without any certain or rooted faith. Knowing, as we do, with what tenacity
> they retain their primitive habits and customs, their sect being, in all points,
> the same as it was four hundred years ago, it appears impossible that they
> should have forgotten their peculiar god, if any peculiar god they trusted.[19]

Gypsies Walking along the Beach in Capri, painting by Rubens Santoro, late nineteenth century.
Léopold Mercier / Roger-Viollet Archives, Paris, France

Borrow's book is a travel diary laced with biblical quotes. He takes seriously the Gypsy account of having been exiled, like the Israelites, from Egypt. But, after confirming that such an Egyptian origin tale exists, he rejects it to concur with an earlier Gypsyologist, Heinrich Grellman, that the Gypsies came from India. "Coming from [India] as they most assuredly did," he argues, "they must have been followers of either Buddh" [Buddha] "or Brahma, those tremendous phantoms which have led . . . the souls of hundreds of millions to destruction." Borrow goes on to argue that by the time the Romas reached Spain, there was no trace of an Indian rite, observance, or original religion to speak of. "They may have been idolaters or atheists, or what they now are: totally neglectful of worship of any kind; and though not exactly prepared to deny the existence of a Supreme Being." What is interesting about this account is that as a devout Christian, he may have indeed believed in his own moral superiority; by the end of his book, in the relationships he has formed with Gypsies and the music and dance he has experienced, he tempers these views and allows the reader a prism into mid-nineteenth-century Gypsy life.

"Sad and weary," Borrow continues in his explanation to the British Bible Society, "must have been the path of the mixed rabble of the Romas, when they left India's sunny land and wended their way to the West, in comparison with the glorious exodus of the Israelites from Egypt, whose God went before them in cloud and in fire, working miracles and astonishing the hearts of their foes." Borrow, in setting up his own tale of origin, compares in a bizarre fashion the exodus and wandering of the Gypsy to the Jew. "There are certainly," he argues, "some points of resemblance between the children of Roma and those of Israel. Both have had an exodus, both are exiles and dispersed amongst the Gentiles, by whom they are hated and despised . . . both speak the language of the Gentiles, possess a peculiar tongue, which the latter do not understand, and both possess a peculiar cast of countenance by which they may . . . be distinguished from all other nations." Borrow then breaks away from his comparison of wandering, lost tribes to concentrate the rest of his book on the Romas.

He makes a stunningly ignorant and, yet, from another perspective, illuminating. statement, "Romas have no history."[20] It is this nineteenth-century European mindset, along with the sheer difficulty of ethnographic research that obfuscates serious attempts to write thorough social and cultural histories of the Gypsy people and their impoverished existence in Spain. In addition, while the Gypsy people have certainly created obstacles to an understanding of their history such as their Egyptian origin story, the prejudice they have faced at Christian hands explains their centuries-long fear of the law and avoidance of writing about themselves.

Because so little evidence exists to prove or disprove an alternative hypothesis that Gypsies first arrived in Spain after the Arab conquest, most Gypsy historians cite the second, clearly documented Gypsy migration from central and northern Europe into Spain in the fifteenth century. This chapter considers both migrations, in an attempt to understand the cultural context within which the art form known as flamenco was born. It is this specifically Spanish Gypsy form of music and dance that delineates Carmen as a fictional character and a Romantic myth to European travelers who, over several centuries, popularized a mythology about the Gypsy femme fatale through travel diaries, letters, and serialized stories in European journals.

Borrow's classic nineteenth-century British perspective dwells on the Gypsy's lack of belief in one God. But what his writing reveals is the ability of the Roma in any country in which they roam to put on the cultural garment of the land and then divest it along the way to their next geographical foothold. This recognition by Borrow of a moving, multicultural, multiethnic situational adaptation by the Gypsy "sect" helps understand how they survived in fifteenth-century Spain and to the present as a living culture.

Further, Borrow claims the Gypsy people as children of "The Eternal, His Son, and Mary," soliciting a new place for them in history by ignoring their convoluted Egyptian tale of origin, which he dismisses outright.[21] Borrow writes that they entered Germany calling themselves "Egyptians," a name bestowed on them by priests wishing to explain their presence. The "grand body of this nation of wanderers," Borrow argues, "made a halt for a considerable time" and speedily overran the country. It was a crime "to offer any violence to the Egyptian pilgrims who were permitted to rob on the highway, to commit larceny, and to practice every species of imposition with impunity."[22] Borrow, in justifying his prejudicial view, quotes a seventeenth-century Spanish writer, Quiñones, who, "in a little book," echoed Aventinus's words: "They do not understand what kind of thing the church is and never enter it but for the purpose of committing sacrilege . . . One of the five whom I caused to be hung a few days ago was baptized in the prison, being at the time upwards of thirty years of age."[23]

What Borrow and the theologians to whom he refers actually expose is the tremendously painful life of the Gypsy in Inquisitional and post-Inquisitional Spain. Borrow mentions Dr. Sancho de Moncada, a Spanish theologian from the University of Toledo who dedicated his treatise *The Expulsion of the Gitanos* to Philip III. Moncada's anti-Gypsy discourse draws, for Borrow, the history of government-sanctioned hatred for the Gypsy. Moncada begins with etymology, trying to trace their history in their name: "In the opinion of respectable writers," he writes, "they are called Cingary or Cinli, because they, in every respect, resemble the bird cinclo, which we call in Spanish Motacilla, or aguzanieve (wagtail), which is a vagrant bird and builds no nest, but broods in those of other birds, a bird restful and poor of plumage."[24]

Moncada justifies his case by introducing the notion of their strangeness:

They are foreigners, though authors differ much with respect to the country from whence they came. The majority say that they are from Africa and that they came with the Moors when Spain was lost; others that they are Tartars, Persians, Cilicians, Nubians, from Lower Egypt, from Syria, or from other parts of Asia and Africa, and others consider them to be descendants of Chus, son of Cain; others say that they are of European origin, Bohemians, Germans, or outcasts from other nations of this quarter of the world . . . There is not a nation which does not consider them as a most pernicious rabble; even the Turks and Moors abominate them.[25]

"The second and sure opinion," Moncada continues, "is that those who prowl about Spain are not Egyptians, but swarms of wasps and atheistical wretches, without any kind of law or religion, Spaniards, who have introduced this Gypsy life or sect, and who admit into it every day all the idle and broken people of Spain. There are some foreigners who make Spain the origin and fountain of all Gypsies of Europe, as they say that they proceed from a river in Spain called Cija, of which Lucan makes mention; an opinion, however, not much adopted amongst the learned."[26]

Borrow does not comment on Moncada's clearly prejudicial treatise but wisely lets it reveal itself. What Moncada's racist musings do, however, is situate Gypsies within Inquisitional Spain of the fifteenth century. Whether they fought for the Christians or the Moors or both, they were left behind after the surrender of Boabdil in July 1492, the expulsion of the Sephardim on 2 August 1492, and perhaps the official expulsion of the Hispano-Arab population in 1508, although it is well documented by Henry Kamen and Americo Castro that many small Muslim landholders remained fighting Christian foes well into the seventeenth and, perhaps, even the eighteenth century.[27] The xenophobic language of Dr. Moncada brings to the surface, shockingly for the contemporary reader, the cultural context of post-Inquisition Spain. A Christian monarchical line moved with quicksilver velocity into the Alhambra palace and all of the landholdings of the Spanish Arabs and set about Christianizing the architecture, the people, the books, the street names, and the open plazas, obliterating their Muslim names but leaving for history the Koranic lettering that ornamented their private apartments and public alcazars. To accomplish the political reunification of Spain—a task completed by their grandson, Carlos V—King Ferdinand II (1452–1516) of Aragon, Sicily, Naples, and Valencia and Queen Isabella I (1451–1504) of Castile and Léon spun a tale of authenticity. They saw themselves, not the Arabs or the Jews, as the true rulers of the Iberian Peninsula. They spoke of fighting for Spain's renewal— *renacimiento*—to bring her authentic state of being back into Christendom and rid her of the uncleanliness and the infidelity of those who had colonized her eight hundred years before.

1423–1492: From the Gypsy Migration to the Defeat of Muslim Spain

Having described their early history in Spain, Borrow then asks himself why the Gypsies were allowed to escape the fires of the Church. He argues that they were cruelly punished by the Spanish Crown for being murderers, robbers, thieves, and sorceresses, and either sent to the galleys, branded, imprisoned, flayed, or, too often, hanged on the gallows. Yet, the Holy Office of the Inquisition left them alone. "Whilst I resided at Cordova," Borrow writes, "I was acquainted with an aged ecclesiastic, who was priest of a village called Puente, at about two leagues' distance from the city. He was detained in Cordova on account of his political opinions . . . We lived together at the same house." He had worked for the Inquisition. "One night, whilst we were seated together, three Gitanos entered to pay me a visit, and on observing the old ecclesiastic, exhibited every mark of dissatisfaction, and speaking in their own idiom, called him a *balichow* . . . On their departing, I inquired of the old man whether he [who] . . . was doubtless versed in the annals of the holy office, could inform me whether the Inquisition had ever taken any active measures for the suppression and punishment of the sect of the Gitanos: whereupon he replied that he was

> "not aware of one case of a Gitano having been tried or punished by the Inquisition . . . The Inquisition always looked upon them with too much contempt to give itself the slightest trouble concerning them; for as no danger either to the state, or the church of Rome, could proceed from the Gitanos, it was a matter of perfect indifference to the holy office whether they lived without religion or not."

Borrow finishes the interview in his own words:

> Religion was assumed as a mask to conceal the vilest and most detestable motives which ever yet led to the commission of crying justice; the Jews were doomed to persecution and destruction on two accounts — their great riches, and their high superiority over the Spaniards in learning and intellect. . . . Much the same causes insured the expulsion of the Moriscos, who were abhorred for their superior industry, which the Spaniards could not imitate; whilst the reformation was kept down by the gaunt arm of the Inquisition, lest the property of the church should pass into other and more deserving hands.[28]

To understand the Gypsy contribution to Spanish art and especially to flamenco, one must understand how the Gypsy lived in Catholic Spain.[29] Again, I return to Borrow for insight as well as to a more comprehensive, fair-minded and better-documented approach to Spanish history by Americo Castro. Let us begin with the laws against the Gitanos, known as the *Pragmaticas*.

While the first published law by the Spanish Crown against the Gypsy as "foreigner" within Spain was drafted in 1478, it was with the expulsion of the Jews and the slow exile (1508) and exodus of the Hispano-Arabs that the Spanish Crown and Church turned their attention to any outsider left on Spanish soil.[30] Excluding the *conversos*, and aside from African slave labor working the fields of Andalusia, the only other "outside" group was, of course, the Gypsies. From their arrival around 1423, the Gypsies experienced substantial social, economic, cultural, and political upheaval caused by the defeat and colonization of the last Muslim Kingdom on 2 January 1492 and the expulsion of the Jews on 2 August 1492. Southern Spain — in particular, Andalusia, in the late fifteenth century — was absolutely rocked by internal wars of conquest and ensuing social change. Whereas heretofore the Gypsies had enjoyed considerable liberty to travel and, at times, to settle in the Arab villages throughout the Iberian Peninsula, Gypsies did not fare so well in the united kingdoms of Castile and Aragon. They had no right to citizenship, as they were neither Spaniards nor citizens of any other country. They were stateless and had no legal, political, or social rights.

There were other issues as well. While they absorbed the Spanish language, they did so into Caló, the Gypsy tongue. Additionally, they dressed like foreigners, in rags, often polka-dotted and brightly colored. The men rarely cut their hair or trimmed their beards; they wore a style of hat that must have appeared immodest to the Spanish court and its hyper-religious advisers. Gypsies danced and sang in public areas, moving their arms, fingers, and hips. This behavior of "lascivious" Gypsy women in public greatly upset the Church. Moncada expressed his opinion to the Crown:

> The *Gitanas* are public harlots. [Their] dances, demeanor, and filthy songs are the cause of continual detriment to the souls of the vassals of your Majesty, it being notorious that they have done infinite harm in many honorable houses by separating the married women from their husbands, and perverting the maidens: and finally, in the best of these *Gitanas* any one may recognize all of the signs of a harlot given by the wise king; they are gadders about, whisperers, always unquiet in places and corners.[31]

Lastly, Gypsies in some places lived in large groups as vagrants and settled into safer, less obvious dwellings — caves or even in the mountains — when able.

Gypsies in the Sacromonte, Granada, Spain, photographer and date unknown.
Roger-Viollet Archives, Paris, France

Designed to stop them from wandering, dressing as foreigners, speaking a foreign tongue, fortune-telling, dancing, singing, castanet or tambourine playing, and stealing, *Las Pragmaticas* were as harsh as the French, German, and British laws against them. If the Gypsies were willing to convert, accept Jesus Christ as their savior, forsake their animist, polytheistic traditions and become true believers as proscribed by the Holy Office, there could be some hope. But Gypsies were expected to stop the wandering existence considered anathema to the reserved, controlled lifestyle proselytized by *Los Reyes Catolicos* and the church, or face exile.[32] In the opinion of the Inquisitional Office, the Gypsies were considered:

idle, vagabond people, who are in no respect useful to the kingdom, without commerce, occupation, or trade of any description; and if they have any it is making picklocks and pothooks for appearance sake, being wasps, who only live by sucking and impoverishing the country, sustaining themselves by the sweat of the miserable laborers . . .

. . . Because they are enchanters, diviners, magicians, chiromancers, who tell the future by the lines of the hand which is what they call *buena ventura*, and are in general addicted to all kind of superstition . . .

The civil law ordains that vagrants be seized wherever they are found . . . Moreover, the emperor, our lord, has decreed by a law made in Toleda in the year 1525, that the third time they be found wandering they shall serve as slaves during their whole life to those who capture them.[33]

The enslavement in the galleys of the male *Gitano* and the mutilation and/or exile of the *Gitana* as a means of converting them and changing their way of life was cruel. While it certainly killed off numbers of Gypsies, it had no lasting effect on their lifestyle. These same rituals and traditions — described from the harshly distorted perspective shown in the above quotations — are practiced by Gypsies to this day.

Fatalism may have entered the flamenco *cante* not just from Arab and Sephardic chant but also from the sense of hopelessness and the sheer wretched existence forced upon the Gypsy by the Spanish Crown. "The Gitanos ought to be condemned to death," wrote Moncada, after the *Pragmaticas* of the Spanish crown. "The reasons are many."[34]

The first, for being spies and traitors to the crown; the second, as idlers and vagabonds . . . The third, because they are stealers of four-footed beasts, who are condemned to death by the laws of Spain, in the wise code of the famous King Don Alonso; which enactment became a part of common law . . . The fourth, for wizards, diviners, and for practicing arts which are prohibited under pain of death by the divine law itself . . . The last and most urgent cause is, that they are heretics, if what is said be truth; and it is the practice of the law in Spain to burn such.[35]

Dr. Moncada continues, moving from this recommendation of the execution of the Gypsy to their expulsion:

They are comprehended as hale beggars in the law of the wise King, Don Alonso, by which he expelled all sturdy beggars, as being idle and useless . . . Secondly, the law expels public harlots from the city . . . Thirdly, as people who cause scandal, and who as is visible at the first glance, are prejudicial to morals and common decency. It is established by the statute law of these kingdoms that such people be expelled there from; it is said so in the well-pondered words of the edict for the expulsion of the Moors: "And forasmuch as the sense of good and Christian government makes it a matter of conscience to expel from the kingdoms the things which cause scandal, injury to honest subjects, danger to the state, and above all, disloyalty to the Lord our God." Therefore, considering the incorrigibility of the Gitanos, the Spanish kings made many holy laws in order to deliver their subjects from such pernicious people.[36]

At the end of Moncada's quotation of the original fifteenth- and sixteenth-century edicts against the Gypsies, he declares in a letter to the King, Don Alonso, that it would be better—more just—to expel them than to kill them. Quoting a colleague, Doctor Salazar de Mendoza, Moncada argues that all the Church doctors, "who are of the opinion that the Gitanos may be condemned to death, would consider it as an act of mercy in your Majesty to banish them perpetually from Spain."[37]

What is interesting is that he refers to them as Spaniards. "And as others profess the sacred orders of religion, even so do these fellows profess gypsying, which is robbery and all the other vices enumerated . . . It is still more [just] to banish them."[38] Moncada feels himself justified in this plea to the king, as it is his Majesty's responsibility to consider the welfare of even the Gitanos if they are Spanish subjects. Appealing to his benevolence, Moncada concludes, "because your Majesty, in the Cortes at present assembled has obliged [me with] your royal conscience to fulfill all the articles voted for the public service . . . deemed expedient that your Majesty command them to quit these kingdoms within six months . . . and that they do not return to the same under pain of death."[39]

Moncada suggests that if the Gypsies are willing to reside in large towns, they should be allowed to do so. At the same time that he admits that it "appears a pity to banish women and children," Moncada points to other European monarchs' rulings to substantiate the request to remove the Gypsy from Spain:

The emperor our Lord, in the German Diets of the year 1548, expelled the Gitanos from all his empire . . . The King of France, Francis, expelled them from thence; and the Duke of Terranova, when Governor of Milan for our lord the king, obliged them to depart from that territory under pain of death . . . Pope Pius the Fifth offered the option to all his princes: "for he drove the Gitanos from all his domains, and in the year 1568, he expelled the Jews, assigning as reasons for their expulsion those which are more closely applicable to the Gitanos . . ."[40]

In 1619, during the reign of Philip III, Gypsies were forbidden to speak Caló. Just as the Holy Office had attempted to remove all trace of Jews, Protestants, and Muslims from its lands, now the Gypsy was to be renamed a Spaniard and expected to fall in line with the philosophy of *limpieza de sangre*, purity of Spanish blood. Anything less would result in death or permanent exile.[41] The problem for the Gypsies was that, prior to their coming to Spain, France, Italy, and Germany, each nation had passed laws discouraging them from ever crossing into its lands. By the mid-seventeenth century, Philip reiterated his charge that the Gypsies were the dregs of society. Gypsies were ordered to disband their tribes and marry outside the clan, into Spanish society, but hardly ever did this happen.

The *Pragmaticas* were repeated over and over again throughout the seventeenth and eighteenth centuries, clearly because they were never adhered to. Twelve anti-Gypsy laws were written between 1499 and 1783;[42] and yet the Gypsy not only survived but did well in Andalusia.

The topography of Andalusia — its steep hills and mountain ranges, winding paths and sharp-edged switchbacks — helped the Gypsy people survive in an inhospitable land that, as Bercovici argued, wrote many laws dictating how they should be punished or die but none explaining how they might live.[43] This wilderness, at times snowy and barren, provided an escape from the law if required. Their ability to disappear into the mountains may well have been the single most important reason that the Spanish authorities could not forcibly assimilate, Christianize, or radically transform the Gypsy people from nomadic to settled, eastern to western, animists to monotheists. This vision of the Gypsy in the inhospitable, wild mountain terrain above the cities of Andalusia inspired both Prosper Mérimée and Georges Bizet.

1783–1820: From the *Pragmaticas* to the Birth of Gypsy Flamenco

Not even topography, however, could make Gypsy life in Spain easier. In the reign of Charles III (1759–1788), all previous laws were reiterated. Gypsies were again told to give up their customs, language, dress, and unsettled traveling lifestyle. But Charles, coming from the Netherlands, allowed Gypsies to choose an occupation or profession. This marked an historic change. Finally, they could participate in the slow proto-urbanization of the growing towns that dotted the Iberian Peninsula. As Andalusians, by virtue of the king's law, became familiar with the Gypsy presence in and around cities, and the Gypsy saw a more welcome reception to that presence, Gypsies remained for longer periods of time in the same locations. Eventually, by the mid-nineteenth century, Gypsies had permanently settled in pueblos throughout the south.

This is not to say that the Gypsy was not already living in the hidden caves of the Sacromonte during what would become the end of eight hundred years of Hispano-Arab presence in Western Europe. Rather, the Gypsy came to be known as an Andalusian, albeit a black Andalusian. A figure from the East, like the Arab and the Jew who no longer walked the city streets of Granada, Cordoba, and Seville, the Gypsy became a reflection, to poet and painter, musician and writer, of civilizations past.

The Birth of Flamenco

So closely connected was the Gypsy to Andalusian ways and manners that Andalusia and *Gitano* became synonymous. Gypsy life, as full as it was and still is with dancing, singing, and the music of the guitar, became an anachronistic reflection of the balladeering of the Arab court and the rich tapestry of Andalusian arts and cultures under the almost-forgotten Muslim rulers.

Borrow, while disturbed by the lack of "faith" on the part of the Gypsy soul, comments upon the harsh treatment of the "few" Gypsy people by the Spanish authorities. "Perhaps," he writes, "there is no country in which more laws have been framed, having in view the extinction and suppression of the Gypsy name, race and manner of life, than Spain."[44] Already several hundred years into a religious, political, and socioeconomic war against many of its citizens, the Spanish Crown, by the time of Borrow's visit to Spain, was well-versed in chasing "the other" from its lands.

Gypsy Entrance into Spain, a Fifteenth-Century History

In his 1707 preface to Grellman's "dissertation," the historian I. Should argues:

> Nobody has ever thought of publishing a circumstantial, connected account of the economy of these people, their opinions and condition, since they have been in Europe. Whatever has appeared, on this subject, has been in detached pieces, occasionally communicated by writers of travels, or by such persons, who, having made particular enquiries about the origin of the Gipsies, formed a system of their own,

Gypsy Circus Rests by the Side of the Road, photographer and date unknown.
Roger-Viollet Archives, Paris, France

concerning them . . . It may not be possible to compile some consistent history of this tribe, which has diffused itself through all the countries of Europe: especially as such a description, by reason of the strange and striking customs of the Gipsies, may be equally useful for entertainment, as for the promotion of the knowledge of manners and mankind.[45]

The field of Gypsy study began with the Gypsies' entrance into Europe in the early fifteenth century. Dozens of horse- and donkey-drawn wagons driven by dark-skinned strangers speaking an incomprehensible tongue arrived in central Europe in 1417.[46] The Gypsies, in their westward migration, are thought to have traveled from Turkey to Bohemia/Hungary, Germany, England, and France. George Borrow has placed the number of Gypsies who entered Europe at this time at between 120 and 400 people, although there is very little substantiation of these figures, as contemporary writing about the Gypsies was so heavily biased against them that it is impossible to know the facts. It is clear, however, in all historical and mythical accounts of their entry into central, northern, and western parts of Europe, that they alarmed and angered local populations and began a lifetime of outwitting the natives through fortune-telling, stealing, and horse trading. Their one legitimate trade was blacksmith work, although even here they often tricked their clients. The notion of Gypsies against the world spread throughout the Gypsy trail from East to West, and this somewhat mythical, somewhat real circumstance led to the European romanticization of Gypsies, laced with severely racist and xenophobic ideas, that ultimately led to their unusually harsh treatment by local authorities.

The notion of the Gypsy as a pilgrim or traveler fueled a romantic mythology encouraged by the Gypsies that slowly spread throughout Europe. The twentieth-century Gypsy historian and anthropologist Walter Starkie gave a lecture at NYU in 1959, quoted by Bertha Quintana, in which he argued that, in 1430, King James I of Scotland "went so far as to conclude a treaty with the Gypsy Chief" the Earl of Little Egypt. In the treaty, King James pledged to support the Gypsies.[47] The myth of the Gypsies migrating into Europe from Egypt and into Spain from Africa led to the adoption of the words *Gitanos*, *Gitanes*, and *Ciganes*, meaning no-mads from Egypt.[48] German philologist/gypsyologist Heinrich Grellmann argues that the Gypsies arrived in France in 1417, in Rome in 1422, and in Santiago de Compostela, Spain in 1423.[49]

For the space of between three and four hundred years, they have gone wandering about, like pilgrims and strangers . . . unsettled wandering robbers: they are found in eastern and western countries, as well as among the rude as civilized, indolent and active people; yet they remain ever, and every where, what their fathers were—Gipsies. Africa makes them no blacker, nor Europe whiter; they neither learn to be lazy in Spain; nor diligent in Germany: in Turkey, Mahomet, and among Christians Christ, remains equally without adoration.[50]

To secure the protection of the Pope, they claimed to be penitents, "condemned to wander throughout the world for seven years because of a curse placed upon their Egyptian ancestors of having refused protection to the Holy Family from Herod."[51] Borrow concurred with Grellmann in 1841 that the Gypsies invented the Egyptian ancestry tale so that "beneath the garb of penitence they could rob and cheat with impunity, for a time, at least."[52] (The Gypsy response to these affronts to their being was disinformation of their own "history" now inserted into the "pure" historical record.) Walter Starkie agreed with Grellmann and Borrow, claiming that the "Gypsies as pilgrims found, at first, open doors everywhere in Europe because they were looked upon as sacred men and women who should be helped to accomplish their penance, for it was the duty of charitable Christians to speed on their way those undertaking the long journey to Compostela and to give them all the assistance they needed."[53]

As a result of their success in surviving in foreign lands, the Gypsies' origin tale became convoluted. To solicit a sympathetic response from what would normally be hostile local populations, the Gypsies were wise enough to claim an aristocratic heritage and called themselves kings, dukes, and earls of a kingdom known as Little Egypt, "from whence they had been driven by conquering infidels."[54]

Gypsy chiefs, dressed in costumes foreign to Europeans, were convincing in their "royal" robes. Considered to be kings, Gypsy chiefs were accorded the same rights and privileges of any royalty. They could only be tried by Gypsy tribunals or by a court whose composition was half Gypsies. They were awarded a papal safe-conduct pass, money, and travel permits to visit pilgrimage shrines throughout Europe.[55] While the Gypsies did nothing to dissuade people over the centuries that they came from Little Egypt, their tale of migration met with another powerful story: the migration of nomads, meaning Gypsies, from Africa through Egypt.[56] (The reigning flamenco Sevillian dynasty, descended from El Farruco, has a relative they call *La Faraona*, the Pharoah.)

Their claims of Egyptian ancestry, hence the name *Egipcianos*, is considered in Gypsy history as the "First Great Trick" played by the Gypsies upon Europeans.[57] Grellmann was among the first philologists to dispute the Egyptian ancestry tale

Gypsy Fortune-teller, Paris, France, photographer and date unknown.
Roger-Viollet Archives, Paris, France

woven by Gypsies throughout Europe to secure royal favors and citizen protection. He discovered in the late eighteenth century that *Romani* contained many Sanskrit words resembling dialects from northwest India. A series of racial theories followed Grellmann's etymological studies. These, beginning in the eighteenth century and extending into the twentieth, argued that Gypsies had typical Indian physical characteristics. But by the early twentieth century, ethnomusicology in the service of Spanish nationalism became one of the most powerful artistic and scholarly means of claiming the Gypsies' Indian heritage, thus dispelling the Egyptian tale. In his 1950 book of musical writings, *Escritos sobre la musica y musico*, Manuel de Falla, like Grellmann, argued that the Gypsies originated in India. Falla based his argument upon their music, finding musical traits common to both Indian and Gypsy rhythm: complex arabesques, infinite gradations of pitch, a single note repeated endlessly, metallic tone, conflicting rhythms played simultaneously by different instruments (voice), falling cadence, etc.[58]

The beginning of the harsh persecution of the Gypsies, resulting in their near-total extermination between 1944 and 1945 at the hands of the Nazis (largely at Auschwitz), is traced by Grellmann to Poland and Germany, where the first restrictive laws against the Gypsies were written in the fifteenth century.[59] At first, Gypsies seem to have enjoyed some years of safe travel, but once the Church understood that they had no intention of practicing Catholicism, both the Vatican and local governments succumbed to xenophobia and real fears of theft by Gypsies. With so many accusations—true and false—against them, nomadic Gypsies had no chance of integration into local society or even of finding safe passage. Accusations against Gypsies ranged from petty thievery to cannibalism, child stealing, poisoning wells, witchcraft (black magic), and failure to stop their nomadic ways and assimilate smoothly into the local culture. These dangerously negative opinions intensified as more bands of Gypsies descended upon local European populations. "By 1438," Walter Starkie argues, "the ranks of what had started out as relatively small bands were being swelled continuously by thousands of Gypsies eager to share in the earlier success of their people."[60]

Under orders at first to donate alms, shelter, and aid to the Gypsies, impoverished townspeople and peasants soon viewed them as "parasitic hoards," and pressured local church authorities to have them excommunicated. By 1447, thousands of Gypsies had fled west and south, traveling from Central Europe and France and Germany, sweeping down into Barcelona, and continuing further south beyond that. Once in Spain, the Gypsies, Walter Starkie argues, returned to their mythic origin tale of fleeing the Kingdom of Little Egypt in search of safe passage as penitential Christians trying to worship the Lord.[61] Most tribes entered Spain from the east and the north through Catalonia, traveling quickly into the more tolerant, multicultural areas of the south.

Fifteenth-century Spain was a complex, still-feudal collection of kingdoms and principalities vying against one another for control of arable land and trade routes. "It was to Granada," argued Quintana, "that the 'Original Band' came in the fifteenth century. They moved into the nearby caves of the Sacromonte, where they still dwell. Because the Gypsies of Granada forged the projectiles used by the Catholic Monarchs to attack the Nasrid fortress and the Alhambra, they were titled the "New Castilians."[62] The caves of the palace hill overlooking the Gypsy quarter of Granada, known as the Albaicín as it is called today, became hidden points of entry into the palace. "We came to Granada," sang a famous *cantaor*, whose *cante* recalled the relationship between the Gypsy and Andalusia, "with los reyes catolicos five hundred years ago," that is to say, in their armies against the Moor. "Since then we have been here in the Sacromonte and the Albaicín, living and dying like our parents before us in the shade of the Alhambra."[63]

While some Gypsies came to Andalusia following a coastal route along the Costa del Sol and the Costa Brava, others followed the royal caravan into the city of Granada in 1492. Along with the northern Catholic Spanish soldiers, they worked for the armies of Ferdinand of Aragon and Isabella of Castile. They were repaid for their work and loyalty by being allowed to settle in Granada.[64]

There were other reasons the Gypsies settled in Granada. As a persecuted people fleeing the anti-Gypsy laws of France, Hungary, Germany, and England, they quickly discovered the caves that began at the foot of the Nasrids' Alhambra Palace and extended all the way up the hill that leads deep into the Albaicín. Though illuminated only by candlelight, the caves were safer places than open-air camps, cool in the hot summer months and warm in the winter.

The second reason the Gypsies were drawn to Granada was the Sierra Nevada, the steep mountain range that rises above the city and descends into the fertile lands on both sides. Both for smuggling purposes (Gypsies were often the mules for supplies that arrived from the coast) and to avoid the law, they often took refuge in these mountains, finding in their endless back trails perfect places to hide from the authorities. Gypsies slipped unseen into and out of the mountains for long periods of time. The rugged terrain also provided excellent places in which to lie in wait for wagon trains passing from one end of Spain to the next, which Gypsies would rob.

Another potent reason why the Gypsies chose Granada might have been its landscape. Under the Nasrids, Granada was (and remains) a stunningly beautiful environment, peaceful and filled with plants and trees. This final Hispano-Arab court cultivated in its gardens, fountains, tree-lined streets, open-air markets, courtyards, and patios a meditative, quiet naturalism enjoyed by anyone who lived there. Their city was rich in greenery and trees, and the deciduous pines, whose tops left pools of light where the sun broke through, gave it an almost wild appearance. "Nature," wrote one travel writer about the Alhambra Palace, "penetrates to the most intimate corners."[65] In the Arab palace and in the city itself, a city-dweller or even a visitor might well experience the intended hypnotic effect of this architectural landscaping.

Perhaps, above all, the Gypsies settled near the Alhambra Palace on the adjacent hillside for the sheer natural beauty of the view. "The Muslim oratory, facing the East with its richly adorned Koranic niche looking out over the Darro and the Albaicín," revealed, to anyone who looked up to see it, beautiful arched windows, porticoes with lateral naves thought by the Nasrid architects to bring the inhabitant and surely the onlooker on a path to spiritual enlightenment.[66] The architectural joining of stone building to running water was extended to the city—the Darro—itself and thus was enjoyed by anyone walking through.

The interpenetration of interior and exterior space was repeated throughout the city, a true incorporation of nature into architectural form that continues in Spanish homes to this day. The idea that a settled dweller still lives outside while at home must have appealed to the Gypsy, whose outside encampments from Turkey to Spain, perched on the sides of hills or the edges of towns, symbolically reflected this urban architecture. Used to living outside, comfortable with the freedom that nature offers, Gypsies in Granada came to live in a landscape of gardens and running water.

The Islamic Contribution to Gypsy Culture

Between 711 CE and the mid-fifteenth century, Muslim kingdoms ruled the Iberian Peninsula, transforming rural villages into caliphal centers of power, commerce, and learning. Erecting tremendous fortresses, cities and villages, palaces, mosques, libraries, gardens, and city dwellings, a series of Hispano-Arab caliphs and their court architects, musicians, and scholars transformed a medieval, barren land into the Baghdad of the Maghreb, or "Far West." George Borrow argued that they moved into Valencia, Extremadura, Nuevo Castilla, and Murcia, all Arab lands: "But far, far, more, Andalusia . . . Andalusia, the land of the proud steed and the stubborn mule, the land of the savage *sierra* and the fruitful and cultivated plain: to Andalusia they hied, in bands of thirties and sixties."[67]

The Spanish Historical Perspective — Americo Castro, Henri Pirenne, and Bernard Lewis

"The Moors," wrote seminal Spanish historian Americo Castro in 1957, "came to Hispaña sustained by two highly efficacious forces: political unity and the impetus of a newly born religion, the expression of everything that the body and soul of the Bedouin could long for."[68] The Bedouin (*Bedu*) wanderer was the nomadic soul-brother to the Indian Gypsy. "The Moors," Castro continued, "progressed elastically with the feeling that they were moved by a central mainspring of religion and politics."[69] Within a short time, Visigothic Hispania succumbed to the Syrian-Berber military advance, as did the northern Spanish provinces as the Arab armies pushed well north of the Pyrénées, only to be stopped by Charles Martel, grandfather of Charlemagne, in 732 CE, and thus began the eight-hundred-year history of Islamic Spain.[70] Americo Castro once referred to the continued Hispano-Arab presence in the post-Reconquest of Spain after 1492 as "the footprints of Islam in Christian Spain."[71]

Flamenco *Cante* and Arab Poetry — Philosophical Fatalism

"The highest achievement of the Arabs," writes Lewis in *The Arabs in History*, "in their own reckoning and the first in order of time was poetry with the allied art of rhetoric . . . Under the Umayyad, the orally transmitted poetry of pre-Islamic Arabia was codified . . . Under the Abbasids, Arabic poetry was enriched by the accession of many non-Arabs, especially Persians."[72] Thus, Islam as it was transported to Spain, "was not only a system of belief and cult. It was also a system of state, society, law, thought and art — a civilization with unifying religion." Islam continued to mean submission to the Prophet, his *hadiths*, and the *umma*, or Muslim community, and, of course, the Caliph, commander of the faithful. Muslim laws came from God through Mohammad, his Prophet, and were dictated directly to him in the Revelations.

All Muslim civilizations were built upon the spoken word as being the dominant source of communication of civil, legal, moral, and spiritual philosophy. Spoken Arabic was used to bear witness both to Arab history and to its rich cultural expression. Lewis tells us that in the eighth century, Bashahar ibn Burd (d. 784) spoke at the Umayyad court in Cordoba. In the ninth century, Ibn Bah, "'al-Jahiz" (d. 869), the grandson of a black slave, became one of the most famous early Islamic poets. In the tenth century, Al Mutanabii (905–65) was considered one of the greatest proselytizers of Arabic prose. By the mid-fourteenth to early fifteenth centuries, Islam's greatest historian, Ibn Khaldun (1332–1406), came to work in Spain from the Middle East.[73]

Some of these and many other poets reinvented the Greek tradition of balladeering, placing poetic verse with musical notes, offering the news of the day, commentary on society, or just a soothing means of entertainment.

Arabic poetic verse, spoken and sung, influenced Gypsy *cante*. In most global cultures of the time, poetry was transmitted orally, from poet to Caliph or person to person. A book, "a physical entity, a bound collection of pages with title and illustrations . . . was first published" in recitation.[74] "The spoken word" was its defining element.[75] Each Muslim, Spanish court employed one or more poets who recited poetry on political, philosophical, religious, and personal themes, playing an important role in court culture. They were frequently in the presence of court subjects and were known for their wit, rhythm, stories, charm, and diction.

While it is certain that Gypsies came to Spain with their own form of singing, there is little doubt that the effect of Muslim culture on an already established form of oral and gestural storytelling was significant. Gypsies, to this day, trans-

mit their history and daily news orally, through *cante*. The *cante*, like the Moorish singing tradition, both entertains and remembers. Stories abound of the Gypsy man's plight as a non-citizen of the country. Some of the finest *cantaors* have given exact descriptions of the prison cells in the local jail. Other songs historicize the Gypsy's relationship to the Muslim court. One such song describes a Gypsy in love with a "beautiful Jewess." Another speaks of a Gypsy man who falls in love with a Muslim woman of the wealthy class. While many if not most songs refer to the famous Gypsy *barrio* of Triana, all Gypsies everywhere have experienced intense hostility and physical abuse at the hands of local authorities. The actual sound of the singing is rough and has an almost jagged edge. In the *rasquedo*, or

Dancers and Musicians Perform in Front of the Casbah of El Kelaa, Morocco, photographer and date unknown.
CAP / Roger-Viollet Archives, Paris, France

vocal chords, are slow descents from major to minor keys that fall into the back of the throat, producing sounds that resonate with pain and suffering, injustice without respite. Gypsy song is considered by ethnomusicologists to contain their *intrahistoria*, or oral history; in Muslim-Sephardic Spain it gained an emotional vocal resonance.

While the person of Carmen emerged from the imagination of a modern French writer, she, like the flamenco song and dance she represents, is a product of an amalgam of the many elements of Hispanic Muslim civilization. If, as Americo Castro has argued, "the hand of Islam can still be seen in the monuments of Cordova, Granada, Seville, and Toledo," then it can surely be seen inside the prism through which Mérimée looked when he studied Spain.[76] Such a powerful cultural consequence has continued to influence both Andalusian life and the perception of those seeking to understand Andalusia, the Gypsy, and Spain.

As the Gypsy is so closely connected to Andalusian ways and manners, Andalusia and *Gitano* have become synonymous. Gypsy life, as full as it was and still is with dancing, singing, drumming, and the guitar, became an anachronistic reflection of the balladeering of the Arab court and the rich tapestry of Andalusian arts and cultures under the Muslim rulers. Like contemporary rap, an urban form with roots in the African American South, flamenco song contains vestiges of earlier cultural attributes. *Cante* is a poetic, metered, abstract singing style. Its raspy, guttural wail bespeaks its subject matter: unrequited love, persecution by the authorities, prison, death — that is, Gypsy existence and identity.

Gypsyologist Jean-Paul Clébert has argued a second migrational path of the Gypsies, in a short book called *Les Gitans* (1963). Romantic Gypsy philologists like

Grellmann wrote that the Gypsies feared water as they came from the dry deserts of Rajasthan in the Punjab region of northwest India, and thus their route into Spain from India was landlocked. But mid-twentieth-century research, like that of Clébert, has revealed that the Gypsies did indeed travel by boat, from North Africa across the Straits of Gibraltar, symbolic of a second wave of "dark peoples" arriving from the East. Clébert, concurring with his Romantic predecessors, agrees that the exact date of their arrival remains speculative. Further, Clébert's research has revealed that while the first exodus took them into and through central and northern European lands, this second journey was a more direct route from Egypt across North Africa and the Mediterranean. Gypsies who had left their countries some centuries previously then encountered one another in Andalusia.

> We do not know the date on which the Gypsies crossed the Strait of Gibraltar . . . Where and when did the meeting of the two groups take place? This also is not known . . . Spanish documents never speak of two different groups of nomads. They simply mention *Gitanos* . . . We remember that the northern Gypsies have arrived in Barcelona in 1447 . . . The arrival of the southern *Gitano* colonies in the south of the peninsula seems to have been established at an earlier date than those of the north: the Sierra Nevada mountains must have given shelter to the first tribes, and the *Gitano* colonies of Andalusia at Granada, Cadiz and Seville have been attested "at all times."[77]

I base my final chapter, "Space and Place in Mozarabic Spain," on Clébert, arguing that Gypsies might well have come with Arab-Berber armies from North Africa to Spain in the first waves of crusade in the early eighth century. But one must ask if there was any evidence of a Gypsy migration from the Punjab prior to 1000 CE. There is some evidence in Persian poetry that the Gypsies were already present in Persia in Roman times during the Persian–Roman Wars, but it is scant.

Grellmann, Borrow, Starkie, and Clébert argue effectively that the largest Gypsy migration occurred in the fifteenth century. However, there is evidence that they also wandered through the Arab empires of the East.[78] While there is much speculation on the subject, it seems that the Gypsy's greatest freedom came in Andalusia, living in lands themselves occupied by Muslims and Jews, many of who had emigrated to Spain from the Middle East. Unlike the less evolved, medieval culture of the northern Christian Kingdoms of Aragon, Navarre, and Castile, Andalusia contained a culture rich in poetry, music, art, and mysticism. The last Muslim *taifa* in Spain, the Nasrid kingdom of Granada, drew the greatest number of Gypsies. Consisting of Sephardic, Hispano-Arab, and Mozarabic (Arabized

Christian) traditions, this rich intercultural fusion offered foreigners a much more familiar and tolerant place to live. In the cities of Andalusia, Arabic, Ladino, and Spanish could be heard daily along with various other languages and dialects belonging to the many foreigners who came to conduct business or just to see the great Muslim kingdom that stood at the edge of Christian Europe.

Adding to the attraction felt by Gypsies to the Nasrid kingdom is what some historians and ethnomusicologists argue is a similar philosophical outlook possessed by both the Hispano-Arabs and the Gypsies: fatalism, a kind of existential spiritualism expressed through poetic, sung verse. Gypsy culture was and is built upon oral tradition, remembering its past through a history passed down from adults to children in song and story.

> Once the *gitano* families . . . arrived in Granada, they settled in neighborhoods
> occupied by the Moriscos . . . This was a neighborhood of many caves and Arabs
> and Gypsies lived together there until the expulsion of the Moriscos in 1610 . . .
> The proclamations only imposed on the Gypsies the requirement that they stay
> in a fixed residence, without wandering, and that they perform manual labor.
> Did many Moriscos of Granada use the illegal possibility of "camouflaging"
> themselves as Gypsies?[79]

As mentioned previously, a third reason for settling in Andalusia were the caves of the Sacromonte, the perfect dwelling place for a people wishing to live freely on the outskirts of town, while allowing certain clan members the ability to continue to wander if desired. With a home base to protect and house them, settled Gypsies could look for work as blacksmiths, mule clippers, horse traders, and minstrels and also wander into large public areas to tell fortunes, dance, sing, and perform tricks.

SETTLING IN THE NASRID TAIFA

Hear me, Albar Fanez and all Knights!
We have imprisoned great wealth in this castle;
The Moors lie dead; few live ones do I see.
Moorish men and Moorish maids we cannot sell,
Nor by chopping off their heads will we gain anything;
Let us keep them inside, for we have the seigniory;
We shall dwell in their houses, and we shall
Make use of them. (616–22)

Poem of El Cid, 1140

Gypsy Family, 1841, engraving by Raffet. Bibliothèque Nationale de France
Roger-Viollet Archives, Paris, France

While there were many attractions for Gypsies in Granada, especially after their time wandering in central and northern Europe, it was perhaps the physical beauty of the kingdom that most attracted them. Like a fairy tale, with fountains of fresh spring water flowing, large public plazas, gardens, and souks (Arab markets), it was the perfect place to earn a living as people passed through daily. It is impossible to ascertain the exact reasons why certain groups of Gypsies settled in the white-washed pueblos of Andalusia. Americo Castro in *The Structure of Spanish History* offers a tremendous argument for the healthy, vibrant confluence of ideas circulating within the Andalusian Hispano-Arab world. Upon first view, the Gypsies found open *plein-air* plazas where they could ply their trades of fortune-telling, singing, dancing, and petty theft. However, this does not explain why they remained, since in every other country they entered, they eventually chose to or were forced to move on. A brief discussion about medieval Spain follows, offering insight into the Gypsies' choice to settle in Andalusia, in the hills of the Albaicín, where they live to this day. I believe that the rich, multiethnic society into which they moved led eventually to the art form known as flamenco.

The political climate of fifteenth-century Andalusia was contentious. Following upon the medieval Islamic feuds of the Almohads and Almoravids, the Nasrid kingdom, "the perfect jewel upon the hill," by the fifteenth century seemed to be signaling its own demise. In 1466, Sultan Boabdil violated a fragile truce with northern, Christian Spain by failing to pay in gold his annual tribute to the Spanish monarchs. Boabdil's hope was to maintain his autonomous Muslim state entirely free of Christian interference.[80]

From 1466 to 1479, King Ferdinand and Queen Isabella left the Nasrids alone. At war with Portugal and administratively weak, Ferdinand and Isabella averted their gaze from Granada and the last Arab kingdom. Having finally established a truce with Portugal, they petitioned the Pope for crusading privileges that were ultimately approved. Beset by internal factional fighting, Sultan Boabdil must have seen the end, although he heard nothing from the Spaniards until they declared holy war upon his kingdom, signaling the final act of war of the eight-hundred-year Christian Reconquest, the *Reconquista*.

War against the Nasrids turned quickly into a bloody power struggle in which the Christians took fourteen actual cities and ninety-seven fortified palaces and castles, as well as outlying lands. In 1481, they began their war in earnest, an armed response to the Muslim surprise attack against the Christian fortress of Zahara, once an Arab stronghold. Aided by power struggles inside the Nasrid court, *Los Catolicos*, as they were called, slowly advanced on the city of Granada.[81]

By 1491, Christian armies had cut off all routes to the city. Camped at the base of the Alhambra in what today is called Santa Fe, Ferdinand and Isabella's troops surrounded the citadel and besieged the city. Beset by famine, in January 1492 Boabdil, the last ruler of his dynastic line, surrendered the keys to the Islamic kingdom. Gypsies seemed to have made both cannons and swords—and spied for both sides.

While documentation of the Gypsy role in the struggle of the Christians to defeat the Nasrids complicates any serious historical account of the Muslim defeat, Bercovici has argued that the Gypsies served as spies for the Muslims and as metalworkers for the Christians. Borrow reasoned that "the *gitanos*, who cared probably as little for one nation as the other . . . doubtless sided with either as their interests dictated, officiating as spies for both parties and betraying both."[82] The gradual decline of Islamic Spain was accompanied by a philosophical fatalism and nihilism, echoes of which are found in the fifteenth-century poetry and song. After eight hundred years of incessant warfare against the Christians, it is perhaps not surprising that the last Arab kingdom fell so easily to Ferdinand and Isabella in 1492.

While the Battle of Granada was the final, celebrated defeat by the Christian armies of the last ruling Muslim dynasty, it was by no means the last battle that would be fought between Moors and Christians. While many historical events may have come to live in the memory of the *cante*, the notion of struggle, of persecution, of historic identity may indeed have begun in the sixteenth century when the idea of Andalusian national identity — long associated with Arab rule — was co-opted by the Spanish crown and metamorphosed into a Castilian, homogeneous national identity. Even so, Americo Castro has pointed out that the "Morisco form of life had [already] been integrated within the life lived together by Mohammedans and Christians" for eight hundred years.[83] The Moors were fond of burlesques, dances, and songs with "bagpipes, timbrels and tambourines."[84] Tales of woe, love, and daily life were expressed in musical verse and dance. While the Inquisitional office of King Ferdinand and Queen Isabella was dedicated to the erasure of any Moorish dynastic presence or Sephardic social, political, or economic influence, there is no question that Moorish identity continued to affect Andalusian life. Many Moors remained in Spain, fighting the Christian armies well into the eighteenth century. Further, as Americo Castro has argued, "it had proved impossible to assimilate the Moriscos through persuasion or violence. These people felt themselves to be as Spanish as the old Christians and their consciousness of nationality had its roots in a glorious past. Don Fernando de Valor (Aben Humeya) a *Tornadizo* or Moor who converted to Christianity and led the revolt against the Christians in Granada in 1568, was quoted as stating: 'Don't you know we are in Spain and that we have owned this land for nine hundred years!'"[85] Aben Humeya continued such declarations in 1568, stating that "the broad empire of Spain is nothing to me, because, believe me, when states reach the pinnacle of their grandeur, they must decline. We are no band of thieves but a kingdom; nor is Spain less abandoned to vices than was Rome."[86]

The Kingdoms of Aragon and Navarre forced upon Andalusia a northern, Castilian Spanish culture whose *modus operandi* was founded in religious unity "and the indisputable seigniory of royal power" and aristocratic lineage.[87] To the sixteenth-century *Nuevo Castilian* mind, wealth and industriousness, symbolized by Muslim-Sephardic Spain, no longer held currency in the Spanish point of view. While eight centuries of Muslim rule took a long time to erase, Catholic Spain worked diligently to construct a theocratic society in which the community that under Hispano-Arab rule was praised as the moral voice of Andalusia was once and for all wiped out. Perhaps it is impossible to say what Andalusian consciousness might have been toward the end of the sixteenth century. Other historians have argued that the search for a soulful existence was a remnant of Moorish, Jewish, and Christian life: "only a pure heart in service to God."[88] Castro expands on this idea:

In spite of their suspect faith, the Moriscos challenged the severities of the Inquisition for more than a century. They enjoyed strong protection. They seduced more than one old Christian with their enticing sensuality as well as their cleverness in making money; they even insinuated into Spanish Catholicism, along with illuminism, some subtle forms of mysticism and they funneled the themes and styles of the Arabic tradition into literature of the 16th and 17th centuries. A centuries' old tradition protected them because important zones in the Hispanic soul had been conquered by Islam . . . With those nine hundred years unfolded before our eyes, why should we find anything strange in the fact that the language, the customs, the religion, the art, the letters and even the living structure itself of the Spaniard require, for understanding, that we bear in mind this interaction that continued for centuries?[89]

This cycle of the Muslim influence on Spain began with the eighth-century invasion, penetrated the Mozarabic Christian world, and ended with the close of the seventeenth century. Only with a complete understanding of this socio-cultural environment, however complex and subtle, can one begin to study the effect of the past nine centuries on the history of flamenco.

Carmen and the *Siguiríya*

This connection of Moorish fatalism to the Gypsy Carmen is key to understanding Carmen's nihilistic approach to her life and death. Prosper Mérimée's reading of history becomes all the more apparent and thorough in his crafting of such a character, for he had to have read histories of the Moorish court to have sketched a character with such a hold on the meaning of life and the human condition. The flamenco dance he must have seen influenced his appreciation for Gypsy sorrow. In the song and dance of the Gypsy *Siguiríya*, which he may have heard and seen, one can appreciate Carmen's awareness of the intractability of fate.

Africans Residing in Granada in the Sixteenth and Seventeenth Centuries

"Slavery," writes Casares, "was a normal institution in Islamic Spain . . . Most of the slaves were black Africans coming from the trans-Saharan slave trade." During the centuries-long *Reconquista* — the south-moving Christian expansion into Muslim territories — Christians and Muslims, Casares argues, took into their possession

Gypsy Couple Dancing, Sacromonte, Granada, photographer and date unknown.
Roger-Viollet Archives, Paris, France

(buying or stealing) each others' slaves.[90] Most slaves were brought to Spain by Portuguese slave traders, although some arrived in Spanish ships as well. As early as 1444, Portuguese merchants had built settlements in Guinea and began what would become, after 1492, the trans-Atlantic slave trade.

Casares discovered in the archives of the Alhambra that three categories of slaves existed in the fifteenth and sixteenth centuries. The first were the slaves who powered the galleys of Arab pirates and the rulers of North Africa. The second category rowed the galleys of Spain. These ships plundered North Africa in search of lost Muslims. The third category to reenter Spain had worked for white and black Moriscos who had left Spain in search of a better life in Muslim countries away from the Christian *Reconquista*.[91]

Many Africans living in Andalusia were freed. Many of these freed slaves, however, were prevented by Spanish law from working in many trades, and remained, like the Gypsy, impoverished. Confined to the trades in which one also found the Gypsy, black Africans continued to toil in the fields, or as metal casters, smelters, workers, carriers and vendors of water and firewood, bakers, butchers, and public executioners.[92] Castigated by the mark of slavery with which their skin color alone branded them, the freed African was oftentimes too poor to do anything but beg for charity. Like the Gypsy, he would go to the public squares where employers arrived looking for cheap labor.[93]

Most interesting, however, is the possible connection between African freed women and *Gitanas*. Many black women sought work as domestics in homes. Others worked in taverns and inns. Granada, Casares has discovered, had some twenty-four public inns and taverns that housed the litigants who came to the Chancery court, the only one in Andalusia. Women who could not find work in these establishments worked as sorceresses, "making love filters, finding lost objects, curing illnesses with herbal remedies."[94] The same ritual professions were found among Gypsy women.

With the collapse of the Kingdom of Granada, Muslims living in more outlying areas, now Christian lands, continued to reside in Spain.[95] Valencia, Aragon, Extremadura, and Castilla de la Mancha were filled with free Arab Muslims who, by the end of the sixteenth century, had been forced to convert to Christianity. Their influence on the Gypsies who worked for them was extensive. Here we might look at a connection between the rich cultures of Arab-Sephardic Spain and the art form known as flamenco. The problem in tracing possible rhythmic roots from Africa to Gypsy flamenco is that most Spanish historians do not look into the origin of the slaves: Casares, for example, writes, "whatever their origin." Without knowing the exact tribe and/or country, it is difficult to understand which rhythms made their way into flamenco. And even then, even if one did know, one would still have to look at the longevity of these rhythms, that is to say, are they the same rhythms or have they changed over time?

Despite their caveats, the possibility of a cultural fusion between Gypsy and African was substantial. It has been suggested that as much as ten percent of the population of Andalusia were black Africans.[96] Moriscos preferred owning sub-Saharan African slaves to North African Arab slaves[97] but, after the 1560 Morisco uprising against the Spanish crown, slave ownership was forbidden to Spanish Arabs and their slaves were either sold to Christians or set free.[98] Substantial numbers of African former slaves now lived throughout the Iberian Peninsula.

Perhaps the most powerful influence on the Gypsies was the presence of African slaves and freed men who also resided in the city, caves, and hills of Granada at the time. "Most of the liberated black Africans lived in the mountains of the Alpujarra or in the Morisco quarter of Granada. There are still several streets in the Albaicín named after the black Africans, such as the Callejon de los Negros (alley of the black Africans), the Placeta de los Negros (square of the black Africans), and the Barranco de los Negros (ravine of the black Africans)."[99] While many slaves came as children from other Spanish slave colonies, like Cuba, it was the older slaves with connections to Africa, called *bozales*, whose drumming and dance might have had the greatest influence.[100]

Gypsies were not the only foreigners who came to live in Granada toward the end of the Islamic state. Black Africans, too, had come to the city from several regions in Africa. Some were Christian, others Muslim, like those brought to Andalusia to work the fields from the sub-Saharan regions of Guinea, Congo, and Angola. Still others were slaves or freed persons from North Africa who had been working in Andalusia for several generations. These free Africans spoke Arabic and practiced Islam; others came from the Canary Islands and were slaves.[101] The question the dance historian must raise (like the tap historian of seventeenth-century America) is what became the socio-economic and cultural relationship between the black African and the Gypsy? Did they work side-by-side in the fields? Did they sing, dance, and drum together? Which sub-Saharan dancing and drumming rhythms might have been absorbed into what ultimately became the flamenco idiom? And, finally, how might African spiritual and aesthetic traditions have contributed to the birth of flamenco style?

What, then, was the possibility of cultural syncretism between the African and the Gypsy living in Granada?[102] Freed Africans who had been slaves were never able to liberate themselves from the stigma of having been owned and could never climb the socioeconomic ladder. This, alone, may have kept Africans living among the Gypsies, who, themselves, never integrated into Spanish society. Secondly, dark skin was commonly and notoriously associated with slavery. As can be seen in the *Pragmaticas* against the Gypsies, that enslaved the men in galleys, any dark-skinned person in post-Reconquest Spain lived a dangerous existence. "It is evident," argues Casares, "that the association between dark skin and slavery was an integral part of the mentality of the time."[103] Both Gypsies and freed Africans were stigmatized by racism.

The Africanist presence in Spain was complex and its remnants might have affected how Mérimée envisioned Carmen. The inability of nineteenth-century Europeans to grasp degrees of freedom based upon one's internal, psychic awareness of liberty, or ascribe their enlightened dreams of freedom to the Other, demonstrates how quick they were to dichotomize and not search for granularity or distinctions between the freed African, the enslaved African, and the Gypsy. The Gypsies retained in every moment of Spanish history a certain autonomy, a pride, unmappable on the exterior, which they protected by refusing to accommodate the homogenizing forces of local authorities. Their tribal, clan-like culture to this day is profoundly unassimilable. Mérimée possessed an archeologist's sensitivity to these degrees of African-ness, layered traces of race as it moves through history. But he too addressed, at least in his fiction, a European audience hungry for an Orientalist fantasia. He embodied the Africanist presence in Carmen whose corporeality, let us not forget, he ultimately compares to the geography of Andalusia where Caesar, in love with his African Queen, fought Pompey.

CHAPTER FIVE

Gypsies in the Dance Cafés of the Islamic Mediterranean

The nomad signifies the great free space. Liberty.
Nomads are free men, sons of the wind.

Nadjm oud-Dine Bammate, *Cités d'Islam*, 1987

The Bedouin doesn't look for God inside of himself:
he is too sure that he is inside God.

T. E. Lawrence, *The Seven Pillars of Wisdom*, 1973

To be free is to feel the wind of space . . .
Oh Woman! Love only the sultan whose turn is space.

Dassine-oult-Yemma 1954[1]

If, in the context of colonial production, the subaltern has no history
and cannot speak, the subaltern as female is even more deeply in shadow.

Gayatri Chakravorty Spivak, *Can the Subaltern Speak?*, 1988[2]

The shape of Orientalism can be mapped like a dance, its bodies moving to and from center stage, crossing and extending back out into space along multiple choreographic routes. For Edward Saïd, author of the groundbreaking theoretical history *Orientalism* (1978), Napoleonic Egypt represented the supreme Orientalist crossroad, located geographically in the French Orientalist mind between the ancient worlds of the Middle East and the proto-capitalist societies of Western Europe. "Placed between Africa and Asia, and communicating easily with Europe, Egypt occupies the center of the ancient continent . . . it is the homeland of the arts."[3]

Cairo, like other cities along the caravan trade routes, became a significant place for Gypsy café dance. The existence and subsistence of these cafés depended on a complex cultural and commercial infrastructure tied to three migrations: the Romantics' search for the Other in their quest to escape the French capital; Napoleon's invasion and distribution of thousands of personnel who remained behind even after the Emperor departed, abandoning his army in 1799; and the Gypsies' migrations to Egypt from other parts of the Middle East. Based upon these populations' entrances into Egypt, a commercial, public form of café performance spectacle emerged in the nineteenth century, opening and funding a desire for and economy of Middle Eastern dance.[4]

The vast socioeconomic and cultural changes engendered by the French Revolution (1789–1799) transformed the literary field of Orientalism and subsequently Europeans' sensibility of the physical geography of the Orient—from barbaric and wild to sensuous, poetic, and mysterious—an urban coast bordered by vast desert topography housing the ancient ruins of the Pharonic dynasties.[5] The link between these disparate landscapes is the Gypsy who crosses empires and geographic expanses from India on her way to Spain. Egypt, in the Gypsy mind, is a stop along the road extending in front of and behind her as she moves through time and space. No point along this endless journey is more significant than any other as, for the Gypsy, migration—dancing—carries the greatest freedom.

The Gypsy forms an essential part of this mutation of literary perspective and Orientalist physiognomy; she emerges out of the desert, walking barefoot into the city to dance for the European, whether stranded soldier or literary tourist. The Ghawazi—Carmen's soul-sisters—are dark, savage, luscious beauties, considered just a step above the African slave.[6] Inside the darkened, male-populated cafés, they danced in a staged fulfillment of their viewers' expectations of being pleasured sexually, if only visually.

Let us explore this phantasm in more detail: women with half-nude torsos covered in ringing bells, beads, and necklaces, undulating their pelvises, executing rapid footwork sequences, multiple revolutions and polyrhythms of the torso, head, wrists, and arms, to the point of frenzied abandon—a release that the male spectator, perhaps a British or French officer or an Arab merchant, expects when he enters the darkened, cave-like room of low tables, dimly lit corners, and dense air. As the dances extend over many minutes, the Ghawazi enters a kind of trance, a threshold space, the infinite, quiet expanse of the desert transported into the confines of the crowded, smoky café. Beads of intimate sweat drip down her face, neck, and torso and onto the floor. The nomadic Gypsy, whose family caravan remains far away from the site of this performative discourse, transforms

Algerian Woman Posing for the Camera, photographer and date unknown.
Roger-Viollet Archives, Paris, France

herself momentarily into an urban site for ethnographic discourse, tourism, and history.

Urban spectacle intersects the geography, cartography, and ancient culture from which the Gypsy emerges onto the café stage. A spectatorship conceived by Orientalists in Paris, London, New York, or Berlin, the Ghawazi became complicit in newly emerging ideas about women, the Middle East, and dance as the mechanism by which both the Gypsy pilgrimage and history are declassed, overwritten like a palimpsest by projected desire.[7]

While her "journey of silence" continues by virtue of their gaze, the Ghawazi still holds power: she generates, controls, and manipulates the very text they read. Her dancing body becomes the new topographical road map "read" by Orientalists upon entry into the city. A popular spot for Orientalist tourism, the café marks the point of intersection between two migrations: that of the Gypsies out of the desert and the Europeans into the phantasmagoric location of desire, escape, and difference. The nomadic desert designates a space of traversal, the passage to an oasis. At the site of the dance café, a provisional settlement for the Gypsy dancer, wandering has ended for the time being. For the European spectator, it is a destination of a very different mode of travel — that of tourism — with its safety net of the return trip home. For the Gypsy, there is no home — no place to which return is possible.

In this nexus, the European too performs, acting out the rites of travel, expectation, and the tourism of desire. Travel of the European Romantic tourist carries the phantasm to the destination, while that of the Bedouin, Berber, and Gypsy nomad carries ancient culture *à l'intérieur*, within the animist space of the desert. The European transports the lustful, escapist sentimentality with him to these places of entertainment. In the meeting place of the dance café, we might speak of an oasis serving two very different deserts. Migration of the imagination on the part of the European, within an unexamined ideology, signaled in effect a libidinous travel of a kind of literary, fictional gratification. This is the migration of the *aller-retour*: for the Gypsy, geography will not be so linear.

Carmen, the literary and musical invention of Prosper Mérimée and Georges Bizet, was born in the port cities along the Islamic Mediterranean coast. Her image owes its historiography to the birth of French ethnography, a field that

Tuareg Dancers and Singers of Guedra, Southern Morocco, photographer and
date unknown. The nomadic Tuareg also are known as the Blue People.
Roger-Viollet Archives, Paris, France

emerged out of the Romantic travelogue diaries from the eighteenth and nineteenth centuries.[8] Perhaps one of the most important ideas informing the *fantasia*
surrounding the myth and semiology of Carmen is the corporeality of her image:
an eastern — Indian — woman who came, at one time, from a faraway place, well
beyond "civilized" European land. This chapter studies the shaping of European
consciousness and mythology about the Gypsy dancer through the spectatorship
of French Romantic writers who frequented the dance cafés.[9]

A French invention, the myth of Carmen belongs to nineteenth-century history,
to Spanish history, and to French Romantic spectacle.[10] But it also belongs to
Carmen, whether she existed or not. She symbolizes Gypsy women — a mysterious
part of the projection of the other within white, Christian Europe. Her character
also illuminates our understanding of poor women, a second level of abjection

or what Gayatry Spivak calls the "subaltern," abused, silenced, in this case, by the Spanish system she mocks with dangerous abandon.

To decipher this Romantic myth-making and to understand Carmen's enduring presence in contemporary culture and in the countries that colonized the Middle East, we must travel back in time. Let us not forget the extent of Orientalism and its expression in music, painting, poetry, and literature. Edward Saïd demonstrates Orientalism to be "a cultural and a political fact" based upon the western notion of the Orient that he painstakingly reconstructs. The Orient, Saïd tells us, is "an idea that has a history and a tradition of thought, imagery, vocabulary that have given it reality and presence in and for the West. The two geographical entities thus support and to an extent reflect each other."[11]

Orientalism, Saïd continues, can only exist if the Orient exists in peoples' minds. The Occident — the West — in the nineteenth-century European mind was considered clean, virtuous, and safe. Conversely, the Orient was characterized by western writers as strange, sensual, feminine, archaic, Muslim, foreign, unsafe, and unknown. Orientalism was an eighteenth- and nineteenth-century colonial European intellectual movement that "bound together" an archive of Orientalist/racist information that colonial powers used to support colonial, economic, political, social, and cultural activity. Orientalism endowed Orientals — peoples from the Near and Middle East of Islamic faith, from Southeast Asia of Hindu tradition and the Far East of Buddhist tradition — with a "mentality, a genealogy, an atmosphere; most important [Orientalism] allowed Europeans to deal with and even to see Orientals as a phenomenon possessing regular characteristics." Europeans, Saïd argues, split the world into a simplistic binary. There was the familiar West = "us" and the strange East = "them."[12] With this "knowledge," or point of view, European colonials entered foreign lands, treating "Orientals" inhumanly having reduced them within an intellectual matrix to a morally, racially, and religiously weaker group of sub-humans.

With Saïd's scholarship in mind, let us explore with some granularity the notion of the liminal city of spectatorship where the Orientalist traveler roamed.

Why is Carmen located, at a crucial juncture in her development, in the port city of Seville? Historically, Gypsies traveled into cities for short periods of time to earn money in public spaces where larger populations of city-dwellers might pass to see a Gypsy dance or have their fortune told. In the Spanish *café cantante*, both the Spanish bourgeoisie and the Napoleonic army went in expectation of having a Gypsy female dancer entertain them. Imagine the café where flamenco evolved as the center of a series of concentric circles of Gypsy geography.[13] At the micro level, we have the *café cantante* of Lillas Pastia as Carmen's geography. Surrounding the café we have the larger shape of the port city, a place of trade, exchange of goods, ideas, and sensations—a liminal, border space where cultures collide and interact. The city, in Carmen's hands, becomes a place of illegal smuggling, prostitution, and spectatorship.

A city has been a clearly circumscribed notion since antiquity. Egyptians had a hieroglyph for *city* that consisted of a cross enclosed in a circle.[14] It signified a crossroad within walls. The city was the locus of commerce, of the exchange of goods as well as of information and security. Until the nineteenth century, the city had walls, or at least a vestigial wall, separating it from the "outside," which was either wilderness (forest, plains) or farmland. In an emergency such as war, peasants and nomads rushed to the city. In the Middle Ages, a drawbridge was raised and the city gate closed to transform the city into a sanctuary.

The Greek word for *city* was *polis*, referring to an administrative body rather than a physical place, hence our word *political*. The Latin synonym was *civis*, from which the words *civic* and *civilization* come. Romans had another word, *urbs*. *Civis* gave rise to *ciudad*, *cité*, and *city*. All of these words then evolved into words expressing the same idea: *polite*, *civil*, and *urbane*. The city was where civilization—culture—was located. *Urban* was opposed to *wild*, *sauvage*, or *rural* and *rustic*; *urbane* became the antithesis of *uncouth*.

During the French Revolution, there arose a need to distinguish urban centers from rural spaces when the rural became worthy of recognition. Urban culture became a tautology. When the word *culture* came to be anthropologically expanded into a value-free term, notions of primitive culture and rural culture emerged. The binary oppositions *urban-rural* and *urban-rustic*, *urban-provincial*, *urban-primitive* continue to exist in modern discourse. But in terms of culture and of dance, *urban* suggests polite society versus folk society. Folk dance is not urban, but it can be made urban through domestication, gentrification, purification, and philosophical discourse. This leads me to my neither rural nor fully urban topic—a mélange of Gypsy dancers on the North African and Western European stage.

Gypsy dance and song, whose modern shape is known to the world as flamenco, has come to represent an infinite bohemia: the touching, emotional deep song and dance cycles of the persecuted, the homeless, and the undocumented.[15] Gypsies, Jean-Paul Clébert explains, were manual laborers, related to the Hindu caste of *Dom* people. They worked as street entertainers, fire-eaters, snake charmers, jugglers, acrobats, and animal trainers. Gypsy women are described as having clairvoyant powers. They are also described as an illiterate, non-Sanskrit-reading clan that married only Gypsies and whose identity was preserved and handed down through song, dance, and storytelling. Gypsies were and are considered one step beneath the caste of Untouchables, who too often live in great poverty on India's crowded streets.[16] With the ninth-century invasion of northwest India—Rajasthan—by Muslim horsemen, many Gypsy clans fled.[17] Only 15,000 Gypsies remain in Rajasthan today. "Between Basra and Baghdad there was a zone of lagoons inhabited by a small tribe of Gypsy people. In July 834 the Caliph Mottassim, by a stroke of genius, sent against them rebles [*sic*] from the Nile delta."[18]

By foot, on the back of a donkey, or, if lucky, inside the protected, cooling shelter of a caravan, Gypsies wandered through Afghanistan, Persia, Turkey, Greece, Europe, and North Africa. (The pilgrimage of St. Jean de Mars, a yearly, month-long Gypsy celebration honoring the Madonna and Christ that extends from Santiago de Campostelo to Bordeaux, is reenacted from South America to the western coast of France.) Some Gypsies hid among desert peoples—Bedouins and Berbers in the Saharan desert lands—as they felt safer when removed from cities.[19] Others, Borrow writes, traveled as far north as England and as far West as America; there are records of Gypsies living in Philadelphia in the early eighteenth century.[20]

The Gypsy presence, as recorded by monarchs, ministers, writers, and local administrators, seems always to have caused anger and, oftentimes, violence against its people. Wherever Gypsies roamed, although they tended, for the most part, to adapt and assimilate to language and custom, they remained nation-less, mysterious outsiders whose permanently nomadic existence upset the balance of local civic life. Gypsies were wild, savage, not from the city. They came from the outside; some Europeans, as early as the fourteenth century, perceived that they came from the desert sands, from Egypt, from the East. They were seen as not sharing the Christian God. They were faithless and thus beneath contempt.

Along their route, Persian and Turkish sultans, eastern and western European monarchs, and even local village sheikhs made proclamations against the Gypsies for their tirelessly dangerous and unruly behavior. Though the majority of Gypsies continued to roam, picking up odd jobs in towns along the way, most never settled. In 1478 Ferdinand and Isabella of Spain wrote a series of decrees forcing Gypsies, known as *fellah mengus*, or foreigners, into ghettos called *gitanerias*. The Spanish under Carlos III wrote a law against all Gypsies, forcing them to "leave their vagrant life or face exile or death."[21] In the late seventeenth century, Louis XIV (1648–1715), King of France, wrote a series of decrees forcing Gypsies to "give up foreign habits and dress" like everyone else; in other words, to give up their Eastern culture. By the mid-eighteenth century, Carlos III, King of Spain, who, like King Louis, reigned with enlightened absolutism, enacted a series of harsh anti-Gypsy laws in an attempt to solidify his reign by distinguishing the outsider—the Gypsy—from the insider—the Spanish citizen.

The most active period of migration, though, extended from the later Middle Ages—the ninth and tenth centuries—until the late Renaissance, the fifteenth century, when many *Rom*, whether called Bohemians, Egyptians, or Tziganes, seem to have confined their movements to a single region such as Andalusia, or to Hungary and Romania in Eastern Europe. Their common language—Caló—and their music and dance and fortune-telling linked all Gypsies.[22] Their foreign-ness—their dress of cascading skirts, beaded necklaces, and headscarves, and their violins, tambourines, ankle bells, and long, sparkly earrings—shocked most of the populations with whom they came into contact, as few Europeans at that time ventured more than fifteen kilometers away from the place in which they were born and died. Only the traveler and the wealthy, with tales of the Crusades, the Holy Land, and the Black Moor, could have recognized in the Gypsy something familiar, and that something was usually feared if not despised.[23]

Out of what Jean-Paul Clébert considers to be six million nomadic Gypsies, it is estimated that in Europe alone several million settled over centuries on the outskirts of villages, where the men found manual labor and the women either begged, told fortunes, or danced on the street or in the homes of the wealthy. Once "settled," Gypsies began to absorb local customs—*la couleur locale*—and the religions (Catholic or Muslim) of their host countries, assimilating and adapting somewhat to local tradition whenever possible. Most eyewitness accounts place Gypsy caravans in Europe and North Africa, in semi-hidden spaces: in forests, near riverbanks, on the outskirts of town.

Although there is much to be said about the early evolution of Gypsy dance from the sixteenth to the eighteenth century in Spain, this chapter will focus on the birth and evolution of urban Gypsy performance—but not primarily in the West—for these cafés originated in Muslim countries: Syria, Egypt, Algeria and, finally, in Spain, once a Muslim and now a Catholic country. Gypsy dance and song in cafés was an eighteenth- and nineteenth-century phenomenon. Performing for tourists and indigenous male spectators, the dancers were all female,[24] and the nineteenth-century café represented one of the first public performance spaces for young Gypsy girls.

One French author, Charles Didier, visiting Cairo in the 1870s after governor 'Ali's ban on dance was lifted, wrote of his passion for the Ghawazi dancers: "I was consumed with a desire to see them. God knows how much I had searched, how many inquiries I had made into the matter. I had asked the help of others, some of them very important powerful people."[25]

Apart from the cafés of Spain, it is almost impossible to trace an aesthetic or technical evolution of female Gypsy performance throughout the Middle East. Those who left behind literary accounts of these performances were almost always looking from the outside in. Most were travelers although there are some local accounts of Gypsy dance. To study these performance moments, one must begin to excavate the romantic, tourist language that describes the Eastern dancer as foreigner, the Gypsy café dancer in Egypt being twice foreign. She represents a sensuous, earthly delight, the physical embodiment of a non-Christian, uncivilized, un-European exhibitionist. Gustave Flaubert (1821–1880), for example, finds her sexual, public display of femininity indecent; no European woman was allowed to reveal raised skirts and bare feet in public. [26]

One might argue that the birth of cross-cultural, Middle Eastern Gypsy dance in Arab street cafés is most likely the result of travelers willing to pay to see women — not local women — dance as only Gypsies could do. Without spectators, the dancers may never have found a way to make their living. By 1834, most were banished to Upper Egypt by the governor/viceroy Mohammad 'Ali Pasha who, in an attempt to Europeanize his cities, determined the Ghawazi to be lascivious.[27] Most, however, hid away and could only be found if you knew where to look.

Gypsies were already viewed as having foreign habits — the idea of a Muslim man allowing his daughter or wives to display themselves publicly would have been unacceptable. Gypsies, by contrast, had liminal status, marginalized as "belonging" neither to the East nor to the West. At first, nineteenth-century European travelers who paid to see them found them indistinguishable from imagined harem dancers, girls they had seen in the paintings of Jérome and Délacroix. From Istanbul to Damascus, Cairo, Algiers, and Seville, Gypsy "girls" were recorded by foreigners and locals alike as dancing in crowded streets and then disappearing at night, back to their families. Not to be confused with prostitutes, the Ghawazi appear to have only danced for money. There were at least three styles of Gypsy performance: the Ghawazi Gypsy dancing girls who performed *danse du ventre*, or belly dance, along Cairo's infamous 'al-Hoshe Derbek (Street of the Open Hall);[28] the Tuareg dance of the blue veils, an improvisational dance of one or more women on a Berber theme performed solely for men at the Café d'Algiers, already a tourist destination; and the Sevillian café performance of the Gypsy style developed for public (mostly male) consumption.[29] This dance fed the Romantic inclination of nineteenth-century Europeans to search for—create the pre-history for—an opera like *Carmen*.

As German Romanticist Frederich Schlegel writes, "we must see the supreme Romanticism in the Orient."[30] It is impossible to discuss the foreign observation and notation of Gypsy dance without considering Napoleon Bonaparte's Cairo-based Oriental Institute's twenty-three-volume publication, *Déscription de l'Égypte*, whose writing commenced in 1809 and ended in 1828.[31] This work, in some sense, prepared observers for an occidental view of the Arab-Orient, the Gypsy of course remaining at the forefront of this growing palaver about the feminine exotic: the dancer as one symbol of the sensuous East.[32] *Déscription de l'Égypte* sketches for the French reader a complex Orientalist geography of entrance into and conquest of the Arab Middle East in the form of a map. Its textural and spatial descriptions profess a desire to conquer, to be inside the lands of the East, to have absorbed and consumed its spatial, temporal, and exotic design and flavor and discursively mapped its constituent spaces and temporalities.

"A veritable pilgrimage of Europeans to the Orient began during the first half of the nineteenth century," following General Bonaparte's Egyptian campaign.[33] Alexandre Dumas (1802–1870), "wanting to show the limitless capacities of human nature . . . preferred to place heroes" in his more than three hundred books, "in unusual conditions," the Orient—Egypt—being but one.[34] In his quest to imagine for his French readers an exotic, Oriental space, Dumas drew—spatialized—a map of the Romantic Orient, pulling readers into an invented universe of Romantic Orientalism laced with ancient Eastern wisdom and violence.

The second major influence on the European traveler before he set foot in the Middle East was the popular European press, with its infinite musings about faraway, exotic lands. The third great influence was Prosper Mérimée, whose 1846 novella, *Carmen*, limned an archetypal figure who was all things rolled into one: foreigner, Gypsy-Jewess-Moorish other, la Carmen. Her sensuality posed a threat to the Romantic ballerina. She was the anti-sylph. She took on colossal and mythic form in the European collective consciousness, such that all Gypsy dancers become known in the French daily press as "Andalusian dancers" or "Spanish dancers *au style Andalou*." The emerging literature describing café performances was written almost solely by men, sometimes from the countryside and mostly from abroad, men who could not distinguish the foreigner from the local on the stage.

Nor can these touristic review accounts, being "snapshots," track an evolution or assessment of the form. "[It] becomes thus extremely difficult to distinguish what is most likely still a demi-Bedouin-Gypsy performance in an urban North African café, the Syrian Café du Fleuve."[35]

One English painter, James Augustus St. John, observed the Ghawazi dancers in a small coffee house located near Cairo. In 1845 in Cairo, he witnessed another performance of "girls" between sixteen and thirty to whom he referred as "tall and admirably proportioned." His description exudes astonishment and makes the connection between dance, thought, self-control, and mastery:

> Their eyes shot fire; their bosoms heaved and panted and their bodies assumed the most varied attitudes and inflexions. They twined round each other snake-like, with a suppleness and grace such as I had never seen before. Now, they let their arms drop, and their whole frames seemed to collapse in utter exhaustion; then might you see how a new thought arose within them, and strove to express itself in impassioned gestures. All this while the music continued to play, and in its very simplicity was like a pale background to the picture, from which the glowing figures of the girls stood out in so much stronger relief.
>
> After a pause, the second dance began. One of the *ghawazee* took a little glass, filled it with rose water between her teeth and held it so without spilling a drop, whilst she executed the most rapid and difficult movements. She repeated nearly the whole of the preceding dance, and it was certainly no trifling effort of skill to go through it without emptying the glass. At last, she stepped up to one of the male spectators, and clasping him round the middle with both arms, she bent backwards and continued her gesticulations without ceasing; at last she leaned forward and slowly poured the rose water over his clothes, let the glass drop, kissed his lips, and bounded back into the middle of the room.[36]

The solo female Gypsy performer in North Africa and southern Spain fulfilled the French and British intellectuals' quest for the inner Orient, the spiritual Orient, an archetypal female presence that allows foreigners the mytho-poetic right of return to self via the Holy Land, as if they, like Gypsies, once belonged. "Preoccupied by what was forbidden in their own country," comments Middle Eastern dance scholar Wendy Buonaventura, "many observers saw in Arabic dance only its thrilling eroticism."[37] These dancers might be the Ghawazi of Egypt, the café dancers of Syria and Yemen, the Berber-Bedouin-Gypsy Ouled Nail dancer seen in Algerian and Moroccan café-clubs or, of course, the Spanish Gypsy who, toward the mid- to late nineteenth century, emerges as the ultimate symbol.[38]

Most travel writers never distinguish between the Gypsy and the Arab dancer, and perhaps it is an unconscious passport they give the Gypsy dancer, unbeknownst to her. As Anouar Louca wrote of Victor Hugo, "the Orient no longer resided outside but, rather, inside the geographical experience such that interiorization of Orientalism springs forth a psychological space of liberty and imagination."[39] A recognizable and recognized confluence of non-western cultures was most easily seen in the dancing combination of the Indic Gypsy and the Arabian Alméh. Buonaventura argues that the Ghawazi/Almeh (Almée) performed a dance throughout the 1860s and 1870s known as the *baladi*. The *baladi* was a women's solo dance of acrobatic skill and isolation and control of different body parts.[40]

The image of these dances belongs to what art historian Linda Nochlin terms the "Imaginary Orient," a mental map so deeply felt that it can be communicated, subtly, through the body: the extended arms, the coquetry of the veil, the gentle and then frenetic movements of the waist and the swaying of the hips as dancers moved past café tables. "The most recurring features," writes Christian Poche, "of an Ouled Nail performance at the Café d'Algiers was the gliding alternation of arms away from hips and feet in ecstatic moments of rhythmic assault, culminating in subtle courtship with an absent partner."[41] Like the Guedra dancers of Morocco, the Tuareg or blue people of Morocco and Algeria—"les anges blues—who, at times, lived side-by-side Gypsies," would come into the cities to earn money, carrying with them Berber, Gypsy, Arab, and Turkish dance traditions.[42]

According to one British traveler's account of 1842 in a Marrakech café:

The young girl, long black hair, and delicate, bronzed skin, and almost daintily thin fingers, four of which had attached little cymbals which she played to sonorous effect, wore a blue veil whose edges were adorned by rounded pieces of tin or metal that resounded together as she moved like an accompaniment to her sensuous swaying of hips and her stamping of feet which she achieved, alternating hips, and then shaking (shimmying) her entire pelvic region to my near astonishment. Later she asked me if I wanted anything else. There were many people in the café that day.

They say that she had traveled in to town.

It seems that the castellation of arms lifted away from the body in preparation to play wooden (Indian) or metal (Arabian) castanets or finger cymbals (Greek/Turkish) remained a permanent, rhythm-making feature of belly dancers.[43] Although the castanet playing of the *Gaditanes* Gypsy girls remains a common part of café performance to this day, emphasis in the Spanish café dance fell to the leg and, in particular, the power of the foot to sound rhythm. In regions where Gypsy women's primary work was to be found outside the harem, Ghawazi and other café dancers oftentimes were invited to dance inside the harem for sultans and for women of the harem. Dance, in this locale, like the geography of the Middle East, remained highly sexual, with emphasis placed in the pelvic region, neck, and shoulders. Among the Ghedra of Agadir, as in Indian Kathak and Spanish flamenco, the hands and feet remained mainstay performance features when Bedouin and Gypsy dancers performed in urban areas. Whereas most Egyptian dancers were accompanied by a team of male musicians or could even sing for themselves, as did the Alméh, the Spanish Gypsy might have a guitarist with her or she might create her own rhythm through clapping, chant, and foot percussion.

In 1924 an excellent work of dance ethnology was written by W. L. Westerman entitled "The Castanet Dancers of Arsinoe." Published in the *Journal of Egyptian Archaeology*, it describes the westward migration of Gypsies to Egypt and claims that they settled along the Nile. It was the "perfect place for westerners to see the *zambra mora*," an all-woman's dance that Gypsies performed in a circle, alongside other Egyptian dancers.[44] The women stretched out their arms, tiny castanets attached to their fingertips, their hair falling down their back, dressed in pants and skirts, as they moved to the sound of percussion and flute of male musicians. "Swaying from side to side, sometimes, holding hands," wrote one Nile traveler, "the dancer lifts her arms outward in a serpentine motion and dances a lascivious dance, swaying her hips and singing to herself."[45]

Spanish dance historian Marina Grut has argued that the Hispano-Arab word *zambra* can mean three things: "an entertainment, a dance and the group of musicians who play together."[46] It originated, Grut argues, in Caliphal Cordoba in the eleventh century, shortly before Seville became the center of power in Muslim Spain. Grut asserts that slaves from North and Eastern Africa, Bedouin, and Gypsies were thought to have danced together in public spaces to the music of the Moorish lute. The dance included a "sensuous swaying of the hips," later found in the Spanish *Sarabande* of the early Renaissance.[47]

According to Poche in *La Danse Arabe*, the Egyptian *raqs sharqi*, or "dance of the almehs," performed by poor Egyptian dancing girls/prostitutes and by Gypsies, was recorded by the French traveler Savary as early as 1785. Savary describes café dance as voluptuous, lascivious, and filled with erotic attitudes and postures, meaning body stances. The *raqs sharqi* was a dance form that terminated in a supreme exaltation with faster body and foot movements throughout. In the end, "la danse Arabe" culminates in a succession of tableaux, sensuous poses that increasingly become a type of rhythmic song—a physical *mawwal*.[48] It is important to note that these dance motions were "read" by the travel writers as generated for the purposes of their seduction. To their minds, they conquered the female, absorbing her undulations into their desirous imaginations in psychic parallel with Napoleon's conquest of Egypt.

"As we peered through the courtyards," wrote Richard Ford of a Tangier café in 1830, "several women sat on the floor in two rooms. They either covered or turned away their faces as we passed from room to room. As a tambourine sounded, two young girls, coyly veiled, uncovered their faces . . . Their eyes were glorious and one could see at a glance where the women of Spain got their wonderful eyes. There was a roguish expression on their Moorish faces and a fascinating smile as they danced—not the forced sickly smile of European ballet girls, but the natural, sweet smile of girls belonging to a race among which women depend for their happiness in life on their power to please men."[49] Is this to say that the urban city café connotes the unveiling of the Moorish-Gypsy dancer? The wealthy European often paid money for the dancer to reveal herself on the café stage.

One might comment, as did Maxime du Camp of Egyptian dancers in his "Travel Notes," that in the Alexandrian dance, the "cabalistic lore of the dancer [becomes] so thoroughly interwoven with a religious ceremony that the inner Orient is illuminated by the undressing of the female performer. This interweaving acts specifically as a conflation of *la danse d'almeh* and *la danse sacré*. Sacred earth collides in the textual travel log with the body of the dancer."[50]

If art, as Victor Hugo and Gustav Flaubert believed, has the power to change life, then those who were mystically, spiritually, or sexually touched and, at times, confused by this physical apparition of "the other," in this case the oriental dancer, could truly feel the spiritual essence of occidentalist aesthetic philosophy reaching out and touching, through observation and heightened desire. "Anywhere! Anywhere!" pronounced Baudelaire, "Anywhere out of this world!"[51] How much further could one travel than a Syrian café, located in the center of Damascus? As Flaubert would describe it: "Oh! To feel you bending, swaying on a camel's back. I want to see the frenzied native dancers in the dances that end in death," surely a nomadic desire to touch Carmen.[52] Perhaps it is as Savary wrote in 1785, the male public, discovering "la danse arabe . . . in front of the public expression and conceptions of the feminine dancer."[53] But can we distinguish between the Arab dance and the Gypsy dance? Do they become one? Is the whirling an Indic quality, the swaying of the hips a Ghawazi quality?

In the mid-nineteenth century, the Damascan Rives du Barada, like similar sites in Cairo and Alexandria, was literally lined with cafés where one could see any number of dancers from any number of countries. Lamartine (*Voyage en Orient* published 1835) compared the "outdoor cafes" with girls dancing to the civility of Paris. The most frequented, the Café du Fleuve, the Café des Roses, and the Café de la Porte-du-Salut (1833–35), wrote Lamartine, offered a "delicious array of people and events." Alexander Dumas on his visit to the Middle East between 1849 and 1850 called the cafés "elegant." Some of them could, as early as 1745, hold as many as 500 people. Almost all cafés, particularly the Bab Gayrun, were associated with heavy tobacco usage. In 1854, Laorty-Hadji wrote of the music and dance at the Bab Gayrun, describing dancers in Arab silhouettes who charmed in animated dance scenes, alongside beautiful Almehs who sang for their sisters. "From time to time, a visitor would distinguish a Bedouin dancer from an Arab dancer. Usually the description distinguishes the nomadic dancer's heavier use of castanets and footwork from the pelvic movements of the *danseuse du ventre*."

This departure from an undulating pelvis and toward an increased attention to feet and hands follows the development of flamenco in Spain in the *cafés cantantes* of Seville and Madrid. All movement was centered not in the hips but in the upper torso, the head, the neck, the eyes, hands with castanets, and the feet. Flamencologist Gerhard Steingrass has done important work in this area, beginning with the Sevillian *Café sin nombre*, attempting to track through travelers' iconography and written accounts the actual technical style of flamenco. Steingrass argues, and I concur, that the heavy emphasis on the feet does not appear in Andalusian Gypsy performance until the late nineteenth century. This he finds a northern Spanish and French phenomenon. The more delicate swaying of hips and arms, a style closer to African *danse du ventre*, was most likely influenced by the Andalusian folk dance known in the mid-nineteenth century as the *Seguidilla Boleras,* today the *Sevillanas*. There were also academic forms of dancing popular at the Teatro Real de Madrid: the *Bolero*, the *Jota*, the *Valenciana*, and the *Majo Fandango*. The *Cachucha* became an important trans-continental European dance, taught by the Spanish *prima bailarina* Dolores Serral of the Teatro Real de Madrid to Paris Opéra prima ballerinas Fanny Elssler and Elis Noblet. In an attempt to shield Madrid's Royal Ballet stars from the civil strife of the 1830 revolution, Dr. Veron, director of the Paris Opéra, invited Serral and her compatriots to dance in Paris. One can see in the deep side bends of Petra Camara, described by Dumas and Gautier and Gypsies like Antonio el de Triana, that Gypsies and opera dancers had seen and imitated each other's dance styles.

Last, with regard to footwork, the style of the high shoe we know today — the flamenco dancer's *zapata* — seems to have been first built by French shoemakers in the mid-nineteenth century, and only toward the end of the nineteenth century by the Madrilian shoemakers the Ramirez.[54]

For other travelers, the Orient was to be found, excavated, and evaluated. This was not necessarily a spiritual quest but rather a thing to be located, like an Oriental *tel*. Dumas described the Orient as filled with "young subalterns." In Spain, making no distinction between the Spanish Orient and the Syrian Orient, Dumas wrote, "dancing is a joy to the dancer herself," an illuminating comment that seems to move from the usual Orientalist perspective toward a more empathic descriptive modality.[55] "She delights in every toss of her head, every flicker of her hands. Her feet spurn the ground, she whinnies with excitement and the magnetic current of her passion streams out to galvanize every man who watches her . . . the Gypsy Orient is produced for him . . . the delirious joy of fifty or sixty Spaniards applauding a dancer in the upper room of a café in Seville!"[56] He ends these passages by stating that a six-month veteran of the bolero-café-theatre named Carmen asks in a whisper whether or not he can find her work in a French theatre.[57]

By the 1820s and 1830s, French press receptivity to foreign influence in art was as strong as any interest in indigenous French tradition. Tobacco — *Gitanes Cigarettes* — became synonymous with exotic pleasure and Oriental tastes. (Where does Carmen work? In a cigar factory.) The alien Gypsy element eventually became the French love of the exotic. Perhaps, in France, the Gypsy dance, termed "Andalusian" or "Egyptian," and sometimes confused with "Arab-Bedouin," began to be tolerated by the people, its mysterious flair absorbed into mainstream French culture. In Gautier's reviews and many others in *La Presse* of the "Spanish dancer," the distinction between Andalusian Gypsy and Castilian *bolero* is not made, except in the case of a few dancers such as Mariano Cambrubi, Dolores Serral, and Petra Camara. But no distinct category is made for the Gypsy dancer. (Could performers have transformed the *Jaleo de Jerez* into a more airborne, ethereal form of bolero and jota?) The earthy, sensuous Gypsy dance, either of the hips or of the shoulders, back and hand gestures, now resides à l'Orient, cleaned up for the French *café chanson* and Parisian variety theater with a kind of peculiar reprise at the Folies-Bergères by the early part of the twentieth century.

However, this is an analysis of a foreign art that came to Paris. Most interesting, I feel, is the ability of the Gypsy dancer, whether Egyptian or African, to inspire. The French conquest of Algeria, which began in 1830 and officially ended in 1962, permanently transformed French receptivity to the East and, of course,

Arab-Gypsy dance. Owing to the nineteenth-century war on Algeria and the strong defense waged against the French, the East had yet another incarnation. East became synonymous with violence, danger, and lack of control. In dance, the café girl is no longer only from the streets of Cairo, but also the product of Abd el-Kader, who fought back with one hundred thousand men only to be defeated and captured in 1842.

Yet the Romantic call of the Orient continued into the twentieth century, as Antoine de Saint-Éxupéry wrote: "The desert. It is that which was born in us, that which we understand on our own."[58]

The desert in the modern European imagination, however, remains the purest, most exotic, and impenetrable space, the most foreign experience. "In the desert," says Jean-Marie LeClézio, "we discover our ancient past: the echo of the urban, of the civilized, the sacred."[59]

By the late nineteenth century, Orientalist descriptions of dance, like those of pyramids, became somewhat more detailed and even offered the idea that the dance was becoming commercial, an urban form of performance whose patrons were only male. French historian Édouard Driault, in his 1898 *La Question d'Orient*, declares the necessity of changing Muslim habits, such as dancing girls and harems, in order to become a secular, modern state—a civilization that had been renewed in the eyes of the West.

There is no question that the few descriptions we have of dancing girls in Egypt, Syria, Algeria, and Spain, as observed by foreigners, continue the mystification of the Orient as female, sexual, absent of law and order and, thus, tempting. It is what Linda Nochlin termed "an iconic distillation of oriental colonial ideology."[60] Even Félicien David's 1844 ode-symphonie *Le Désert*, a pre-symbolist attempt to bring the sensuous escapism of Bedouins and *Egipcianos* to the French lyric opera stage, reveals an exotic approach to the spiritualism of the desert and its wandering peoples. Inspired by his 1833 to 1835 trip to the Near East and Egypt, *Le Désert* was admired by Romantic Parisian critic Théophile Gautier for the eastern charm of its *Danse d'Almées*.[61]

The narrative relationship between Orientalism and Occidentalism can be obliquely captured through the prism of Spanish Gypsy culture and the emergence of public, commercial dances in the cafés of the Middle East. Europeans' descriptions of exotic bodies, clothing, and movement and "local" reaction to European tourism in the coastal cities of the Middle East, speak to an emerging discourse centered on western views of the Near East and North African views of western visitation, all inscribed on the female body. Dumas wrote: "L'Afrique

Spaniard Drinking, painting by Paul Ortiou, Salon of 1912.
Neurdein / Roger-Viollet Archives, Paris, France

commence aux Pyrénées" (Africa begins at the Pyrenees). If the Gypsy is already performing within the West, when the West loses the ancient Eastern villages to war and industrialization, the Gypsy remains a constant reminder of our ultimate universality as human beings and of the relativity of cultural perceptions of interior and exterior.

This western surveying of the solo female dance practitioner "invading" from the wild, uncivilized eastern forest, entering town not through a gate or a doorway — a proper entrance — but, rather, on foot, will never depart the European stage. For modern Africans, the reception in Dakkar of *Karmen Gei*, a bisexual Carmen who runs barefoot along the sea away from an island prison and the female warder for whom she has performed to gain her freedom, was so hostile that Senegalese theatres showing the film had to be closed. *Karmen Gei* is the most current version of La Esmeralda, Victor Hugo's dark Gypsy dancer from the *Hunchback de Notre-Dame*, and a challenge to the observer. The reaction of Gringoire (a young poet who marries the Gypsy Esmeralda) to the foreign Esmeralda is one of complete surprise, as if "this young female was not a human being." It is only through her dancing — "She picked up from the ground two swords which she balanced on their points upon her forehead and made them turn round one way, while she turned the other" — that Gringoire knows she is an "Andalusian . . . her complexion dark as she danced, whirled, turned around on an old Persian carpet carelessly spread on the pavement and every time her radiant face passed before you as she turned, her large black eyes flashed lightning."[62]

Most useful in my own attempt to find Carmen has been tracing the technical evolution of Gypsy dance on the café stage through the articles written by North African French (and, mostly female) ethnomusicologists and sociologists who, in an attempt to recover their own histories, have contributed detailed descriptions of café performance in several cities in the mid-to-late nineteenth century.

Muslim feminist scholar Fawzia Afazel-Khan, in her September 2001 commentary for *The Drama Review*, recognizes the prescience of French Orientalist approaches to Gypsy performance and the Eastern, sexual, lascivious, abandoned dancing of Egyptian dancers on French soil: "Labels," writes Afazel-Khan, "place all people into a single, often mutually contradictory group, suppressing the heterogeneity of dissenting voices, people like myself who are both 'inside' and 'outside' the Orwellian whale."[63] Carmen, like Schéhérazade, metamorphoses in the early nineteenth-century French reader's imagination into an orientalist totem of erotic dancing girls. Whether she is an Egyptian from Cairo, a Tzigane from Hungary, or an Indian from Rajasthan we will never know, left to the unspecific and totalizing cultural conflation of Near Eastern male Occidentalists and tourists to the Near East (imagined and real). From Lady Mary Montagu, the wife of the British Ambassador to Turkey in the eighteenth century, we gain a somewhat accurate and extremely detailed description of the Turkish Sultan's harem. (It was Lady Montagu who introduced smallpox variolization to the British court, a custom that she observed in Constantinople.)

Beyond Montagu, we will have to wait for Matisse and the modernist perspective to see distinctions between the picturesque quality of the desert landscape and the physical reality of Moroccan women. Writing to Camoin in the autumn of 1914, Matisse observes: "When Delacroix's imagination deals with a subject, it remains anecdotal which is too bad. This is because of the quality of his mind." According to Delacroix, "I began making something passing out of my trip to Africa only after I had forgotten all the little details . . . in my pictures, [retaining] only the striking and poetic side. Until then, I had been pursued by the love of exactness which most people mistake for truth."[64]

In the end, we can observe a curious interplay among the texts produced by orientalist, romantic travel writers such as Chateaubriand, Victor Hugo, Lady Mary Montagu, Fromentin, Gautier, Flaubert, Maxine du Camp, Gerard de Nerval, Alexander Dumas, Prosper Mérimée, Marihalt, the painting of Delacroix, and the lyric, exoticizing operas of Félicien David.[65] The Seductive Orient and later, during the Second Empire, the Exotic Orient merge into a single, late Romantic vision of a single country, one found in Volney's *Voyage en Série et en Égypte* of 1787 and followed by Napoleon Bonaparte's scholars' *Déscription de l'Égypte 1808–1828*. The Orient begun by an Oriental such as Cervantes, who describes the Roman emperor's dancing girls as having "honey in their undulating hips," was completed on the other side of the Pyrénées between the revolutions of 1830 and 1848, the Franco-Prussian War of 1870–1871 and finalized in the last work of Georges Bizet, *Carmen*, whose 1904 rendition contained no less than one hour of flamenco dance in the second act.[66]

CHAPTER SIX

Picasso, the Bull, and Carmen

We peer back toward a past that seems to have independent being distant
from the present; in body memory the past is enacted in the present as a kind
of immanence.

Henri Bergson

In the large country of Gypsies in art, Picasso is the greatest Gypsy
of them all. It is necessary to know Spain to understand . . . From his
birthplace of Malaga.

Michel Leiris, *Romancero du Gitan*[1]

His spirit is Latin, but his rhythm is Arabic.

Guillaume Apollinaire[2]

The natural steadiness of [Picasso's] character is rooted in his Spanishness,
which has decisively stamped the man and his work. His daring pathos, his
eternally unsatisfied striving, which Brandi describes as Faustian, his humor
reminiscent of that of Cervantes, Gongora, and Goya, and above all the
fantastic image of man he offers us in his works, identify him as a son of
Spain. "That is his homeland, the country of men of temperament, the freest
men ever produced by the human race" (Cassou). His genius is governed not
by norm, but by the spirit of the "capricho," which endows his personality
with a curiously flickering, restless quality.

Guillaume Apollinaire [3]

Picasso and Carmen

In the history of the Mediterranean world, the bull and the moon goddess survive,
absorbed into new rituals, those of the Madonna and the bullfight being the most
significant. Carmen's sacredness as a woman is associated with her beauty, will, and
independence—the inability on the part of men to possess her. Her sensuality,

a mark of the female Gypsy, evokes the mythic moon goddess of antiquity. She and the sacred bull, with which she comes into contact in the fourth act of the opera, are both sacrificed.

As a symbolic representation of the fertility goddess of the ancient Mediterranean world, Carmen's immanent stage presence fascinated modern artists—chief among them Pablo Picasso. Her mythic origins, taken from the Afro-Iberian world, inspired Picasso explicitly to identify his origins with hers. Beginning in 1896 and continuing until 1957, Picasso played with the thematic tapestry of Carmen, weaving it into his worldview. Between 1937, when he made his final trip to Spain, and his death in 1973, he again used her as a conduit for a new phase of his artistic exploration in drawing, painting, ceramics, and found objects. Using distinct media—crayons, pencils, paints, charcoals—Picasso chose Carmen as a subject to which he returned with obsessive regularity. Like Bizet who adopted her, Picasso reinterpreted Carmen's character in modernist language, engaging viewers in a conversation about her universality and survival in popular culture. In his work, Carmen was reborn yet again.

Carmen provided a powerful, figurative access to a mythic world through which he could revel in Hispanic themes and Spanish geography: Gibraltar, Cordoba, and Seville. He nurtured a lifelong attraction to Prosper Mérimée's fictive character. Her liaisons with Don José, with Lucas in the novella, and Escamillo in the opera, and with her fellow Gypsies become, for Picasso, a space from which to draw inspiration for his work. As in literature, Carmen in the hands of Picasso becomes a channel for the expression of a Hispanic and bohemian sensibility. Like the water colors that outline her face or the wicker basket used to construct Picasso's bull-mask, Carmen's kaleidoscopic beings—magician, fantasy, woman, geography—give the artist a route to his own self-expression of Hispanic masculinity, a bridge to his itinerant Andalusian identity and to those archetypes with whom he identified: Gypsy, Matador, Murderer, and Lover.

The image of Carmen resonated with Pablo Picasso's creative imagination. She was a force of nature crafted into form by the artist's hands. Like her, Picasso became his own fictional embodiment. The myth and the man share the following characteristics, a study of which follows: Andalusian, nomadic, erotic, and sacrificial. We begin with a history of the painter.

> *Don José*: "You are at least an Andalusian? I fancy I can detect as much in your soft accent."
>
> *Carmen*: "I believe you are of the Holy Land—a few steps from Paradise."

Mérimée: "I had learnt this metaphor, which refers to Andalusia, from my friend
 Francísco Sevilla, the well-known picador."

Don José: "Then you must be Moorish, or—I stopped, not liking to say, 'a Jewess.'"

Carmen: "Go along! Go along! You see quite well that I am a Gypsy. Do you wish
 me to tell you 'la baji—good-fortune'? Have you ever heard of La Carmencita? I
 am she!"[4]

Like Carmen, a Gypsy born of myth and a novella, Picasso was an Andalusian
who saw himself as a kindred spirit.[5] Pablo Diego José Francísco de Paula Juan
Nepomuceno María de los Remedios Cipriano de la Santísima Trinidad Clito
Ruíz y Picasso (1881–1974), was born in Malaga which, at the end of the nineteenth century, was an impoverished, pre-industrial city that he later claimed he
hated. He would eventually desert his homeland for good, traveling out of Catalonia toward Galicia, crossing into southern France and heading north to Paris.
But he would often return to the South where he traveled close to the border of
France and Spain, to the ancient Arab and Roman *corridas* of Arles, Nîmes, Beaucaire, Bayonne, and St. Maries de la Mer, site of the annual Gypsy pilgrimage to
the sea.

Picasso's lifelong obsession with and integration of Hispanic, Moorish, and
Iberian Spain was profound, deeply coloring his *oeuvre*. Alongside Federico García
Lorca, Miguel de Unamuno, Pio Baroja, José Ortega y Gasset, José Bergamín,
Antonia Mercé, *La Argentina*, Manuel Ortíz, and Manuel de Falla, Pablo Picasso
identified himself, his painting, and sculpture with the political anarchism and
artistic radicalism—laced with Gypsy elements—of southern Andalusia, from
which he unearthed the source material for his most overtly political testament:
Guernica. Picasso returned for the last time to Spain in 1937 to the province of
Catalonia to research a commission from the Second Spanish Republic.

More than almost any other Spanish exile, Picasso spent his life in France in
the company of Spanish exiles—Gypsy flamenco singers touring France, painters
such as Manuel Ortíz, writers and poets—trying to safeguard their traditions.[6]
His obsessive identification in exile with the customs and values of his Hispanic
and, in particular, Andalusian heritage worked to inextricably tie this colossal
modern master to Spain in his art work and daily life. He was influenced by
the late nineteenth-century Spanish painter Ricardo Canals (1876–1931), who
satisfied through his art the French craze for things Spanish. *Hispañolism*, as it was
referred to in the French press of the 1830s, dated from Napoleon I's brutal war
against Spain. In turn, Picasso developed a hypermasculinist Andalusian identity

that merged with Surrealist values of myth, archaic knowledge, and erotic visual metaphors of Hispanic, Andalusian identity.

The Cartography of Exile

Picasso absorbed diverse cultural influences into his artwork. In his thousands of drawings, paintings, and ceramic objects he left behind meditations on Spain that are laced with the *noir* of Goya, the political power of Velazquez, the spiritual height of El Greco, and the draughtsmanship of John Singer Sargent and Toulouse-Lautrec.

Picasso suffered the geographical changes his father and, later, chance forced upon him. Such upheaval is perhaps the most prominent reason that his work reveals a restless, powerfully insightful man caught between worlds. His permanent sense of self-exile helps to explain why, once in France, he moved very little, living in Paris or renting homes in southern France for months or years on end. The first such exile occurred in 1891, when he was a little boy. His father moved the family from Picasso's beloved Andalusia north to Galicia, the land of the Basques. By 1895, he moved the family again, to Madrid, where Picasso enrolled in the art school La Llonja.

In 1896, at the age of fifteen, he went to Barcelona where he rented his first studio.[7] Like his father, the young Picasso wandered the streets of Barcelona's *reforma* neighborhood. He lived close to an impoverished group of bohemian artists, prostitutes, and Gypsies, frequenting zarzuelas, sex shows, and brothels in the *barrio* Xino.[8] The image of Carmen emerging from this milieu already energizes his early work.

In 1898, at the age of seventeen, Picasso drew a hooded woman: Carmen. He imagined a *Sevilliana*, a dark-haired, oval-eyed sensuous beauty, part-European with her blood-red lips and ivory skin, part-Andalusian with her curly jet-black hair. In 1899, he drew her again. Using thick black charcoal lines, he outlined her blackened face in profile. A mantilla covers her black hair. Her left hand, webbed like an insect's, grasps an open fan. A mix of human and creature in form and feel, it is the portrait of an indigent woman, someone from the streets of Barcelona — a Gypsy perhaps.

Two years later, in 1900, Picasso drew another Carmen, this time an abstraction. She appears as part of a study of drawings, her head floating above a room. While only a sketch, she is unmistakably Carmen:

She was pretty, young, well made [with] very large eyes . . . Her eyes were obliquely set but large and full; her lips rather thick, but well cut . . . She was of a strange and savage beauty—a face which at first surprised you, but it was one you could never forget. Her eyes had an expression at once voluptuous and fierce which I have never noticed in any human eyes.[9]

Picasso drew a perfect oval face, giving her almond-shaped eyes and thick black eyebrows. A flower tied into her hair complements her red lips. On top of her face, he drew lines as if to remove her from us, making her the stuff of myth or history rather than the real present. These lines lend a quality of distance and layering to his evocation.

In 1902, he drew another Carmenesque figure, *Femme aux bas verts*. This time, he imagined her from the back. Using a thick, crooked line, he outlined a woman's shoulders, neck, chin, and back. It is an uneven, inconsistent line that gives her body an asymmetrical quality so as to hint at an unattractive deformity. She wears green stockings with a Moorish design of dots and lines in black and orange. She stares out with red lips, oval, Etruscan-looking eyes and dark red hair tied up in a bun, on top of which sits a red rose. With a thicker black line, Picasso draws a necklace and an earring. Painted on wood, she seems to be from another world—from the past—floating in the center of the small rectangular frame.

It is not surprising that Picasso should have gravitated to the brothels that his father had frequented and where he could listen to *cante jondo*, the only music his biographer, John Richardson, claims he loved.[10] Barcelona's Gypsy quarter was called *Chupa y Tira*, or *suck and throw*. There lay the remains of a Moorish castle—the Gibralfaro—and Arab markets, living quarters, and a mosque—the Alcazaba "with its labyrinth of hanging gardens and crumbling walls and flocks of peacocks."[11] In the shadow of the Alcazaba were the shacks of *Chupa y Tira*, where beggars and gypsies "sat . . . in the sun among whiffs of orange flower and drying excrement and children up to the age of twelve ran naked. The neighborhood was called Chupa y Tira because people were so poor," Picasso told fellow artist José Sabartes "that all they could eat was a chowder made with clams.[12] And all their backyards were filled with clamshells, which they had thrown out of their windows after having sucked out . . . their very souls." Picasso's love of *cante jondo* originated when he was just a boy. He even learned to dance a rudimentary flamenco. "There was no end," said Picasso, "to the tricks I learned from the Gypsies."[13]

Could the broken and, at times, jagged lines of his female portraits, beginning in 1899, have resonated with the *queíjo*, the gutteral cry of the *cantaor* in flamenco? His prostitute images are mournful. They peer out, skinny, desperate, sad-looking, like a Gypsy's cry to bear witness to her suffering. One ancient flamenco *letra* from Granada says: *The town jail has twenty-four cells. I have seen twenty-three.* These Carmen-like images never place a woman anywhere specific: she has no precise geography. Rather, each figure hangs in the space of the frame, alone with no belongings, destitute and isolated.

Between 1898 and 1899, Picasso bore witness to a great deal of urban poverty in both Madrid and Barcelona. Having survived scarlet fever in 1898, he moved between Horta de Ebro and Barcelona where he developed his Blue Period. A series of almost *film noir* drawings accompany his paintings. Men beat and rape women. Couples embrace so violently as to negate the act of kissing.

Perhaps one of the darkest paintings to emerge from this period is an 1899 portrait, *Couple d'Andalou*, painted on a tambourine. Using the chiaroscuro technique of Goya, Picasso offers us a Gypsy couple shrouded in the dark, swirling mystery of black lines and impressionist paint. A dark woman in white robes with her hair pulled back and a flower over her head looks at a man who holds her arm as they dance. He is dressed like a *gaucho*, a *caballero*, with flat black hat and black suit, his legs parallel and bent at the knees as if beginning an intense series of *zapateado*, or footwork. The *caballero* Gypsy dances the *farruca*, a stunning show of male prowess, quicksilver feet, and speed. The couple's feet end at the tip of the tambourine whose middle section is dotted with metal disks — tiny castanets that resonate with the Gypsy dancers on its face.

Between 1899 and 1903, Picasso expanded his Goyaesque iconographic cycle of Carmenesque work, painting furies, witches, monsters, and killers. Deeply affected by the urban poverty he both experienced and witnessed in Spain and France, his work became dark: a mélange of cool blues, charcoal blacks and blood-reds with single, cubist lines that outlined entire bodies. Picasso's use of a wide range of dark colors helped him to commiserate with the Gypsy, the beggar, and the prostitute. This was Goya's world as well and, of course, the environment of the characters populating *Carmen*. The colors submit to the narrative or draw her out in a range of emotions that bears witness to pain and suffering. The idea is a modernist one; the artist's *raison d'être* is no longer to please the viewer but, rather, to shock him/her, raise his/her conscience — to bear witness. This tradition is clearly already strong in the work of Goya, and continues to unfold in more abstract guises in that of Picasso.

Living in self-exile in France for most of his life, Picasso seems never to have ceased feeling like a Spaniard in a foreign land. Unlike the hot, sun-filled land-scapes of Spain, Paris was damp and cold most of the year. Between 1900 and 1904, Picasso traveled to Paris three times in an attempt to settle there, but poor and unable to support himself, he returned each time to Madrid or Barcelona. By 1904, having sold three drawings to the dealer Berthe Weill, he moved perma-nently to Paris. In 1909 and 1910, he had sufficient money to rent summer homes in southern Spain, but did not return to Spain again until 1933, traveling from Cannes to Barcelona.[14] Having moved from Paris to Boisgeloup, in the south of France, Picasso was then able to travel extensively in Spain where, in 1934, he would have seen Greco-Roman ruins and artifacts.

The notion that the Gypsy Carmen lived in exile in her host country resonated with Picasso's own form of exile in France, at first self-imposed and, later, enforced by General Franco's thirty-six year dictatorship. Living away from Spain for almost sixty years, Picasso had to find ways of coping with his unending nostalgia for his country. He transformed these feelings into art, musings laid bare in pigment or revealed in his large collection of bullfight tickets and matador postcards. Picas-so's masculinist obsession with *toreros*, *corridas*, Minotaurs, and women could be expressed through the figure of Carmen. As he strove to balance his self-portraits as Minotaur and bull in the ring with the vulnerability of the feminine, the figure of Carmen continued to be the route by which he could access both animus and anima. Picasso's interest in translating traces of her libertine spirit into modern form is more complicated than mere narrative. To Picasso, Carmen, while mythic, appeared iconically Spanish, a hybrid of cultural traces, rather than a verifiable place, setting or story.

One of the most potent themes in Mérimée's novel is that of exile: the forced exile of the Gypsy people. Perhaps one of the most powerful messages that Carmen embodies is that of journey, of exile. As Picasso's art reveals a man constantly in search of self-exploration, Mérimée's cartography of exile in the *Carmen* novella recapitulates itself in Picasso's life and art. Picasso, too, lived in exile—an exile of the artist who, like the Gypsy, stands on the periphery, watching, translating, and documenting through his/her medium.

Painting Gypsies, prostitutes—the underside of life in Barcelona—Picasso began to translate Carmenian themes into modernist art. He pursued his dark vision, often political—sympathetic to the poor, the homeless, and the indigent, and colored by Francísco Goya's (1746–1828) social consciousness.[15] By 1904, after emigrating to France, Picasso began a series of Spanish portraits that he would continue to paint until 1914 and the start of the First World War. Two years into the War, Picasso executed a series of mytho-tauromachic drawings, lithographs, and engravings whose subject he continued to explore until 1930. In that year, by then more prosperous, Picasso rented larger summer homes throughout southern France. There, he painted *toros* and *toreros*, as he attended afternoon *corridas* in the arenas of Arles, Nîmes, Avignon, Beaucaire, and other neighboring towns.

Watching the Nazi rise to power in 1933 and the beginnings of the Spanish Civil War, Picasso turned to Surrealism for a methodological perspective on Hispanism. Much like Goya before him, the transition away from a previous perspective—in Picasso's case that of Cubism, in the case of Goya, figurative representation—became the path to revelation for the artist. By revelation, I mean an unabashed staging of sexuality, eroticism, and violence as autobiographical and masculinist themes. While images of the bull and the bullfight always laced his art, the years 1933 to 1934, in particular Picasso's flirtation with Surrealism, find *toreros* dominating his *oeuvre*.[16] These works will be discussed below in an attempt to connect Pablo Picasso's Hispanic modernism to the idea that Carmen connects us to the ancient past.

Drawing Carmen

In 1946, Picasso moved into a demi-self-exile in the south of France. He chose first Antibes and later Vallauris where, influenced by an indigenous ceramic style, his art became suffused with mythic figures.[17] An explicit reference to the character of Carmen emerged during this time. Centaurs, bacchantes, solar festivals—*la corrida*—make their way onto Picasso's vases, plates, and other pottery as if he was painting in an ancient world. Many afternoons he drove to Arles or Nîmes, France's largest arenas, to attend *corridas*.[18] With Françoise Gilot now living with him, Picasso began to draw *picadoras*, one of whom was real: Conchita Cintron, nicknamed "the blond goddess." Picasso's photographic collection reveals a pop culture obsession with anything Spanish. Between 1946 and 1948, surrounding himself with this reinvented Hispanic world, Picasso began a series of thirty-eight drawings on the character of Carmen.[19]

In 1949, Picasso actually illustrated Prosper Mérimée's novella, *Carmen*. He produced thirty-eight burin engravings and four aquatint images, among them many Carmens, each more abstract than the last.[20] Entitled *Le Carmen des Carmens*, they were executed in intense shades of black, white, and grey. Again, he envisioned her in profile, like the ancient Cretan women on the walls at Knossos.[21] This Carmen feels colossal, her face absorbing the empty space of the frame. Picasso places her immense eye at the center of the frame. He understood she was not from his world; she was from the East. As one approaches the drawing, her gaze draws one in even though she looks away. Almost the size of her entire face, Carmen's eye is an amulet to be worn for protection against the evil eye. Thin black lines define and protect her eye. Her lips are full, her nose Roman, her gaze intent, as if she is meditating on her fate. Ultimately, she is composed of cubist lines and shades of color that begin as one body part and end up as something else. The disorientation of Cubism is perfect for Carmen as it resonates with and illuminates the chaotic existence of a Gypsy.

All of the characters drawn by Picasso in *Carmen des Carmen*—Don José, Micaëla and Lucas—appear in tiny spaces alongside Mérimée's text. Their bodies live in harmony on the page with the story, becoming visual glosses of the character development and plot. They are trapped in the same destined universe fated to lose love: Micaëla who seems to have no control over her destiny; Don José who cannot help loving Carmen; Escamillo, whose famous songlines, "Et songe bien, oui, songe en combatant qu'un oeil noir te regarde et que l'amour t'attend," announce the destiny awaiting the bull in the ring.[22] Picasso plants a little bull, seemingly harmless, next to a text surrounded by a wreath of flowers. Picasso's design of the bullfight, in the case of these illustrations, follows the French and Spanish medieval traditions of bullfighting.

Picasso titled the work *Carmen of Carmens*, referring to the many Carmens with whom he was involved. Etymologically, Carmen is derived from the Latin for light, magic, or charm—*charmer–chanter*, to sing. Carmen for Picasso is inspiration and myth, a reason to paint. In pigment and crayon, the artist seems to be having a conversation with Carmen. So many years removed from Spain himself, Picasso imagines her at the border, inside the cities where he used to roam. For Picasso, Spain, like Carmen, becomes mythic. Out of Mérimée's textual account of Carmen, as well as from his own relationship to her, Picasso created an iconographic system of Hispanic themes that all seem to refer back to her.

An allegorical figure, Picasso's Carmen modernizes Mérimée's romantic imagination: a diabolic creature whose libertine ways unleashed the downfall of every man she met and the disgust of polite society. Picasso was no prude—his art bears witness to this. As a young art student, he covers Carmen's body with a peasant's mantilla, a simple hooded length of cloth in which a poor woman could take cover. Perhaps it is the spirit underneath the fabric that Picasso hopes to reveal.

A second Carmen also appears on a page across from the text. Picasso has drawn a circle, two eyes, a nose, and a mouth. It is a death mask—a mask of ritual sacrifice. A third Carmen still retains the circle and two tiny eyes and nothing else. Perhaps the most powerful image is of her death. In the adjacent text, Don José tells our narrator that he has just killed Carmen and does not want to reveal where her body lay.

Throughout Mérimée's narrative, Carmen travels from Andalusia to Gibraltar and back north into the mountains of the Sierra Morenos. She is disquieted, her sense of fury leading to flight; she feels profoundly unsafe in the mortal world, having dealt her own death card. While her body is sensual, beautiful, anatomically harmonious, and desirable, her fate—*moira*—is ritual bodily sacrifice, preceded by a cartography of exile. Ousted from the tobacco factory, she comes and goes frequently from her Triana haunt either to make a living stealing and smuggling or to avoid vicious lovers, husbands, and the law. She can never be found in one place or in one guise; she is always changing moods, friends, and locations. Her lack of geographic stability heightens her image as homeless and unsafe. Gypsies were despised and feared as strange foreigners who could not stay in one place, assimilate, or adopt local customs; Carmen is seen as coming from that same nomadic tradition.

Surrealism and Picasso I: Eros and Thanatos

My paintings, finished or not, are the pages of my journal.
Pablo Picasso[23]

In 1904, Picasso went to Paris for the second time—the art dealer Ambroise Vollard had arranged an exhibition of his work for sale. There, Picasso encountered artists who would come to define the Surrealist movement. He rented a room with the poet Max Jacob, who introduced him to the poet Guillaume Apollinaire, a great force in the Surrealist camp.[24] Apollinaire and Jacob became as interested in the Spanish artist as he was in their use of words to "draw" a page. To them, Picasso was a free spirit like Carmen—a lightning bolt of creativity.

The Surrealist Manifesto written by André Breton in 1922 proposed the notion that images allow the artist to excavate the unconscious mind.[25] In essence, these images expose one's identity through an exploration of dreams and ego. Picasso's interest in the mythology of the ancient Mediterranean world led him, as did the newly found cave paintings of Altamira, Spain, and Dordogne, France, to embrace the Cretan Minotaur. By virtue of its savage physiognomy—half man, half beast—the Minotaur became a surreal object in the hands of Picasso, a symbolic image of animal lust and potential physical violence, like the bull upon which he had fantasized since he was a child.

Picasso revisited his self-reflexive, Carmenian themes of sensuality, eroticism, and death in his many paintings and drawings of *corridas*. Following his obsession with writing, he returned to drawing full-time and produced a series of Minotaurs, bull-men from the ancient Greek world that live at the center of a maze. The Minotaur, like the centaur and the bull, plays multiple roles in the artist's work. Sexually-charged themes of being and existence set powerfully inside the compressed, filmic scenes that Picasso drew or painted bear witness to his need as an immigrant to identify himself with more ancient cultural themes. A polymorphous creature, Picasso chose the half-human Minotaur with purpose; like Carmen, the Minotaur accepts his death sentence — after a life in the prison of the labyrinth. Drawing hundreds of Minotaurs, Picasso locates in his body an erect bull of many faces.[26] In some drawings he conquers women, taking them at will. In others, like the *Figure Defeated by a Youth in the Arena* from 1933, a once fierce Minotaur bows down to a young athlete, his head tucked low near his hooves, and is slain by the youth, an image that recalls the Greek legend of Theseus who slays the Minotaur.[27]

The concept of the Minotaur, like the bull and the horse, is in a constant state of metamorphosis in both form and meaning. At one pole are the hero types, the artist and classical youth, and at the other is the beast that dies a miserable death as the fighting bull in the arena.[28]

Herschel Chipp

"All this takes place on a mountainous island in the Mediterranean," Picasso explained, like Crete. "It is there, along the coastline, where the Minotaurs live."[29]

Françoise Gilot

Picasso's identification with the mythical Minotaur can best be seen in his transformation — self-annihilation — into a bull-man in 1937. "Picasso," wrote one art historian "appoints the semi-human monster as the trustee of the vicissitudes of his problematic existence."[30] In *Picasso tenant une tête de taureau en osier*, he holds in his left hand a smoking cigarette and in his right a bull-mask made of wicker, a present from the bullfighter Luis Miguel Dominguin.[31] "The Minotaur is, beyond any doubt, Picasso's alter ego, the character who reflects his different states of mind."[32] The Minotaur is also one of the "fundamental themes in [Picasso's] work. Inseparable from taurine motifs, Picasso's Minotaur joins elements from the Cult of Mithras . . . with the legend of Minos itself and the Spanish bull-fighting tradition."[33] Picasso's first bullfighting image was painted in 1896. In 1917, the bull theme reemerged in his work, now transformed into the spectacle of the bull violently goring the horse. By 1919, in his designs for the ballet *Le Tricorne*, the audience sees a bullfighter reclining on the bull's back, an image that will reappear in *Minotauromaquia* in 1935. In 1928, the first Minotaur appears in Picasso's work. Working in conjunction with the Catalonian publisher Gustavo Gili Roig, Picasso completed an initial seven etchings for *La tauromaquia* by Pepe-Hillo.

Drawings and etchings of a raging Minotaur—like the bull at the heart of a *corrida* in the act of raping or killing innocent women—continue to appear frequently throughout the interwar period and are best understood in Picasso's illustrations of Ovid's *Metamorphoses* (1931) and Aristophanes' *Lysistrata* (1934), as well as for the *Suite Vollard*. Married to Olga Koklova, the Ballets Russes dancer whom he met while designing *Le Tricorne*, and in love with the youthful Marie-Therese Walter, Picasso executes *Minotauromaquia*, "the direct forerunner to *Guernica*."[34] The Minotaur, we come to understand, has a second hidden identity; he will soon be transformed into the bull.

Continuing to investigate the unconscious power of the Minotaur as self, Picasso drew a series entitled *La Fin d'un monster*. Within a monster, wounded by a spear, he agonizes as he sees his reflection in a mirror held out to him by a young girl on a shore. Here we see Picasso's exploration of a Freudian theme being touted by the Surrealists: narcissism. Picasso, the wounded, dying monster, must take in the vision of his own death, as shown to him by the taboo object of his longing.

By 1933, in his Minotaur series, Picasso used the Cretan bull-man as an extension of Hispanic themes running through his work: Carmen and the *corrida*.[35] The Minotaur's body embodies a literal representation of a dangerous metamorphosis. A bull's head, a terrifyingly non-human mask with bulging eyes, sharp horns, and curly hair, sits atop a human body that is almost Grecian in its muscular beauty. The collision of bull with man is uncanny and frightening. A symbol of myth, it was recycled by Picasso as a Surrealist nightmare. In a true investigation of Surrealism's manifesto, he drew a nightmare. It is the artist facing himself. In *Dying Minotaur* (1933) an immense Minotaur lies dying. Six women witness his death. They sit in the *sol*, the first row of seats, squeezed shoulder to shoulder. One woman, filled with compassion for the dying beast, reaches out to touch his

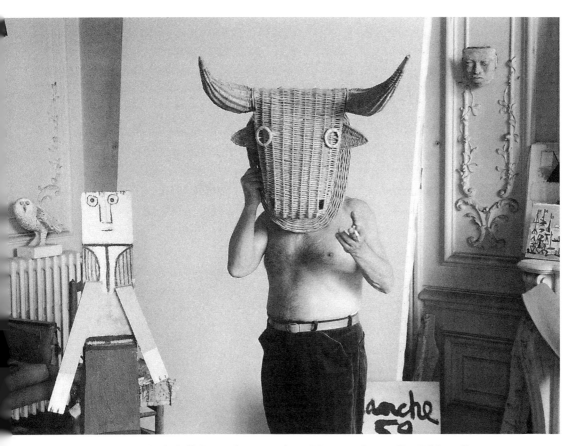

Donning a wicker mask of a bull, Picasso becomes a living Minotaur. Cannes, "La Californie," 1959. Photo by Edward Quinn, © edwardquinn.com

back. His hairy hand clutches at his heart, his nostrils and eyes reaching for the sky. His human feet and legs give way as he gasps for breath. The space is compressed. A solitary dagger lies beside the Minotaur's left arm. He dies alone. The outstretched hand of the one woman draws us empathically into the space with her. In the ritual voyeurism of the women watching the bull-man die, our senses awake to the complicity of their passivity as the Minotaur lays dying.

The Minotaur, like the centaur and the bull, plays multiple roles in the artist's work. Picasso's self-portraits as the rapacious Minotaur, violently making love with the picador's fallen horse or carting a woman and child away, hold as significant a place in Picasso's obsession with masculinity, identity, and Hispanic memory. So numerous are these drawings in his mid-century *oeuvre* that they become a kind of visual grammar for his intimate life and his inner landscape — his psychological state of mind and identity.

Further, the dualism of Carmen and the bull suggests the following thematic bridges: female horse/male bull; human matador/animal bull; passive horse/raging bull; death and violence in the *corrida*. Repeatedly, Picasso's drawings portray acts of love alongside physical violence. He drew literally hundreds of Minotaurs forcefully embracing nude women, their horns protruding up into the air, their hands grabbing at the fated woman's body, drawing her into harm's way. This theme of the hyper-masculine bull-man dominating a woman without her consent is repeated in the *corrida* with the bull and horse. In this case, the bull, rather than goring the picador on horseback, rapes or moves as if to rape the horse as he kills her.

Surrealism and Picasso II: Writing as Figure

> Picasso's poetry is a verbal tide in which his torrential imagination latches
> on to experienced sensations . . . tangible proofs of automatic writing.
> Tristan Tzara, 1953[36]

Picasso's connection to Surrealism extends as well to automatic writing. Between 1934 and 1959, he wrote three hundred and forty-odd texts, including two plays. Between 1934 and 1940 alone, he wrote two hundred and eighty poems and prose works. Picasso had long been associated with journal illustration, one of his great gifts to Jacob, Apollinaire and Breton, frequently illustrating Surrealist journals and reviews. His turn-of-the-century association with a bohemian Catalan group of painters, with whom he painted portraits on the walls of the café El Quatre Gats, ignited his interest in drawing as populist illustration. He illustrated journals, transliterating words into images, especially those of legend and fantasia. Picasso developed an iconic *écriture* in the style of Toulouse-Lautrec. As a young man, he contributed writing-drawings to *Arte Joven* (Young Art) and the Spanish newspapers *La Tribuna* and *El Liberal*.

In 1924, the Surrealists paid homage to Picasso during a performance of the ballet *Mercure*, for which he had designed both the set and the costumes. In November 1925, Picasso participated in an exhibition of Surrealist painting at the Pièrre Gallerie. Breton began to write about Picasso's contribution to Surrealism, stating that he was "enormously responsible" for Surrealism's energy. Breton later wrote in 1935 in his work, *Picasso Poéte*, that the Spaniard had made a "sudden choice" in favor of "the written language to the exclusion of all others."[37] Later, Picasso claimed that it was "the worse period of [his] life."[38] In 1925, Greek publisher Christian Zervos birthed an important art magazine, *Cahiers d'art*. Its contents — poems, drawings and prose essays — became "an umbrella for publications devoted entirely to the dissemination of contemporary art and documents revealing the contemporariness of the discoveries of ancient civilization."[39] By 1928, when Picasso drew his first Minotaur, *Cahiers d'art* had become the vanguard venue that printed both Picasso's writings and drawings. Picasso's use of motifs ranging from Cycladic to paleo-Christian to classical iconography appealed to Zervos and the Surrealists. *Cahiers d'art's* message of the contemporariness of themes from the ancient world—the visual beginnings of French post-modernism—appealed to Picasso.

A connection can be made between Picasso's drawings on newspapers, known as *papiers collés*, and his interest in Surrealism. Drawing or writing in the "margins of printed pages and writing on any piece of paper, Picasso found a newfound language whose syntax met at the intertext between image and word."[40] Picasso explored the multiple meanings elicited by an odd arrangement of words or a strange design of the page. He generated, for example, new verbal and semiotic meanings behind words and images by placing incongruous drawings of bulls and bullfights next to odd bits of text in the Spanish newspapers *Sol y Sombra* and *Le Torero*. These loose forays into what would be termed automatic writing was one method Picasso used to explore the landscape of the surreal. He introduced a Surrealist choreography of the printed page, composed of single and double lines with images that presented the reader with anti-narrative associations.

In developing this technique, Picasso used newspapers and journals, reading materials one associates with a chronological, self-explanatory stream of information that is quickly and easily consumed. His *modus operandi* was to copy down and spontaneously illustrate a poem. Examples include illustrations for Verlaine's *Fêtes Galantes* (1905), as well as poems by Baudelaire, Rimbaud, and Edgar Allan Poe.

In May of 1935, Picasso stopped painting altogether and began writing poetry. He wrote in French and Spanish, an unpunctuated and scrambled free verse.[41] References to his homeland abound, even though the majority of his writing is in French, not Spanish.[42] "Picasso," Christine Piot writes, "also remained imbued with the popular, largely oral tradition of the airs and refrains of bullfights" and with flamenco *cante jondo*.[43] It was from his closest friends, Max Jacob and Guillaume Apollinaire, that Picasso came to understand that poetry, like flamenco *cante* and the *corrida*, could be a living art rather than mere artifact.[44] The work of Verlaine, Rimbaud, and Mallarmé also seduced Picasso. The lyricism in their words became a kind of rhythmic visual tapestry, like the footwork in flamenco, whose impressionistic resonance was almost impossible to capture in a traditional drawing or poem.

In 1933, Picasso drew the cover for the journal *Minotaure*.[45] In 1934, "Picasso's profile filled a square of the 'Surrealist checkerboard,' a photomontage by Man Ray reproduced in *La Petite Anthologie du Surréalisme*."[46] One year later, a Picasso painting appeared in the International Exhibition of Surrealism in Ténérife, an island off the coast of Spain. From 1935 until 1942, Picasso participated in some way in every Surrealist exhibition, signaling the Surrealists' acceptance of the painter-poet as "one of their own."[47] "The emotion experienced" wrote Surrealist poet Pièrre Reverdy at the start of the movement in 1924, "before one of his canvasses, so new in appearance, is an outgrowth of that inspired by pure, true poetry."[48] Picasso said of a poem of Reverdy's: "It is almost a drawing in itself."[49] Colleague Tristan Tzara echoed Reverdy's statement that "poetry could be found in a painting or sculpture."[50]

It was no accident that the Surrealists chose the mythic Minotaur as the namesake for its magazine. Half-beast, half-human, the Minotaur is ambiguous, akin to a dream image. Waking from unconsciousness to consciousness also constitutes an ambiguous state of being as one remembers parts of things—not the whole dream, just its geography and emotional effect. "The Surrealists [drew] from the Minotaur his surreal, extra-human condition, everything that makes him fight against man and his social system and, ultimately, die in combat."[51]

Picasso's painting and drawing style, to the Surrealist mind, was Surrealist. He drew, for example, a bull with the rhythm of a stampede and echoed this rhythmic expressiveness in the words he might draw over the image, creating a temporal and graphic choreography that unites movement and text on drawing paper. Psychic automatism might be one way to describe the speed with which Picasso referred image to word and text to image. "In most of his texts, images are linked according to the analogical laws of the unconscious, influenced" by collage and phonetic association.[52] In their *Dictionnaire Abrégé du Surréalisme*, Breton and Éluard refer to Picasso, or "the Bird of Benin" as "the painter who, through his work, has been an active participant in Surrealism since 1926," and as "the author of Surrealist poems, 1935–1938."[53]

Picasso Plays Carmen

In 1937, Man Ray and his wife, Kiki, visited Pablo Picasso and Dora Maar in Golf-Juan, west of Juan-les-Pins, a little French village located on the Mediterranean coast.[54] The two couples traveled along the Cote d'Azur. In Arles, they went to a bullfight in the ancient Roman arena whose outer archways stand tall above ruined columns. It is a stunning amphitheatre, colossal with the weight of the stone fences that circle the stadium's floor. There, Man Ray shot footage of a *corrida*, capturing the slow, calculated death of the *toro* and the choreographic cacophony of a bull goring a horse and picador.

Like Picasso, Man Ray was fascinated by the bullfight. But he was born into a Jewish family in Philadelphia and love of *la corrida* was not in his blood. He shows the still dangerous but bloodied bull outnumbered, cornered by several matadors as the picador's lances weaken him for the final kill. He has no chance of survival. It is a cruel, sacrificial dance to the finish.

In 1929, Man Ray edited some of this footage into a short documentary entitled *La Corrida*. He catches a bull goaded by five matadors simultaneously as he lays his hooves down on the dirt to die. We first see only the death scene. A quick edit and we see a picador running from a much smaller bull with very sharp horns. The bull is fast, angered by the lances that have been plunged into his neck. The camera pans to the arena, perhaps the well-preserved Roman stadium at Nîmes, filled to the rafters with thousands of people. Here, we see a picador thrust a lance into a bull while the matador stands by with his cape. In a close-up shot, Man Ray's camera captures the cruelty of the bull rushing the horse and rider, allowing the picador to plunge the *banderilla* deep into the bull's neck. The camera pulls out and reveals a matador moving his cape close to a bull who is weak and about to die. Four *banderillas* then surround the bull, forcing him to circle as he is challenged by the colored capes of the *torero*.

The camera cuts to a different scene of a bullfighter and a lone bull facing off. The bull rushes the matador's cape. The matador moves dangerously close to the bull. The camera swivels to the packed stands and the crowd's applause for the brave matador and the bull in their dance of death. Then it pans to the arena and another bull about to meet his death. Cut after cut, Man Ray shows each bull goaded by the matadors preparing the kill before the cheering crowd.

Another bullfight film takes place in the Roman arena of Arles. Entitled *Course Landaise* (1937), the film is also silent. It is a documentary about the southern French bullfight in which the bull is chased and goaded by *sauteurs* who jump, like the Cretan bull-dancers, over the bull's horns, dashing over a fence so as not to be gored. Rather than a dance of ritual sacrifice in which all elements play toward the death of the bull in the skill of the men who bring him, literally, down—to the earth—where he is carted off by horses, the *Course Landaise* has a very different story arc.

A third, untitled, Man Ray film shows Picasso dressed as a Gypsy woman wearing a mantilla, endlessly lighting a cigarette.[55] Picasso is dressed as a matador.[56] In this particular Man Ray shot, he borrows a woman's headscarf. He places it on his head, lights a cigarette, feminizing his gestures and facial movements and turning himself into a Gypsy character the likes of Carmen. The visual paradox — the man whose self-portraits place him in the ancient, mythic saga of minotaur-beast and perfect female beauty morphing into the *gitana* — pulls the viewer into this close-up shot of the *Übermensch* becoming woman, a modern-day totem for the kind of community that Picasso frequented in the summertime. The film consists of a single close-up shot of Picasso dressed as the character Carmen. She sits nervously in the stands of a bullring, repetitively trying to light a cigarette that will not stay lit. It is an ironic view of the Minotaur painter, known at the time as the "Toreador of Painting." Picasso's head is shrouded with the modest head attire of a Spanish mantilla; red lipstick brings attention to the round, black, Gypsy-girl eyes that remind one of Carmen.

Observing Picasso in the stands of a *corrida* must have come as no surprise to the French public as it was known that he lived for the bullfight. But to see the hyper-masculinist painter cross-dressing, transforming his physicality into that of a female, the antithesis of his role as Dionysian matador, presents an enigma. Perhaps this is an echo of Surrealism's manifesto to shock, disorient, and daze through unconscious detail. In the short, tightly edited silent black-and-white film Man Ray performs his own cinematic metamorphosis of the bull into a bacchante. Picasso/Carmen stares out at us with seductive eyes, smoking a Gitane cigarette.[57]

In Carmen, Picasso discovered his anima to complement his overarching animus: "Je suis une femme. Toute artiste est une femme." "I am a woman. Every artist is a woman."[58]

Picasso and the Bull

> Yet how delicate must be this business of approaching
> so subtle an organism as Picasso's bull.
> Frank D. Russell, *Picasso's Guernica*[59]

While the sexuality, archaism, and anarchism in Carmen fascinated Picasso, so too did the aggressive masculinity of the bull. Picasso seizes upon the *corrida*'s imagery as a model for passion, life, and death. In obsessive acts of ritualistic repetition, Picasso drew and painted images from the *corrida*, just as he had done with the Minotaur. Placing himself inside the frame, Picasso's revelation of himself as ravenous bull comes to light. Seminal art historian Rudolf Arnheim presents a cogent summary of the themes at play in this topos:

> The bull, an impressive animal, has a long and noble history in the culture of the Mediterranean peoples. It suffices to recall the images of Mithras subduing the sacred bull, who was created by the God of light and from whose corpse sprang the life of the earth; or the friezes of Knossos, the home of the dreaded Minotaur; in the bullfights, he is the dark fiend, adversary of the human hero who wears the traje de luces, the suit of light; at the same time, he is respected as worthy of his partner; two points of the torero's hat which resemble the two-pronged horns of the bull. The bull's elusive character is faithfully reflected in the life work of Picasso.[60]

To Arnheim, the bull, like the painter, is a totem of the Iberian Peninsula, its peoples, and history.

The same kind of passionate identification is true for Picasso. The bull symbolizes Spain and her history. For Arnheim, the shape of the bull becomes a "conveyor of meaning" as much about Picasso as about the animal. What follows is an analysis of the bull in Picasso's work and of Picasso's identification of himself as a man with the bull.

The bull is Picasso, protector: like Mithras, a gatekeeper who controls women.[61]

> A human consciousness runs beneath the power of Picasso's bulls . . . Half human in essence, the bulls are all, in a sense, Minotaurs.[62]
>
> Frank D. Russell

> For the bull of heaven shall fell the horses of the sun.[63]
>
> Gongora

Beginning with his first drawings, Picasso identified his painting with Spain. After being taken by his father Don José Ruíz Blasco (a painter associated with the School of Malaga, a teacher of drawing at the local Escuela de Bellas Artes, and a frequenter of *café cantantes*, brothels, and cockfights) to his first bullfight in 1890, Picasso sketched a bullring in black and white, the first of thousands of bullfighting images drawn throughout his entire life.

I must have been ten years old when my father took me to see El Lagartijo fight. I remember his hair was snow white. In those days bullfighters didn't retire so young as they do now. Well, the bulls were different then too, huge — and they charged horses as much as twenty times. And the horses dropped like flies, their guts everywhere. Horrible! Those days were different, and so was the bullfight . . .

I also knew Cara Ancha, even if I never saw him fight. I was very young and my father, a great aficionado, took me to his hotel room in Malaga, either before or after the bullfight. I can't remember. It's one of my most vivid childhood recollections. I was on his lap looking at him, overwhelmed.[64]

Pablo Picasso

The bull which all men carry within them.[65]

Vicente Marrero

The Spaniard, when he refers to the bull . . . makes it an agent of danger.[66]

Vicente Marrero

Picasso's *oeuvre* between 1890 and his final taurine work in the year of his death, 1973, included a series of meditations on the bull. At the age of nine, he drew his impression of a bullfight. It consists of an immense bull, his horns protruding out in front of him, chasing after a lone horse that runs away. His second drawing in 1917 shows a bull goring a horse. The horse grimaces in pain, pushed by the bull. The horse's front legs are splayed out in front of him, barely able to support his immense body, now crashing to the ground, gasping for air. The physical violence of the aggressive bull against the passive horse comes to represent most of Picasso's bullfights, the torero as central figure no longer even in the frame. He reduces the cruelty of the spectacle to a battle between a defenseless, blindfolded horse unable to defend itself, and a powerful, domineering, dangerously aggressive bull out to kill anything in his path.

By 1932, Picasso draws a crucified horse — a horse's distorted bones stacked up on a cross. It is an image of animal sacrifice so astute as to reconfigure and communicate the essence of the bullfight: the bull murders the horse and eventually dies at the hands of man. Nobody protects the horse. He is sacrificed for the ultimate show between matador and bull.

A totem that migrated with invading armies and peoples from the eastern shores of the Mediterranean to Gibraltar and the Iberian Peninsula, the bull as ritual object derives from the religious rituals of Ancient Crete, Persia, Rome, and Iberia. Pablo Picasso knew well the meaning of the bull to the ancient Mediterranean world. Although already exiled from Spain for several decades, he heard of a Mithraic image, dating from the second century CE, discovered in 1952 in the fields near Cabra along the Guadalquivir: "a bull overthrown and sprawled on the ground in his death throes, while a young hero on horseback leans down, though his eyes are turned to the sky, to thrust a wide knife into the beast's neck."[67] Picasso's father taught him that the dance of death between *torero/a* and bull, which mimics the movements of the *bailaor* in *los bailes*—the *Farruca* and *Soleá por Bulerías*—represented something sacred. Perhaps he had visited the Mithraic sanctuary at Merida as a child.

> A great kingdom, that of the divine bulls, extends across the Mediterranean world from Asia Minor to Spain.[68]

"The key," writes Vicente Marrero, "to Picasso's vision of the *corrida*, is the myth of dark and light."[69] This notion that the sun—*Helios*—was divine, engaged continuously in a battle with the forces of evil that reside in the darkness, a binary relationship that called the artist to place sun and darkness on opposite ends of the bullring, engaged Picasso in his own cosmic dance, with himself, his families and Spanish history. The myth of the Sun God in a struggle with darkness—represented by a ferocious animal that inspires fear—embodied the human race. The bullring, for the artist, was not simply the primordial site for a spectacle of death but, rather, a locus for the spectacle of life itself, in which a man (the torero) and a bull face off. A cosmic game is constructed such that the myth of light and dark can be played out in public, like a Greek drama.

What Picasso understood about the *corrida* was its essence: a dangerous bull kills a defenseless horse on his way to trying to kill a man who tempts him with a red cape. The closer the man gets to the bull—the closer he is to his own death, physically and spiritually—the greater the ritual response from the audience. For they, too, are essential players in this dance of life and death.

Picasso drew, sculpted, and painted thousands of images of the bull, revisiting in endless repetition the archaic spirit of pre-Islamic and Islamic Mediterranean cultures. Picasso's bull derives from Vedic India, Pharonic Egypt, Babylonia, Crete, and the Muslim Middle East. Deriving its sacred status from its horned—winged—iconographic relationship to the moon and thus to female fertility, Taurus was also the object of cult worship: Mesopotamian, Mithraic, Indo-Aryan, and Grecian.

To Picasso the bull, as animal of blood and earth, was the supreme image of Spain, a symbol of transcendent masculinity, chaos, and destruction. Whether or not he was influenced by the bullfights he attended or the painters who chose to paint the *corrida*, Picasso emphasized the bull's duality: the brutal role it played in

Spanish history alongside the historic, quasi-religious importance of the bull's symbolism to Spanish society. Absorbed through the ages as an Hispanic obsession, the bullfight called Picasso to question on canvas the role of the bull with his cruel domination over and, oftentimes, murderous goring of the horse—Pegasus—a winged, gentle, innocent creature forced into combat with a dangerous force. Picasso's brilliance in representing *la corrida* was in his plastic understanding that the unequal battle between horse and bull was what brought tragedy and pathos to the fight. A helpless, blindfolded creature, the horse has inadequate protection against the raging monster that comes at him. "The horse," said Picasso in describing his most famous *cheval* (*Guernica*), "represents the people. Pain inflicted on the poor, bleeding horse" represented the supreme sacrifice. His role is simply to take the edge off the bull at a cost to him of his life. This bull's death, ultimately, saves the *torero* and from this ritual sacrifice, the crowd draws its catharsis.[70]

Bad person of a bull.[71]

Rafael Alberti

In 1959, Picasso drew a sketch of a picador lying helpless on the ground. To his left lies a wounded horse and, to his right, a bull that lowers his horns in preparation for his goring. In the center is Christ on the Cross. It is an image of a dying God who, with *torero* beneath him, is sacrificed for the public good. Christ unwinds his loincloth, extending it into the shape of a cape in an attempt to divert the bull from the picador and save his life. In the painting of the sketch, Christ merges with the horse, becoming the bullfight, long associated with Christianity and ritual sacrifice.[72]

Guernica

The new bombardment lasted thirty-five minutes, enough to transform the town into an enormous furnace . . . We heard that the glow of the buildings had been seen from Lequito, two kilometers away . . . When it grew dark the flames of Guernica were reaching to the sky and the clouds took on the color of blood, and our faces too shone with the color of blood.

Robert Payne[73]

Guernica, the most ancient town of the Basques and the centre of their cultural tradition, was completely destroyed yesterday afternoon by insurgent air raiders. The bombardment of the open town lasted three hours and a quarter, during which a powerful fleet of aeroplanes consisting of three German types, Junkers and Heinkel bombers and Heinkel fighters, did not cease unloading on the town bombs weighing from 1000 lbs. downward and it is calculated more than 3000 two-pounder aluminum incendiary projectiles. The fighters, meanwhile, plunged low from above the centre of the town to machine-gun those of the civilian population who had taken refuge in the fields. The whole of Guernica was soon in flames except the historic Casa de Juntas, with its rich archives of the Basque race, where the ancient Basque Parliament used to sit. The famous oak of Guernica, the dried old stump of 600 years . . . was also untouched. Here the kings of Spain used to take the oath to respect the democratic rights (fueros) of Vizcaya and in return received a promise of allegiance as suzerains with the democratic title of Señor, not Rey Vizcaya.

London Times[74]

In January of 1937, the socialist Spanish Government in Exile commissioned Picasso to paint a mural for its building at the World's Fair in Paris. The commission required him to "convey in one image the sense of the drama of his fatherland ravished by the fascists."[75] Picasso, already fifty-six years of age and an artist who had mobilized many artistic movements between the nineteenth and twentieth centuries, had not painted in two years. While Picasso had never before accepted a commission, news of the Spanish Civil War, its fatalities and the possibility that Spain's socialist government might collapse, moved him and he began work on the enormous oil painting.

The subject was the Spanish Civil War and the technique was Cubism, Picasso's language of modern art. Picasso executed the first sketch for *Guernica* on 1 May, five days after the town was savaged by Hitler's pilots flying for Franco. Picasso painted from the description in the newspaper. The airplanes bombed during the day when families were out walking around town and men were in the fields working. The death toll for women and children was high. Franco sent an unmistakable signal: "devastation of a peaceful human community . . . brutality in its universal sense . . . in the consciousness of every Spaniard, the town of Guernica symbolized ancient pride and freedom."[76] Picasso chose a single light bulb, placed above the animal/human dying figures, to symbolize the bombing.[77]

Picasso, child of the century, in painting terrible, repellent bulls expresses a truth regarding the period of history in which we all must live. His protest and revolt are the protest and revolt of the artist.[78]

Vicente Marrero

One afternoon in the south of France, Picasso's best friend from Malaga, Manuel Ortíz, also a painter following in his fellow Malagueñan's cubist, footsteps, came down from Paris to visit. A great lover of *cante jondo*, Ortíz pulled up a chair and sang *soleás* for Picasso and friends. "My husband loved flamenco," his wife has said. "Touring flamenco artists—Gypsies—used to visit his studio in Paris. They would sing and play and dance into the night. See this wooden floor, it resonates. Perfect for flamenco!"[79] Did Picasso hear the Gypsy cry—the famous *queíjo*—as he painted *Guernica*? Jackson Pollock criticized Picasso for using epic figurative representation—narrative—in *Guernica*. He and Clement Greenberg thought of it as old school.[80] Maybe they did not understand. Maybe flamenco's "Black Sounds" were as inspiring to Picasso as jazz was for Pollock.

Guernica, Pablo Picasso's poetic, Surrealist, epic *homenaje* to death and the destruction of democratic hope in Spain, resonates with the Gypsy *Siguiríya*. Descendent from Sephardic, Hispano-Arab quasi-religious chanting, the *Siguiríya* embodies the geographic cry. Sharp black lines that outline figures' anatomy "stab like arrows into the sensitive points" of the image, criss-cross like roads in a frenzy of human death traffic. "A hymn to Mediterranean man," *Guernica* represents the artist, a "perpetual traveler" across his own animated scene.[81] Filled with pain and death, its Hispanic imagery symbolizes this Catalonian apocalypse—the day the earth came to a standstill. Even the background, on top of which the figures literally rest, has a deep black hue, pushing the victims' oversized white faces into relief like a newspaper article. It takes an electric light, situated to the left of center and a woman carrying a candle, to bring any clarity of vision at all.[82]

This white on black or white from black effect both animates and dehumanizes the scene, giving it the power of myth. The story within the canvas moves like an animated strip from right to left, death blow to death blow, pulsing with tragic overtones in black, gray and white, "a chromatic mysticism," a eulogy to the dead.[83] Like flamenco's Africanist polyrhythms, *Guernica*'s multiple shades echo semiotically the clashing, crashing sounds that leave the *cantaor*'s lips.

A gray window hovers above the desperate cries of a woman whose outstretched arms and splayed hands are painted with shades of white as if to lace her skin with innocence. The warrior holds out his dead hand revealing a *stigmata* embodying the pain and suffering of Christ and of Spain. Toward the middle of the painting, a sliver of a white wall emerges out of the darkness, only to be plunged at its lower half back into gray and then submerged in the dark black of the ground. One of the central figure's faces, mouth gaping as if in shock, floats through the air, her skin porcelain white. Does she bear witness to the tragedy or is she swept up into its deathblow? A collapsed house crushes another woman, pressing her breasts into the ground. Her rounded neck tries to support her tiny face a little while longer.

While *Guernica* is filled with mythic association, its design is boldly abstract. Fragments of concrete reality merge with abstract expression. We read and feel the women's pain and suffering but, as a picture plane with no depth, the painting's figurative associations, the synthesis of space and volume, and the weight of the primitive as representation confuse and mystify us.[84] We stand back in wonder at its atavistic essence.

For Mérimée, Picasso, and Lorca the bull symbolized a totemic geography, a signifier for country, nation, history, memory, and space imaged by the bullring. Its body is the size of Spain, what Garcia Lorca referred to as a bull's hide. Its head contains the twin symbols of the ancient fertility cults: crescent moons carrying wisdom and power, femininity and masculinity. To Lorca, the bullring, shaped like a full moon, symbolized an ancient temple, a ring-altar where, in Iberian times, sacrifices to the mother goddess occurred at specific moments of the year.

In Picasso's work, the many strands of this totemic geography, ancient and modern, are bound together by the themes of the masculine mortal bull and the eternal female Carmen, both a symbol of the reincarnation of the Mediterranean goddess and of the destitute Gypsy, forever on the move.

CHAPTER SEVEN

Space and Place in Islamic Spain

THE ARCHEOLOGY OF FLAMENCO

The essence of life is a feeling of participation in the flowing onward [history] expressed in terms of space. The poetic image offered takes root in us, bringing out the quality of the original . . . we begin to have the impression that we created it.

Gaston Bachelard, *The Poetics of Space*, 1964

Inside the artist is the spectator — the painting has been there before inside of them — the first spectator of the work is the artist. As the artist made the painting, he/she viewed it moving toward the spectator's vision of viewing and the spectator thus retrieves the experience of the painter upon first viewing — this forges communion with the artist seeing-in — the capacity for seeing the work as representing human emotion.

E. H. Gombrich, *Art & Illusion*, 1964

Let us retrace our steps through the architecture and landscapes of Mozarabic Spain, as a path to kinesthetic empathy with the Gypsy experience and a movement toward the archeology of flamenco. Gypsy Flamenco developed in the whitewashed pueblos along the Iberian Peninsula, in particular in Seville, the city of Carmen's birth.[1] This chapter explores how the Hispano-Arab culture of Islamic Spain influenced the use of poetry, song, and choreography in the art of flamenco.

In its incorporation of Mozarabic architecture into physical expression and ritual chant, Gypsy flamenco becomes an historical and artistic reflection of the Sephardic, Christian, and Muslim civilizations — civilizations that pre-existed the world into which Gypsies traveled in 1423.[2]

"Islamic Spain" also refers to two Arabic phrases: Mudejar—art influenced by Muslim-ruled Spain—and Mozarabic—the Christian, Sephardic and Muslim cultures influenced by Arab rule. Mozarabic influence is reflected throughout the poetry, songs, architecture, dance, and languages of Andalusia. Arabic was the *lingua franca* of Andalusia and could be heard on the streets of Granada well into the early sixteenth century.[3] In the years preceding the Expulsion of the Jews in 1492 and the conquest of Granada, Andalusia became the geographic focus for the cultural development of Gypsy Flamenco.[4]

Gypsy *toque*, *cante*, and *baile* evoke an earlier time; these arts express a Middle Eastern quality of singing and dancing whose ethos lies in sacred chant and tribal ritual. Flamenco music and dance are, in large part, creations of the Middle Eastern Islamic and Arab cultures through which the Gypsies passed in Persia, Egypt, and North Africa on their way to southern Spain.

Flamenco choreography, in particular, represents a mapping of space and needs to be re-read in a larger context than previous flamenco scholarship has established. This reading requires in particular a reflection of the Islamic architectural tradition whose *alcazars*—public buildings—were frequented by *all* peoples living in medieval Andalusia. Flamenco's ornamental, gestural vocabulary known as *floreo y braceo*—a flowering of the hands, wrists, and arms—reflects the Islamic architectural archive of southern Spain. It also reverberates the musical and poetic languages whose inscriptions are to be found on the walls of its public, secular buildings, libraries, nature walks, and fountains, as well as its sacred spaces, such as mosques and their minarets. The physical geography or architecture of the body in flamenco—in the Gypsy *Siguiríya*, for example—recalls the spatial design of *mesquitas* in Cordoba and Granada; that is to say, a *bailaora*'s use of torso, hands, and feet expresses a physical historiography that resonates with the Mozarabic architectural legacy of medieval Spain.

In order to elucidate and clarify the way in which we understand or view "Gypsyism" and our larger concept of Gypsy geography, it is necessary to recall the multiple paths of Islam as it penetrated and spread across the Middle East and North Africa. Let us first define medieval Muslim Spain. Mozarabic connotes "People of the Book"—Christians and Jews who lived with religious tolerance in a Muslim-ruled society. Mozarabic geography extended in space and time from the first Spanish Muslim city, Madinat 'al-Zahra in the eighth century near modern Cordoba, to the city of Granada, surrendered by the last Muslim Caliph living in Spain, Boabdil—Mohammed Abu Abdullah, "el chico,"—on 2 January 1492.[5]

Gypsy Girl Dancing in the Sand [at the annual Gypsy pilgrimage to the
Feast of Saintes-Maries de la Mer, France], photographer and date unknown.
Roger-Viollet Archives, Paris, France

The Creation of a Hispano-Arab Geography

Let us understand the conquest of southern Spain and France by Arab and Berber forces. The eighth-century army described by Arab geographers as an extraordinarily well-organized military force rose in the year 710 in the Atlas Mountains and landed at the southernmost tip of the Iberian Peninsula, pushing north in successive military campaigns through the Christian Visigothic kingdom and Provençe, conquering Nîmes and Narbonnes and eventually reaching Poitiers and Tours. Historian Henri Pirenne describes in *Mohammed and Charlemagne* the first famous battles between Muslims and Christians on European soil.[6] These early eighth-century campaigns, organized from the seat of Muslim power in Damascus, entailed thousands of Arab and Berber soldiers enlisted by their military leaders to fight Christian armies.[7] The idea was not necessarily to remain in Spain but to convert all of Christendom to the belief in the "one, true God: Allah."

Muslim Middle Eastern culture had a profound impact on Visigothic Spain. The culturally rich civilization of Iberia was a coalescence of many other cultures past and contemporary: Phoenician, Greek, Roman, Gothic, and Iberian. Muslim Spain conquered and assimilated civic and rural cultures whose economies depended upon the fertility of a land that produced wine and olives and still used the aqueducts, roads, buildings, art, languages, and religions of the older society. This complex economic and cultural synthesis created a heterogeneous and wealthy Andalusian society.

One of the most compelling arguments for a continuous historiography between the world into which Gypsies settled in the early fifteenth century and their present-day performative language as seen in Andalusia comes from North African cultural practice itself. While reading of the first of many expulsions of Muslim Spaniards from Spain in 1508 in the excellent histories by Richard Fletcher and Bernard Lewis, I came across a memory box. Both describe the foyers of North African families whose lineage once extended to 'al Andaluz. In homes in Marrakech and Fez, "keys to properties in Almería or Ronda, Malaga and Granada, hung in readiness for a return to 'al Andalus." Al-Maqqari's history of the Maghreb (1630), describing the Maghreb reaction to the departure of the Muslims from Spain, noted: "may Allah return it to Islam," referring to her coastal cities.[8]

A powerful historical connection that links the memory of Mozarabic civilization with flamenco is the metaphysical idea, expressed architecturally, of the Muslim portal as window to God. Architecture here is not a static physical entity but a gateway—a place to move through toward spiritual consciousness.

I believe that this meditative choreography/architecture is found throughout the five musical sections of deep song *soleá* dancing and is echoed in the high cries of the *cantaor*. Bachelard reflects:

> To isolate the transforming action of the poetic imagination in the detail of the variation of the images . . . To consider an image not as an object and even less as the substitute for an object, but to seize its specific reality. For this, the act of the creative consciousness must be systematically associated with the most fleeting product of that consciousness.

Flamenco is an act of creative consciousness that houses architectural memory. It is not an icon of worship, but rather a performative enactment, "a fleeting product of consciousness" for both the Gypsy and the spectator.

The Great Mosque of Cordoba

The center of Islam shifted from Damascus to Baghdad after the fall of the Middle Eastern Umayyad Caliphate in 750 and its subsequent rise in Spain under its sole surviving relative: Abd 'al Rahman I.[9] The architecture of Cordoba reflects the commercial, cultural, and religious life of Baghdad, its larger and more powerful sister-city to the East. "Drawing the city to the banks of the Quadalquivir River," Abd 'al Rahman's 785/786 construction of a place of Muslim identity and spiritual tranquility, the mosque became a symbol for Christians, Jews, and Muslims of a "Muslim presence on the Iberian Peninsula."[10] The history of the mosques "chronicles the development of a Muslim language of forms on the western frontier of Islam and the creation of potent visual symbols" that were abstract.[11] What are the principal architectural forms of the mosque and how might they resonate with flamenco?[12]

Like the *mesquita* in Cordoba, flamenco embodies an auditive metaphor for time and space. Its essential properties are Middle Eastern, homegrown in Islamic Spain with sounds and physical embodiments — a predatory circling of the stage, the self-isolation of prayer and devotional ritual practice, a firm pressing by the dancer's feet and legs of weight into the floor, a non-western practice of connecting body to earth, soul to music, that surrounds the dancer rather than drops from heaven above. The emotionally and physically explosive qualities build slowly in the dance through repetition and inwardly directed concentration — away from the audience and toward self-reflection exposed to the *umma* that surrounds the stage.[13]

Soledad Barrio, Soleá, performance by Noche Flamenca,
New York City, 2006.

The Cordoban mosque's prayer wall, stunning in its design and largesse, consists of ten arcades of twelve bays each scattered throughout the main hall, dispersed to the western eye in a random manner that allows no single focal point. Walking through it, I was awestruck at the sight of the arches—nine hundred in all—that "depend upon the repetition of a single support" structure to create a hall for community prayer.[14] Dizzying in their monumental profile of slender, semi-circular arches that cut through the space with alternating *voussoirs* of deep red and black brick and cool white stone, these horseshoe shapes embody a three-dimensional maze in which "constant echoes of arches and unruly staccato colors confuse the viewer, presenting a challenge."[15] An intellectual dialogue is built here between building and spectator that evolves as the person who inhabits the space is slowly transformed by the hallucinatory and therefore meditative quality of the building.[16] Begun by 'al Rahman I in the design of his family's Damascan mosque as a strong symbolic reminder, the internal, illusive qualities of the Cordoban structure psychologically transform anyone who walks through the space, confirming the arrival of the Umayyad caliphate from the East to the southwestern reaches of Europe. The sheer power of this structure as a central place for anyone passing through 'al Andaluz is breathtaking.[17]

In the early ninth century, continuing his father's magnanimous legacy, Abd 'al Rahman II added Persian music to the development of an emerging Islamic Spanish culture along the Iberian Peninsula. Thought to be the finest poet/singer alive for having memorized ten thousand songs, a Persian-trained musician by the name of Ziryab (b. 789), known as "the black nightingale," arrived in Andalusia at the Caliph's invitation in the early ninth century. Ziryab, who some think might have been an African slave, was learned in the Persian musical style heard today in flamenco.

Ziryab brought a Persian instrument—the lute—to which he added a fifth string: this became a precursor of the modern guitar. He also imported the Persian *melismata*, a hypnotic, twenty-two-count song cycle that later inspired Sufi musicians. Like flamenco *cante*, Sufi-inspired mystical phrases, as in the poetic songs of Ziryab, told stories of human emotion—love, anger, loss, love of God—as does contemporary flamenco. Further, as in classical and scriptural Islamic literature, poetic stanzas referred to daily experience and heroic tales. Poems symbolized historical documents that, like flamenco *cante*, revealed a history and culture of Middle Eastern and Persian descent. "The poet, in Moorish culture, represented history and was woven into court society and left a geographer a reflection of the times."[18]

A ninth-century Arab geographer, Ibn Qutayba, described poetry as follows:

> Poetry is the mine of knowledge of the Arabs, the book of their wisdom, the muster roll of their history . . . the rampart protecting their heritage . . . the truthful witness on the day of dispute . . . he who binds [history] with rhymed verse, knots them with scansion and makes them famous through a rare line. . . . made eternal against time, preserved them from negation, averted the plot of the enemy and lowered the eye of the envious.[19]

The historical influence of Persian poetic and musical culture on an emerging Andalusian culture can be traced through a study of flamenco. I look to phenomenological ideas to connect the obvious Middle Eastern and Persian resonance in flamenco to its Islamic Spanish past. What first led me to this exploration was the carving of space and contemplative gesture that dominate flamenco. These seemed to me to represent quasi-religious, and, at times inside a solo dance, transcendental acts of performance, complex in geography and public meditation. No other dance form in the world houses dancers—male and female—who use the stage as a bullring. Suzanne Langer describes a "magic circle" in which the dancer centers, re-centers, and centers again, walking around the space clockwise and then counterclockwise, marking personal time with each step she takes and reconfiguring her place on stage in a confessional manner. This mapping allows the audience to see this very private meditation as musicians tune and retune their instruments waiting for a moment of blowout—of transcendence, or *duende*. To me, these motions embody meditation, creation, contemplation, and worship. Paradoxically, they enable agency for the subaltern while simultaneously expressing layered historical meaning, including architectural meaning, cultural amalgamation, and feminist consciousness. It is an archival dance of survival.

The Gypsy *Siguiríya* and the Dialectics of Islamic Space

The dance is essentially a personal prayer, or *Du'a*, in Arabic, despite the pressure of musicians and audience. It begins and ends in choreographic meditation, building in intensity as the dancer expands into space to the accompaniment of *cantaor* or *muezzin*, and collapsing in exhaustion back into private space, resonating with *desplante*, the finale of five movements of a flamenco cycle that embodies the end of a spiritual journey taken with caller and musician. As in Persian music or calls to prayer, five movements define five places on stage and five newly begun sections of the dance phrasing. At the beginning of each movement, the *bailaora* circles

Soledad Barrio, Siguiríya, performance by Noche Flamenca, New York City, 2006.

around herself, at times with outstretched arms that seem to beckon the audience into her private space—the space closest to her body. At other moments, with downcast eyes and a rapacious circling around herself (as if she were devouring herself), the singer knows that she is signaling the *cantaor* to sing for her. Hitting the ground with her right foot so that the nails in her shoe resound, she calls to him—*una llamada*—to begin his storytelling.

As in *Qu'ranic* verse, the *cante* in the *Siguiríya* solo performance is entirely metaphorical with hints of place and time. Its metric beat keeps time for dancer and singer but its abstract wordplay, delivered inside complex *compás* (Gypsy rhythms), presents a puzzle for the outsider. Here, again, flamenco resonates with a Middle Eastern value: the power and beauty of the sound of poetry in tandem with musical accompaniment is considered high praise of the listener as, in its inherent religiosity, it is a call to God.

Like the red, white, and black repetition in color and line discovered throughout Andalusian mosques—columns that swing wildly up into nine hundred repetitions of cross-vaulted arches or just drop into the floor—a spatial design is reflected both in building construction and in the richly textured arabesques created by *bailaora*.

Like no other dance in the flamenco canon, the *Siguiríya* is a confessional dance of devotion: devotion to rhythm, to dancing, to space. It is, at its base, a dance of worship: worship of the song—its poetry and poetic phrasing; worship of the rhythm and its intricacies; and worship of one's ability to mark time in new ways. The dance, descendent from the Moorish *Zambra*, is a call to prayer: a personal devotion expressed publicly on stage. The *cantaor*, like the Muslim *muezzin* and the Sephardic *chazan*, calls to the dancer five times, as the people of Cordoba were called five times to pray toward Mecca.

Like the Great Mosque at Cordoba, the most ancient of the flamenco dances, the *Siguiríya*, has a structure that expresses religious intensity and spatial patterning. Dizzying in its rhythmic complexities like the horseshoe arches of the first Muslim mosque, *mesquite*, in Cordoba, the *Siguiríya* is one of the oldest dances in the Gypsy pantheon, its roots reaching back to the early Hispano-Arab dances.[20] In its rhythmic structure, the *Siguiríya* is inspired by the Muslim-Sephardic *cante*, the *Saete*, which University of Seville-based flamencologist Gerhard Steingrass claims contains the chanting of the Kol Nidre service and the high-pitched, nasal *queíjo*, or lament/cry to prayer, performed by Muslim *muëzzin*, or cantor, from atop the minaret.[21]

Dance and Song as Portals to God

The *Siguiríya* is a private meditation between singer and dancer that recalls a His-pano-Arab-Sephardic past.[22] (*Sepharad*, or *Sefarad*, means Spain in Hebrew.) Like sister musical forms that date from medieval Mozarabic Spain—the *zambras, zarabandas, pandas de verdiales, cañas, tiranas, jaberas, malagueñas, calescras, zorongas,* and various solo *cantes*—the *Siguiríya* represents an historical document, evidence of the "Oriental music" that survives inside of flamenco.[23] This living archive is notable for its use of microtones—tones smaller than a semitone sliding from one tone to another. These tonal scales repeat a single sound over a long period of time, lending a hypnotic quality to the singing and guitar playing. Melodies "flow within a small tonal range rather than jump by large intervals. The use of microtonal and semi-tonal ornamentation gives expressiveness to the music as does the use of a descending cadence (in conjunction with the phyrigian mode)."[24] There is a lack of harmonization on the part of the singer and guitarists—that is to say, the music sounds melodic, not harmonic. Complex rhythms and cross-rhythms—harsh, nasal-sounding tones, vocally and instrumentally—can be heard in a single performance. And tuning on stage during performance—opening up the process of musical creation to the audience—creates an emphasis on the emotional quality of the playing and of the timbre of the music.[25]

The *muezzin*'s call to prayer, what Bachelard might refer to as a "sonority of being," an offering to the people of *élan vital* (vital aliveness in space and time that is infinite and the essence of that call)—is echoed clearly by the *cantaor* in *cante jondo.* He cries, *Olé!* as the guitarists tune. The word derives from the Arabic *Allah,* and thus the sacred nature of this musical *cantiga* is confirmed.

> If in connection with poetic images we are able to isolate a sphere of pure sublimation; of a sublimation that sublimates nothing, which is relieved of the burden of passion and freed from the pressure of desire . . . by thus giving to the poetic image at its peak an absolute sublimation, I place heavy stakes on a simple nuance. The poetic image is under the sign of a new being.[26]

Bachelard's notion of "poetic image" refers to visual metaphor or imagined space/place, sparked from an extreme attention to detail, to nuance, to the language of the perceived, not the perceiver. I borrow this term, the poetic image (quite similar in spirit to Benjamin's "dialectical image"), to connect the physical, psychic, musical, memorialized relationship of the singer and dancer in flamenco to

Soledad Barrio, Siguiríya, performance by Noche Flamenca, New York City, 2006.

the complex Mozarabic language of architectural form found in Andalusia. Outdoor space in Mozarabic Spain was filled with the beauty of nature—fountains, ponds, plants, trees, walkways that created a harmonious relationship between the individual and the world. Indoor space was defined by the "codification of an early Islamic space for prayer without the intervention of clergy or liturgy," a place of communal gathering unaffected by hierarchy and transformative in its transcendent use of space and light.[27] In its choreography and music, flamenco holds both of these ideals in the bounds of form, translating into deep song tradition the architecture, poetic meter, and civic life of Muslim Spain.

Mosque architecture, experienced by anyone who has wandered through Andalusian public spaces, gives the individual spectator a sensation of an all-pervading light. This diffusion of light awakens a particular physical sensibility in the *flâneur*, who walks through the architectural remains of Andalusian *mesgrids*, or mosques. The play of light and space in the Cordoban *mesquita*, in particular, generates a metaphysical sensation of energy in the viewer that leads to the perception that one stands in a holy place. Perhaps such an experience is what Bachelard, Bergson, and others refer to as *élan vital*, an energy that gives the spectator a sense of liminality, a bridge between intervals of pasts and presents. Its essence is what Bachelard calls a "threshold of being" that joins the present body to its surrounding space, including its layered past, in harmonious union.[28]

A maze-like prayer hall housing an immense open space divided by alternating shapes, ornament—latticework—and columns that dizzy the eye and quiet the mind, the Cordoban mosque's immense hall creates a non-verbal dialogue between the viewer and the structure. Empty niches pointing east, toward Mecca, express the purpose of the hall even in the absence of its original architects and inhabitants. Walls lined with Koranic verses chiseled into stone and painted gold stand in relief as light seems to emanate from underneath the letters, giving the viewer the impression, like the space in which the characters reside, that the words of God are floating. They look like "letters of light" to anyone who circles the columns on which they are inscribed.[29]

Flamenco also carries a scriptural language, spelled out by hands and arms, eyes and feet as the dancer traces centrifugal shapes around her head, body, and surrounding space. The internalization of the inherently contemplative design of Muslim architecture by anyone who wanders through a *mesquita* is reflected in the physical design of the body moving through space in flamenco *soleá*. The *bailaora* seems to embrace this sense of transformative space filled with ornamental intricacies as she slowly surrounds her own body with stylized arm and hand shapes and motions, akin to the complex, enfolding latticework found at the tops of arches and columns in Mudejar art.[30]

Extending out into space, she forms tiny *rondes de jambe* with her toes and legs. In a meditative motion, the dancer constructs an S with her slowly moving limbs, creating shapes that embrace the surrounding space. She reaches out to the four corners of the earth, dragging each corner closer through sustained toe-tracing shapes along the floor, pulling the space into herself until she is exhausted from the movements' ritualistic repetition, a mapping of space and self.

Is the self-enclosure by the dancer an attempt to hide or to express? Perhaps a study of Andalusian structures may reveal the historical relationship between dance and architecture. Andalusian homes house inner spaces, hidden from the street: enclosed patios (in Arabic, *fondak*) with fountains and plants—a reflection of how Mozarabs "took root in their corner of the world." (The very word for garden, *jardin*, is an Arab word.) It is the woman who gestures so intimately with her body; sustaining these arm gestures throughout long solo performances, she reminds us

Soledad Barrio, Soleá, performance by Noche Flamenca, New York City, 2006.

of the femininity of the home—a feminine space, secluded and hidden, as isolated as the *bailaora* becomes as she falls into a trance.[31] Whenever the male singer walks toward her, she hides her face, turning quickly around so that he cannot lay eyes on her. As he follows her around the space, she quickens her step, separating herself from him. She holds forcefully to her own space.[32] It is a personal, meditative space that she designs for herself, an empowering self-isolation.

The intended seclusion of women designed and ensured by the *fondak* is both absorbed and erased by the flamenco dancer as she circles around herself, gesturing to the surrounding space, beckoning it with outstretched fingers, hands, and slow articulations of her wrists. Why do we say erased? The non-Muslim, non-Sephardic, Gypsy flamenco dancer performs, perhaps unknowingly, a destruction of the seclusion of women. She rescues the freedom of the architecture and extends it to women, metaphorically returning their spatial deprivation while celebrating (subliminally) the rich Islamic cultural legacy that remains in the ruins. It is as if she absorbs the architectural space around her, transplanted now to a stage space, repeating the ritual feeling of wandering through the *mesgrid* or *mesquita* in the choreography of her solo meditation.

Music also reflects a Muslim past. The *cantaor*, whose chant and verse embody historical reflections of the Muslim court *rawi*, reciter of poems and songs, holds the history of his people in his song. A material reality, the *cantes*, or songs, chronicle the history of the Gypsy people in accompaniment to the dancer's physical tracings of space in time and place. The actual choreographic gesturing of the dancer becomes a material reminder of the sacred, public (mosques, plazas), and private (gardens, caves) spaces through which Gypsies passed in tri-cultural, fifteenth-century Spain.

While we have been tracing all possible contours of Carmen's body and Gypsy geography, we cannot overlook the importance of the *cantaor(a)* to history, though he/she may remain unnamed. From one perspective, this figure is the animus, the necessary companion to Carmen's anima, for dance and song are like a couple, who call and respond to one another, carrying history within.

One further phenomenological connection resonating in flamenco *baile* is in the masculine dance: the *farruca*. Like the minaret that shoots up into the sky, the *bailaor* effortlessly and repetitively rises onto the tips of his boots, extending his whole body up, reaching for the sky with extended, sharp gestures. He then promenades slowly around himself, distilling his cool balance and male bravura into an image of controlled self-inscription. Carmen shares this masculinity, like the matador, in her very strength, brutality, and flirtation with death.

The *Siguiríya* represents an atavistic flamenco dance whose sheer, explosive rhythmic sequences repeat five times throughout a *soleá*, building in intensity as the dancer reaches the end of a performance—blowout, transcendence, *duende*. This final *desplante*—a moving into the earth—carries the audience on a journey with dancer, singer, and guitarist that communicates to the spectator the transcendental quality of the dance. Descended from the Moorish *Zambra*, these Hispano-Arab-inspired solo performances are considered by Andalusian scholars to come from the eighth century.

Gaston Bachelard explored the notion of poetic imagination. He saw a "fundamental reverie" or imagined memory as one's psychophysical connection to space. People, he argued, experience space on sensorial and metaphysical grounds that recall place, time, and memory.[33] What poetic effect did Muslim architecture have on the creation of Gypsy choreographic design? If Bachelard is correct, then one's experience of form generates imagined landscapes. It is this rich historic complexity that touched and intrigued Mérimée and Bizet as each sought to capture the essence and mystery of Carmen.

Studying Carmen is a task of bringing what Benjamin calls the "dialectical image to its legibility in the present." Could Bachelard's notion of a "spatialization of time" open new ways of understanding this? Gypsy geography as an evocation of the ancient? Gaudin raises an important point with the concept of "image-language"—allowing something to speak in the double voice of the past and present. At its most essential, entering into the image of history, in this case through performance, allows the viewer an "excavation" instead of a mere "reading." It is what Walter Benjamin hoped to reveal in his quoting of Jules Michelet: "Each epoch dreams the one that follows."[34]

What is Gypsy geography? It is a moving architecture, a theatre of nomadology, a borderless stage that spills into Spanish history, pushing against more colonial interpretations. It is a living, breathing space that may not appear on any map but whose historiography or meta-geography is repetitive, alive, and vital to an understanding of history itself.

CHAPTER EIGHT

Carmen, a Close Reading of a Nomadic Opera

As described in Chapter 2, the first performance of *Carmen* was a flop. Its disastrous reception killed Bizet, who was heartbroken and ill at ease with the press. Today, the global list of past and present *Carmen*s since its 1875 premiere is extensive — a genealogy in itself. With HD movie-theater screenings, it now reaches an enormous audience, unimaginable in Bizet's time. Performed annually in almost every opera house in the world, *Carmen* has become a global cultural phenomenon that has traveled well beyond its genesis as a great work of both literary and musical composition.

The very diversity of *Carmen*'s production history — its repetition and difference — is key to understanding its nature. *Carmen* maintains a consistent live stage presence in ballet, flamenco, modern dance, film, and street genres such as hip hop. Bizet's score has been fused with myriad forms of music. Contemporary avant-garde directors admire *Carmen*'s malleability, opening pathways for performance in new media, open-air festivals, public film screenings, and even sidewalk presentations.

Just as Gypsies absorbed and assimilated cultural artifacts such as dance and music from the many lands through which they traveled, *Carmen,* the opera and Carmen, the spirit-being have been appropriated and renewed as a cross-cultural phenomenon. Carmen now moves in reverse, seeking to pollinate the global cultures from which she emerged many centuries ago. *Carmen* itself is nomadic and ubiquitous.

As a compelling work of art, *Carmen* can be neither confined nor retained as something solely French or Parisian. There is no definitive *Carmen*. One discerns in each performance the subliminal desire on the part of the director and conductor to seek points of contact with the 1875 premiere. *Carmen*'s first Carmen, Célestine

Galli-Marié, embodied the Gypsy woman Mérimée had imagined, robust with tremendous *élan vital*.[1] While these first thirty-three performances were deemed disastrous by the conservative French press, Galli-Marié was in fact the first in a succession of great Carmens. Bizet imagined a dancing Carmen—a Gypsy dancer—mobile, ever-changing, unattainable, and Galli-Marié, to a certain extent, fulfilled his Romantic vision. Her performance became the kernel for the future success of the opera.[2]

Carmen has no walls, no borders, no boundaries, no "correct" manner of staging and production. It is a story that lends itself to any culture. *Carmen* and Carmen have been used for every imaginable social, cultural, aesthetic, political, and ideological purpose. Before analyzing possible reasons for the unanticipated proliferation of *Carmen*, let us lay out several key markers in the production history of the opera. What follows is a description of heightened moments in several especially powerful performances in the recent past.

Karmen Gei

In 2001, Senegalese director Joseph Gaï Ramaka directed *Karmen Gei*. Here we find a bisexual Carmen, her Africanist presence introduced to us within an immense drum circle of polyrhythmic intensity. Unlike Bizet's version of the story, in Ramaka's, Karmen's prison warder is a lesbian with whom she sleeps in the hopes of being released from jail. A powerful contemporary interpretation of the Mérimée tale, *Karmen Gei* so enraged local chiefs that they firebombed movie theaters in Dakkar, causing the film to be banned throughout Africa.

In the first scene, Ramaka transformed the tobacco factory into the sandy plaza of a women's prison located along the Senegalese coast, from whence slave ships once departed. We find Karmen seated, dressed in long black robes. Smiling, she opens and closes her legs provocatively, revealing a bright red underskirt. Barefoot, she slowly rises and begins to dance with rhythmic intensity, gyrating her hips to the percussive sounds of brass band and African drums. Encouraged by her fellow prisoners' whistles and screams, Karmen performs a virtuosic solo. Catching sight of the warden, Karmen fixes her gaze on her, moving slowly toward her to invite her to dance. Karmen moves closer to the warden, lifting her by the chin out of her chair, bestowing on her sexual advances. They dance until a whistle blows and the prisoners rush into the jail. In the following scene, Karmen enters the warden's bedroom where she offers her sexual favors. Afterward, Karmen finds a gate left ajar and, thus, she escapes.

Alberto Alonso's *Carmen Suite* Ballet

In 1967, at the height of the Russo-Cuban political alliance, Cuban choreographer Alberto Alonso (brother of Alicia, one of Fidel Castro's supporters)[3] reinterpreted *Carmen* for *prima ballerina assoluta* Maya Plisetskaya, known for her political activism and courage.[4] Alonso's *Carmen*, part pointe ballet, part Spanish bravura, is a powerful commentary on authoritarian surveillance, set inside a bullring whose wooden slats rise high above the stage. The top of the arena — a ritualistic semi-circular amphitheater — holds twelve chairs with tall, thin backs. In each chair sits a masked man who stares down at the *corrida* where Carmen, now a sacrificial subject, dances. Like a row of tarot cards in a Roman coliseum, they will decide her fate. Trapped inside the ring, Carmen dances the narrative of *Carmen*. A blood-red background illuminates the bullring; its massive size foretells the violent death to come.[5]

Carmen in the French Corrida

In a number of southern French nineteenth-, twentieth- and twenty-first-century productions of *Carmen*, real bullfights occur in the fourth act. Several bulls are killed before Don José murders Carmen.[6] The twin sacrifice of bull and woman symbolizes the appropriation of the violence in *Carmen* into a spectacle that draws thousands. Despite extensive scholarly research, the exact origin of the bullfight-*Carmen* remains a mystery.[7]

Another potent reason for the integration of the *corrida* into the opera is architectural. In both Arles and Nîmes, massive Roman coliseums stand as central architectural monuments. While Nîmes' coliseum is the more impressive, both buildings remain mostly intact, their colossal, ancient sandstone walls and Egyptian-style arches frame the outside of the ring through which the bulls and the opera singers enter. Each building stands as the central physical site of cultural activity and civic, political identity. (Beside the Nîmes coliseum is the city's impressive Musée des Cultures Taurines — Museum of Bullfighting.) Inside, each town remains committed to the ancient Moorish bullfighting tradition that appeared in France in the Middle Ages.[8] Influenced by his hometown's bullfighting culture, Arles-born Christian Lacroix — famous for his high-fashion matador jackets — designed the costumes for a 1989 production of *Carmen* in which both singers and bullfighters wore his ornate, *corrida*-influenced jackets and skirts.

Salvador Tavora's *Carmen*

Yet another significant moment in the history of *Carmen* is the environmental flamenco-theater performance by La Cuadra de Sevilla, directed by Salvador Tavora
in 2001. Tavora's *Carmen*, accompanied by live Spanish and flamenco music and
the recorded music of Bizet's opera score, opens to the blasting cry of thirty-two
cornets, a symbol of Spain's anti-democratic military bands of Franco's era. At
the end of the cornet call-to-arms, Don José enters. He dances a long, intense
footwork sequence, drilling his heels unrelentingly in a show of bravura that
translates as anxious pathos, a sign of his growing obsession that drives the plot of
Carmen. Exhausted, he extracts a large knife from his jacket and plunges it into the
center of the stage. Satisfied, he turns to leave, only to be replaced with a second
calling by the cornet-players, whose sonic blast echoes the tragedy that awaits us.

As the cornets fade, a woman enters, wearing a red dress and a red flower in her
hair. Moving toward center stage, she spies the knife. Stunned at first, she reacts
by lifting her powerful, long arms up to the sky and circling many times around
herself, weaving a protective shield. As she turns to leave, the picador Escamillo,
riding a beautiful white horse, enters. The horse, in a balletic gesture of his leg,
asks her to dance. Carmen, unafraid, mirrors the horse, dancing around him,
then touches his forehead and gestures for the animal to move with her. Carmen
and the horse circle one another many times until the Bizet "Toreador" musical
passages end, and both leave the stage.

Antonio Gades and Christina Hoyos

One of the finest translations of Carmenian themes can be found in a 1969 film
danced by Antonio Gades and Christina Hoyos. The many themes of Carmen as
nomad, as Gypsy, as clairvoyant, as peripheral to society, as artist and as healer,
can be found in the Gypsy *Siguiríya*.

In an empty, white space a male dancer stands looking at his singer. To the
subtle strumming of the guitar, Gades, dressed in the traditional matador costume,
begins to move. In the distance we hear the soft roll of castanets. The camera
pans to reveal a beautiful dark woman wearing a long, white *bata de cola*. Like a
panther seeking its prey, she inches closer, calculating the distance between them.
Aggressive, she thrusts her weight into the ground while lifting her arms out to
the sides. El Lebrijano, one of the greatest of flamenco *cantaors*, calls out to her.
She walks toward the song, in the direction of her partner.

The camera recedes to reveal the serpentine cascade of the *bailaora*'s dress, its length the extension of her body into space. She slides her snake-tail along the floor, walking toward her conquest. Like Carmen after spying Don José, Hoyos circles Gades, checking out his movements in threatening whips of her dress. It is as if she plans to swallow him in the folds of the dress. Tentative, he remains very still. The singer's lamenting voice fills the space with a sad energy that establishes the tragic nature of the *Siguiríya*. He reacts by lifting himself onto his toes like a matador about to charge the bull.

Francesco Rosi's and Antonio Gades' *Carmen*

The final *Carmen* performance to add to this short list of Carmenian moments comes from a 1984 film directed by Francesco Rosi and choreographed by Antonio Gades. While Gades had choreographed *Carmen* for Spanish director Carlos Saura's interesting double-narrative interpretation of the Mérimée/Bizet plot, Rosi's film concentrates solely on the operatic tale. Here we find what nineteenth- and twentieth-century critics considered to be the perfect Carmen: the earthy and dangerous performance by Julia Migenes-Johnson who, unlike most mezzo-sopranos, dances the entire opera, performing barefoot and establishing herself not merely as a vocal power nor a physical beauty, but as a raw, unabashed, and unfettered woman. Migenes-Johnson offers us a portrait of a reverse ethnography: rather than an orientalist tale of *femme fatale*, she dances, sings, and restlessly walks the stage, comfortable nowhere. The power in her dangerous energy and her bold approach to sexuality establish this Carmen as larger than life.

Performing beside the great tenor Placido Domingo, who plays Don José as a meek and desperate character, Migenes-Johnson fulfills her destiny as a dancing sorceress. Rather than retiring to the side of the stage, as do most Carmens, she articulates her nomadic presence in the erotic sway of her hips and the strut of her legs. This Carmen offers the transmutation of the Middle Eastern dancer who has negotiated her peripheral status, ultimately writing her own history.

Soledad Barrio in *Soleá* Inherits the *Mantilla* of the Iconic *Carmen*

The geographical mapping of identity critical to the choreographic art of flamenco, as well as to our understanding of Carmen's Gypsy geography, can be understood through the contemporary, feminist performance of Soledad Barrio. Barrio, more than any other female performer today, commits her onstage being to the archeology of the Gypsy female spirit. In her renowned *Soleá*, performed at New York City's East Village Theatre 80, Barrio explains with subtle, powerful arm and leg movements the dialectical relationship between history and the Gypsy. In so doing, she liberates, as no historian has done, the *gitana* from what Gayatry Spivak calls her "journey of silence."

Barrio stands alone on a darkened stage.[9] She strikes her hands together and follows the timbre by dragging her toe along the floor, drawing small circles in front of her cascading black robe. Turning suddenly away from the audience, she raises her arms and begins to accompany her movements with heelwork — *zapateado*. A guitar strums, signaling the introduction of the *cante*. A singer cries out *alé*, Andalusian for *olé*, meaning "Allah." She stops moving as if listening to the lamentation of one singer who is then joined by a second singer. Both *cantaors* offer Barrio their mournful *melismata*, now a capella, as the guitar strumming has dropped out. As the *cantaors* sing their final notes, the guitarist offers a single chord and Barrio begins to turn again, slowly, around herself, as if drawing a map of the space surrounding her.

Her sensual fingers reach out to test the space around her. She circles herself again, energy exuding from her back. Her gaze is dropped and she moves as if we were not there watching her every gesture. Slowly she walks toward a single offstage light source. She quickens her *floreo*, gesturing with hands and wrists in space and calling her singers to her timing.[10]

She lifts her arms high toward the sky. She is discovering her place on each plane — vertical, horizontal, and sagittal — understanding where she ends and the landscape begins. She walks on the tips of her toes like a matador in the ring approaching the bull, and pulls away quickly as if in fear. With her spatial mapping, she signals the guitarist to change *compás* (rhythms) and explodes into a rapid, quicksilver footwork sequence that sends driving beats into the wooden stage.

Every *escobílla* (entrance into a new phrase) is filled with an intense energy as if she were sinking into the earth. Then abruptly, like a toreador, she circles the bull in its final moments of life.

Barrio then drops out of the musical conversation, silencing her feet and grabbing the air with her hands. But when she looks at her hands, she has nothing in them to show for her efforts.[11] Barrio recovers from the existentialism of her gestural self-confrontation and returns to a series of circular walks. She bends her knees low toward the ground, rising each time by jumping quickly, metallic heels striking the stage as she beats out a harsh counter-rhythm to the lilting sound of the guitar's *rasquedo* (strumming).

The *cantaors* continue to enter and exit the dance, their sonorous presence at times forceful and domineering and, at other moments, subtle and polite. Barrio recaptures our attention over and over as she quickens and slows her heel and toe-work in the famous rhythmic sequence required of a *bailaora* wishing to prove herself in the ring.

As she pulls in from larger arm and hand gestures to tiny, quick beats, she drives into the ground, encircling herself, drawing small and then larger circles, her focus turning further inward. It is as if she is attempting to extinguish herself, sweat pouring down her face, her hair becoming disheveled continuing the pulse of her *zapateado* (footwork). She rests: one *cantaor* calls out to God, *ahhhhhhhhhhh*, singing of the Gypsy barrio of Triana, the space of Carmen's home.

Again Barrio circles the stage, rediscovering a provisional center, and then stops her larger patterns to pay attention only to the space beneath her two feet. She hugs her body tightly, pulling all of her energy as close to her skin as possible, and commences a seemingly endless series of circles around herself, becoming dizzy and almost invisible.[12] Having lost her youthfulness in the exhaustion of her dancing, she hunches over like an old, arthritic woman, grabbing her skirt and showing us the antithesis of the youth she professes at the beginning of her *soleá*. She stands up and breaks in her hips, assuming the position of a Hindu Kathak dancer, a stylized body alien to Western European dance. To the minor-key notes of her guitarists' accompaniment, she begins a Middle Eastern sequence in which she throws her weight not into the floor as a Gypsy usually does but rather into her pelvic region as a Middle Eastern dancer might do.

She brings her dancing to an end, moving as close to one *cantaor* as possible, asking the dance and the song to fuse into an inextricable weave of history and consciousness.

Conclusion

Carmen is an opera, a myth, a story, a legend, a woman, a fictional being—a member of a wandering tribe. In the moment of performance on the global stage, *she* lives, transmigrating from medium to medium, stage to stage, performer to performer. While I embedded feminist perspectives (implicitly rather than explicitly) in the exploration of a diverse set of facets of the prism that is Carmen, it is the focus on notions of performativity by Judith Butler's 1990 *Gender Trouble* that gave me insight into the cultural construction or enactment—in this case, cross-cultural staging—of *Carmen*.[13]

Butler defines performativity—something living in the moment of performance—as a series of stylized, repeated acts. Gender, in Butler's theory, is constructed culturally inside of these moments.[14] If we translate Carmen's dancing, walking, living being on stage into a series of performative actions, then it follows that the historical layers of Carmen become manifest on stage.

At the same time, each actual staging of *Carmen* adds a layer to Carmen's history-as-palimpsest. The variegated strata of the past that have been explored throughout this book emerge as present in performance; conversely, the haecceity of performance draws upon the rich past that extends into "prehistorical" terrains.[15] Geography and temporality are intimately intertwined for Carmen, the Gypsy geographer.

Throughout *Carmen, a Gypsy Geography*, I have attempted to open the field of dance history to the uninscribed. I have taken both historical and aesthetic approaches to the subject of the Gypsy who stands resistant, outside of history. I have done so in order to merge the paradoxical nomadology of the Gypsy aesthetic housed inside *flamenco puro* and the body of Carmen with mythology, feminism, and social history. I finish this chapter with few real answers on the feminist notions of écriture. What seems most apparent at the end of my journey is the idea of the Gypsy artist as historian, writing her own history in the dance, which I take to mean energy flow or migrational route. While I had hoped to unearth these answers in feminist, historical discourse, it was only in the dancing *act* of Carmen's moving body where ultimately I could hope to understand and perhaps even retrace her historical importance. This is not so much an act of retrieval of Gypsy history as an ephemeral moment of bearing witness to her life and its layered meaning.

In the previous chapter, I argued theoretically the possibility that the nomadic movements of the *bailaora* through the sacred, public religious spaces of Hispano-Arab Spain became defining architectural layers surrounding the dancing body. Further, I argued that the inscriptional movements of arms in *flamenco puro* along choreographic planes through which the dancer moves, reconfiguring religious space into artistic space, further define flamenco as emanating not just from the surrounding space but also from the physiognomic space within. *She* moves from the inside out, as do most modern dancers.

I turn now to French philosopher Gilles Deleuze for final thoughts on the nomadology of *Carmen, a Gypsy Geography*.[16]

No more than the transcendental field is defined by consciousness can the plane of immanence be defined by a subject or an object that is able to contain it.[17]

Carmen's shifting layers of Gypsy history reveal that she is caught in the sweep of time. Each *escobílla*—danced phrase—or *llamada*—call to God or to singer and guitarist to change tempi and direction—signal Carmen's attempt to carve out a planar surface through which, in the dance, she passes, thus self-positioning. Her movements flow from her torso, energy radiating out from her arms and legs, crystallizing in centrifugal motions of the wrists and fingers, the bodily architecture of *flamenco puro*. In distilled moments of performance, Carmen sheds her mythic being. She displays anguish and pain at the points in space that trace and thereby remember so much geographic loss. Throughout the course of her dancing, she becomes a generative space for *la gitana flamenca*.

We witness in her *soleá* that her history, while previously unwritten, or rather erased, is emanating from her body, out into the world. Carmen is bearing witness to her own space of being, prescient energy that oozes out of her body, reenacted anew in each turn of the wrist. She turns endlessly, enclosing her self within herself. Carmen's immanence comes to be: geographic layers spinning out from her body, sweat pouring from her skin, peeling back layers of ecstasy and mourning.

Carmen as Gypsy geographer dances on an immanent field that represents her journey. The geometry of her dancing route recapitulates a tribal migration, the memory-path of an historic nomad who, at the core, performs the physiognomic remembrance of the mother goddess.[18] Carmen's body houses a performing history, a moving palimpsest. In Deleuzian conceptual terms, she dances a "pure immanence that is A LIFE . . . A life is the immanence of immanence, absolute immanence: it is complete power, complete bliss."[19]

If she writes, she writes in space. She leaves traces without authorship, writing herself back into time and space, places from which previously she had been ousted by Romanticism, Orientalism, and identity politics that elide performativity as historical agency of the dancing body. Carmen's *way of being*—her dancing—cannot be captured by patriarchal discourse because it evaporates into evanescence. Latent and layered in the body, history only gets written in the act of performance, which is itself ephemeral and yet, paradoxically, leaves a series of traces. We have seen these traces in a *novella*, an opera, the cultures of the ancient Middle East, Islamic Mediterranean dance cafés, the paintings of Picasso, the

LEFT *Gypsy Soloist, Sacromonte, Granada*, photographer and date unknown. Roger-Viollet Archives, Paris, France

BELOW *Hungarian Gypsy Children Dancing*, photographer unknown, 1928. Jacques Boyer / Roger-Viollet Archives, Paris, France

Islamic architectural patterns of southern Spain, the diasporic production history of *Carmen*, and, finally, in the dancing act of the *bailaora*.

Like any skilled nomad, she disappears upon being discovered; she spins and spins throughout her dance only to reconstitute, stilled as the dance comes to its close with the final strumming of the guitar. She perceives new pathways in and out of her body, flowing again into new surroundings. It is not safe to stand still — to be — and, thus, Carmen and *Carmen* keep moving.

Appendix

THE FIRST CAST OF *CARMEN*

The first production was reviewed by Arthur Pougin. *La Chronique Musicale* (15 March 1857), 275–81; Charles de Senneville, "Les Premières," *La Comédie* (14 March 1875). The opera's cast of characters is as follows: Morales, an officer (bass); Micaëla, a peasant girl (soprano); Zuniga, a lieutenant of dragoons (bass); Don José, a corporal of the dragoons (tenor); Carmen, a Gypsy girl (soprano); Mercedes and Frasquita, Gypsy friends of Carmen (mezzo-sopranos); Escamillo, a toreador (baritone); El Remendad and El Dancaïro, Gypsy smugglers (tenor and baritone); cigarette girls, dragoons, Lillas Pastia, smugglers and dancers. The original production, according to records at the Bibliothèque Nationale de l'Opéra, called for 40 male choral members; 38 female choral members; 30 dancers (15 men and 15 women); 20 townspeople and 24 children in Act I; in Act II, 40 male and 38 female choral members; 16 male and female Gypsy dancers; one old woman and one young girl; Act III: 78 male and female smugglers; and 3 guards; Act IV, 40 male and 38 female choral members; 24 townspeople, 6 elegant ladies, 8 background people; female and male dancers consisting of upper-class women, vendors, bullfighters, picadors, and extras; 12 upper-class ladies, 8 soldiers, and one major.

A great deal, as has been noted, has been written about the performance and compositional histories of *Carmen*. The Opéra-Comique version as written by Bizet had only thirty-four performances. The grand opera score is the version performed to this day. Bizet's staging manual is a work that illustrates clearly Bizet's Delsartian search for the perfect synthesis among music, movement, and gesture, as well as a sensitivity to the characters required by the composer of all his principal singers. The difference between the first and second versions of the score has to do with the removal in the grand opera score of the spoken dialogue and the replacement of these parts with sung dialogue. It is important to note that, to this day, the Opéra-Comique theater continues to perform Bizet's version of *Carmen*, with its long passages of spoken versus sung dialogue. Guiraud removed the spoken passages in order to tighten a score that did not go over well with the French public. This version exists to the present day.

Guiraud, while trying to help save his friend's score, was considered to have cut too much. The wonderfully ethnographic detail of Bizet's score, some argue, has been lost in his editing. These musical passages provided "background, explained motivations, or developed character" (*Carmen*, 1875–1969 [Dossier d'oeuvre], BN-Opéra, 75).

Notes

Preface

1. Georges Bizet. "La Habanera," orchestral score for *Carmen*. BN-Opéra [Bizet]. It is interesting to note that Bizet's wife was related to François Delsarte (1811–1871), the Paris Conservatoire professor who helped singers and performers to discover an inner emotional relationship to their bodies, movements, gestures, and rhythm.

2. I spent two years reading the French press's reviews of nineteenth-century productions of *Carmen* at the Opéra-Comique and Paris Opéra. I also studied important *Carmen* choreographers and ballet mistresses, such as La Mariquita, in an attempt to write a history of the evolution of Spanish and Gypsy dance, technique, and style on the French stage.

3. See Chapter 8 for a close reading of Tavora's *Carmen*.

4. Carolyn Abbate, *Unsung Voices: Opera and Musical Narrative in the Nineteenth Century* (Princeton: Princeton University Press, 1991); Catherine Clément, *Opera, or the Undoing of Women* (Minneapolis: University of Minnesota Press, 1988); Mina Curtiss, *Bizet and His World* (London: Secker and Warburg, 1959); Winton Dean. *Bizet* (London: J. M. Dent, 1975); Lou Charnon-Deutsch. *The Spanish Gypsy: A History of a European Obsession* (University Park: Pennsylvania State University Press, 2004); Evelyn Gould, *The Fate of Carmen* (Baltimore: Johns Hopkins University Press, 1996); Susan McClary, *Georges Bizet: Carmen* (Cambridge: Cambridge University Press, 1992).

Theoretical Introduction

1. Richard Ford, *Hand-book for Travellers in Spain and Readers at Home, Describing the Country and Cities* (London: J. Murray, 1845).

2. Gerald Brenan, *The Spanish Labyrinth: An Account of the Social and Political Background of the Civil War* (Cambridge, UK: Cambridge University Press, 1943).

3. Walter Benjamin, "Paralipomena to 'On the Concept of History,'" *Theses on the Philosophy of History* (published posthumously), 403 (hereafter "On the Concept of History").

4. Raymond Carr, *Spain: A History* (Oxford: Oxford University Press, 2000), 6.

5. Here I must also credit the groundbreaking theoretical writing on dance by Susan Foster, *Reading Dancing: Bodies and Subjects in Contemporary American Dance* (Berkeley: University of California Press, 1986), and *Choreographing History* (Bloomington: University of Indiana Press, 1995).

6. Friedrich Nietzsche, *On the Advantages and Disadvantages of History for Life* (1873), quoted by Walter Benjamin in "On the Concept of History."

7. Chris Marker, *Immemory* (liner-notes by blind librarian to interactive CD-rom), 1994: http://www.chrismarker.org/2008/10/immemory-re-released-by-exact-change/.

8. Benjamin, "On the Concept of History," from *Theses on the Philosophy of History*, written in Paris and Lourdes between February and May of 1940, just four months before Benjamin died fleeing the Nazis in the city of Port Bou, in the French Pyrénées on his way to Spain, hoping to reach America.

9. Benjamin, "On the Concept of History," 390.

10. On the subject of consciousness, Spanish poet Federico García Lorca once wrote, "I am used to suffering from things that people do not understand, do not even suspect. Being born in Granada has given me a sympathetic understanding of those who are persecuted—the Gypsy, the black, the Jew, the Moor which all Granadans have inside them." Federico García Lorca, *Deep Song and Other Prose* (New York: New Directions, 1975), ix. Lorca believed the Gypsy deep song, known as the *Siguiríya*, to be Spain's and, in particular, Andalusia's historical vessel of pain and memory. Between 1933 and 1934, several years before his execution, Lorca traveled to Argentina and Uruguay, reading these ideas aloud in a series of lectures on *The Play and Theory of Duende* and historical consciousness.

11. Henri Bergson, *The Creative Mind* (New York: Philosophical Library, 1946), 185–87.

12. Gilles Deleuze discussing Henri Bergson.

13. Henri Bergson, *The Creative Mind*, 200. For Benjamin, this meant to intuit and experience its light.

14. Ibid., 200. See also Federico García Lorca, "Deep Song," *Deep Song and Other Prose* (New York: New Directions, 1975), 23–41.

15. Marcel Proust's mother was Jewish, as was Henri Bergson's.

16. Henri Bergson, *Matter and Memory*, trans. Nancy Margaret Paul and W. Scott Palmer (New York: Zone, 1994), 208–9.

17. Gilles Deleuze, *Immanence: Essays of a Life* (New York: Urzone, 2002). Italicization in original.

18. Bernard Lewis, *The Arabs in History* (London: Hutchinson's University Library, 1956); *Cultures in Conflict: Christians, Muslims, and Jews in an Age of Discovery* (New York: Oxford University Press, 1995); *The World of Islam: Faith, People, Culture* (New York: Thames & Hudson, 1992); *Islam and the West* (New York: Oxford University Press, 1993); *The Jews of Islam* (Princeton: Princeton University Press, 1984); *The Middle East: A Brief History of the Last 2,000 Years* (New York: Scribner, 1995); *A Middle East Mosaic: Fragments of Life, Letters & History* (New York: Random House, 2000); *The Multiple Identities of the Middle East* (London: Weidenfeld & Nicholson, 1998); and *The Muslim Discovery of Europe* (New York: W. W. Norton, 1982).

CHAPTER ONE Inventing *Carmen*

1. *The Works of Walter Pater: Miscellaneous Studies* (London: Macmillan, 1901), 20.

2. Roland Barthes. *The Responsibility of Forms*. Trans. Richard Howard (New York: Hill and Wang, 1985), 307.

3. *Carmen* in Latin means tune, song, strain, poem. The plural of *carmen* is *carmina*, meaning part of a musical—instrumental or choral—composition. According to the Oxford Dictionary of Music, the word *carmen* was used "during the Middle Ages and the Renaissance to refer to various kinds of vocal music." *The Oxford Dictionary of Music* (New York: Oxford University Press, 2012).

4. Mérimée's descriptions of her body read as though he were describing an archeological site of discovery; corporeally, Carmen has the scent and walk of a woman from the East.

5. For evidence of Mérimée's political conservatism and full support of the Second Empire versus the Second French Republic, consider the following statement: "The writer," comments Alistair Horne, "and friend of the regime, Prosper Mérimée described the atmosphere as 'like that aroused by Mozart's music when the Commendatore is about to appear.' His name might be reread as Otto von Bismarck." See Alistair Horne, *Seven Ages of Paris* (New York: Alfred A. Knopf, 2002), 268–69.

6. Mérimée finished *Carmen* on 16 May 1845. *Carmen* was first published in serial form on 1 October 1845 in *La Revue des Deux Mondes. Carmen, la novella* was first published as a book on 29 May 1847 by Michel Lévy, having been registered with the Bibliothèque Nationale on 14 February 1847. See *Prosper Mérimée: exposition organisée pour commémorer le cent cinquantième anniversaire de sa naissance. Décembre 22, 1953–février 28, 1954* (Paris: Bibliothèque nationale de France, 1953), 3.

7. Biography from the Académie Française and the Académie des Inscriptions, quoted in the chapter "Prosper Mérimée. Son caractère et sa tournure d'ésprit," *Études sur le XIX siècle.* (BN-Opéra, Mérimée). His parents married on 22 June 1802 in the 8th arrondissement.

8. Barrymore Laurence Scherer, "Prosper Mérimée, Storyteller," *Opera News* (14 March 1987), 32.

9. *Études sur le XIX siècle,* 325. For a discussion of the exotic as Spanish, see Louis Maigron, *Le Romantisme et la mode* (Paris: Slatkine Reprints, 1989).

10. Scherer, "Prosper Mérimée, Storyteller," 32.

11. For an account of the friendship between Mérimée and Stendhal (1783–1842), see Prosper Mérimée, *Lettres libres à Stendhal* (Paris: Arléa, 1992).

12. A seminal British art historian once described Mérimée's gift for writing as follows: "With a natural gift for words, for expression, it will be his literary function to draw back the veil of time from the true greatness of old Roman character . . ." See Pater, *The Works of Walter Pater,* 15.

13. Mérimée began a liaison with Madame Delessert in February of 1836. See *Prosper Mérimée: exposition organisée pour commémorer le cent cinquantième anniversaire de sa naissance,* 2.

14. Pater, *The Works of Walter Pater,* 18–19.

15. Ibid., 327. See also *Encyclopaedia Britannica,* 11th ed., s.v. "Mérimée, Prosper"; Pater, *The Works of Walter Pater,* 11.

16. The setting is Granada, home to the last Hispano-Arab dynastic line of the Nasrids.

17. Mary Dibbern, *Carmen, a Performance Guide* (Hillsdale, NY: Pendragon Press, 2001), "Introduction to the Literary Sources," 239.

18. *Encyclopaedia Britannica,* 11th ed., s.v. "Mérimée, Prosper."

19. *Mateo Falcone* was first published in the *Revue de Paris* on 3 May 1829, before being published in the collection *Mosaïque* in 1833. See Prosper Mérimée, *Mosaïque* (Paris: M. Lévy Frères, 1833).

20. Scherer, "Prosper Mérimée, Storyteller," 34. See also Marion Cousin-Régnie, *Mateo Falcone; La Vénus d'île* (Paris: Gallimard, 2001); and Oscar Mandel, *Plays on Hispanic Themes* (New York: P. Lang, 2003).

21. Prosper Mérimée, *La Vénus d'île,* quoted in Scherer, "Prosper Mérimée, Storyteller."

22. BN-Opéra c. 12064. Prosper Mérimée. *Carmen, la novella.* (London: Folio Society, 1949), 28.

23. Ibid.

24. Harold Kurtz, *The Empress Eugénie* (Boston: Houghton Mifflin, 1964).

25. Scherer, "Prosper Mérimée, Storyteller," 34.

26. Doña Mañuela took her daughter to Paris to be educated and to avoid the civil revolts in Madrid, beginning in the 1830s. Mérimée became Eugénie's tutor and remained Mañuela's confidant. For several decades, he educated Eugénie in literature and languages, guiding her through her courtship with Napoleon III and through much of her life. This professorial relationship became the basis for Mérimée's continued standing at court. In May of 1866, he was promoted to Grand Officer of the Legion of Honor. With this new standing, he admitted to Mañuela that France could have made wiser geopolitical decisions because "no one has any really clear idea of the danger, everybody is frightened. Bismarck has become the universal bogeyman. His words are weighed and reweighed, and people think he wants to swallow us whole . . . If you could see the way our poor country is split, the lack of patriotism, the love of money and high living, you would not recognize the French of the past, and you would dread a war for them, even against an enemy of inferior strength."

Mérimée's Left Bank house on the Rue de Lille was destroyed, according to fellow author Théophile Gautier, during the Prussian siege of 1871. His famous library was "reduced to ashes." See Alistair Horne, *Seven Ages of Paris*, 248, 275.

27. *Encyclopaedia Britannica*, 11th ed., s.v. "*Prosper Mérimée*."

28. Ibid., 166–67.

29. Mérimée left France for Spain in June of 1830, traveling throughout the country until December.

30. On the meeting of Mérimée and the Countess of Montijo, see Otto Friedrich, *Olympia: Paris in the Age of Manet* (New York: Harper Collins, 1992), 46.

31. Prosper Mérimée to the Countess of Montijo, 1845.

32. A further point about Mérimée's use of first-person narration—his successful ability to place himself as a subsidiary character within the story—results in the author's ability to use realistic details as fictive elements.

Mérimée worked on *Carmen* from 1830 to 1845.

33. Americo Castro in his seminal text, *The Structure of Spanish History*, puts forth a radical argument on the multicultural—multireligious, multilinguistic, and multiethnic—twentieth-century relationship among Castile, Andalusia, Galicia, and Catalonia as being representative of the Hispano-Arab (Moorish), Mozarabic (Christian-Arab) world of the Middle Ages. Castro argues that eight hundred years of Islamic Spanish and Sephardic-Mozarabic cultural history cannot be erased. It is written into the walls of buildings, chiseled into the living memory of what is Spain. Writing during Franco's reign, Castro carefully negotiated a delicate bridge between the southern and northern provinces of Spain that stood geographically, linguistically, and politically at quite a distance from each other. A figure like Rondino or Don José, who reminisces about "home"—a faraway place and a figment of his imagination—is literally referring to a province so distant from the one in which he lives as to evoke the notion of a foreign country. This geographical split opens a temporal one, serving to deepen the reader's sense that the character does not belong to the present moment—that a narrative rupture must occur and that the protagonists live, somehow, in some other liminal space, the threshold being the land between where they are and where the path, inevitably, will lead them: somewhere we will never go, as it is in the distant past.

34. On 31 July 1830, the monarchical government of Charles X suddenly collapsed. After the Peninsular Wars and the fall of Bonaparte's French Empire, the reinstalled Bourbon line had directed

their efforts toward the institutional revival of the monarchical state. The result of the Napoleonic occupations of Spain (1795–1798 and 1804–1805) still reverberated even fifteen years after Bonaparte's capture and subsequent imprisonment on the South Atlantic island of St. Helena. Napoleon and the French had occupied much of Spain (and Europe) and Napoleon had placed his brother, Joseph Bonaparte, on the throne of Spain. This led to a series of wars on the soil of the Americas as Europe attempted to wrest control of a number of Spain's restive colonies. The late eighteenth century and early nineteenth century witnessed the rise of both liberal and reactionary forces that fought each other for control of the government. In the twentieth century this conflict of ideas and parties would further destabilize Spain. Unfortunately for the Spanish people, General Franco's nationalist dictatorship resolved the dispute once and, cruelly, for all in 1939 after a bloody Civil War.

35. *Carmen, la novella* was published in 1846. Preceding the publication of *Carmen* was the publication of many Paris Opéra and Opéra-Comique *livrets* with bohémien protagonists. I list a few here: De Montalembert, *La Bohémienne supposée*, Hotel de Montalembert (17 March 1786); Gustav Lémoine and Paul de Kock, *La Bohémienne de Paris*, Théâtre de la Gaité (24 February 1844) c. 11498 (9) T.4; Léo Scribe. *La Bohémienne ou l'Amérique en 1779*, Théâtre de Madame (1 June 1829), c. 11498 (4bis) T.11; D'Énnery and Grangé. *La Bohémienne de Paris*, Théâtre de l'Ambigu-Comique (27 September 1843), c. 11498 (10) T.4; Laurencin et Desvergere, *La Gitana*, Gymnase Dramatique (28 January 1839), c. 11498 (4bis) T.16. While numerous operas *à la Gitane* preceded *Carmen*, perhaps the most famous was A. Marliani's *La Gipsy* from 1839 (BN-O, Res. 136).

36. Please see the excellent description of orientalist ballet spectacle in Susan Foster, *Choreography and Narrative: Ballet's Staging of Story and Desire* (Bloomington: Indiana University Press, 1996).

37. 'Al Tariq was the Syrio-Berber warrior who raised an army "out of the sand" of Arab-Berber jihad soldiers who crossed from North Africa the Straits of Gibraltar in the year 711 and into southern Spain. Forcing the gates of the city open, 'al Tariq continued with his men from Andalusia through Spain and across the Pyrénées into France, pushing as far as the outskirts of Paris where they were met by the French army.

38. Antonia Fonyi's remarkable analysis of Prosper Mérimée, author, is further analyzed in the preface to this book.

39. Carl F. Braun, trans., *Carmen* (privately printed edition, 1952): 3.

40. *Bellum Hispaniense*, written by an anonymous Roman author, presents a detailed account of Julius Caesar's colonial wars of conquest in Spain between 48 and 45 BCE.

41. In 1564, King Philip II granted the title of Duke of Osuna to the fifth Count of Ureña. The town of Osuna from then on became, according to the Spanish monarchy, the capital of Andalusia. In 1830, when Mérimée was living and working in Spain, the eleventh Duke of Osuna was only twenty years old. He died in his thirties and his brother, to whom the title passed, died shortly thereafter. Five years after the publication of *Carmen*, the twelfth Duke of Osuna represented Spain at the marriage of Eugenia de Montijo to Emperor Napoleon III in 1853.

42. The notion of *arché* writing is elaborated upon by Jacques Derrida, *Of Grammatology* (Baltimore: Johns Hopkins University Press, 1998).

43. Fonyi, 198.

44. Ibid.

45. All of the following excerpts from the novel appear in Prosper Mérimée, *Carmen, la novella* (Philadelphia: Henry Altemus, 1899).

46. Prosper Mérimée, *Carmen, la novella*.

47. Ibid., 37ff.

48. Ibid., 40.

49. Ibid.

50. Ibid., 43–44.

51. Ibid., 58–59.

52. Ibid., 59.

53. Ibid., 62–63.

54. Ibid., 63.

55. Ibid., 64.

56. Ibid., 68–69.

57. An interesting connection between Carmen's story and the 1846 Mazilier ballet *Paquita* might be drawn here. In the libretto for the ballet, the protagonist Paquita is stolen by Gypsies and raised in a Gypsy camp, away from her noble family. A French royal officer, Lucien, who falls in love with her, discovers her true identity. Determined to marry her, he must prove that she is not Gypsy but, rather, French Catholic of aristocratic lineage.

58. Prosper Mérimée, *Carmen, la novella*, 70–71.

59. Ibid., 72–73.

60. Ibid., 104.

61. Ibid., 109.

62. Ibid., 138–39.

63. Ibid., 147–51.

64. Pater, 16.

65. Ibid.

66. Ibid.

67. Ibid., 36.

68. Ibid., 31.

CHAPTER TWO Georges Bizet and the Genealogy of *Carmen*

1. Americo Castro. *The Structure of Spanish History*, trans. Edmund L. King (Princeton: Princeton University Press, 1954), viii.

2. Ibid., 276.

3. Ibid.

4. Bizet was born at 26 Rue de la Tour d'Auvergne. See Winton Dean, *Georges Bizet: His Life and Work* (London: J. M. Dent, 1965), 1.

5. Numerous comprehensive biographies of Georges Bizet exist. One of the finest is Mina K. Curtiss, *Bizet and His World*, London: Secker & Warburg, 1959. Several fine French biographies of Bizet are Célestine Galli-Marié, *Mémoire de Bizet* c. 7553 (3); Raoul Laparra, *Bizet et l'Éspagne* (Paris: Librairie Delagrave, 1934); and Charles Pigot, *Georges Bizet et son oeuvre* (BN-O c. 7409) 1886. A fine biography of the opera *Carmen* was written by the critic Henri Malherbe, *Carmen* (BN-O, c. 9159) 1951.

6. The original score for *Carmen* was published by Éditions Choudens in 1875. Parts of the music for various instruments and re-editions of the score, especially those by Ernest Guirard, were also published

by Choudens. I studied the following scores on microfilm: Georges Bizet (BN-Musique, VM5 873) *Carmen*, "Partition Chant et Piano de Carmen Opéra-Comique," (Paris: Choudens, March 1875); *Carmen*, Partition Chant et Piano arranged by the author (BN-O Res. 1088) Paris: Choudens; *Carmen* partitioned score from the 1900 production at the Opéra-Comique. Notes most likely by Dolferoni Éditions: Choudens. *Carmen*, Livret de Henry Meilhac et Ludovic Halevy. Librairie Théâtrale, Gerard Billaudot, ed., 1981; *Carmen*. Livret (BN-O Liv. 116) Paris: Calmann-Levy, eds. 3 Rue Auber.

7. Marcia B. Siegel, "Modern Dance," in *The Living Dance: An Anthology of Essays on Movement and Culture*, ed. Judith Chazin-Bennahum (Dubuque, Iowa: Kendall-Hunt, 2007), 94. See also François Delsarte and Genevieve Stebbins, *Delsarte System of Expression* (New York: Edgar S. Werner, 1887).

8. Having studied singing at the Paris Conservatoire, Delsarte created a system of training singers called "The Science of Applied Aesthetics" in which voice, breath, and movement became linked, training an artist to develop an emotional connection between all parts of the body. If, for example, one's hand moved with the same feeling and rhythm as one's voice, a singer could develop the acting and vocal skills needed for a harmonious presentation of a character on stage.

9. Dean, *Georges Bizet*, 4. Mina Curtiss argues that Bizet began music classes at the Conservatoire in 1847, but that he passed his piano examinations in 1848 and was then officially accepted as a student.

10. Ibid., 5.

11. Ibid.

12. Dean, *Georges Bizet*, 11. Gounod was Zimmerman's son-in-law. In 1855, Gounod wrote two symphonies: the *Symphony #1 in D Major*, said to have been the inspiration for Bizet's *Symphony in C* composed in the same year, and the *Symphony #2 in E Flat Major*. Gounod won the Prix de Rome in 1839 and spent his sojourn in Italy studying sacred masses and the intellectual rigor of J. S. Bach's and Félix Mendelssohn's keyboard compositions. He considered entering the priesthood. His music, like his religiosity, merged the sacred with the improvisational. In this way, Gounod's musical style influenced his young student Bizet, with whom he shared a rich correspondence about music and composition.

13. *New Grove Dictionary of Music*, s.v. "Bizet, Georges," 642.

14. Fromental Halévy was the son of a cantor who taught Hebrew and served as secretary to Paris's Jewish community. The student of Cherubini at the Paris Conservatoire, Halévy won the Prix de Rome in 1819 for a cantata. His work was religious in tenor and hue, written at times in Hebrew. *De Profundis* (1819) was dedicated to Cherubini and performed in Hebrew at the synagogue in the Rue St. Avoye in 1820. He rose to the position of chorus master at the Paris Opéra and in 1827, he became a professor of harmony and accompaniment at the Conservatoire. By 1833, he was professor of fugue and, by 1840, of composition. In 1836, he was elected to L'Institut de France. *La Juive* (1835) was a tremendous popular success; the title role of Eléazar was later sung by the famous tenor Enrico Caruso at the Metropolitan Opera on 22 November 1919. *La Juive* told a romantic story of unrequited love between a Christian man and a Jewish woman. When Halévy died in Nice, he left his final opera, *Noé*, unfinished; Bizet completed it for him.

15. Bizet's repertoire would surely have been more extensive had he not felt out of place artistically in mid-nineteenth century France. While he abandoned many of the works he had begun to compose, those he completed were *Symphony in C Major* (1855); *Les Pécheurs de Perles* (1863); thirty-seven published songs (1866); *Variations Chromatiques de Concerts* (1868); *Jeux d'Enfants* (1871); *Djamileh* (1872); *L'Arlésienne* (1872); and *Carmen* (1875).

16. Henry Gauthier-Villars, *Bizet* (Paris: Librairie Renouard, 1920), 7.

17. Louis XIV and his minister Colbert founded the Prix de Rome in 1666. It is awarded to students and professionals who show excellence in any performing or visual art form. The Conservatoire's rules as laid out by its patron—the French government—came with an obligation that the winner spend two years residency in Rome and one in Germany and, upon returning to Paris, two years on a living allowance. During that time, one had to produce new work. Winning the Prix de Rome opened connections, theaters, and concerts throughout the city of Paris. It helped launch graduates of the Paris Conservatoire into a world of performance, composition, and critique.

18. Ellen H. Bleiler, *Carmen* (New York: Dover, 1970), 3.

19. Curtiss, *Bizet and His World*, 50. It is said that Bizet did not accomplish much musically during his tenure in Rome.

20. Ibid., 68–92.

21. Victor Hugo, Preface to *Les Orientales* (1829), translation by Susan McClary, 30.

22. Dean, *Georges Bizet*, 5.

23. The work was not performed until 1906.

24. Curtiss, *Bizet and His World*, 92–93.

25. BN-Opéra [*Le Désert* (1844). Dossier d'oeuvre].

26. Bizet did go to the summer festival at Baden-Baden in 1862 to assist on a production of *Erostate*.

27. John W. Klein, "Bizet and Wagner," *Music & Letters* 28 (January 1947): 51.

28. Jouvin quoted by Winton Dean, 52.

29. *Tannhäuser* opened at the Salle Le Peletier on 13 March 1861. Albert Wolff, "Le Courrier de Paris," *Le Figaro*, 24 March 1861; John W. Klein, "Bizet and Wagner," 51. Part of the reason for the French audience's outrage was the fact that Wagner, as per the rules of the Opéra, had to insert a ballet. Rather than inserting it into the final act, he inserted it where it would cause the least amount of disruption, in Act 1. This angered the aristocratic public who were accustomed to arriving late, just in time for the ballet.

30. Prosper Mérimée, quoted by Curtiss, *Bizet and His World*, 108.

31. Susan McClary, *Georges Bizet: Carmen* (Cambridge: Cambridge University Press, 1992), 47–48.

32. Ibid.

33. Ibid., 48.

34. Georges Bizet quoted by John W. Klein, "Bizet and Wagner," 51. French poet Charles Baudelaire also fell in love with *Tannhäuser* and published an article in *La Revue européen* entitled "Richard Wagner et *Tannhäuser à Paris*," on 1 April 1861, in defense of Wagner. In a letter dated 26 May 1871, Bizet wrote to his mother-in-law, Madame Halévy, referring to Wagner as a "revolutionary genius" and a "great artist . . . The fascination of his music is indescribable. It is all voluptuousness, tenderness, love. If I could play you this music for a week, you would rave about it . . . The whole of nineteenth-century German thought is incarnate in this man." Georges Bizet to Madame Halévy, quoted by Klein, 56.

35. Théophile Gautier, "*La Jolie Fille de Perth*," review for *Le Moniteur universel* (1866), quoted by Curtiss, *Bizet and His World*, 211.

36. Berlioz, quoted by Curtiss, *Bizet and His World*, 140–41.

37. Jean was told that Adolphe, his grandfather, was his father.

38. *Les Pêcheurs de Perles* was originally entitled *Leila*. Dean, *Georges Bizet*, 50.

39. A parody of a Romantic-themed opera, *Les Pêcheurs de Perles* tells the story of Nadir (tenor) and

Zurga (baritone), two Ceylonese fishermen who fight over a woman, Leila, the village temple *devadasi*. Leila loves Nadir, causing Zurga to become so jealous that he denounces them to the priesthood and, as her societal role is that of virgin, the two are condemned to death. Feeling guilty, Zurga sets fire to the village, enabling Nadir's and Leila's escape. It was premiered by the famous Carmen, Emma Calvé, at the Metropolitan Opera in 1911.

40. Gustave Bertrand said in *Le Ménestrel Universel* that Bizet should have pretended to have been dragged onstage. Dean, *Georges Bizet*, 52.

41. Benoît Jouvin quoted by Dean, *Georges Bizet*, 46; Jouvin quoted by Curtiss, *Bizet and His World*, 139.

42. Bertrand quoted by Curtiss, *Bizet and His World*, 140–41.

43. Hector Berlioz. "Théâtre-Lyrique," *Journal des Débats*, 8 October 1863. Berlioz's *Les Troyens à Carthage* was performed at the Théâtre-Lyrique just after Bizet's opera closed.

44. "Emma Calvé to Retire," *The New York Times* (8 August 1920). Calvé was considered one of the greatest Carmens since Galli-Marié. She monopolized the role of Carmen for over twenty years. A music critic for the *London Globe* was quoted as saying that Calvé's singing brought him close to a "revelation of the character of the gypsy as it existed in the imagination of Prosper Mérimée when he wrote his novel. She came upon the stage as Mérimée's heroine stepped into his pages, poising herself on her hips like a filly from a Cordovan stud, and with a fine simulation of unconsciousness she seemed every moment about to break into one of those dances . . ." "Emma Calvé to Retire."

45. Berlioz, "Théâtre-Lyrique," *Journal des Débats*.

46. Dean, *Georges Bizet*, 51.

47. The Metropolitan Opera is said to have grossed $10,000 per performance of *Carmen* in 1893 and in 1920, $100,000. Each time Emma Calvé sang the role of Carmen. *The New York Times* wrote of the 1893 *Carmen* season at the Met: "The public of New York never paid a greater tribute to one woman's genius . . . Emma Calvé's Carmen is a creature of her own imagination." W. J. Henderson, "Emma Calvé," *The New York Times*, 6 December 1896. Wikipedia cites *Carmen* as "perhaps the most famous *opéra-comique*."

48. Jouvin quoted by Curtiss, *Bizet and His World*, 139.

49. *Encyclopaedia Britannica*, 11th ed., s.v. "Bizet, Georges."

50. Bizet's mother's family, the Delsartes, who were extremely religious, objected vociferously to the marriage because Geneviève was Jewish. The Halévy family was also conservative, socially. Associated with wealthy banking families, the Rothschilds and Pereiras, the Halévys also disapproved of Bizet because he was neither financially stable nor Jewish. Bizet was unable to manage the little that he earned, spending it foolishly and quickly. He also had an illegitimate child. In the end, the couple was married by the mayor of the *arrondisement*. Eleven years after Bizet's death, Geneviève re-married, this time to an extremely wealthy man, Émile Strauss, and was able to set up a salon later frequented by Marcel Proust and other writers.

51. Geneviève's father had died in 1862, her sister only two years later, which may have contributed to her emotional instability.

52. *New Grove*, "Bizet, Georges."

53. Georges Bizet, quoted by Bleyel, 14.

54. Léon Carvalho (né Carvaille) commissioned Bizet for over a decade. An innovative theatrical director who was once a singer himself, Carvalho went bankrupt in 1868 and was forced out of the

Théâtre Lyrique and the Théâtre de la Renaissance. He migrated to the Théâtre du Vaudeville where he commissioned Bizet's *L'Arlésienne* in 1872. By 1876, Carvalho became the director of the Opéra-Comique. Most significant about Carvalho was his commitment to the new French composers: Berlioz, Saint-Saëns, Massenet, Gounod, Delibes, and Bizet.

55. *Carmen*–BN-Opéra [Col. Bizet, Georges].

56. Ivor Guest, Lecture for the Society of Dance History Scholars, University of Oregon, Eugene, June 1998.

57. *Carmen*–BN-Opéra [Col. Bizet, Georges]. Célestine Galli-Marié (1840–1905) was taught by her father, a tenor at the Opéra who eventually became a conductor. Galli-Marié sang the Italian premier of *Carmen* in Naples and went on to sing Carmen in London and Madrid. Her final appearance as Carmen was in 1890. Beloved by Bizet, she was considered a Mériméen Carmen.

58. Ludovic Halévy, "La Millième Répresentation de *Carmen*," *Le Théâtre* (1905).

59. Ibid.

60. Ibid.

61. Susan McClary, *George Bizet: Carmen*, 23.

62. Ibid., 23.

63. Metropolitan Opera Association Press Department, *Carmen* file, Metropolitan Opera Archives, no date.

64. Ibid.

65. Richard Somerset-Ward, *L'Histoire de l'opéra* (Paris: Editions de la Martinière, 1991), 175. While the connection between Bizet and the *zarzuela* is mine, Somerset-Ward offers a wonderful history of the *zarzuela* as a broad Hispanic form of composite spectacle: music, dance, and spoken word.

For a more complete history of the seventeenth- and eighteenth-century dance forms and their relationship to grand opera and popular theater, see Carlo Blasis, *Code complet de la danse* (London: J. Bulcock, 1828); and Marina Grut, *The Bolero School: An Illustrated History of the Bolero, the Seguidillas and the Escuela Bolera* (Alton, Hampshire, UK: Dance Books, 2002). K. Meira Weinzweig argues that the *Escuela Bolera* was thought to have been founded by Anton Boliche, "possibly nicknamed 'El Bolero.'" She writes of Boliche, "he was probably a *gitano* born in Murcia or Seville who died in Cádiz in 1794." See K. Meira Weinzweig, *Border Trespasses. The Gypsy Mask and Carmen Amaya's Flamenco Dance*. Unpublished Dissertation. Temple University, 1995, 33. Two Gypsy flamenco dance forms, the *Fandanguillo* and the *Soleá*, share similar rhythms and choreographic structures.

66. Following Bizet's score for *Carmen* were a series of Spanish-inspired scores written by French composers: in 1883, Chabrier wrote *España*; in 1905 Debussy composed *Ibéria*; in 1875, Lalo wrote *Symphonie Espagnole for Violin and Orchestra*, dedicated to Pablo de Sarasate; in 1907, Maurice Ravel wrote *Vocalise en forme d'Habanera*, *La Rhapsodie Espagnole*, *L'Heure espagnole*, *Le Boléro*, *L'Alborada del gracioso*, and songs from *Don Quixote à Dulcinée*. Also in 1907 Fauré composed *Pas Espagnole* and Saint-Saëns wrote *La Havanaise*. Russian composers contributed to this Spanish frenzy as well: Glinka composed *Jota Aragonese*, *Nuit d'été à Madrid*; Balakirev wrote *Overture on Spanish Themes* and *Spanish Serenade for Piano*; and Rimsky-Korsakov wrote *Capriccio Espagnole*. One must also mention the composers whose scores Antonia Mercé, *La Argentina*, used: Isaac Albeníz, Enrique Granados, and Manuel de Falla.

67. For a specific review of the difficulty in reworking the opera's premiere, see Evan Baker, "The Scene Designs for the First Performance's of Bizet's *Carmen*," *19th- Century Music* XIII, no. 3 (Spring 1990).

68. Cigarettes were not manufactured in Spain in the 1820s. Cigarettes and cigars were rolled in Cuba and throughout the Spanish and French Afro-Caribbean slave colonies. Alluding to tobacco in France signaled the trans-Atlantic slave trade. [BN-Opéra–original program reference].

Bizet's score, in and of itself, provides a history of *Carmen*. Due to the failure of its premiere and the premature death of Bizet three months after the opening, the score sustained many changes that Bizet could not approve.

69. For a discussion of the possible destruction of the original designs in a fire of 1887 and their reconstruction by Bertin, see Evan Baker, "The Scenic Designs for the First Performances of Bizet's *Carmen*," *19th-Century Music* XIII, no. 3 (Spring 1990).

70. The Almohads were more ethnically Berber than Arab. The Almohads and the Almoravids, fundamentalist Berber Islamic powers from North Africa, entered Andalusia after the fall of Toledo in 1085 in response to the *Taifa* leaders' pleas for help in repelling the Christian armies of northern Spain composed of princes from Castile, Aragon, Navarre and Portugal. At the Battle of Las Navas de Toloso in 1212 in the Sierra Morenas (where the third Act of *Carmen* takes place), the Almohads were defeated, never to rise again as a political force in Spain. Cordoba and Seville fell to Christian armies soon after and the Almohads eventually returned to Africa.

71. Sir Richard Eyre's 2010 production of *Carmen* for the Metropolitan Opera banishes the factory altogether. At their break, Gypsy women emerge from a hole in the stage, sweaty and in need of water. This is a poor design choice, an attempt to replace the grand plaza in front of La Cortuja with the remains of the Roman bullring (which in reality is located on the other side of the river).

72. In 1614, Philip III decreed that all tobacco grown in the Spanish colonies must be shipped to Seville for processing. In 1758, the Royal Tobacco Factory was opened.

73. Dale Fuchs, "Tobacco Industry Stressed in Europe: Days Numbered for Carmen's 'Heirs?'" *The New York Times* (Saturday, December 18, 2004).

74. Ibid.

75. Ibid.

76. Original watercolors by Émile Bertin (1878–1957) from the BN-O, Carmen, ésquisse de décor, d (1). I must thank the chief music librarian at the Bibliothèque Nationale de l'Opéra, Romain Feist, for copies of Bertin's original drawings of the four acts of *Carmen*. For evidence of Émile Bertin as the opera's most influential scenic designer, see Evan Baker, "The Scenic Designs for the First Performances of Bizet's *Carmen*."

77. Micaëla, although young and innocent, a virgin, and coming as she does from a small town, is more courageous than one might think. She somehow manages to follow the Gypsy smugglers into the high mountains above the city, tracking Don José to his lookout between jagged boulders and dangerous precipices. While her virginity separates her from Carmen's worldliness, the fact alone of Micaëla's solo journey complicates previous notions of what constitutes innocence and purity.

78. Eyre's 2010 production of *Carmen* added a fantastic stroke of realism in showing one Gypsy woman breastfeeding her child above the steamy factory at lunch, as the chances of a working woman being able to make the long trek home to the Gypsy *barrio* of Triana located across the river in time to return to work were slim.

He further intensifies the sexually aggressive, perhaps violent, abusive behavior by the dragoons of the *gitanas*. Their manhandling of Micaëla as she searches for Don José in their office is a fine ethnographic addition to the Metropolitan Opera's new production.

79. Rampart means the ancient, walled heart of Seville, built by the Moors with its winding alleyways of whitewashed buildings with blue doors.

80. Ernest Guiraud's recitative states that it is two months later.

81. *Carmen*, Libretto (Chester, New York: G. Schirmer, 1959). All excerpts are from this edition. Note the self-deprecating words Carmen utters, "the same old song," as she refers to the *Seguidillas*. As the *Seguidillas* historically signals both the history of flamenco and of eighteenth-century Spanish aristocratic court dance, such a prejudicial statement gives today's reader pause; the librettists allowed Carmen, reduced to the level of common minstrel, to see no value in the very act she performs for the audience while she sings of it. This anti-Gypsy view was the only way in which the tale of a seductress like Carmen could be justified by librettists Halévy and Meilhac before a bourgeois audience in nineteenth-century France.

82. Ibid., 9.

83. Ibid., 11–16.

84. Bizet, *Carmen*, orchestral score, 68–69.

85. *Carmen*, Libretto, 19.

86. Ibid., 20–22. It is interesting to note that Carmen sings in minor keys and Micaëla in major keys.

87. Perhaps one of the most evocative *bata de colas* worn by Carmen was designed by Rob Howell for Sir Richard Eyre's 2010 production of *Carmen* at the Metropolitan Opera in New York City. In the fourth act, Carmen enters on Escamillo's arm, wearing a cascading black *bata de cola*. A décolleté neck and tight corset reveal Carmen's bust and exquisite neckline. One lacy strap rests comfortably on Elina Garanca's left shoulder. A thick, blood-red line drops from the *bata*'s center to its base, playing off the blackness of the rest of the dress and presaging Carmen's death a few minutes later at the violent hands of Don José. Much like Isamu Noguchi's sculpted black-and-white dresses designed for Martha Graham's Grecian heroines, Rob Howell's costume for Carmen serves both the plot and character of *Carmen*.

88. *Carmen*, Libretto, 23.

89. Baker, 69. Baker makes an important point: "It has been pointed out that Bizet and his librettists violated the ceremonial order of the *cuadrilla* and that the *espadas*, who were two, not just one, should enter first" (70). This said, many directors since 1875 have envisioned the entrance of the *cuadrilla* in myriad ways. Space was tight in Eyre's latest production at the Metropolitan Opera as the majority of the stage was occupied by a colossal Roman arena resembling the ruined one in Nîmes. This left a sliver of downstage space for the entrance of the *cuadrilla* and, thus, while the correct number of men entered, they almost escaped the attention of the audience, hurried as they were to get through the crowds.

90. There exist several versions of Bizet's score—Bizet's, Guiraud's, and the most commonly used, which is a streamlined version of the original score. This leaves the fourth act open to interpretation.

91. *Carmen*, Libretto, 24–25.

92. *New Encyclopaedia Britannica*, 1092.

93. "Georges Bizet" correspondence in Mina Curtiss, *Bizet and His World*, and quoted in the *New Encyclopaedia Britannica*, 1092.

94. *New Encyclopaedia Britannica*, 1093.

95. Ibid.

96. Ibid.

97. As will be discussed in Chapter 5, the etymology of the Spanish word for rhythm, *compás*, is very recently being expanded to include the influence upon Gypsy singers of African slaves and freed men and women working and living beside them in Andalusia.

98. For a working definition of the *Seguidillas*, see Ninotchka Devorah Bennahum, *Antonia Mercé: El flamenco y la vanguardia española* (Barcelona: Global Rhythm Press, S. L., 2009).

99. Matteo, *The Language of Spanish Dance* (Norman: University of Oklahoma Press, 1990), 225.

100. Marina Grut, *The Bolero School* (London: Dance Books, 2002), 13.

101. Jean Henri Dupin, librettist of more than two hundred light operas, was a frequent visitor to Meilhac's home, where he went to play billiards. "He arrived early the morning after the Carmen premiere." Quoted in *Opera News* (14 March 1987), 37.

102. Klein, 61. "Bizet's Admirers and Detractors," *Music and Letters* 19 (October 1938).

103. Ibid., 59.

104. In 1878, *Carmen* was performed more times in that year in Germany than any other opera, including Wagner. According to musicologist John Klein, Bizet's German success "challenged the hegemony of the German Titan in his own country." Klein, 61.

105. Friedrich Nietzsche quoted by Herbert F. Peyser, "For Deeper Enjoyment of *Carmen*," *Opera News* (15 March 1943), 18.

106. Ibid.

107. "From Mérimée it still has the logic in passion, the shortest line, the harsh necessity . . ." Friedrich Nietzsche, "The Case against Wagner" (Leipzig: Verlag von C. G. Neumann, 1888).

108. On the notion of narrativity in opera and music as an interpretation of text, see Carolyn Abbate's *Unsung Voices: Opera and Musical Narrative in the Nineteenth Century* (Princeton: Princeton University Press, 1991).

109. On *Gesamtkunstwerk*, please see Paul Henry Lang, *Music in Western Civilization* (London: J. M. Dent, 1941).

110. Ibid., 889–90.

111. Abbate, *Unsung Voices*, 11.

112. The following is the entry on *Carmen* and Bizet in the *Dictionnaire Lyrique* of Clément and Larousse. It appeared shortly after the premiere of the opera.

113. Henry Stuart Oliver, *Paris Days and Evenings*. (London: T. Fisher Unwin, 1896) 907.

114. Peter Rabinowitz, "Singing for Myself," *Audible Traces: Gender, Identity, & Music* (Zurich: Carciofoli, 1999), 38.

115. Abbate, *Unsung Voices*, ix. See also Catherine Clément. *Opera, or the Undoing of Women* (Minneapolis: the University of Minnesota Press, 1988); Arthur Groos, "Deconstructive Postscript," *Reading Opera* (New York Times Book Review, 1 January 1989); Nelly Furman, "The Languages of Love in *Carmen*," in *Reading Opera*, ed. Arthur Groos and Roger Parker (Princeton: Princeton University Press, 1988).

CHAPTER THREE Mythic Space and Ancient Carmen

1. F. de Rougement, "Des mythes primitives," *Le people primitif, sa réligion, son histoire et sa civilization, Révue Contemporaine* 2 (1 September 1855).

2. Paleolithic, from the Greek meaning Old Stone Era, distinguished by historians for humans'

first use of stone tools—a new technology. The Paleolithic Era is thought to have begun roughly 2.5 to 2.6 million years ago and to have extended to the introduction of agriculture, roughly 12,000 years ago. The introduction of agriculture brings human history to the Mesolithic Era. The Neolithic Era or New Stone Age, in which agricultural tools such as the hoe and the wheel were discovered, began in roughly 9500 BCE in the small villages of the ancient Middle East that occupied what is now known as Mesopotamia, the land between the Tigris and Euphrates rivers. The Neolithic Age was critical to the development of food supplies that could be stored through long winter months, leading the way to cities and the development of urban civilizations with ruling classes that distinguished wealth from poverty, mortal from immortal, and male from female.

3. BN-Opéra [*Carmen*, dossier d'oeuvre]. For a deepened, more archeological understanding of the figure of Carmen, please see Bizet's many versions of his score—the stages through which he passed as composer—housed in the Paris Opéra Music Archives.

4. The Gypsies' lack of physical, geographic space and, ultimately, of nationhood will be discussed in Chapter 4.

5. In Gypsy cosmology and daily spiritual practice, the Hindu goddess Kali remains the most important female deity. Like Shiva, Kali is considered creator, protector, and destroyer of the universe; her cosmic powers allow her to create good and evil. As Gypsies were forcibly converted to Catholicism between the Spanish Inquisition and the eighteenth century, Kali, like other deities in the Gypsy pantheon, was hidden from view, her expressive face and long, thick, curly hair imaged in votive form, housed in caravans and caves. Masked by the luminous face and delicate frame of the Virgin Mary, earthy, muscular Kali became the "underside" of the pure, innocent Mary, two spiritual mothers inextricably intertwined. Kali, also spelled Cali after the Gypsy language Caló, is dark like the Virgin of Guadalupe. At Easter time during the *Semana Santa*, the Gypsy Virgin is carried on pedestals through the streets of Andalusian villages like Tarifa and Gibraltar.

Carmen possesses Kaliesque attributes; she does not fit entirely as a human with Kali attributes, nor as a spirit with human qualities. Choreographed in a liminal space, Carmen protects neither Don José nor herself, nor does she create anything but a dance—the *Seguidillas*—on a tabletop at her Gypsy friend Lillas Pastia's tavern in the second act of the opera. Bizet chose for Carmen's only symbolic creation probably the most important dance from the Spanish-Gypsy idiom, as inside the *compás* of the *Seguidillas* is the history of Gypsy dance, known to the world as flamenco. How interesting that Carmen's creation should be a dance, an amorphous, physical embodiment that lasts as long as its performance.

6. Archeologists refer to "BCE" as "before present."

7. For detailed references on the emergence of goddess worship in post-Ice Age Europe, see Elaine Pagels, *The Gnostic Gospels* (New York: Random House, 1979); Johann Bachofen, *Myth, Religion, and Mother Right: Selected Writings of J.J. Bachofen.* (Princeton: Princeton University Press, 1967); Elise Boulding, *The Underside of History: A View of Women through Time* (Boulder: Westview Press, 1976); Robert Briffault, *The Mothers: The Matriarchal Theory of Social Origin* (New York: Macmillan, 1931); and Gerda Lerner, *The Creation of Patriarchy* (New York: Oxford University Press, 1986).

8. Lerner, *The Creation of Patriarchy*, 146.

9. Ibid.

10. Ibid., 147.

11. Ibid., 148.

12. Ibid., 149.

13. Ibid., 145.

14. Layne Redmond, *When the Drummers Were Women* (New York: Random House, 1997), 30–31.

15. See Lerner, *The Creation of Patriarchy*, and William McNeill, *The Rise of the West* (Chicago: University of Chicago Press, 1963), 8–28.

16. McNeill, *The Rise of the West*, 12.

17. The *New Grove Dictionary of Music* cites the grain sieve and frame drum as having the same word in ancient Sumer. *The New Grove Dictionary of Music* (Washington, DC: Grove's Dictionaries of Music, 1980).

18. McNeill, *The Rise of the West*, 12.

19. Fernand Braudel, *Memory and the Mediterranean* (New York: Vintage Books, 2002), 39.

20. Ibid.

21. Ibid., 45.

22. Redmond, 51.

23. Feminist musicologist Carolyn Abbate makes a wonderful point in her book when she raises the idea of "intelligent resonance," which she discusses when exploring the sonorous presence of Carmen in Bizet's *Carmen*. See *Unsung Voices: Opera and Musical Narrative in the Nineteenth Century* (Princeton: Princeton University Press, 1991).

24. Redmond, 53.

25. Ibid.

26. Ibid.

27. See also the excellent work by Page duBois. *Sowing the Body: Psychoanalysis and Ancient Representations of Women* (Chicago: University of Chicago Press, 1988).

28. Lerner, *The Creation of Patriarchy*, 153.

29. Ibid., 154.

30. *Encyclopedia Judaica*, 980. This clearly demonstrates the ability of women to divorce men before Hebrew law was written down.

31. The Sumerians were referred to as the black-headed ones.

32. A comparison here might be drawn between the absorption of the goddess into historical memory and the reformulation of the sacred in African drumming when enslaved Africans throughout the diaspora were stripped of their instruments. Ritual worship in music was thus transferred from the drum to the body, rhythmic consciousness and memory hidden by the body in the absence of the drum.

33. Ma. Po. "Eve," *Encyclopedia Judaica*. The tablets on which the *Myth of Enki and Ninhursag* was written were discovered in 1849.

34. Lerner, *The Creation of Patriarchy*, 151.

35. See Samuel Noah Kramer, *Sumerian Mythology: A Study of Spiritual and Literary Achievement in the Third Millennium BCE* (New York: Harper & Row, 1961), and Kramer, *Enki and Ninhursag: A Sumerian "Paradise Myth,"* New Haven: Yale University Press, 1945.

36. Ibid., 185.

37. Lerner, *The Creation of Patriarchy*, 188.

38. Ibid.

39. Joseph Campbell has a wonderful analysis of this myth. Please see "Initiation," *The Hero Has Many Faces* (Princeton: Princeton University Press, 1968), 97–108.

40. Campbell, 108, and Campbell quoting James Joyce's *Finnegan's Wake*, 92.

41. Lerner, *The Creation of Patriarchy*, p. 126.

42. Ibid., 126–27.

43. McNeill, *The Rise of the West*.

44. Lerner, *The Creation of Patriarchy*, 128.

45. For a contemporary view of the placement of inner sanctuaries inside large homes, please view the disturbing Afghan film *Osama*, shot in Kabul in 2003, *Osama*, directed by Siddiq Barmak. Released by United Artists, Persian with subtitles.

46. Lerner, *The Creation of Patriarchy*, 135.

47. Ibid.

48. Lerner, *The Creation of Patriarchy*, 135, quoting Pritchard.

49. Ibid., 136.

50. Ibid., 140.

51. Ibid.

52. Surprisingly, veiling and seclusion never occurred in Judaism.

53. Lerner, *The Creation of Patriarchy*, 187.

54. Ibid.

55. Ibid., 183.

56. Sarah Grimké quoted by Lerner, *The Creation of Patriarchy*, 184.

57. Redmond, 116.

58. Ibid.

59. Louis Ginzberg, *Legends of the Jews* (Philadelphia: The Jewish Publication Society of America, 1925), 87–88.

60. While Lilith is never mentioned in the *Torah*, the Rabbis refer to her in fragments in the *Midrash* (the legends of the Jewish People) and the *Talmud* when Adam says of Eve: "This one at last is bone of my bone and flesh of my flesh." The words "at last" signal that Adam has been married before. In conversation with Rabbi Joel Chazin, August 10, 2012. For further reading on the subject of Eve and Lilith, please see: Louis Ginzburg. *Legends of the Jews* (Philadelphia: Jewish Publication Society, 2003).

61. See McNeill. *The Rise of the West*.

62. Campbell, *The Hero with a Thousand Faces*, 106.

63. Ibid.

64. Ibid., 108.

65. Redmond, 118.

66. Women lost power after agriculture developed, around 12,000 years ago, as early agriculture required land (property) and storage of grain. In Mesopotamia and Egypt, priestly cults developed for storage, distribution, and documentation and male warrior cults for defense against marauders. Once "property" developed, women's fertility was controlled by law to assure inheritance—i.e., one always knows who the mother is, but not always who the father is. Patriarchal warrior tribes descending from the Russian steppes and elsewhere often conquered lands in Greece and the Near East, leading to suppression but not abolition of the female goddesses such as Athena and Astarte. For more on this radical historical transition, please read Gerda Lerner, *The Creation of Patriarchy*.

67. Redmond, 118.

68. On the subject of the Dithyramb and women in Greek dance, see the fine work of Maurice Emmanuel, *The Antique Greek Dance, after Sculpted and Painted Figures* (New York: John Lane, 1916). On the

subject of the removal of women from the Dithyrambic chorus and the Greek stage, see Sue Ellen Case, "Classic Drag: The Greek Creation of Female Parts," in "Staging Gender" printed in *Theater Journal* 37, no. 3 (October 1985): 317–27.

69. There is significant, critical literature on the subjects of myth and feminism. Please see Simone de Beauvoir, *The Second Sex* (New York: Vintage Press, 1989); Susan Bordo, *Unbearable Weight: Feminism, Western Thought and the Body* (Berkeley: University of California Press, 1993); Judith Butler, *Gender Trouble. Feminism and the Subversion of Identity* (New York: Routledge, 1990); Anne Fausto-Sperling, *Myths of Gender: Biological Theories about Women and Men* (New York: Basic Books, 1992).

70. Ananda K. Coomaraswamy, "Akimcanna: Self-Naughting," *New Indian Antiquary*, vol. 3 (Bombay, 1940).

71. On Flugel's link between spirituality and the female, please see: Joseph Campbell. *The Hero with a Thousand Faces*, 113–14.

72. For a reconstruction of the Dionysian dithyrambic dance, see Emmanuel, *The Antique Greek Dance.*

73. A stunning, recent work of cinematography that attempts to simulate the experience of cave artistry can be seen in director Werner Herzog's 2010 film *Cave of Forgotten Dreams*. Written, directed, and narrated by Werner Herzog and released by Sundance Selects. Director of Photography, Peter Zeitlinger.

74. Lerner, *The Creation of Patriarchy*, 125.

75. There is no question that Carmen has retained her tragic reputation, like that of other literary figures who die, among them Madame Bovary and La Dame aux Grilles.

CHAPTER FOUR The Gypsy Inside and Outside of History

1. Salvador de Madriaga, *Spain, a Modern History* (New York: Frederick A. Praeger, 1958), 18.

2. Sa'id ibn Ahmad al-Andalusi poem "Northerners, Seen from Andalusia (1068)," translated by Bernard Lewis, *A Middle East Mosaic: Fragments of Life, Letters and History* (New York: Modern Library, 2001), 31.

3. Geographic historian Tom Conley argues in his exquisite work *The Self-Made Map: Cartographic Writing in Early Modern France* (Minneapolis: University of Minnesota Press, 1996) that Renaissance cartography—the world into which the Gypsies wandered as they entered Barcelona in the early fifteenth century—brought Europeans an emerging sense of self, nationhood, and cultural identity, inextricably tied to ideas of public space and place in the universe. See also Steven Erlanger, "Expulsion of Roma Raises Questions in France," *The New York Times* (20 August 2010), A4.

4. Jean-Paul Clébert, *The Gypsies*, trans. Charles Duff (New York: E. P. Dutton, 1963), xvi–xvii.

5. Telephone interview with Flamenco guitarist Pedro Cortés, 4 October 2010.

6. This point of view is confirmed by interviews with the Gypsy artists Mario Maya and Manolete, as well as with flamenco singer and dancer La Conja.

7. Bernard Lewis and Henri Pirenne have given me a sense of the tenth- and eleventh-century Arabist worldview. For accounts of this first moment of contact, see Henri Pirenne, *Mohammed & Charlemagne* (London: Allen & Unwin, 1939), and Bernard Lewis, *The Muslim Discovery of Europe* (New York: W. W. Norton, 2001).

8. 'Al Masudi quoted by Bernard Lewis, *A Middle East Mosaic: Fragments of Life, Letters and History* (New York: Modern Library, 2001), 30.

9. Ibid.

10. The methodological discipline of Gypsyology—the study of the geographical origins of the Gypsy people—emerged in the late eighteenth century with Napoleonic invasions of southern Europe and Egypt.

11. See Gretchen Williams, *Buen Metál de Voz: The Calé and Flamenco Cante Jondo*. Unpublished Master's Thesis. The University of New Mexico, Albuquerque, 2002; K. Meira Weinzweig, "Sonidos Negros: a Meditation on the Blackness of Flamenco," conference paper, The International Flamenco Festival, The University of New Mexico, Albuquerque, 10 June 2012, and *Border Trespasses: The Gypsy Mask and Carmen Amaya's Flamenco Dance*. Unpublished Dissertation. Temple University, 1995; Claus Schreiner, ed., *Flamenco: Gypsy Dance and Music from Andalusia* (Portland: Amadeus Press, 1990).

12. Lewis, *A Middle East Mosaic*, 27–37.

13. Clébert, *The Gypsies*, 5.

14. Ibid., 16–17.

15. Ibid., 17.

16. George Borrow, *The Zincali: An Account of the Gypsies of Spain* (London: J. M. Dent, 1924), 88–89.

17. Animism (or *anima* from the Latin meaning soul life) is a spiritual philosophy practiced often by nomadic peoples—desert wanderers—who believe that spirits and souls exist not just in humans but also in animals, rocks, sand, and in natural phenomena like mountains, rivers, rain, and sunshine. *Webster's Dictionary New Universal Abridged Dictionary* (New York: Barnes & Noble, 1992), 59.

18. Borrow, *The Zincali*, 92.

19. Ibid., 90–92.

20. Ibid., 88–89.

21. For a twentieth-century historian's perspective on the Gypsy myth of their Egyptian origin, read Clébert, *The Gypsies*, 5–10.

22. Aventinus, *Annales Boiorum*, 826, cited by Borrow, *The Zincali*, 92.

23. Quiñones, quoted by Borrow, *The Zincali*, 93.

24. Moncada, quoted by Borrow, *The Zincali*, 98–99.

25. Ibid.

26. Ibid., 98–99.

27. Henry Kamen, *Spain, 1469–1714. A Society of Conflict* (New York: Pearson/Longman, 2005).

28. Borrow, *The Zincali*, 95–96.

29. Flamenco is an Arab, Sephardic, and Mozarabic form of modern art.

30. The Edict of Expulsion of the Jews, known as the Alhambra Decree, was written 31 March 1492. All Jews were to vacate Spain and their properties by 31 July 1492.

We have only to look at France and Europe's policies toward "les nomades" to confirm their continued resistance to the Gypsy population. See Suzanne Daley: "Roma Test Europe's 'Open Policies,'" *The New York Times*, 17 September 2010, front page. "Above all else," Jean-Paul Clébert writes in 1963, "Gypsies are feared . . . they are not liked . . . their invisible presence is attested by a notice, 'No nomads' or 'No Gypsies.'" Clébert, *The Gypsies*, xv.

31. Dr. Sancho de Moncada quoted by Borrow, *The Zincali*, 100.

32. Looking back from the twenty-first century with the benefit of hindsight, it is bizarre that the Gypsy in Europe was forced to either stop wandering or permanently leave a country in the face of the rapid colonial trade and conquest in which most European nations were involved. Spain, in

particular, sent thousands of missionaries, soldiers, and builders to the Americas. It was acceptable to move anywhere outside of Europe but nowhere inside of Europe. This double standard persists in imperialist and "globalist" thinking and practices in the present.

33. Dr. Sancho de Moncada quoted by Borrow, *The Zincali*, 99, 101.

34. Ibid.

35. Ibid., 101–2.

36. Moncada, quoted in Borrow, 102–3.

37. Ibid., 103.

38. Ibid., 104.

39. Ibid., 105.

40. Ibid., 105–6.

41. While the concept of *limpieza de sangre*, or purity of blood, was used against the Jews and Gypsies, it originated in Jewish thought.

42. Bertha B. Quintana and Lois Gray Floyd, *Que Gitano!* (Prospect Heights, Illinois: Waveland Press, 1986), 20.

43. Ibid., 21.

44. Borrow, *The Zincali*, 107.

45. I. Should, "Preface," *Dissertation on the gipsies being an historical enquiry, concerning the manner of life, economy, customs and conditions of these people in Europe, and their origin* (London: G. Bigg, P. Elmsley, and T. Cadell in the Strand, and J. Sewell, in Cornhill, 1787), i.

46. Clébert, *The Gypsies*, 29–31. For the Gypsies' entrance to Beaucaire, France, in 1300, Clébert cites H. de Galier, *Filles nobles et magiciennes* (1913). Clébert, quoting Brian Vesey-Fitzgerald's 1944 *Gypsies of Britain*, cites the specific date of 22 April 1505 "as the date of the first official reference to Gypsies in Britain, a very brief note in the accounts of the Lord Treasurer for Scotland . . . Item to the Egyptians be the Kinge's command," Clébert, *The Gypsies*, 36.

47. Starkie, quoted in Quintana and Floyd, *Que Gitano!*, 12.

48. Quintana and Floyd, 13, 15.

49. Heinrich Moritz Gottlieb Grellman, *Dissertation on the gipsies being an historical enquiry, concerning the manner of life, œconomy, customs and conditions of these people in Europe, and their origin*. Written in German, translated into English by Matthew Raper, 1808. For further research on the Sanskrit linguistic root of *Romani* and of the dates or the Gypsies' entrance into Europe, please see the following sources: Martin Block, *Moeurs et coutumes des Tziganes* (London, 1936); Jules Bloch, *Les Tziganes* (1953); Bataillard, *De l'Apparitions des bohémiens en Europe* (1844); Hutton, *Les Castes de l'Inde* (1949); Alexandre Vexliard, *Introduction à la sociologie du vagabondage* (1956); Graberg, *Doutes et Conjectures sur les bohémiens et leur première apparition en Europe* (before 1817); Lyonnais, *Histoire generale des larrons* (1623–1709); J. A. Vaillant, *Grammaire dialogues et vocabulaire de la langues des Bohémiens ou Cigains* (Paris, 1868); Walter Simson, *History of the Gypsies* (London, 1865); Charles Godfrey Leland, *The English Gypsies and Their Language* (London, 1873); Francísco de Sales Mayo, *Los Gitanos, su historia, sus costumbres, su dialecto* (Madrid, 1869). An extremely interesting and problematic journal publication that helps the researcher to trace the historical origins of the Gypsies of Spain is the *Journal for Gypsy Lore*, begun in London in 1888 by the Gypsy Lore Society, a group of mostly wealthy, educated philologists. The articles, some of which are available on-line or on microfilm, are largely unsubstantiated. Still, they are very interesting and, from time to time, document the writer's research trail.

50. Grellmann, *Dissertation on the Gipsies*, x.

51. Quintana and Floyd, *Que Gitano!*, 13.

52. Borrow, *The Zincali*, 126.

53. Walter Starkie, *The Road to Santiago* (New York: E. P. Dutton, 1957), 146.

54. Quintana and Floyd, 14.

55. Ibid., 14. While the papal decree was meant to encourage Gypsies to visit Christian pilgrimage sites, a radical transformation of religious pilgrimage in Spain and France ensued. Gypsies began to visit certain saints like Sara the Black in St. Marie de la Mer, considered by Christians to be one of three Maries to be visited, decorated, and honored with gifts. Gypsies from all over Europe journey there yearly on pilgrimage. St. Marie de la Mer is an interesting choice for the Gypsies. It feels like a paradox of their pilgrimage, rather than a point of completion—salvation, redemption, and rebirth.

However, that said, the city is not the Gypsies' geographical end-point. Instead, it is the sea into which the Gypsies wander carrying "Sara the Black." Their journey into a living body of water is indeed a communal baptism, a rebirth—the ability to begin again. Shortly thereafter, the Gypsy caravans will turn around and journey in reverse along their path, a contemporary version of their first movements within western and eastern Europe.

56. "The Spaniards," argues twentieth-century Gypsy historian Jean-Paul Clébert, are *Gitanos*, meaning Egyptians. See, Clébert. "Origins," *The Gypsies.*

57. Quintana and Floyd, *Que Gitano!*, 14.

58. Ibid., 15. See Manuel de Falla, *Escritos sobre musica y musicos Débussy, Wagner, el "cante jondo."* *Introduction y notas* (Buenos Aires: Espasa-Calpe, 1950).

59. Grellmann quotes an author speaking of how the Polish laws against Gypsy men who continued a nomadic life were medieval. The Gypsy was whipped until he bled and his nostrils were slit. It is no wonder that, five hundred years later, also in Poland, between six hundred thousand and one million Gypsies should be murdered.

60. Quintana and Floyd, *Que Gitano!*, 16, quoting Starkie, *Road to Santiago*, 147. When one considers the dreadfully impoverished circumstances in which most European peasants lived in the fifteenth century—tilling unfertile, tiny plots belonging to them and large fields belonging to the local nobility, living with disease and cold, illiterate and dependent upon the Church for most news—it is no wonder that they rejected with such prejudicial vehemence the appearance of nomadic, dark, people speaking a strange language they could not understand and who played tricks on them. The medieval persecution of anyone who did not belong—whose ways differed from everyone else's—is a well-known phenomenon. Most Europeans lived and died in the villages where they were born. Most never traveled more than fifteen kilometers in their entire lives, at a time when average life expectancy was less than thirty years.

61. Quintana and Floyd, 16.

62. Ibid., x.

63. Gypsy *cantaor* quoted in Quintana and Floyd, 12.

64. Americo Castro, *The Structure of Spanish History*, 89, refers to a group of *enciados* whom he characterizes as people who "moved between religions and capitalized on their bilingualism, serving as spies. Enciados lived in border towns" such as Extremadura, specializing in smuggling.

65. Francísco Prieto-Moreno, *Granada* (Barcelona: Noguer, 1963), 10. The Alhambra Palace

rises in three sections above Granada formed by the Alcazaba, the Royal Palaces, and the Citadel. "Constructed in 1238 by Sultan Al Hamar who moved his court to a fortified hill from the Albaícin, it reflects the need for a fortified structure," 12.

66. Moreno's description of the Palace, 14.

67. Borrow, *The Zincali*, 45.

68. Castro, *The Structure of Spanish History*, 81.

69. Ibid.

70. Castro refers to the northern Spanish kingdoms as "nonsubject Christendom."

71. Castro, *The Structure of Spanish History*, 83.

72. Bernard Lewis, *The Arabs in History* (Oxford: Oxford University Press, 1958), 146. In Arabia, the *Qu'ran* was the first written work of literature. Its historical accounting began with the Prophet's life, born in 622. Thanks to Muhammad's fourth wife, Aiesha, who was said to have written down the *hadiths*, the Revelations were recorded.

73. Lewis, *The Arabs in History*, 146–47.

74. Ibid.

75. Ibid., 150.

76. Castro, *The Structure of Spanish History*, 84.

77. Clébert, *The Gypsies*, 85.

78. See Clébert, *The Gypsies*.

79. Molina Fajardo, quoted in K. Meira Weinzweig, *Border Trespasses*, 43.

80. Quintana and Floyd, *Que Gitano!*, 17.

81. Ibid., 17–18.

82. See Konrad Bercovici, *The Story of the Gypsies* (New York: Cosmopolitan Books, 1928), and George Borrow, *The Zincali*, 83.

83. Castro, *The Structure of Spanish History*, 350.

84. Castro, *The Structure of Spanish History*, 90. Florencio Janer, *Condicion social de los moriscos*, 1857, 162.

85. Castro, *The Structure of Spanish History*, 92, quoting Janer, *Condicion social de los moriscos*, 144. Don Antonio de Fuenmayor, *Vida y hechos de Pio V*, 1595. Castro tells us that twenty books were written between 1610 and 1613 documenting the power of the Hispano-Arab-Andalusian voice in both forming and swaying public opinion.

86. Castro, *The Structure of Spanish History*, 92, quoting Don Antonio de Fuenmayor.

87. Castro, *The Structure of Spanish History*, 92.

88. Henry Charles Lea, *The Moriscos of Spain: Their Conversion and Expulsion* (Philadelphia: Lea Bros., 1901), 407.

89. Castro, *The Structure of Spanish History*, 95–96.

90. Aurelia Martin Casares, "Free and Black Africans in Granada in the Time of the Spanish Renaissance," in *Black Africans in Renaissance Europe*, ed. T. F. Earle and K. J. P. Lowe (Cambridge, UK: Cambridge University Press, 2005), 250. *Slave* in Arabic is *abid*.

91. Ibid., 254.

92. Ibid., 256. Casares has done an excellent job of researching the Archivo de la Alhambra as well as both the Church and municipal archives in Granada and Seville.

93. Casares tells us that Granada tried to help freed Blacks, while it did nothing to aid the Gypsy. The two confraternities were Nuestra Señora de la Encarnacion y Paciencia de Cristo in the Church

of San Justo y Pastor and San Benito de Palermo in the church of Santa Escolastica. Both helped slaves to obtain their freedom.

94. Aurelia Martin Casares, "La hechiceria en la Andalucia Moderna; una forma de poder de las mujeras?" (Casares, "Free and Black Africans in Granada," 257).

95. All remaining Spanish Muslims were forced to convert to Christianity in 1505. They were, thereafter, called *Moriscos*. By the end of the sixteenth century, many had been labeled as only wearing a mask of Christianity. Eventually, the *Moriscos* were either killed or expelled by the Office of the Inquisition because the Spanish crown and Church continued to fear subsequent Muslim uprisings against the Christian State and institutions she upheld.

96. Alessandro Stella, *Histoires d'esclaves dance la peninsule iberique* (Paris: École des Haute Études en Sciences Sociales, 2000), 76–77.

97. Casares, "Free and Black Africans in Granada," 250.

98. Casares quotes from the law of 1560, ratified by the Cortes de Toledo and reified in 1566.

99. Ibid., 251.

100. Ibid.

101. Ibid., 248. While Dr. Casares is primarily interested in the Spanish etymological reference to the slave or freed person living in Renaissance Spain, I am interested in the exact geographical region from whence the slave came before arriving in Spain, so as to understand how the dances and drumming might have made their way into flamenco.

For further information on slavery in Spain, Casares suggests Stella, *Histoires d'esclaves danse la peninsule iberique*; Alexis Bernard, *Les esclaves a Seville au debut du XVIIe siecle*, Ph.D. Dissertation, University of Lyon, 1998; Albert Ndambe Kabongo, *Les escalves a Cordue au debut du XVIIe siecle (1600–1621)*, Ph.D. Dissertation, University de Toulouse, Le Mirail, 1975; A. C. de C. M. Saunders, *A Social History of Black Slaves and Freedmen in Portugal, 1441–1551* (Cambridge: Cambridge University Press, 1981).

102. Dance scholar Katita Milazzo is conducting research in the area of the effect of African dance and music on Gypsy flamenco at present, and I look forward to her book on the subject.

103. Casares, "Free and Black Africans in Granada," 252.

CHAPTER FIVE Gypsies in the Dance Cafés of the Islamic Mediterranean

1. Quoted in Roselyne Chenu. *Le Désert* (Paris: Les Éditions du cerf, 1994).

2. Gayatri Spivak, *Can the Subaltern Speak?: Reflections on the History of an Idea*, ed. Rosalind Morris (New York: Columbia University Press, 2010).

3. Edward Saïd, *Orientalism* (London: Routledge & Kegan Paul, 1978), quoting Jean-Baptiste-Joseph Fourier, "Préface historique," vol. 1. *Déscription de l'Égypte* (Paris: Imprimerie Impériale, 1809–28), 84.

4. Napoleon Bonaparte's first expedition to Egypt took place in 1798.

5. Marianna Taymanova, "Alexandre Dumas in Egypt: Mystification or Truth?," in *Travellers in Egypt*, ed. Paul and Janet Starkey (London: Tauris Books, 2001), 181. Taymanova writes that "the School of Oriental Languages was established in Paris in 1795," on the heels of Napoleon's passage through Spain and into Egypt. Taymanova discovers an essential distinction between the emerging Orientalist writers. "Some," she tells us, "were looking for the classical past; others for Biblical traditions; yet others were attracted by Oriental exoticism. Several writers (such as Chateaubriand and Nerval) described their travels in diary form, others (like Hugo and Balzac) wrote about the Orient

without having set foot there. Hence literary involvement with the Orient soon became a kind of internal dream. In this respect, one may speak about Romantic Orientalism as a peculiar synthesis, where ancient Oriental wisdom fruitfully merged with European culture." Taymanova, 182.

6. According to Middle Eastern dance scholar Penni Al Zayer, in her book *Middle Eastern Dance* (Philadelphia: Chelsea House, 2004), 30–34, the Ghawazi are thought to have migrated from northern India to the Middle East around the fifth century CE. "Many of them became traveling entertainers. Although it was their habit to adopt the religion of their host countries, they were still considered to be outsiders. So even after the advent of Islam, they were not subject to the same restrictions [on dance] as the local Islamic population." The Ghawazi, Al Zayer argues, are those Gypsy women who traveled from city to city in Egypt, dancing on the streets and in the cafés of Cairo. Some lived in Cairo. Others lived along the banks of the Nile. Known to Napoleon's soldiers as "thieves of the heart," the Ghawazi became a part of the Orientalist "tour" of the Middle East.

7. Middle Eastern dancer and dance scholar Wendy Buonaventura, in "Images of Women in Arabic Dance," *Dancing Times* (July 1997), 925, argues that the Gypsy dancers—the Ghawazi—could be found in company with Egyptian dancers who earned a living dancing in Cairo along the 'al Hoshe Derbek (Street of the Open Hall), 57. The ban against the Ghawazi dancers was lifted in 1866 and all dancers were allowed to return to Cairo from Upper Egypt to perform. Interestingly, Buonaventura argues that the Ghawazi contributed over a tenth of all taxes collected in Cairo (68–69).

8. For a history of French ethnography and a distinction between folklore and ethnography, see Michel Valière, *Ethnographie de la France. Histoire et enjeux contemporains des approaches du patrimoine ethnologique* (Paris: Armand Colin, 2002).

I would argue that the field of ethnography is born in the poetry and literature that emerges in France in the eighth and ninth centuries (*La Chanson du Geste*, "The Song of Heroic Deeds") after the Arab invasions of the early eighth century. Battles fought by the King of France, Charles Martel, between 722 and 732 in southern France and later in the century by his grandson Charlemagne, birthed a literature on the part of both medieval Arab geographers and French priests that spoke to the need to feel superior to the invading army. The notion of "us" versus "them" emerges, shaping a historiography of contact and ethnographic study, however misplaced.

9. French Romanticism in literature commences with the writings of Chateaubriand and Victor Hugo.

10. For further insight into the French Romantic notion of "L'Orient," see Anouar Louca, *Les Sources Marseillaises de l'orient romantique* (Paris: Maisonneuve et Larose, 2001); Sarga Moussa, *Géographie des orientales* (Paris: Maisonneuve et Larose, 2001); Claude Millet, *Le Déspote oriental* (Paris: Maisonneuve et Larose, 2001); and Paul and Janet Starkey, ed., *Travellers in Egypt* (New York: Tauris Books, 2001).

11. Saïd, *Orientalism*, 5.

12. Ibid., 43–44; 45.

13. On the evolution of flamenco in the cafés of Spain and France, see Ninotchka Devorah Bennahum, *Antonia Mercé, "La Argentina"* (Middletown, CT: Wesleyan University Press, 2000).

14. Telephone conversation with Art History Professor T. Kaori Kitao about the history of the city and its etymology, New York City, June 2000.

15. According to John Henry Hutton's *Les Castes de l'Inde: nature, fonction, origines* (Paris: Payot, 1949), Gypsies came to Europe from India out of Egypt. Gypsy beliefs, he argues, were recorded in the ancient Sanskrit text *The Book of Manu* as Hindu-influenced with worship of Cali, the Hindu Goddess

of Destruction. In Egypt and later Spain, Cali would be transformed from a pagan deity into Sara, the Black Madonna.

16. Jean-Paul Clébert, *The Gypsies* (London: Vista, 1963), 41. Also see Jules Bloch, *Les Tsiganes* (Paris: Presse Universitaire de France, 1953.)

17. Konrad Bercovici, *The Story of the Gypsies* (New York: Cosmopolitan Books, 1928), and Frans de Ville, *Tziganes: Tziganes: Témoins des temps* (Brussels: Office de Publicité) 1956.

18. Quoted in Clébert's *The Gypsies*, after *Encyclopédie de l'Histoire*.

19. Clébert drawing from the French *Encylopedie d'Histoire*. See also chapter 1, *Les Tziganes de l'ancien régime.*

20. *Les Roms, histoire vrai bohémiens* (1857); *Les Bohémiens du pays Basque* (1862).

21. Law of Carlos III against the Gypsies, 1633.

22. They became in reality and in the minds of local populations a kind of borderless subculture, living always on the margins of society, taking only temporary jobs, living for freedom and safety purposes on the edge of town, close to a riverbank or forest, either outside, or in caravans.

23. Benserade, who wrote his *Oeuvres* in 1627, speaks to the centuries-long presence of Indic-Egyptian dancers in France, with orientalist palaver but rather, like Lévi-Strauss, as an ethnographer, curious to understand how their *danse bohéme* and local custom meet, at the town crossroads.

24. The only dancer of the mid-nineteenth century known by name was Safiya, also known as Kutchuk Hanem, a Turkish name meaning "Little Princess," Buonaventura, "Images of Women in Arabic Dance," 71. Hanem was the lover of Muhammad 'Ali's son, Abbas Pasha, and was allowed to remain in Cairo during the ban on dancing. An American journalist, G. W. Curtis (1824–1892), met her in the 1850s and described her dancing: "The sharp surges of sound swept around the room, dashing in regular measure against her movelessness, until suddenly the whole surface of her frame quivered in measure with the music. Her hands were raised, clapping the castanets, and she slowly turned upon herself, her right leg the pivot, marvelously convulsing all the muscles of her body. When she had completed the circuit of the spot on which she stood, she advanced slowly, all the muscles jerking in time to the music, and in solid, substantial spasms . . . It was a curious and wonderful gymnastic. There was no graceful dancing—only the movement of dancing when she advanced, throwing one leg before the other as gypsies dance," George William Curtis, *Nile Notes of a Howadji* (New York: Harper, 1852): 134–35. Electronic resource.

25. Charles Didier, *Les Nuits de Caire* (Paris: Hachette, 1860), 329.

26. For Gustave Flaubert's orientalist literature, see *Voyage en Égypte* (1851); *Salammbô* (1862); *La Tentation de Saint Antoine* (1874); and *Trois Contes* (1877). Flaubert visited Egypt in the late 1840s and met Kutchuk Hanem with whom he had a sexual relationship, memorialized by him in his letters to his mistress, the poet and novelist Louise Colet. Flaubert described his encounter with Hanem.

27. The Ghawazi were Gypsy dancers who performed publicly and privately for men who paid them. When Governor 'Ali banned them dancing, Egyptian boys and young men, hoping to take over their living, impersonated them and were found dancing in cafés in Cairo. See Christian Poché, *Les danses dans le monde arabe ou l'héritage des almées* (1996). Governor Muhammad 'Ali Pasha ruled Egypt from 1805 until 1849. During Ali Pasha's reign of "modernization," historian Philip Sadgrove argues there to have been approximately 3,000 Europeans visiting the country in 1836. In 1840, that number comprised approximately 2,000 Italians, 700 to 800 French, and 80 to 100 British. See Philip Sadgrove, "Travellers Rendezvous and Cultural Institutions in Muhammad 'Ali's Egypt," in Paul and Janet Starkey, ed., *Travellers in Egypt*, 257. One of the most interesting facts about Governor 'Ali was that

he was illiterate and yet he possessed a tremendous love of learning, and set up schools throughout Egypt in addition to a national library in 1822 with some 25,000 volumes in various languages (Sadgrove, 258).

British travel writer Edward William Lane (1801–1876), in his extensive 1835 work on Egypt, wrote on the Ghawazi. See E. W. Lane, *An Account of the Manners and Customs of the Modern Egyptians, Written during the Years 1833 and 1835* (London: Charles Knight & Co., 1836).

Governor 'Ali had four hundred Ghawazi publicly whipped and then drowned in the Nile river as a warning to any women who might have been thinking about defying his anti-dance entertainment statutes.

28. *Description de l'Égypte* (1798). Interview with Egyptian costume historian, Hannadi Sileet, Paris, Bibliothèque Nationale à l'Arsenal, Paris, 12 June 2002.

29. Juana, "From the High Atlas to the Desert's Shore," *Dance Magazine* (December 1951), 17.

30. Frederich Schlegel quoted in Michel le Bris, *Romantics and Romanticism* (New York: Skira Rizzoli, 1981), 170.

31. Edward Saïd, *Orientalism*, 84. See also, *Description de l'Égypte ou recueil des observations et des recherches qui ont été faites en Égypte pendant l'expédition de l'armée français, publié par les orders de sa majesté l'empereur Napoléon le grand*, 23 vols. (Paris: Imprimerie impériale, 1809–1828.)

32. According to Alexander Dumas, "toute cette nouvelle page s'ouvre donc avec Bonaparte encadré par deux arabisants provençaux." Dumas, quoted in Marianna Taymanova, "Alexandre Dumas in Egypt: Mystification or Truth," in Paul and Janet Starkey, ed., *Travellers in Egypt*, 182.

33. Marianna Taymanova, "Alexandre Dumas in Egypt: Mystification or Truth," 182. While Dumas traveled extensively through Russia (1858–1859; producing eight volumes of literature afterward called *Voyage en Russie*) one wonders whether he visited Egypt. "Le Sinaï? C'est vrai, je n'y suis guère allé, mais le pachah d'Égypte m'a felicité de mon livre; sans moi, ce pays-là serait inconnu de mes contemporains!" (. . . Without me, this country would have remained unknown to my contemporaries! 186). Still, one wonders whether or not George Borrow ever read Dumas.

34. Taymanova, "Alexandre Dumas in Egypt," 183.

35. Volney, *Voyage en Syrie et Égypte*, 1787. See also Sadgrove. "Travellers' Rendezvous and Cultural Institutions in Muhammad 'Ali's Egypt," 257–67.

36. James Augustus St. John, *Egypt and Nubia: Their Scenery and Their People* (London: Chapman & Hall, 1845), 274.

37. Buonaventura, "Images of Women in Arabic Dance," 70.

38. François de Vaux de Foletier, *Les Tsiganes dans l'ancienne régime* (Paris: Gallimard, 1935); Jean Peyriguere, "Poesie et danse dans une tribu berbere du moyen-atlas," *Études et Documents Berbères* (1998, 15–16), 219–48.

39. Anouar Louca quoting Victor Hugo from *Les Orientales* (1829), *Les sources Marseillaises de l'Orient romantique* (Paris: Maisonneuve et Larose, 2001), 16–17.

40. Buonaventura, "Images of Women in Arabic Dance," 65.

41. Algeria, *Oxford English Dictionary*, and Poché, *Les danses dans le monde arabe*. See also Marino, "Cafés," *Révue du Monde Musulman* 75–76, no. 3 (1995).

42. Poché, *Les danses dans le monde arabe*, 39.

43. For a fine analysis of the use of the hands in Middle Eastern dance, see Wendy Buonaventura, *Serpent of the Nile. Women and Dance in the Arab World* (New York: Interlink Books, 1998).

44. The *Zambra Mora* has an important and interesting history. Emerging in the courts of the

Hispano-Arab caliphs of Muslim Spain, with rhythmic origins in North Africa and the Afro-Caribbean, the *Zambra Mora* was well-known for having its roots in the Arab world. In the context of nineteenth-century Orientalist spectatorship, it becomes all the more enticing a dance, as it is twice-invented, emerging in the East and carried to the Maghreb by musicians and dancers who entered Muslim Spain and then reemerging well after the Inquisition in New Spain. Among the ecstatic, quasi-religious dances of the Bedouin, its performance was protected by virtue of geographic separation from the city and public eyes.

Dancer/flamencologist K. Meira Weinzweig has written that a particular style of *zambra*, called "La Golondrina"—named after María García Cortes Campos, "La Golondrina," born in 1843, whose daughter Carmen Amaya Cortes became "a specialist in the *Soleares* and *Siguiriyas*"—is still danced in the caves of the Sacromonte. See K. Meira Weinzweig, *Border Trespasses: The Gypsy Mask and Carmen Amaya's Flamenco Dance*, Unpublished Dissertation, Temple University (January 1995), 246, n. 85.

45. Quoted in Buonaventura, *Serpent of the Nile*, 43. W. L. Westermann, "The Castanet Dancers of Arsinoe," *Journal of Egyptian Archeology* (London, 1924): 135. Also see "Danse des Femmes," *Le Monde* (10 January 1998), vol. 55, no. 16.

46. Marian Grut, *The Bolero School* (London: Dance Books, 2002), 151.

47. Ibid.

48. Christian Poché, "La Danse Arabe: quelques repères," *Les danses dans le monde arabe ou l'héritage des almées* (1996). See also "Folk Heritage. Arts of the Islamic World," *ART* (1993, no. 23).

49. Richard Ford, *Traveller's Hand-book of Spain* (New York: Scribner's, 1891), 96.

50. Maxine du Camp, quoted in *Flaubert in Egypt* (New York: Penguin, 1972), 61.

51. "L'Usage de l'Opium chez les Orientaux," *Le Voleur* (28 February 1830). This is also poem 48 of the "Spleen de Paris: Petits poems en prose." The title is in English with a French subtitle/translation: "Any Where out of the World / N'importe où hors du monde." It appears in the *Oeuvres completes*, vol. 1 (Paris: Éditions Gallimard. Bibliothèque de la Pléiade, 1975): 356–57.

52. Ibid., 161.

53. Savary, *Lettres sur l'Égypte*. Paris: Chez Onfroi libraire, 1785, quoted in Poché, *Les danses dans le monde arabe*, 46.

54. Interview with Joaquin Enciñas after his interview with Angel Alvarez Caballero, 10 June 2000, Albuquerque, New Mexico, Festival Flamenco International.

55. Alexander Dumas, *Voyage en Orient: quinze jours au Sinai* (Stuttgart: E. Hallberger, 1839), 214.

56. Ibid.

57. Ibid., 220.

58. Antoine de St. Éxupery, *Le Petit Prince* (Paris: Gallimard, 1946).

59. Telephone interview with Mr. LeClézio, June 2002, New Mexico.

60. Linda Nochlin, "The Imaginary Orient," *Art in America* (May 1983). With tourist numbers travelling to Algeria on the decrease, other faraway escapes emerged in the wake of an industrializing, increasingly middle-class Europe. The coast of the Mediterranean was seen as an endless, Zen-like expanse. Like the Arabian Desert lands, the Gobi and the Sahara deserts beckoned the brave traveler.

61. Théophile Gautier, "Le Désert," *La Presse* (16 December 1844).

62. Victor Hugo. *Le Hunchback de Notre-Dame* (New York: Modern Library 1831), 55.

63. Fawzia Afzel-Khan. "Where Are the Muslim Feminist Voices?" *Drama Review* (September 2001): 5.

64. *Matisse in Morocco: The Paintings and Drawings, 1912–1913* (Washington, DC: National Gallery of Art, 1990), 23.

65. Félicien César David (1810–1876) studied music in Egypt between 1832 and 1833, returning to Paris only to lace his French symphonic scores with the "orientalist" sounds he had absorbed during his travels: *Le Désert* (1844); *Moïse au Sinaï* (1846); *Christoph Columb* (1847); *Eden* (1848); *La Perle du Brésil* (1851); *Herculanum* (1859); and *Lala-Roukh* (1862), whose scenery and costumes are among the most sensuous of the era. David was awarded the Légion d'honneur in 1862, following the composition of *Lala-Roukh*, and was given a civil pension for life. See, David Félicien. Cliché B.N.: [C76193. Est. 29] BN - Paris Opéra.

66. BN-Arsénal. Colléction Rondel [*Carmen* Programs and Press clippings.]

CHAPTER SIX Picasso, the Bull, and Carmen

1. Pablo Picasso quoted in Michel Leiris. "Introduction," *Romancero du picador* (Paris, 1960).

2. Ibid., 341–42. "These two aspects of his Spanish nature also dominate his painting . . . He has a Latin anthropomorphic sense of form . . . At the same time his sense of rhythm has enabled him to express his emotions independently of his subject matter. Not one of Picasso's works is the product of his own imagination alone; all of them have been fertilized by something outside of himself . . . to make a masterpiece out of rubbish gratifies his ambition."

3. Ibid., 341.

4. Prosper Mérimée, *Carmen, la novella* (Philadelphia: Henry Altemus, 1899), 40.

5. Picasso's Andalusian sensibility attracted him to Carmen. Andalusia is steamy hot— desert hot. People spend the afternoon into the evening drinking cool red wine or beer laced with lemonade to combat the temperature. The land is arid, like New Mexico, filled with rocks that jut out from hillsides and on dirt roads. One-lane roads are the only way to travel from town to town.

6. See Annie Maïllis, *Picasso et Leiris dans les arènes: Les écrivains, les artistes et les toros . . . 1937–1957* (Paris: Éditions Cairn, 2002), Preface.

7. Wilhelm Boeck and Jaime Sabartés, *Picasso* (New York: Harry N. Abrams, 1955), 511.

8. John Richardson, *A Life of Picasso: The Cubist Rebel, 1907–1916*, vol. 2 (New York: Random House, 1990), 151. See also John Richardson. *A Life of Picasso, 1881–1906*, vol. 1 (New York: Alfred A. Knopf, 2007).

9. Prosper Mérimée, *Carmen, la novella*, 43–44.

10. Richardson, vol. 2, 14.

11. Ibid.

12. Ibid., 27.

13. Ibid.

14. Boeck and Sabartés, *Picasso*, 512.

15. One need only compare Picasso's prophecy *Guernica* to Goya's *Disasters of War* (*Los Désastres de la Guerra*, 1810–1820). Both painters bore witness to cruelty and injustice, each abstracting figurative representation in order to say something universal about inhumanity.

16. Anne Baldassari, *Picasso Carmen: sol y sombra* (Paris: Éditions de la Réunion des Musée Nationeaux, Flammarion, 2007), 7.

17. Ibid., 28. On the subject of Vallauris, see also Françoise Gilot and Carlton Lake, *Life with Picasso* (New York: McGraw Hill, 1964).

18. Picasso kept the ticket stubs—*sol y sombra*—from bullfights in Arles and Nîmes as well as

postcards of famous matadors—his friend Dominguin—Gypsy and Spanish dancers and other Spanish images. Archives, Musée Picasso, Corréspondences. [Écrits. Picasso, 1905–1962.]

19. "Voilà, la gitanilla! Je levai les yeux et je la vis. C'était un vendredi, et je ne l'oublierai jamais." Prosper Mérimée, *Carmen* (Paris: Gallimard, 2000), 70.

20. Boeck and Sabartés, *Picasso*, 515; Christian Dedet, "Minotaurs et Taureaux," *Corrida* 12 (March 1982): 33–37.

21. Pablo Picasso, Prosper Mérimée, Louis Aragon. *Le Carmen des Carmens* (Paris: Editeurs, 1964).

22. Prosper Mérimée, *Carmen des Carmens*; Archives de Musée Picasso. [Classeur 6. Louis Aragon. 25 letters. 1919–1953]; Escamillo. "Toreador Song," *Carmen* Act II. (New York: G. Schirmer, 1959): 10.

23. Pablo Picasso quoted in Françoise Gilot, *Vivre avec Picasso* (Paris: Calmann-Lévy, 1965), 116.

24. The Surrealist Movement was founded by André Breton in 1922, upon the publication of the *Surrealist Manifesto*. Writers such as Jacob, Apollinaire, Leiris, Baron, Heine, Cocteau, Prévert, Bataille, Desnos, Vitrac Ribemont-Dessaignes, Tzara, Éluard, Péret, Hugnet, Man Ray, Zervos, Sabartés, Dalí, Fernandez, Gonzalez, Miró, and Picasso contributed to the rich literary and visual tapestry that represented Breton's manifesto.

25. "A surrealist before surrealism came to be," Breton maintained close ties to Picasso, about whom he wrote in 1934: "Picasso is Surrealist in cubism." André Breton, *Qu'est-ce que le surrealisme?* (Paris: Actuel/Le Temps qu'il fait, 1986). Picasso illustrated two of Breton's books: *Clair de Terre* (1923) and *Anthologie de l'Humour Noir* (1940); the latter contained two Picasso poems.

26. Breton, *Qu'est-ce que le surrealisme?*, 66.

27. The myth of the Minotaur emerges from Crete, the first Greek civilization, twelve or thirteen centuries before the Common Era. The myth goes as follows: King Minos had several wives who all tried to give him an heir. Their entrails produced nothing but snakes and scorpions. Finally Pasiphae birthed normal children, Phaedre and Ariadne. Minos offended the God Poseidon who took revenge by making Pasiphae fall in love with a bull. Pasiphae married Daedalus, an Athenian engineer with whom she conceived the Minotaur. King Minos ordered Daedalus to construct the labyrinth in which to hide the Minotaur, as well as himself. But instead, Daedalus built himself and the Minotaur wings of wax and together they rose into the sky.

28. Herschel Chipp, *Picasso's Guernica: Histories, Transformations, Meanings* (Berkeley: University of California Press, 1988), 112.

29. Françoise Gilot describes Picasso's series in *Life with Picasso*.

30. Paloma Esteban Leal, "Picasso/Minotauro," *Picasso/Minotauro* (Madrid: Museo Nacional Centro de Arte Reina Sofia, 2001), 226.

31. Leal, "Picasso/Minotauro," 224.

32. Ibid.

33. Ibid., 225. See also Nagai Takanori, "Picasso and the Minotaur," *Picasso: The Love and the Anguish, the Road to Guernica* (Kyoto: The National Museum of Modern Art, 1995), exhibition catalogue.

34. Leal, "Picasso/Minotauro," 226. Picasso met Olga Koklova in 1917. They married in 1918 and had a child, Paulo, in 1921. Later, in 1935 (and while still married to Olga), Picasso's mistress, the very young Marie-Therese Walter, had a child, Maya, by him. Picasso, still a Spanish citizen, was unable to obtain a divorce.

35. Carmen does not possess a man's physical strength. Like the matador squaring off against the bull toward the end of the fight, moving ever so close for the final blow, taunting him with cape and gesture, Carmen must rely on her intelligence to defeat her opponent.

36. Tristan Tzara, "Picasso et la Poésie," *Commentari*, vol. 4, no. 3 (July–September, 1953): 181–203.

37. Christine Piot in "Picasso and the Practice of Writing," *Picasso Collected Writing* (Paris: Editions Gallimard, 1989), xxxii, quoting Antonio Jimenez Milan and André Breton.

38. Pablo Picasso quoted by Christine Piot, in "Picasso and the Practice of Writing," xxvii.

39. Jean Leymarie, "Picasso, the New Ulysses," *Picasso and the Mediterranean* (Humlebaek, Denmark, 1996), 21, exhibition catalogue.

40. Piot, "Picasso and the Practice of Writing," xxvii.

41. Leal, "Picasso/Minotauro," 244.

42. Piot, "Picasso and the Practice of Writing," xxviii.

43. Ibid.

44. Ibid.

45. André Breton, "Guillaume Apollinaire," *Les Pas Perdus*, 1924, and "Picasso dans son Élément," *Point du jour* (Paris: Gallimard, 1934).

46. Piot, "Picasso and the Practice of Writing," xxviii.

47. Ibid.

48. Pièrre Reverdy, "Pablo Picasso et son oeuvre," *Nord-Sud, Self Défence et autres écrits sur l'art et la poésie* (1917–1926), *Oeuvres Completes* (Paris: Flammarion, 1975), 203. In 1924, Reverdy had defined Cubism as "plastic poetry."

49. Picasso quoted by Piot, "Picasso and the Practice of Writing," xxix.

50. Tristan Tzara, *Surréalisme au Service de la Révolution*, no. 4 (Paris, 1932): 20.

51. Leal, "Picasso/Minotauro," 228.

52. Piot, "Picasso and the Practice of Writing," xxx. Piot is quoting Breton's "Le Méssage automatique," *Point du jour* (Paris: Gallimard, 1934): 195.

53. Piot, "Picasso and the Practice of Writing," xxix.

54. Man Ray was born Emmanuel Radnitzky in Philadelphia. He was born in 1890 and died in 1976, just three years after Picasso. Man Ray was one of dozens of artists who visited Picasso in southern France before and after the German occupation of the country.

55. Man Ray, *Madame Errazuriz, Picasso et Olga*, 1924, *Musée Picasso*, 2007. Visiting Gypsy flamenco choreographer and dancer Mario Maya at his Sevillian home in 1995, I was taken on a tour of his house. In the center of an empty bedroom a chair was placed. On the chair rested an exquisite matador's jacket and pants.

56. Ramon Gomez de la Serna, "Le Toréador de la Peinture," *Cahiers d'art*, no. 3–5, 1932. On the history of Picasso's profound love of the bullfight, I studied the following sources: Marie-Laure Bernadac, "1933–1940 Del Minotauro à Guernica," *Picasso, Toros y Toreros* (Paris: Musée Picasso, 1993); José Delgado (born Pepe Illo, matador), *El carnet de la Tauromaquia* (Barcelona: Editorial Gustavo Gili, S.A., 1963). Illo died in the *corrida*, 11 May 1801; Luis Miguel Dominguin (matador), *Toros y Toreros* (Paris: Éditions Cercle d'Art, 1961); Jaime Sabartés, *À los toros avec Picasso* (Monte Carlo: André Sauret, Éditeur, 1961); Archives de Musée Picasso [Billets d'entrée à la corrida (42 pieces)]. 1926–1963, Lettres reçue et documentation sur la corrida. 1917–1963. A.18, and Pablo Picasso with José Bergamín, Exhibition Catalogue for *Guernica*, 1937, Barcelona.

This was not the first time that Man Ray had photographed Picasso. In 1924, he shot Picasso and Olga together at the costume ball of Count Etienne Beaumont.

57. *Gitane* is the French word for Gypsy.

58. Pablo Picasso quoted in Michel Leiris, "Introduction," *Romancero du picador* (Paris, 1960).

59. Frank D. Russell, *Picasso's Guernica: The Labyrinth of Narrative and Vision* (Montclair, NJ: Allenheld & Schram, 1979), 297, n. 61.

60. Rudolf Arnheim, *The Genesis of a Painting: Picasso's Guernica* (Berkeley: University of California Press, 1962): 22–23.

61. Read Arnheim's text on *Guernica*, 27. See also Rudolf Arnheim, *Toward a Psychology of Art: Collected Essays* (Berkeley: University of California Press, 1966).

62. Russell, *Picasso's Guernica*, 63.

63. Gongora, quoted in Vicente Marrero, *Picasso and the Bull*, trans. Anthony Kerrigan (Chicago: Henry Regnery, 1956), 67.

64. Picasso interviewed in 1981 and quoted in Richardson, 2, 9.

65. Marrero, *Picasso and the Bull*, 78–79.

66. Ibid., 57.

67. Ibid., 20. The piece is now in the Archeological Museum of Cordoba.

68. Franz Altheim and E. Trautmann-Nehring, *Italia und Rom* (Amsterdam, 1941); Marrero, *Picasso and the Bull*, 23.

69. Marrero, *Picasso and the Bull*, 13.

70. Arnheim, *The Genesis of a Painting*, 45.

71. Rafael Alberti. Quoted by Vicente Marrerro. *Picasso and the Bull*. Trans. Anthony Kerrigan (Chicago: Henry Regnery Co., 1956), 68.

72. Picasso loved the psycho-sexual bloodsport of the *corrida* and attended every summer in southern France. He brought his entourage with him, always, to the *corridas*. Surrealist poets and painters and visiting flamenco singers all joined him in the bleachers. Picasso even brought his children Paloma and Claude.

73. Robert Payne, *The Civil War in Spain, 1936–1939* (New York: Putnam, 1962).

74. *London Times*, 26 April 1937.

75. Rudolf Arnheim. *The Genesis of a Painting: Picasso's Guernica* (Los Angeles: University of California Press, 1962; 2006): 18.

76. Arnheim, *The Genesis of a Painting*, 19.

77. Anne Maïllis, *Picasso et Leiris dans l'arène: Les écrivains, les artistes, et les toros . . . (1937–1957)* (Paris: Éditions Cairn, 2002): 15.

78. Marrero, *Picasso and the Bull*, 73.

79. Interview with Madame Brigitte Ortíz, 4 rue de l'Odéon, Paris, February 1986.

80. Clement Greenberg referred to *Guernica* as "Bulging and buckling . . . this huge painting reminds one of a battle scene from a pediment that has been flattened under a defective steam-roller. It is as if it had been conceived within an illusion of space deeper than that in which it was actually executed. . . . *Guernica* is the opposite of a breakthrough." Clement Greenberg quoted in Timothy Hilton, *Picasso* (London: Thames & Hudson, 1975), 246.

81. Ibid.

82. The metaphor of the horse for the Gypsy is clear. The horse represents autonomy, movement, freedom, the ability to leave, travel, disappear—values worshipped by Gypsies within the peripheral lifestyle to which they are condemned by Europeans and their historic *pragmaticas*.

83. Ibid.

84. Ibid

1. Flamenco is a complex art form, not easily understood. Its music and dance rhythms and poetic phrases require knowledge of Spanish, the Gypsy language, Caló, and the artistic relationship between singer and dancer. To understand the aesthetic power of flamenco is to understand a history of the form; to understand a technical history of flamenco is also to become fluent in Islamic Spanish culture. Thus we must travel to consider the root sources of Flamenco.

2. The titular leader of Mozarabic Spain was known as the "Caliph." Caliph means "commander of the faithful," supreme leader of law and faith. He rules over all peoples either born into or converted to Islam. The faithful share a transnational kinship. For example, the Umayyad dynasty ruled over all peoples from Damascus to Cordoba between 661 and 750 CE. Abd 'al Rahman I, the last-surviving son of the Umayyad dynasty, destroyed by the Abbasids in a murderous take-over, proclaimed himself commander of the faithful of Spain.

3. For a fuller discussion on the linguistic survival of Arabic in Andalusia after the Expulsion of the Moors in 1508, see Americo Castro, "Islam and Hispania," *The Structure of Spanish History*, trans. Edmund L. King (Princeton: Princeton University Press, 1954).

4. For a more comprehensive study of Muslim-Christian political and religious wars following the year 1492, please read Henry Kamen, *Empire: How Spain Became a World Power: 1492–1763* (New York: HarperCollins, 2003).

5. John Edwards, "The War against Islam," *Ferdinand and Isabella. Profiles in Power* (London: Pearson Longman, 2005): 48–68. Madinat 'al Zahra was constructed by the first self-proclaimed Caliph, Abd 'al Rahman I, living outside Damascus in 785/786.

6. Henri Pirenne. *Mohammed and Charlemagne* (New York: Norton Books, 1939), chapter 1.

7. For a discussion of social class distinction in early eighth-century Muslim armies, see Bernard Lewis, *The Muslim Discovery of Europe* (New York: W. W. Norton, 1982; 2001).

Islamic civilization in Spain began in the heart of the Muslim Middle East in the eighth century, in the city of Damascus in the year 710. The Umayyads, rulers of the Shi'ite dynasty, believed themselves directly descended from Mohammad the Prophet. Following the Prophet's teachings, they set up a well-organized bureaucracy—one that would be replicated in Spain—they collected taxes and ruled from Syria over Arabia, Sasanid Iran, and Palestine. After the death of Mohammed in 632 CE, Damascus became Islam's first civic center.

8. Richard Fletcher, *Moorish Spain* (London: Weidenfeld & Nicolson, 1992), 171. Bernard Lewis discusses the profound loss of homeland and cultural identity to Andalusian Hispano-Arabs and Sephardim exiled to North Africa in the late fifteenth and early sixteenth centuries. Lewis discovered that fleeing Andalusian citizens kept the keys to their Andalusian homes and hung them in their new North African homes.

9. For two fine histories of early Umayyad rule in Spain, please read Henri Pirenne, *Mohammed & Charlemagne* (New York: Norton, 1939) and Bernard Lewis, *The Arabs in History* (New York: Oxford University Press, 1993).

10. Jerrilynn D. Dodds, ed., *Al Andalus. The Art of Islamic Spain* (New York: Metropolitan Museum of Art), 11.

11. Ibid.

12. "The light of 800 lamps filled with fragrant oil made the crystals in the mosaic-work flash like

pearls and produce on the pavement, the arches and the walls a marvelous play of color and reflection
. . . The mosque of Cordova is . . . by universal consent the most beautiful temple of Islam and
one of the most beautiful monuments in the world," Charlotte M. Yonge, *The Christian and the Moor*
(London: Macmillan, 1879), 78.

13. *Umma* in Arabic means community.

14. Dodds, ed., *Al Andalus*, 11.

15. Ibid., 15.

16. We are close here to the concept of the sublime as explored in Kant's *Critique of Judgment*, where
he illustrates an overwhelming of the metabolic capacity of rational processing, using the example of
St. Peter's in Rome. In relation to large-scale Western religious architecture, the mosques might be
termed "meta-sublime." See Immanuel Kant, *Critique of Judgment*, trans. James Creed Meredith (Cosimo
Classics, 2007), 67. [Section 26: "Of that estimation of the magnitude of natural things which is
requisite for the Idea of the Sublime."]

17. A substantial travel literature extending from the time of the Muslims in Spain through the
conquest of Spain by Napoleon Bonaparte's troops in the 1790s and throughout the nineteenth and
twentieth centuries is absolutely worth reading to gain truth and legendary tales about the splendid
architectural remains of Muslim Spain. Paco Sevilla, "Flamenco: the Early Years," *Guitar & Lute*
(November, 1982): 24–27.

18. See Bernard Lewis, *Music of a Different Drum: Classical Arabic, Persian, Turkish & Hebrew Poems*
(Princeton: Princeton University Press, 2001), Introduction. On the significance of Arab poetry to
Castilian identity, see also Americo Castro, "Islam and Hispania," *The Structure of Spanish History*, trans.
Edmund L. King (Princeton: Princeton University Press, 1954).

19. Lewis, *Music of a Different Drum*, 32–33.

20. Flamencologists draw a relationship between every cultural dancing tradition that ever swept
through the Iberian Peninsula and flamenco. In particular, they cite the Roman Gaditanes dancing
girls, whom both the Roman poet Martial and Cervantes described as "dancing with honey in their
hips" for the Roman Emperors, and Gypsy flamenco. One can point to a rhythmic relationship
between the Greek use of finger cymbals and the Spanish Gypsy use of castanets. For further reading,
please see José Blas Vega and Mañuel Ruíz, *Diccionario enciclopédico ilustrado del flamenco* (Madrid: Editorial
Cinterco, 1988), and Angel Alvarez Caballero, *Gitanos, payos y flamencos en los origenes del flamenco* (Madrid:
Editorial Cinterco, 1988).

21. At the International Flamenco Festival in 1996, Gerhard Steingrass introduced his idea of
the *Saete* as "housing" in the *cante* musical influences from Sephardic chant. See Gerhard Steingrass,
Sociologiá del cante flamenco (Jerez: Centro Andaluz de Flamenco, 1993), and *Sobre flamenco y flamencología*
(Sevilla: Signatura Ediciones de Andalucía, 1998).

22. "Sephardic" refers to Jews of the *Sefarad*—the Jews of Spain—who came with the Romans as
slaves around 450 BCE. By the fifteenth century, close to one million Jews lived in Spain. "Had they
not been expelled," writes Jane Berger, "they would have by now had two millennia of continuous
presence in the Iberian Peninsula . . . Only Babylonian Jewry, which lived for two millennia in the
territory now called Iraq, had a longer record of continuous existence in one country." See Jane
Berger, *The Jews of Spain: A History of the Sephardic Experience* (New York: Free Press, 1992), 10.

23. Sevilla, "Flamenco: The Early Years," 24–27.

24. Ibid., 25.

25. Ibid.

26. Bachelard, *The Poetics of Space*, xxviii.

27. Ibid., 12.

28. Bachelard, *On Poetic Imagination and Reverie*, 36.

29. Dodds, *Al Andalus*, 37.

30. It is remarkable that, to my knowledge, these architectural influences from Mozarabic Spain on flamenco have received no speculation in the broad history of flamencology.

31. For a more comprehensive discussion of feminine spaces in Arab culture, please read Pièrre Bourdieu, "The Berber House," *The Anthropology of Space and Place* (Oxford: Blackwell Press, 2003), 131–41.

32. See Dodds, *Al Andalus*, chapter 1.

33. Colette Gaudin, "Introduction," *On Poetic Imagination and Reverie* (Putnam, CT: Spring Publications, 2005): liv–lv.

34. Walter Benjamin quoted Jules Michelet, "Paris, the Capital of the Nineteenth Century," *The Arcades Project* (Cambridge: Harvard University Press, 1999), 4.

CHAPTER EIGHT *Carmen*, a Close Reading of a Nomadic Opera

1. There is a popular story that on 2 June 1875, while singing Act III's card scene in which Carmen chooses the death card, Galli-Marié had a premonition about Bizet's death. She is said to have fainted backstage. Bizet died that night.

2. On the subject of the many famous Carmens, see Almaviva, "Les Interpretes de Carmen," *Le Figaro* (27 October 1938). Almaviva lists these great interpreters of the role who followed Galli-Marié: Deschamps-Jehin (1881), Adèle Isaac (1883), Emma Calvé (1892), Charlotte Wyns (1894), Eléna Sanz (1897), Mérentié (1897), Marie Brèma (1898), Marié de l'Isle (1902), Suzanna Brohly (1904), Martha Chenal (1911), Alice Raveau (1919), Ninon-Vallin (1919), Conchita Supervia (1930), Leontyne Price (1963), Grace Bumbry (1967), Regina Resnik (1965), Regine Crespin (1975), Julia Migenes-Johnson (1984), Elena Garanca (2010).

3. See Ninotchka Bennahum, "Alicia Alonso at 72," *Dance Pages* (Winter/Spring 1993).

4. See Janice Ross, "Jewish Culture and Identity in the Russian Ballet: The Case of Leonid Jacobson," *Jewish Folklore & Ethnology Review* 20, nos. 1/2 (2000).

5. The Maryinsky (Kirov) performed *Carmen Suite* at the Metropolitan Opera House on 15 July 2011. Also see the original production made for film: Plisetskaya Dance *Carmen Suite*, Corinth Films, 1988.

6. Henri de Curzon and Louis Schneider, "Carmen à Nîmes," *Le Théâtre* (May 1901).

7. To research southern French *Carmen* productions with bullfights, one must read the southern French bullfighting press. These can be found at the BN-Tolbiac and the Municipal Library in Nîmes: *Le Toreador, Revue de Toros, Le Touring-Sport, Midi-Taurin, Midi-Toros, La Mise à Mort, Le Moustic Nîmois, La Muleta, Nîmes Taurin, La Puntilla, Toros-Revue, La Corrida, L'Echo Taurin, Le Furet Nîmois, Gazette de Nîmes, Le Journal du Midi, Toros et Toreros, Le Toreo Illustré, Alais-Journal, Revue Tauromachie, Chronique du Toreo*.

8. During the Occupation, the Nazi Party staged massive Nazi pageants inside Nîmes' bullring. Oftentimes, these pro-Nazi rallies were followed by a bullfight. Outside of the coliseum, the Nazis executed French Resistance fighters. See Annie Maïllais: *Picasso et Leiris dans l'arène: les écrivains, les artistes et les toros . . . (1937–1957)* (Paris: Editions Cairn, 2002).

9. Soledad Barrio with Noche Flamenca, *Soleá*, Theater 80 on St. Mark's Place, New York City.

10. *Una illamada*—a call by dancer to musicians—is "a fully articulated functional signal occupying at least one measure." K. Meira Weinzweig, *Border Trespasses: The Gypsy Mask and Carmen Amaya's Flamenco Dance*, Unpublished Dissertation, Temple University, 199533. n. 427.

11. This moment resonates with Lorca's character Yerma and her sexual abandonment and frustration of her husband Juan.

12. It is as if she is saying "there's no place I'm allowed to stand": *Bury me standing*.

13. See Judith Butler, "Subjects of Sex/Gender/Desire," and "Subversive Bodily Acts," in *Gender Trouble. Feminism and the Subversion of Identity* (New York: Routledge, 1990).

14. "Gender is the repeated stylization of the body, a set of repeated acts . . . " Judith Butler, *Gender Trouble*, 33.

15. Haecceity, from the Latin *haecceitas*, meaning the essence of a thing; its thisness, or the characteristics, properties, or discrete qualities that make something particular.

16. A student of both French phenomenologist Gaston Bachelard and philosopher J. Wahl (the latter the student of Henri Bergson), Gilles Deleuze (1925–1995) graduated with a Masters from the Sorbonne in the History of Philosophy in 1948. A close friend of Michel Foucault and collaborator for over twenty-five years with Félix Guattari, Deleuze was a Professor of Philosophy at the University of Paris VIII at Vincennes from 1969 until his early retirement in 1987.

17. Gilles Deleuze, *Immanence: Essays of a Life* (New York: Urzone, 2002), 27. "Immanence: A Life" was originally published in *Philosophie 47* in 1995, just before Deleuze's premature death.

18. Please consider other great migrations: that of the Jews forcibly marched by Babylonian conquerors from Jerusalem in chains; that of Africans from ancestral homelands herded onto ships and into slavery; that of Native Americans thrown off their land, and forcibly marched west by American soldiers.

19. Deleuze, *Immanence*, 27.

Glossary

Albaicín Spanish from Arabic, meaning Gypsy neighborhood of Granada, downhill from the Alhambra Palace

Alcazar Arabic, meaning royal palace

'Al Andaluz Arabic, meaning blue-green lands of southern Spain

Almée/Almeh French, meaning Middle Eastern dancer/singer

Andalusia From the Arabic, meaning blue-green lands; southern coast of Spain, also referred to as the Iberian Peninsula

Baile Spanish, meaning dance

Bailaor(a) Spanish, meaning flamenco dancer

Baladi Arabic, meaning women's solo dance of acrobatic skill

Bolero Spanish and Afro-Cuban dance form that emerged in the eighteenth century; danced by a soloist who, at times, plays castanets or by a group in ¾ time to the music of the guitar

Café cantante Spanish, meaning singing café, where flamenco singers and dancers performed throughout the nineteenth and twentieth centuries

Caliph Arabic, meaning King and Commander of the Faithful

Caliphate Arabic, meaning Muslim Empire/dynasty

Caló The Gypsy language, part-Spanish, part-Romani with Sanskrit words

Cantaor Spanish, meaning Flamenco singer

Cante Spanish, meaning Flamenco song

Cante Jondo Spanish, meaning Gypsy flamenco deep song tradition

Compás Spanish, meaning Gypsy rhythm or phrasing

Contrabandistas Spanish, meaning smuggler

Cuadrilla Spanish, meaning matador's team

Danse du ventre French, meaning Middle Eastern dancer

Dar-al-Islam Arabic, meaning House of Islam or pan-national Islamic World

Du'a Arabic, meaning personal prayer

Duende Spanish, meaning transcendence

Élan vital French, meaning vital aliveness or the impulse to surge forward; term used by French philosophers

Escobílla Spanish, meaning dance passage

Fandango Spanish word deriving from Arabic, meaning "go and dance"; danced throughout Andalusia in quick triple time

Farruca Gypsy flamenco solo dance performed at first only by men until Carmen Amaya; refers to the gaucho tradition of horse-riding and Spanish bullfighting

Flamenco Puro Spanish, meaning a Gypsy style of flamenco deriving from African, Sephardic, Hispano-Arab, and Indian roots

Florea y braceo Spanish, meaning flowering of wrists and hands; Gypsy flamenco style of expressive dancing

Fondak Arabic, meaning fountain

Ghawazi Arabic, meaning dancing/singing traveling entertainers thought to be Gypsies, having migrated into Egypt from northern India and Persia in the fifth century BCE during the Roman–Persian wars

Gitane French, meaning Gypsy

Gitanerías Spanish, meaning Gypsy neighborhoods; Triana, the Gypsy part of Seville, is located across the Guadalquivir from the center of town

Gitano(a) Spanish, meaning Gypsy

Habanera Spanish dance that, like the *Guajira*, was imported from the Spanish Caribbean

'Al Hoshe Derbek Arabic, Street of the Open Hall

Una Illamada Spanish, meaning calling of Flamenco musicians and dancers to one another on stage

El Jardín Spanish, meaning garden

Kathak From the Sanskirt word *Katha*, meaning story; *Kathak* means storytelling of Hindu mythology; an Indian of rhythmic dance, originally performed in Uttar Pradesh, North India

Letra Spanish, meaning Flamenco verse

Madinat Arabic, meaning city

Maghreb Arabic, meaning the "Far West"; referred to Spain and farthest reaches of Muslim empire

Melismata Spanish, deriving from Arabic, meaning shrill sound; refers to early twentieth-century style of flamenco singing

Mesgrid Arabic, meaning mosque

Mesquita Arabic, also meaning mosque

Mozarabic Arabic, meaning People of the Book—Christian, Sephardic and Muslim

Mudejar Art influenced by Muslim-led Spain

Muezzin Arabic, *muzim*, meaning chosen person at a mosque who leads call to prayer (*adhan*) atop the minaret in the direction of Mecca; he "calls" people to the mosque five times a day

Olé Spanish word of encouragement for a flamenco dancer; it derives from the Arabic word for *Allah*

Ouled Nail Algerian nomadic tribe known for their belly dance

Quejijo Spanish, meaning lamentful cry of flamenco singer

Raqs Sharqi Arabic, dance form in quick meter

Rawi Arabic, meaning reciter of poems and songs

Rom, from *Romani* Romani, meaning Gypsy, Bohemian, Egyptian

Sarabande Spanish Renaissance court dance, slow and stately in ¾ time

Seguidillas Spanish, meaning small successions, is a quick-paced dance in ¾ or ⅜ meter; from Castile and Andalusia; the *Seguidillas* appears in Act 1 of *Carmen*

Seguidillas Manchegas Manchegas is Arabic, short for ' *al Mansha*, meaning the dry land or wilderness between Castile and Andalusia

Sephardic Ladino, Hebrew, and Spanish, meaning Spanish Jew

Sevillanas Spanish dance of Seville, derives from *Seguidillas Manchegas,* once performed only during Holy Week; danced by all at fairs, markets, parties

Siguiríya Gypsy mournful song and dance, poetic, sad

Soleá Spanish, meaning solo, pertaining to a Gypsy solo dance of serious intent

Tel Greek, meaning hill or mound above hidden archeological site

Triana Gypsy neighborhood of Seville, where Carmen lives

Tsigane French, meaning Gypsy

Tuareg "Blue People," nomadic, matrilineal tribe of the Sahara deserts

Umma Arabic, meaning community

Zambra Mora Arab-Gypsy flamenco dance of Hispano-Arab Spain with rhythmic origins in African dance

Zapateado Spanish deriving from Arabic, meaning footwork. *Zapata* means shoe.

Zarabande Arabic, meaning Sarabande, dance in ¾ meter; danced throughout the Afro-Caribbean colonial world of the sixteenth and seventeenth centuries

Bibliography

Books

Abbate, Carolyn. *In Search of Opera.* Princeton: Princeton University Press, 2001.

————. *Unsung Voices: Opera and Musical Narrative in the Nineteenth Century.* Princeton: Princeton University Press, 1991.

Albaric, Alain. *Les Saintes Maries de la Mer.* Camargue Editions du Vent Large, 2003.

Alloula, Malek. *The Colonial Harem.* Minneapolis: University of Minnesota Press, 1986.

Alvarez Caballero, Angel. *Historia del Cante Flamenco.* Madrid, 1981.

Altheim, Franz, and E. Trautmann-Nehring. *Italia und Rom.* Amsterdam: Pantheon, 1941.

Amicis, Edmondo des. *Spain and the Spaniards.* 2 vols. Trans. Stanley R. Yarnell. Philadelphia: Henry T. Coates, 1895.

Al Zayer, Penni. *Middle Eastern Dance.* Philadelphia: Chelsea House, 2004.

And, Metin. *A Pictorial History of Turkish Dancing.* Ankara: Dost Yayinlaru, 1976.

Arnheim, Rudolf. *The Genesis of a Painting: Picasso's Guernica.* Berkeley: University of California Press, 1962.

————. *Toward a Psychology of Art. Collected Essays.* Berkeley: University of California Press, 1966.

Bac, Ferdinand. *Louis Ier de Baviere et Lola Montes.* Paris: Louis Conard, 1928.

Bachelard, Gaston. *On Poetic Imagination and Reverie,* ed. Colette Gaudin. Putnam, CT: Spring Publications, 2005.

————. *The Poetics of Space. The Classic Look at How We Experience Intimate Places.* Boston: Beacon Press, 1969.

Bachofen, Johann J. *Myth, Religion and Mother Right: Selected Writings of J.J. Bachofen.* Princeton: Princeton University Press, 1967.

Baker, Evan. *The Scene Designs for the First Performance's of Bizet's Carmen.* Berkeley: University of California Press, 1990.

Baldassari, Anne. *Picasso Carmen: sol y sombra.* Paris: Éditions de la Réunion des Musée Nationeaux, Flammarion, 2007.

Bammate, Nadjm oud-Dine. *Cités d'islam.* Paris: Arthaud, 1987.

Banes, Sally. *Dancing Women: Female Bodies on Stage.* Middletown, CT: Wesleyan University Press, 1998.

Barkin, Elaine, Lydia Hamessley, and Benjamin Boretz. *Audible Traces: Gender, Identity, and Music.* Zürich: Carciofoli, 1999.

Bataillard, Paul. *De l'apparition des Bohémiens en Europe.* Paris, 1844.

————. *Notes et questions sur les Bohémiens en Algérie.* Paris: impr. de A. Hennuyer, 1873.

Bataille, Georges. *Story of the Eye.* (*L'Histoire de l'oeil.*) (1928) New York: Urizen Books, 1977.

Bates, Katharine Lee. *Spanish Highways and Byways.* New York: Macmillan, 1900.

Baudrimont, Aléxandre. *Les Bohémiens du Pays Basque.* Bordeaux: G. Gounoilhou, 1862.

Beard, Mary R. *Woman as Force in History.* New York: Macmillan, 1946.

Beauvoir, Simone de. *The Second Sex*. New York: Knopf, 1953.

Bellaigue, Camille. *Promenades Lyriques*. Paris: Nouvelle Librairie Nationale, 1924.

Benjamin, Walter. *Illuminations*. Essays and Reflections. New York: Schocken Books, 1968.

Bennahum, Ninotchka Devorah. *Antonia Mercé, "La Argentina": Flamenco & the Spanish Avant-Garde*. Middletown, CT: Wesleyan University Press, 2000.

———. *Antonia Mercé: El flamenco y la vanguardia española*. Barcelona: Global Rhythm Press, S. L., 2009.

Bergamín, José. *Picasso Dibujos. Sala Gaspar*. Barcelona: Consejo de Ciento, 1961.

Berger, Jane. *The Jews of Spain: A History of the Sephardic Experience*. New York: Free Press, 1992.

Berger, John. *Success and Failure of Picasso*. New York: Penguin, 1955.

Bergson, Henri. *The Creative Mind*. New York: Philosophical Library, 1946.

———. *Matter and Memory*. Trans. Nancy Margaret Paul and W. Scott Palmer. New York: Zone, 1994.

Bercovici, Konrad. *The Story of the Gypsies*. New York: Cosmopolitan Books, 1928.

Bernard, Alexis. *Les esclaves á Seville au debut du XVIIe siècle*. Ph.D. Dissertation. University of Lyon, 1998.

Bernard, Henri. *Moeurs des Bohémiens de Moldavie et de Valachie*. Paris: Maisonneuve et cie, 1869.

Bizet, Georges. *Lettres à un ami, 1865–72*. Paris: C. Levy, 1909.

Bizet, Georges, Ludovic Halévy, and Henri Meilhac. *Carmen*. 1875. New York: G. Schirmer, 1959.

———. *Carmen*. 1875. English and French ed. New York: Dover Publications, 1983.

Blache, Jean-Baptiste. *Choreography*. 1852.

Blasco, Paloma Gay y. *Gypsies in Madrid: Sex, Gender, and the Performance of Identity*. New York: Berg, 1999.

Blasis, Carlo. *Code complet de la danse*. London: J. Bulcock, 1828.

———. *The Code of Terpsichore*. London: J. Bulcock, 1828.

Bleiler, Ellen H. *Carmen*. New York: Dover, 1970.

Bloch, Jules. *Les Tsiganes*. Paris: Presse Universitaire de France, 1953.

Block, Maurice. *Moeurs et coutumes des Tziganes*. Paris: Payot, 1936.

Blondel, Eric. *Nietzsche. The Body and Culture: Philosophy as Philological Genealogy*. Stanford: Stanford University Press, 1991.

Blunt, Anthony. *Picasso's Guernica*. New York: Oxford University Press, 1969.

Blunt, Isabel. *The Inner Life of Syria, Palestine, and the Holy Land: From My Private Journal*. London: Henry S. King, 1875.

Boeck, Wilhelm, and Jaime Sabartés. *Picasso*. New York: Harry N. Abrams, 1955.

Bolitho, W. *Zwolf-Ggen das Schicksal*. Potsdam: Muller & I. Keipenheur, 1931.

Bordo, Susan. *Unbearable Weight: Feminism, Western Thought and the Body*. Berkeley: University of California Press, 1993.

Borgese, Elisabeth. *Ascent of Woman*. New York: Braziller, 1963.

Borrow, George. *The Bible in Spain or Journeys, Adventures and Imprisonments of Englishmen in an Attempt to Circulate the Bible*. London: J. Murray, 1843.

———. *Les Bohémiens du pays Basque*. 1862.

———. *Lavengro: The Scholar, the Gipsy, the Priest*. London: Oxford University Press, 1904.

———. *The Romany Rye*. London: Cresset Press, 1948.

———. *The Zincali: An Account of the Gypsies of Spain*. 1841. London: J. M. Dent, 1924.

Boulding, Elise. *The Underside of History: A View of Women through Time*. Boulder: Westview Press, 1976.

Bouza, Fernando. *Communication, Knowledge, and Memory in Early Modern Spain*. Philadelphia: University of Pennsylvania Press, 1999.

Boyle, Leonard. *St. Clement's Rome.* 1960. Rome: Collegio San Clemente, 1989.

Braudel, Fernand. *A History of Civilizations.* New York: Penguin Books, 1993.

———. *The Mediterranean and the Mediterranean World in the Age of Philip II.* New York: Harper & Row, 1972.

———. *Memory and the Mediterranean.* New York: Vintage Books, 2001.

Braun, Carl F., trans. *Carmen.* By Prosper Mérimée (privately printed edition), 1952.

Brenan, Gerald. *The Spanish Labyrinth: An Account of the Social and Political Background of the Civil War.* Cambridge, UK: Cambridge University Press, 1943.

Breton, André. "Guillaume Apollinaire," *Les Pas Perdus.* 1924.

———. *Nadja.* Paris: Gallimard, 1964.

———. "Picasso dans son Élément." *Point du jour.* Paris: Gallimard, 1934.

———. *Manifestoes of Surrealism.* (1924). Trans. Richard Seaver and Helen R. Lane. Ann Arbor: The University of Michigan Press, 1969.

———. *Les Vases Communicants.* Paris: Gallimard, 1955.

Briffault, Robert. *The Mothers: The Matriarchal Theory of Social Origin.* New York: Macmillan, 1931.

Bris, Michel le. *Romantics and Romanticism.* New York: Rizzoli, 1981.

Brooks, Lynn Matluck, ed. *Women's Work. Making Dance in Europe before 1800.* Madison: University of Wisconsin Press, 2007.

Brown, Irving Henry. *Deep Song: Adventures with Gypsy Songs and Singers in Andalusia and Other Lands.* New York: Harper, 1929.

Brown, Jonathan, ed. *Picasso and the Spanish Tradition.* New Haven: Yale University Press, 1996.

Browning, Barbara. *Samba: Resistance in Motion.* Bloomington: Indiana University Press, 1995.

Buonaventura, Wendy. *Serpent of the Nile. Women and Dance in the Arab World.* New York: Interlink Books, 1998.

Burckhardt, John L., and William Ouseley. *Arabic Proverbs: Or, the Manners and Customs of the Modern Egyptians.* London: J. Murray, 1830.

Burt, Ramsay. *Alien Bodies: Representations of Modernity, "Race," and Nation in Early Modern Dance.* London: Routledge, 1998.

Burton, Sir Richard. *The Jew, the Gypsy, and El Islam.* Chicago: Herbert S. Stone, 1898.

Butler, Judith. *Gender Trouble. Feminism and the Subversion of Identity.* New York: Routledge, 1990.

Caba, Pedro y Carlos. *Andalusia, su comunismo y su cante jondo.* Barcelona, 1969.

Caballero, Angel Alvarez. *Gitanos, payos y flamencos en los origenes del flamenco.* Madrid: Editorial Cinterco, 1988.

Calleja, Seve. *Un pueblo trashumante: los gitanos.* Bilbao: Ediciones Mensajero, 1993.

Campbell, Joseph. *The Hero with a Thousand Faces.* Princeton: Princeton University Press, 1968.

Canaday, John. *Mainstreams of Modern Art.* New York: Simon and Schuster, 1959.

Cansinos, Assens Rafael. *La Copla Andaluz.* Madrid: Ediciones Démofilo, 1976. *Carmen.* Chester. New York: G. Schirmer, 1959.

Carr, Raymond. *Spain: A History.* Oxford: Oxford University Press, 2000.

Casares, Aurelia Martin. "La hechiceria en la Andalucia Moderna; ¿una forma de poder de las mujeres?" *Pautas históricas de sociabilidad feminina: Rituales y modelos de representación*, ed. Mary Nash and María José de la Pascua. Spain: Servicio de Publicaciones de la Universidad de Cadiz, 1999. 101–12.

Castro, Americo. *The Structure of Spanish History.* Trans. Edmund L. King. Princeton: Princeton University Press, 1954.

Césaire, Aimé. *Corps perdu.* Paris: Editions Fragrance, 1950.

Cervantes Saavedera, Miguel de. *Adventures of Don Quixote de la Mancha.* London: Routledge, Warner & Routledge, 1869.

———. *La Bohémienne de Madrid.* Paris: Hachette, 1853.

———. *Don Quixote.* Trans. Walter Starkie. New York: Macmillan, 1957.

———. *Exemplary Stories.* New York: Oxford University Press, 1998.

———. *La Gitanilla.* Buenos Aires: A. Estrada y cía, S.A., 1942.

Chase, Gilbert. *The Music of Spain.* New York: W. W. Norton and Company, Inc., 1941.

Chateaubriand, François-René. *Atala ou les amours de deux sauvages dans Le désert.* Paris: Garnier Frères, 1801.

Chateaubriand, Francois-René, and Jean B. B. Anville. *Itinéraire de Paris à Jérusalem et de Jérusalem à Paris: en allant par la Grèce, et Revenant par l'Égypte, la Barbarie et l'Espagne.* Paris: Le Normant, 1822.

Chatwin, Bruce. *The Songlines.* New York: Penguin Books, 1987.

Chazal, Gilles. *La nuit Espagnole. flamenco, avant-garde et culture populaire, 1865–1937.* Paris: Musée Beaux-Arts de la Ville de Paris, 2008.

Chebra, Djamila Henni, and Christian Poché, eds. *Les danses dans le monde arabe ou l'héritage des almées.* Paris: L'Harmattan, 1996.

Chenu, Roselyne. *Le désert. Petite anthologie.* Paris: Éditions du Cerf, 1997.

Chipp, Herschel. *Picasso's Guernica: Histories, Transformations, Meanings.* Berkeley: University of California Press, 1988.

Claudon, Francis, ed. *Dictionnaire de l'opéra comique français.* Bern: Peter Lang Publishers, 1995.

Clébert, Jean-Paul. *Les Gitans.* New York: E. P. Dutton, 1963.

———. *The Gypsies.* New York: E. P. Dutton, 1963.

Clément, Catherine. *The Feminine and the Sacred.* New York: Columbia University Press, 2001.

———. *Opera, or the Undoing of Women.* Minneapolis: University of Minnesota Press, 1988.

Cobban, Alfred. *A History of Modern France.* Baltimore: Penguin, 1965.

Collins, Roger. *The Arab Conquest of Spain 710–797.* Oxford: Blackwell, 1989.

Conley, Tom. *The Self-Made Map: Cartographic Writing in Early Modern France.* Minneapolis: University of Minnesota Press, 1996.

Coon, Carleton Steven. *The Origin of Races.* London, 1963.

Cooper, Martin. *Georges Bizet.* Westport, CT: Greenwood Press, 1971.

Cordova, Francísco de. *Histoire de los gitanos.* Barcelona: J. N., 1832.

Curtis, George William. *Nile Notes of a Howadji.* New York: Harper, 1856.

Curtiss, Mina Kirstein. *Bizet and His World.* London: Secker & Warburg, 1959.

Daix, Pièrre. *Picasso: Life and Art.* New York: Icon Editions, 1987.

Danses de Carmen. Covent Garden: Royal Italian Opera, 1882.

David, Félicien. *Le Désert. ode-symphonie en trois parties avec strophes déclamés, airs, chants, choeurs, et grand orchestra.* Poésie par d'Auguste Colin. Paris: Heugel et Cie,

de Falla, Manuel. *Escritos sobre musica y musicos Débussy, Wagner, el "cante jondo." Introduction y notas.* Buenos Aires: Espasa-Calpe, 1950.

Dean, Winton. *Bizet: His Life and Work.* London: J. M. Dent, 1975.

———. *Carmen by Prosper Mérimée with a Study of the Opera of the Same Name.* Illus. Francisco de Goya. London, 1949.

———. *Essays on Opera.* New York: Oxford University Press, 1990.

Decourdemanche, Jean-Adolphe. *Grammaire du Tchingané ou langue des Bohémiens errants.* Paris: P. Geuthner, 1908.

Delgado, José, aka Pepe Illo. *El carnet de la Tauromaquia.* Barcelona: Editorial Gustavo Gili, S.A., 1963.

Deleuze, Gilles. *Spinoza: Practical Philosophy.* San Francisco: City Lights, 1988.

———. *Immanence: Essays of a Life.* New York: Urzone, 2002.

Delsarte, François, and Genevieve Stebbins, *Delsarte System of Expression.* New York: Edgar S. Werner, 1887.

Dibbern, Mary, *Carmen, a Performance Guide.* Hillsdale, NY: Pendragon Press, 2001.

Didier, Charles. *Les Nuits de Caire.* Paris: Hachette, 1860.

Dominguin, Luis Miguel (toreador). *Toros y toreros.* Paris: Editions Cercle d'Art, 1961.

Derrida, Jacques. *Of Grammatology.* Baltimore: Johns Hopkins University Press, 1998.

Dodds, Jerrilynn D., ed. *Al Andalus. The Art of Islamic Spain.* New York: Metropolitan Museum of Art, 1992.

Dominguin, Luis Miguel. *Toros y Toreros.* Paris: Editions Cercle d'Art, 1961.

Dos Passos, John. *Orient Express.* New York: Jonathan Cape and Harrison Smith,

Driault, Edouard. *La question d'Orient depuis ses origines jusqu'à nos jours.* Paris: F. Alcan, 1898.

Drillon, Ilyana. *Quejio: Informe.* Madrid, 1975.

Duff-Gordon, Lady Lucie. *Lettres d'Égypte, 1862–69.*

Dumas, Alexandre. *Voyage en Orient. Quinze jours au Sinai.* Stuttgart: E. Hallberger, 1839.

Dumas, Danielle. *Coplas flamencas.* Paris: Aubier-Montaigne, 1973.

Duncan, David Douglas. *Picasso's Picasso.* New York: Ballantine Books, 1968.

Ebers, Georg. *Egypt: Descriptive, Historical and Picturesque.* 2 vols. New York: Cassell, 1878–79.

Edwards, John. *Ferdinand and Isabella: Profiles in Power.* Edinburgh: Pearson Gate, 2005.

Emmanuel, Maurice. *The Antique Greek Dance, after Sculpted and Painted Figures.* New York: John Lane, 1916.

Falla, Manuel de. *Escritos sobre musica y musicos Débussy, Wagner, el "cante jondo." Introduction y notas.* Buenos Aires: Espasa-Calpe, 1950.

Fausto-Sperling, Anne. *Myths of Gender: Biological Theories about Women and Men.* New York: Basic Books, 1992.

Figes, Eva. *Patriarchal Attitudes.* New York: Stein & Day, 1970.

Flaubert, Gustave. *Flaubert in Egypt: A Sensibility on Tour,* ed. Francis Steegmuller. New York: Penguin, 1972.

Fletcher, Richard. *Moorish Spain.* London: Weidenfeld & Nicolson, 1992.

Foletier, François de Vaux de. *Les Tsiganes dans l'ancienne régime.* Paris: Gallimard, 1935.

Fonesca, Isabel. *Bury Me Standing: The Gypsies and Their Journey.* New York: Vintage Books, 1995.

Fonyi, Antonia. *Prosper Mérimée: écrivain, archéologue, historien.* Paris: Droz, 1999.

Ford, Richard. *A Hand-book for Travellers in Spain and Readers at Home, Describing the Country and Cities, the Natives and Their Manners, the Antiquities, Religion, Legends, Fine Arts, Literature, Sports, and Gastronomy, with Notices on Spanish History.* London: J. Murray, 1845.

———. *Traveller's Hand-book of Spain.* New York: Scribner's, 1891.

Formby, The Reverend Henry. *A Visit to the East. Germany and the Danube, Constantinople, Asia Minor, Egypt and Idumea.* London: James Burns, 1848.

Foster, Susan Leigh. *Choreographing History.* Bloomington: University of Indiana Press, 1995.

———. *Choreography and Narrative: Ballet's Staging of Story & Desire.* Bloomington: Indiana University Press, 1996.

———. *Reading Dancing: Bodies and Subjects in Contemporary American Dance.* Berkeley: University of California Press, 1986.

Franko, Mark. *Dance as Text: Ideologies of the Baroque Body.* Cambridge: Cambridge University Press, 1993.

Freud, Sigmund. *Totem and Taboo: Resemblances between the Psychic Lives of Savages and Neurotics.* New York: Vintage Books, 1918.

Friedman, Ellen G. *Spanish Captives in North Africa in the Early Modern Age.* Madison: University of Wisconsin Press, 1983.

Fulcher, Jane F. *The Nation's Image: French Grand Opera as Politics and Politicized Art.* Cambridge: Cambridge University Press, 1987.

Gallet, Louis. *À la mémoire de Georges Bizet, vers dits le 31 Octobre 1875, au concert du Châtelet, par Mme Galli-Marié.* Paris: impr. de Motteroz, 1875.

Gallwitz, Klaus. *Picasso at 90.* New York: G. P. Putnam & Sons, 1971.

Gautier, E. F. *Sahara, the Great Desert.* Trans. Dorothy Ford Mayhew (Emile Félix). New York: Columbia University Press, 1935.

Gautier, Théophile. *L'histoire de l'art dramatique en France depuis 25 ans.* Vols. 1–6. Leipzig: Edition Hetzel 1859.

———. *La Musique.* Paris: Charpentier, 1911.

———. *Voyage en Espagne.* Paris: G. F. Flammarion, 1981.

Gauthier-Villars, Henry. *Bizet.* Paris: Librairie Renouard, 1920.

Geertz, Clifford. *Interpretation of Cultures.* New York: Basic Books, 1973.

———. *Local Knowledge: Further Essays in Interpretive Anthropology.* New York: Basic Books, 1983.

Ghalib, Abu. *The Contentment of the Soul in the Contemplation of the Ancient Remains of Spain.*

Gilligan, Carol. *In a Different Voice: Psychological Theory and Women's Development.* Cambridge: Harvard University Press, 1982.

Gilman, Charlotte Perkins. *Women and Economics.* 1898. New York: Harper & Row, 1966.

Gilot, Françoise. *Vivre avec Picasso.* Paris: Calmann-Lévy, 1965.

Gilot, Françoise, and Carlton Lake. *Life with Picasso.* New York: McGraw Hill, 1964.

Gimblett, Barbara Kirschenblatt. *Destination Culture: Tourism, Museums, and Heritage.* Berkeley: University of California Press, 1998.

Gimbutas, Marija. *Goddesses and Gods of Old Europe.* Berkeley: University of California Press, 1982.

Gimké, Sarah M. *Letters on the Equality of the Sexes and the Condition of Women.* Boston: Isaac Knapp, 1838.

Ginzberg. Louis. *The Legends of the Jews.* Vol. 5. Philadelphia: The Jewish Publication Society, 1925.

Gombrich, E. H. *Art and Illusion: A Study in the Psychology of Pictorial Representation.* Washington, D.C.: Trustees of the National Gallery of Art, 1960.

Gould, Evelyn. *The Fate of Carmen.* Baltimore: Johns Hopkins University Press, 1996.

Grabar, Oleg. *The Formation of Islamic Art.* New Haven: Yale University Press, 1973.

Graberg. *Doutes et conjectures sur les Bohémiens et leur première apparition en Europe.* [before 1817].

Grammont, Henri Delmas de. *L'Histoire du massacre des Turks à Marseilles en 1620.* Paris, 1879.

Grande, Felix. *Memoria del flamenco.* Vol. 2. Madrid: Espasa-Calpa, 1979.

Grangé, Eugène. *Les Bohémiens de Paris, drame en 5 actes et 8 tableaux, par Mm. Adolphe d'Ennery et Grangé. [Paris, Ambigu-Comique, 27 Septembre 1843.].* Paris: Marchant, 1843.

Graslin, L. F. *L'histoire de l'Iberia. Ou essai critique sur l'origine des premières populations de l'Espagnes, l' ancien consul de France à Santander,* no. 1. 8 vols. Paris: Chez Leleux, 1838.

Graves, Robert. *The White Goddess: A Historical Grammar of Poetic Myth.* New York: Farrar, Straus and Giroux, 1983.

Grellman, Heinrich Moritz Gottlieb. *Dissertation on the Gipsies Being an Historical Enquiry, concerning the Manner of Life, Œconomy, Customs and Conditions of These People in Europe, and Their Origin.* Trans. Matthew Raper. London: C. Bigg, 1787.

———. *Histoire des bohémiens.* 1810.

Grut, Marina. *The Bolero School: An Illustrated History of the Bolero, the Seguidillas, and the Escuela Bolera.* Alton, Hampshire, UK: Dance Books, 2002.

Guest, Igor. *The Ballet of the Enlightenment: The Establishment of the Ballet d'Action in France 1770–1793.* Princeton: Princeton Book Company, 1997.

Hanna, Nabil Sobhi. *Ghagar of Sett Guiranha: A Study of a Gypsy Community in Egypt. Cairo Papers in Social Science.* Vol. 5. Cairo: American University, June 1982.

Hawk, Minnie. *Memories of a Singer, Minnie Hawk (Baroness De Wartegg).* N.p., 1925.

Hemingway, Ernest. *Death in the Afternoon.* New York, 1932.

Highwater, Jamake. *Myth & Sexuality.* New York: Meridian, 1988.

Hilton, Timothy. *Picasso*. New York: Praeger, 1975.

Horne, Alistair. *Seven Ages of Paris*. New York: Alfred A. Knopf, 2002.

Hugo, Victor. *Le Hunchback de Notre-Dame*. New York: Modern Library, 1831.

Hureaux, Alain Daguerre de. *Délacroix: Voyage au Maroc*. Paris: Aquarelles, 2000.

Hutton, John Henry. *Les Castes de l'Inde: nature, fonction, origines*. Paris: Payot, 1949.

Imbert. P. L. *L'Espagne. splendeurs et miseres. Voyage artistique et pittoresque*. Paris: E. Plon et Cie Imprimeurs-Éditeurs, 1875.

Irving, Washington. *Tales of the Alhambra*. Granada: Miguel Sánchez, 1992.

Jones, Jo. *Paintings and Drawings of the Gypsies of Granada*. Detroit: Folklore Associates, 1969.

Kabongo, Albert Ndambe. "Les escalves á Cordue au debut du XVIIe siècle (1600–1621)." Ph.D. diss. Université de Toulouse, Le Mirail, 1975.

Kamen, Henry. *Empire: How Spain Became a World Power, 1492–1763*. New York: Harper Collins, 2002.

——. *Spain, 1469–1714. A Society of Conflict*. New York: Pearson/Longman, 2005.

Kirsch, Jonathan. *The Harlot by the Side of the Road: Forbidden Tales of the Bible*. New York: Ballantine Books, 1997.

Kramer, Samuel Noah. *Enki and Ninhursag: A Sumerian "Paradise Myth."* New Haven: Yale University Press, 1945.

——. *History Begins at Sumer*. London: Thames & Hudson, 1958.

——. *Sumerian Mythology: A Study of Spiritual and Literary Achievement in the Third Millennium BCE*. New York: Harper & Row, 1961.

Kurtz, Harold. *The Empress Eugénie*. Boston: Houghton Mifflin, 1964.

Laffon, Rafael. *Seville*. Barcelona: Editorial Noguer, S.A., 1963.

Lamartine, Alphonse de. *Pilgrimage to the Holy Land*. Philadelphia: Carey, Lea and Blanchard, 1838.

——. *Voyage en Orient*. Paris, 1835.

Lamoreaux, John C. *The Early Muslim Tradition of Dream Interpretation*. Albany: State University of New York Press, 2002.

Lane, E. W. *An Account of the Manners and Customs of the Modern Egyptians, Written in Egypt during the Years 1833*. London: J. Murray, 1860.

——. *The Modern Egyptians*. London: J. M. Dent, 1936.

Lang, Paul Henry. *Music in Western Civilization*. London: J. M. Dent, 1941.

Laparra, Raoul. *Bizet et l'Éspagne*. Paris: Librairie Delagrave, 1934.

Lawrence, T. E. *The Seven Pillars of Wisdom*. Fordingbridge, Hampshire: J. and N. Wilson, 2004. Original published in 1922.

Lea, Henry Charles. *The Moriscos of Spain: Their Conversion and Expulsion*. Philadelphia: Lea Bros., 1901.

Leal, Paloma Esteban. *Picasso/Minotauro*. Madrid: Museo Nacional Centro de Arte Reina Sofia, 2001.

Leblon, Bernard. *Les Gitans d'Espagnes*. Paris: P.U.F., 1985.

——. *Musiques Tziganes et flamenco*. Paris: L'Harmattan, 1990.

LeClézio, Jean Marie. *Mondo et autres histories*. Paris: Gallimard, 1978.

Leland, Charles Godfrey. *The English Gypsies and Their Language*. London, 1873.

Lemon, Ralph. *Geography: Art/Race/Exile*. Middletown, CT: Wesleyan University Press, 2000.

Lerner, Gerda. *The Creation of Feminist Consciousness: From the Middle Ages to 1870*. New York: Oxford University Press, 1993.

——. *The Creation of Patriarchy*. New York: Oxford University Press, 1986.

——. *The Majority Finds Its Past: Placing Women in History*. New York: Oxford University Press, 1979.

Lévi-Strauss, Claude. *The Raw and the Cooked*. Chicago: Chicago University Press, 1983.

———. *Tristes Tropiques.* New York: Modern Library, 1997.

Lewis, Bernard. *The Arabs in History.* London: Hutchinson's University Library, 1956.

———. *Cultures in Conflict: Christians, Muslims, and Jews in an Age of Discovery.* New York: Oxford University Press, 1995.

———. *Islam and the West.* New York: Oxford University Press, 1993.

———. *The Jews of Islam.* Princeton: Princeton University Press, 1984.

———. *The Middle East: A Brief History of the Last 2,000 Years.* New York: Scribner, 1995.

———. *The Middle East: 2000 Years of History.* London: Weidenfeld & Nicholson, 1993.

———. *A Middle East Mosaic: Fragments of Life, Letters & History.* New York: Random House, 2000.

———. *The Multiple Identities of the Middle East.* London: Weidenfeld & Nicholson, 1998.

———. *Music of a Different Drum: Classical Arabic, Persian, Turkish & Hebrew Poems.* Princeton: Princeton University Press, 2001.

———. *The Muslim Discovery of Europe.* New York: W.W. Norton, 2001.

———. *The World of Islam. Faith, People. Culture.* New York: Thames & Hudson, 1992.

Lexova, Irena. *Ancient Egyptian Dances.* Prague: Oriental Institute, 1935.

Liron. *Question curieuse, si l'histoire des deux conquetes d'Espagne par les maureu est un Romain.* Paris, 1708.

Liszt, Franz. *Des Bohémiens et de leur musique en Hongrie.* 1881. Bologna: Forni, 1972.

Lorca, Federico García. *Deep Song and Other Prose.* Ed. and Trans. Christopher Maurer. New York: New Directions, 1975.

Louca, Anouar. *Les sources Marseillaises de l'Orient romantique.* Paris: Maisonneuve et Larose, 2001.

Lux, Joseph Aug. *Lola Montez.* Berlin: Verlag von Rich, 1912.

Lyonnais. *Histoire générale des larrons.* 1623–1709.

Madden, Richard Robert. *Egypt and Muhammad Ali.* London: H. Colburn, 1841.

———. *Travels in Turkey, Egypt, Nubia and Palestine in 1824, 1825, 1826, and 1827.* 2 vols. London: Henry Colburn, 1829.

Madriaga, Salvador de. *Spain, a Modern History.* New York: Frederick A. Praeger, 1958.

Mafouz, Naguib. *Akhenaten: Dweller in Truth.* New York: Anchor, 2000.

Maigron, Louis. *Le Romantisme et la mode.* Paris: Slatkine Reprints, 1989.

Maïllis, Annie. *Des femmes et des toros.* Paris: Éditions Cairn, 2003.

———. *Picasso et Leiris dans les Arènes: Les Écrivains, les Artistes et les Toros . . . 1937–1957.* Paris: Éditions Cairn, 2002.

Malherbe, Henry. *Carmen.* Paris: Michel, 1951.

Mansel, Philip. *Paris between Empires: Monarchy and Revolution 1814–1852.* New York: St. Martin's Press, 2001.

Marrero, Vicente. *Picasso & the Bull.* Trans. Anthony Kerrigan. Chicago: H. Regnery, 1956.

Marvin, Garry. *Bullfight.* Urbana: University of Illinois Press, 1994.

Mauss, Marcel. *The Gift: Forms and Functions of Exchange in Archaic Societies.* London: Cohen & West, 1954.

McClary, Susan. *Georges Bizet: Carmen.* Cambridge: Cambridge University Press, 1992.

McEvedy, Colin. *The New Penguin Atlas of Medieval History.* New York: Penguin, 2006.

McNeill, William. *The Rise of the West.* Chicago: University of Chicago Press, 1963.

McPherson, J. W. *The Moulids of Egypt.* Cairo: N. M. Press, 1941.

Meilhac, Henri, and Ludovic Halévy. *Carmen.* Composed by Georges Bizet. New York: Dover Publications, 1989.

Menocal, María Rosa. *The Ornament of the World: How Muslims, Jews, and Christians Created a Culture of Tolerance in Medieval Spain.* New York: Back Bay, 2002.

Mérimée, Prosper. *Carmen.* Paris: Michel Lévy Frères, 1875.

———. *Carmen.* Paris: F. Rouff, 1927.

———. *Carmen.* Paris: Gallimard, 2000.

———. *Carmen, la novella.* Philadelphia: Henry Altemus, 1899.

———. *Carmen, la novella.* 1845. London: The Folio Society, 1949.

———. *Carmen: The Story of Bizet's Opera.* Adapt. Robert Lawrence. Illus. Alexandre Serebriakoff. New York: Metropolitan Opera Guild, 1938.

———. *Chronique du règne de Charles IX.* Paris: 1829.

———. *Chronique du règne de Charles IX.* Paris: Calmann-Lévy, 1890.

———. *Columba.* Paris: Charpentier, 1862.

———. *Columba and Carmen.* London: Heinemann, 1945.

———. *Études sur l'histoire romane.* Paris: V. Magen, 1844.

———. *Une Femme est un diable.* 1825.

———. *Lettres d'Espagne. 1830–1833.* Paris: Editions Lemarget, 1927.

———. *Lettres Libres à Stendhal.* Paris: Arléa, 1992.

———. *Mosaïque.* Paris: Fournier Jeune, 1833.

———. *Notes d'un voyage en Corse.* Paris: Fournier Jeune, 1840.

———. *Notes d'un voyage dans le midi de la France.* Paris: Fournier, 1835.

———. *Oeuvres Complètes.* Paris: Champion, 1881.

———. *Le Théâtre de Clara Gazul.* Paris: Calmann Lévy, 1898.

Millet, Claude. *Le Déspote oriental.* Paris: Maisonneuve et Larose, 2001.

Mirecourt, Eugène de. *Lola Montés.* Paris: Gustave Havard, 1857.

———. *Mérimée.* Paris: G. Havard, 1859.

Mitchell, Timothy. *Colonizing Egypt.* Cambridge: Cambridge University Press, 1988.

Montes, Lola. *Aventures de la célébre danseuse racontées par elle-même.* Paris: chez tous les Libraires, 1847.

Montesquieu, Charles de Secondat. *Persian Letters.* London, 1892.

Moreno, Casado José. *Los gitanos desde su penetración en España su condición social y Juridica.* Granada, 1949.

Moussa, Sarga. *Géographie des orientales.* Paris: Maisonneuve et Larose, 2001.

Mulouk, Qamar El (Edwina Nearing). *The Mystery of the Ghawazi.* Habibi III. 1984.

Nerval, Gerard de. *Journey to the Orient.* Trans. Norman Glass. New York: New York University Press, 1972.

Neruda, Pablo. *Toro.* Poem presented at the Congrés des Intellectuels pour la Paix, read 27 October 1960.

Neuville, J. *Les Joyeuses dames de Paris. Le réveil de Paris, mabille.* Paris: chez tous les Libraires, 1867.

Northcott, Richard. *Bizet: A Sketch of His Life and Compositions, and a Record of His Opera "Carmen."* London: Press Printers, 1916.

Ochsenwald, William, and Sydney Nettleton Fisher. *The Middle East: A History.* New York: McGraw Hill, 2003.

Ohanian, Armen. *The Dancer of Shamahka.* Trans. Rose Wilder Lane. New York: E. P. Dutton, 1923.

Oliver, Henry Stuart. *Paris Days and Evenings.* London: T. Fisher Unwin, 1896.

Pagels, Elaine. *The Gnostic Gospels.* New York: Random House, 1979.

Pamuk, Orhan. *My Name Is Red.* New York: Vintage Books, 2001.

Parker, D. C. *Georges Bizet: His Life and Works.* Harper, 1926.

Parouty, Michel. *L'Opéra-Comique.* Paris: Asa Editions, 1998.

Parry, J. H. *The Spanish Seaborne Empire.* London: Hutchinson, 1966.

Pater, Walter. *The Works of Walter Pater: Miscellaneous Studies.* London: Macmillan, 1901.

Payne, Robert. *The Civil War in Spain, 1936–1939.* New York: Putnam, 1962.

Picasso, Pablo. *Écrits.* Paris: Reunion des musée nationaux, 1989.

Picasso, Pablo, with José Bergamín. Exhibition Catalogue for *Guernica,* 1937, Barcelona. *Toros y Toreros.*

Picasso, Pablo, Prosper Mérimée, and Louis Aragon. *La Carmen des Carmens*. Paris: Editeurs, 1949, 1964.

Pigot, Charles. *Georges Bizet et son oeuvre*. Paris: 1886.

Piot, Christine, and L. Bernadac. *Picasso, Les Écrits*. Paris: Gallimard, 1989.

Pirenne, Henri. *Mohammed & Charlemagne*. London: Allen & Unwin, 1939.

Pizzigoni, Davide. *Carmen*. New York: Abbeville Press, 2002.

Pohren, Donald. *The Art of Flamenco*, Jerez de la Frontera: Spain Jerez Industrial, 1962.

———. *Lives and Legends of Flamenco*. Madrid: Society of Spanish Studies, 1964.

Poole, Sophia Lane. *The Englishwoman in Egypt: Letters from Cairo, Written during a Residence There in 1842*. London: Charles Knight, 1844–1846.

Pradels, Octave. *30 Ans de café concert*. Paris: Societé d'Édition, n.d.

Prieto-Moreno, Francísco. *Granada*. Barcelona: Noguer, 1963.

Proust, Marcel. *Swann's Way*. New York: Modern Library, 1928.

Pushkin, Alexander. *Poems*. Boston: Cupples and Hurd, 1888.

Quintana, Bertha B., and Lois Gray Floyd. *Que Gitano!* Prospect Heights, IL: Waveland Press, 1986.

Raeburn, Michael. *The Chronicle of Opera*. London: Thames and Hudson, 1998.

Redmond, Layne. *When the Drummers Were Women*. New York: Random House, 1997.

Richardson, James. *Travels in the Great Desert of Sahara in the Years of 1845 and 1846*. London: Richard Bentley, 1848.

Richardson, John. *A Life of Picasso*. New York: Alfred A. Knopf, 2007.

———. *A Life of Picasso: The Cubist Rebel, 1907–1916*. Vol. 2. New York: Random House, 1990.

———. *A Life of Picasso: The Cubist Rebel, 1888–1906*. Vol. 1. New York: Random House, 1991.

Roberts, Samuel. *The Gypsies, Their Origin, Continuance and Destination*. London: Longman, 1836.

Robinson, David. *Muslim Societies in African History: New Approaches to African History*. Boston: Cambridge University Press, 2004.

Romi. *Petite Histoire des cafés concerts Parisiens*. Paris: Editions Chilry, 1950.

Rosaldo, Michelle, and Louise Lamphere. *Women, Culture and Society*. Stanford: Stanford University Press, 1974.

Ross, Dorien. *Returning to A*. San Francisco: City Lights, 1995.

Royce, Anya Peterson. *The Anthropology of Dance*. London: Dance Books, 2002.

Rubenstein, Richard E. *Aristotle's Children: How Christians, Muslims, and Jews Rediscovered Ancient Wisdom and Illuminated the Dark Ages*. New York: Harcourt, 2003.

Ruby, Pechon de, aka Gentilhomme de Breton. *La Vie généreux des gueux, mercelots et Boesmiens*. 1596. Paris: Stendhal et cie, 1927.

Russell, Frank D. *Picasso's Guernica: The Labyrinth of Narrative and Vision*. Montclair, NJ: Allenheld & Schram, 1979.

Sabartés, Jaime. *Á los toros avec Picasso*. Monte Carlo: André Sauret, Éditeur, 1961.

Sachar, Abram Leon. *A History of the Jews*. New York: Alfred A. Knopf, 1955.

Said, Edward. *Orientalism*. London: Routledge & Kegan Paul, 1978.

Saint Éxupery, Antoine de. *Le Petit Prince*. Paris: Gallimard, 1946.

Sales Mayo, Francísco de. *Los Gitanos, su historia, sus costumbres, su dialecto*. Madrid, 1869.

Sand, George. *Consuelo*. Boston: W. D. Ticknor, 1847.

Saunders, A. C. de C. M. *A Social History of Black Slaves and Freedmen in Portugal, 1441–1551*. Cambridge: Cambridge University Press, 1981.

Schreiner, Claus, ed. *Flamenco. Gypsy Dance and Music from Andalusia*. Portland: Amadeus Press, 1985.

Shandler, Jeffrey, and Beth S. Wenger, eds. *Encounters with the "Holy Land": Place, Past and Future in American Jewish Culture.* Hanover: University Press of New England, 1997.

Simson, Walter. *History of the Gypsies.* London, 1865.

Sklar, Deidre. *Dancing with the Virgin: Body and Faith in the Fiesta of Tortugas, New Mexico.* Berkeley: University of California Press, 2001.

Somerset-Ward, Richard. *L'Histoire de l'opéra.* Paris: Editions de la Martinière, 1991.

Sontag, Susan. *On Photography.* New York: Farrar, Straus and Giroux, 1973.

Spivak, Gayatri. *Can the Subaltern Speak? Reflections on the History of an Idea*, ed. Rosalind Morris. New York: Columbia University Press, 2010.

St. John, Bayle. *Village Life in Egypt.* New York: Amo Press, 1973.

Starkey, Paul, and Janet Starkey, eds. *Travellers in Egypt.* London: Tauris, 2001.

Starkie, Walter. *Cervantes and the Gypsies.*

———. *Don Gypsy. Raggle-Taggle: Adventures with a Fiddle in Barbary, Andalusia and La Mancha.* London: J. Murray, 1956.

———. *In Sara's Tents.* London: J. Murray, 1953.

———. *A Musician's Journey through Time and Space.* Geneva: Edisili, 1958.

———. *The Road to Santiago.* New York: E. P. Dutton, 1957.

———. *Scholars and Gypsies: An Autobiography.* London: J. Murray, 1963.

———. *Spanish Raggle Taggle: Adventures with a Fiddle in North Spain.* London: J. Murray, 1934.

Steingrass, Gerhard. *Sociologiá del cante flamenco.* Jerez: Centro Andaluz de Flamenco, 1993.

———. *Sobre flamenco y flamencología.* Sevilla: Signatura Ediciones de Andalucía, 1998.

Stella, Alessandro. *Histoires d'esclaves dance la peninsule iberique.* Paris, 2000.

Straton, Suzanne L. *Spain, Espagne, Spanien: Foreign Artists Discover Spain 1800–1900.* New York: The Equitable Gallery/The Spanish Institute, 1993.

Sturman, Janet L. *Zarzuela: Spanish Operetta, American Stage.* Urbana: University of Illinois Press, 2000.

Thomas, Helen. *The Body, Dance and Cultural Theory.* New York: Palgrave Macmillan, 2003.

Thompson, Robert Farris. *African Art in Motion.* Los Angeles: University of California Press, 1974.

———. *Flash of the Spirit: African & Afro-American Art & Philosophy.* New York: Vintage Books, 1983.

———. *Tango: The Art History of Love.* New York: Vintage Books, 2005.

Thornton, Lynn. *Picturing the Middle East: A Hundred Years of European Orientalism: A Symposium.* New York; Dahesh Museum of Art, 1996.

Vaca, Cabeza de. *Adventures in the Unknown Interior of America.* Albuquerque: University of New Mexico Press, 1961.

Vaillant, Jean Alexandre. *Grammaire dialogues et vocabulaire de la langues des Bohémiens ou Cigains.* Paris, 1868.

———. *Les Romes: histoire vraie des vrais Bohémiens.* Paris: E. Dentu, 1857.

Vaillat, Léandre. *Ballets de l'Opéra de Paris.* Paris: Co. Française des arts Graphique, 1943.

Van Vechten, Carl. *The Music of Spain.* New York: A. A. Knopf, 1918.

Vega, José Blas, and Mañuel Ruiz. *Diccionario enciclopédico ilustrado del flamenco.* Madrid: Editorial Cinterco, 1988.

Verba, Cynthia. *Music and the French Enlightenment: Reconstruction of a Dialogue, 1750–1764.* Oxford: Clarendon Press, 1993.

Vexliard, Alexandre. *Introduction à la sociologie du vagabondage.* Paris, 1956.

Les Vies des femmes célèbres de France. Paris: Grangé, 1766.

Ville, Frans de. *Tziganes.* Brussels: Office de Publicité, 1956.

Volney. *Voyage en Syrie et Égypte.* Paris: Desenne, 1787.

Weinzweig, K. Meira. *Border Trespasses. The Gypsy Mask and Carmen Amaya's Flamenco*

Dance. Unpublished Dissertation. Temple University, 1995.

Williams, Gretchen, *Buen Metál de Voz: The Calé and Flamenco Cante Jondo.* Unpublished Master's Thesis. The University of New Mexico, Albuquerque, 2002.

Williams, Simon. *Richard Wagner and Festival Theater.* Westport, CT: Greenwood Press, 1994.

Wolff, Stephane. *Un demi-siècle d'opéra-comique (1900–1950).* Paris: Éditions Andre Bonne, 1953.

Wood, Melusine. Historical Dances. London: C. W. Beaumont, 1952.

Yonge, Charlotte M. *The Story of the Christians and Moors of Spain.* London: Macmillan, 1879.

Yors, Jan. *Tziganes.* Paris: Phébus, 1990.

Journals and Book Chapters

Afzal-Khan, Fawzia. "Where Are the Muslim Feminist Voices? A Question Asked in September 2001." *Drama Review* 46, no. 1 (Sept. 2006): 5–9.

Alberti, Raphael. "Picasso le rayon interrompue," *Toros y Toreros.* Paris: Cercle d'Art. (n.d.)

Aviator. "Otero dans les Airs." *La Livraison Illustré* (24 Aug. 1895).

Baker, Evan. "The Scenic Designs for the First Performances of Bizet's *Carmen.*" *19th-Century Music* XIII, no. 3 (Spring 1990): 230–42.

Barr, Alfred H. "Minotauromachy, a private allegory," in *Picasso. Fifty Years of His Art.* New York: MoMA, 1946.

Bauer, Henry. "Mme. Galli-Marié." . . . *Paris* (7 May 1887). "*Carmen 1875–1969*: Dossier d'Oeuvre," Bibliothèque Nationale de l'Opéra collection, Paris.

Benjamin, Walter. "Paralipomena to 'On the Concept of History.' Theses on the Philosophy of History," *Illuminations. Essays and Reflections.* New York: Schocken Books, 2007; 1968. 253–64.

———. "Paris, the Capital of the Nineteenth Century." *The Arcades Project.* Cambridge: Harvard University Press, 1999. 3–13.

Bennahum, Ninotchka Devorah. "Flamenco." *Oxford International Encyclopedia of Dance.* 1998.

———. "Flamenco Dance. Dancing in the Deserts of Spain and New Mexico." In *The Living Dance: An Anthology of Essays on Movement and Culture,* ed. Judith Chazin-Bennahum. Dubuque: Kendall/Hunt, 2007. 61–90.

Berlioz, Hector. "Théâtre-Lyrique," *Journal des Débats,* 8 October 1863.

Bernadac, Marie-Laure. "1933–1940 Del Mintaoro à Guernica." *Pablo Picasso: Toros y Toreros.* Paris: Musée Picasso, 1993.

Bizet, Georges. "Causerie Musicale." *La Révue Nationale et Etrangère* (3 Aug. 1867).

———. "Lettres. Impressions de Rome, 1857–1872." In *La Commune,* 1871, ed. Louis Ganderax.

Boll, Andre. "Carmen et ses decorateurs." 1959. "*Carmen 1875–1969*: Dossier d'Oeuvre," Bibliothèque Nationale de l'Opéra collection, Paris.

Bourdieu, Pièrre. "The Berber House." *The Anthropology of Space and Place.* Oxford: Blackwell, 2003. 131–41.

Bourgeis, J. "Carmen à l'Opéra." *Engelbert Magazine* (March 1960). "*Carmen 1875–1969*: Dossier d'Oeuvre," Bibliothèque Nationale de l'Opéra collection, Paris.

Breton, André. *La Révolution Surréaliste* (1 Dec. 1924): 4–5.

Breval, Lucienne. "Carmen." *Paris-Soir* (13 Apr. 1925). "*Carmen 1875–1969*: Dossier d'Oeuvre," Bibliothèque Nationale de l'Opéra collection, Paris.

Buonaventura, Wendy. "Images of Women in Arabic Dance." *Dancing Times* (Jul. 1997): 925.

Busser, Henri. Letter about the "new Carmen." 1959. "*Carmen 1875–1969*: Dossier d'Oeuvre," Bibliothèque Nationale de l'Opéra collection, Paris. T.s.

Bussy, Charles de. "Caroline Otero." *Femme de France* (18 Mar. n.d.).

"*Carmen*, ciudadana de Europe." *Ballet 2000 2* (Aug. 1992).

Carrau, Gaston. "1000th Carmen." *La Liberté* (26 Dec. 1904). "*Carmen 1875–1969:* Dossier d'Oeuvre," Bibliothèque Nationale-Opéra collection, Paris.

Casares, Aurelia Martin. "Free and Black Africans in Granada in the Time of the Spanish Renaissance." In *Black Africans in Renaissance Europe*, ed. T. F. Earle and K. J. P. Lowe. Cambridge, UK: Cambridge University Press, 2005. 247–60.

Case, Sue Ellen. "Classic Drag: The Greek Creation of Female Parts," in "Staging Gender," *Theater Journal* 37, no. 3 (October 1985):

Chantavoine, Jean. "Quelques Inédits de Georges Bizet." *Le Ménestrel*, 4 Aug.–22 Sept. 1933.

———. "Le Centenaire de Georges Bizet." *Le Ménestrel*, 21–28 October, 1938.

Chareau, Ludovic. *La Gitana, Grand Opéra en 4 Actes et 7 Tableaux, Paroles de M. Ludovic Chareau, Musique de M. Étienne Rey. (Bordeaux, Grand-Théatre, 22 Février 1864).* Bordeaux: impr. de E. Bissei, 1864.

Charpentier, Gustave. "La Millième de *Carmen*." *Le Figaro*, 23 Dec. 1904.

———. "La Millième de 'Carmen.'" "*Carmen 1875–1969:* Dossier d'Oeuvre," Bibliothèque Nationale de l'Opéra collection, Paris.

Coomaraswamy, Ananda K. "Akimcanna: Self-Naughting." In *New Indian Antiquary*. Vol. 3. Bombay, 1940.

Curtiss, Mina K. "Bizet, Offenbach, and Rossini." *Musical Quarterly* (July 1954).

Curzon, Henri de. "Carmen à Nîmes." *Le Théâtre* (May 1901).

Daley, Suzanne. "Roma Test Europe's 'Open Policies'." *New York Times*, 17 Sept. 2010: 1.

Daix, Pièrre. "La Tauromachie vue par Goya et Picasso." *L'Oeil*, August, 1982.

"Danse des Femmes." *Le Monde*, 10 Jan. 1998: 55.16.

Dedet, Christian. "Minotaurs et Taureaux," *Corrida* 12 (Mar. 1982): 33–37.

Delage, A. "Les Saintes Maries de la Mer." *Études Tziganes* (Oct. 1956).

Deleuze, Gilles, and Félix Guattari. "1227: Treatise on Nomadology—the War Machine." *A Thousand Plateaus: Capitalism and Schizophrenia.* Minneapolis: University of Minnesota Press, 1987. 351–423.

Duhamel, C. "Le Palais de la danse à l'exposition de 1900." *Le Théâtre* (Nov. 1899): 1.

Erlanger, Steven. "Expulsion of Roma Raises Questions in France." *New York Times*, 20 Aug. 2010: A4.

Fauré, Gabriel. "La Millième Réprésentation de *Carmen*." *Le Figaro*, 23 Dec. 1904.

"Folk Heritage. Arts of the Islamic World." *ART* 23 (1993).

Fuchs, Dale. "Tobacco Industry Stressed in Europe: Days Numbered for Carmen's 'Heirs?'" *New York Times*, 18 Dec. 2004. Web. 17 Sept. 2010.

Furman, Nelly. "The Languages of Love in *Carmen*." *Reading Opera*. Eds. Arthur Groos and Roger Parker. Princeton: Princeton University Press, 1988.

Galabert, Edmond. "La Maladie et la mort de Bizet." *La Passant* (Feb. 1888).

Gaudin, Colette. "Introduction." *On Poetic Imagination and Reverie.* Putnam, CT: Spring Publications, 2005. liv–lv.

Gautier, Théophile. "Danses Espagnoles." *La Presse*, 24 July 1837.

———. "Le Désert." *La Presse*, 16 Dec. 1844.

———. "Nostalgie d'obélisques," *La Presse*, 4 Aug. 1851.

———. "Un Nuit de Cléopâtre." *La Presse*, 29–30 Nov. 1838.

Godechot, Jacques. "La Course Maltaise le long des côtes barbaresques à la fin du XVIII siècle." *Revue Africaine* (1952): 105–13.

Gondreourt, M. de (Lieutenant aux saphis d'Oran). "Études sur les Moeurs des Arabes-Bédouins." *Le Constitutionnel* (12 Aug. 1838).

Gounod, Charles. "Lettres à Georges Bizet." *Révue de Paris* 6, no. 15 (Dec. 1899).

Groos, Arthur. "Deconstructive Postscript," *Reading Opera*. *New York Times Book Review*, 1 January 1989.

Haddad, Leila. "Maghreb et moyen-orient. La danse des mille et une nuits." *Dancing Times* (July 1997).

Halévy, Ludovic. "La Millième réprésentation de *Carmen*." *Le Théâtre* (Jan. 1905).

Harris, Rivkah. "Women in the Ancient Near East." *The Interpreter's Dictionary of the Bible*. Nashville: Abingdon, 1976.

Henderson, W. J. "Emma Calvé," *New York Times* (6 December 1896).

Holff, Cornelius. "La Señora Pepita Oliva." *Chronique des Théâtres* (31 July 1892).

Hughes, Robert. "Anatomy of a Minotaur." *Time*. 1 Nov. 1971. Accessed 17 Sept. 2010. http://www.time.com/time/magazine/article/0,9171,905485,00.html.

Jahyer, Félix. "Lola Gomez." *Camers Artistiques* (11 Feb. 1880).

Jakobsen, Thorkild. "Primitive Democracy in Ancient Mesopotamia." *Journal of Near Eastern Studies* 2, no. 3 (July 1943).

Juana. "From the High Atlas to the Desert's Shore." *Dance Magazine* (Dec. 1951): 17–19, 43–46.

Julien, Adolphe. "Revue Musicale." 20 Feb. 1898. "*Carmen 1875–1969:* Dossier d'Oeuvre," Bibliothèque Nationale de l'Opéra collection, Paris.

Klein, John W. "Bizet's Admirers and Detractors." *Music and Letters* 19 (Oct. 1938).

———. "Bizet and Wagner." *Music and Letters* 28 (Jan. 1947).

———. "Nietzsche and Bizet." *Musical Quarterly* 9, no. 4 (Oct. 1925).

Kramer, Samuel Noah. "The Weeping Goddess: Sumerian Prototypes of the *Mater Dolorosa.*" *Biblical Archaeologist* 46, no. 2 (Spring 1983).

Lawrence, T. E. "The Changing East." In *Oriental Assembly*, ed. A. W. Lawrence. London: Williams and Norgate, 1939. 71–102.

Lémoine, Gustav, and Paul de Kock. *La Bohémienne de Paris, Théâtre de la Gaité.* 24 Feb. 1844.

Leymarie, Jean. "Picasso, the New Ulysses." *Picasso and the Mediterranean*. Denmark: Humlebaek, 1996. 21.

Marino, Brigitte. "Cafés et cafetiers des damas aux XVIIIe et XIXe siècles." *Révue du Monde Musulman* 75–76 (1995): 275–94.

Marsan, Eugene. "Carmen, Théâtre de Clara Gazul de Prosper Mérimée." 31 Dec. 1927. "*Carmen 1875–1969:* Dossier d'Oeuvre," Bibliothèque Nationale de l'Opéra collection, Paris.

Mérimée, Prosper. "Carmen." *La Révue de deux Mondes* (1 Oct. 1845).

———. "Encore quelques mots sur l'attitude de l'Espagne." *Bulletin Hispanique* (1899).

———. "Lettres à un inconnue." *La Revue des deux mondes.* Paris, 1829.

———. "Des mythes primitives: *Le peuple primitif, sa réligion, son histoire et sa civilization.*" *Révue Contemporaine* 2 (1 Sept. 1855): 5–21.

———. "Voyages archéologiques en France." *Révue de Paris.* Paris, 1829.

Michelet, Jules. "Paris, the Capital of the Nineteenth Century." *The Arcades Project* (Cambridge: Harvard University Press, 1999).

Montepin, Xavier de, and Jules Dormay. *La Gitana at the Théâtre Beaumarchais*, 22 Dec. 1869.

Nietzsche, Friedrich. "The Case against Wagner." Leipzig: Verlag von C. G. Neumann, 1888.

Niles, Doris. "El Duende." *Dance Perspectives* (1966).

Nochlin, Linda. "The Imaginary Orient." *Art in America* (May 1983): 118–31, 187–91.

Nozière. "Otero," *Le Théâtre* (28 July 1904).

"Origin and Wanderings of the Gypsies." *Edinburgh Review* (July 1878): 117–46.

Peyrat, Alphonse. "Paris, 19 Juillet." *La Presse*, 20 July 1837.

Peyriguere, Jean. "Poesie et danse dans une tribu berbere du moyen-atlas." *Études et Documents Berbères* 15–16 (1998): 219–48.

Peyser, Herbert F. "For Deeper Enjoyment of *Carmen.*" *Opera News* (15 Mar. 1943): 18.

Piot, Christine. "Picasso and the Practice of Writing." *Picasso: Collected Writings.* Paris: Editions Gallimard, 1989.

Ponthierry. "Chez Mme. Emma Calvé." *La Liberté* (26 Dec. 1904). "*Carmen 1875–1969*: Dossier d'Oeuvre," Bibliothèque Nationale de l'Opéra collection, Paris.

Pougin, Arthur. "La Légende de la chute de *Carmen* et la mort de Bizet." *Le Ménestrel* 69, no. 15 (Feb. 1903).

"Quand Jane Enfant vocalisant, on fermait les fenêtres." n.d. "*Carmen 1875–1969*: Dossier d'Oeuvre," Bibliothèque Nationale de l'Opéra collection, Paris.

Rabinowitz, Peter J. "Singing for Myself: 'Carmen' and the Rhetoric of Musical Resistance." *Audible Traces: Gender, Identity, & Music.* Zurich: Carciofoli, 1999: 133–52.

Reverdy, Pièrre. "Pablo Picasso et son oeuvre." *Nord-Sud, Self Défence et autres écrits sur l'art et la poésie (1917–1926), Oeuvres Complètes.* Paris: Flammarion, 1975.

"Revue Musicale, Théâtre de l'Opéra-Comique, with Galli-Marié." *La Liberté*, 15 Dec. 1890. "*Carmen 1875–1969*: Dossier d'Oeuvre," Bibliothèque Nationale de l'Opéra collection, Paris.

Rorhlich-Leavitt, Ruby. "State Formation in Sumer and the Subjugation of Women." *Feminist Studies* 6, no. 1 (Spring 1980).

Rougement, F. de. *Le peuple primitif, sa réligion, son histoire et sa civilization, Révue Contemporaine* 2 (1 September 1855).

Sadgrove, Philip. "Travellers' Rendezvous and Cultural Institutions in Muhammad 'Ali's Egypt." In *Travellers in Egypt*, ed. Paul and Janet Starkey. 257–67.

Saint-Victor, Paul de. *Le Moniteur.* 3 March 1875.

Saleh, Magda. "The Ghawazi of Egypt: A Preliminary Report." *Arabesque* 19, no. 2 (July/Aug. 1993): 8–12.

Scherer, Barrymore Laurence. "Prosper Mérimée, Storyteller." *Opera News* (14 Mar. 1987): 32–35.

Schneider, Louis. "Le Théâtre en Provence. Carmen aux arènes de Nîmes." *Le Théâtre* (12 May 1901).

Scribe, Léo. *La Bohémienne ou l'Amérique en 1779, Théâtre de Madame.* 1 June 1829.

Senneville, Charles de. "Les Premières." *La Comédie* (14 March 1875). "*Carmen 1875–1969*: Dossier d'Oeuvre," Bibliothèque Nationale de l'Opéra collection, Paris.

"Les sept plaisirs capitaux de l'Orient." *Qantara: Magazine des Cultures Arabe et Méditerranéenne* 40 (été 2001): n.p. Paris: L'Institut du Monde Arabe.

Serna, Ramon Gomez de la. "Le Toréador de la Peinture." *Cahiers d'art* (1932) nn. 3–5.

Sevilla, Paco. "Flamenco: The Early Years." *Guitar & Lute* (Nov. 1982): 24–27.

Should, I. "Preface." *Dissertation on the Gipsies Being an Historical Enquiry, concerning the Manner of Life, Œconomy, Customs and Conditions of These People in Europe, and Their Origin.* London: G. Bigg, P. Elmsley, and T. Cadell in the Strand, and J. Sewell, in Cornhill, 1787. i.

Siegel, Marcia B. "Modern Dance." In *The Living Dance. An Anthology of Essays on Movement and Culture*, ed. Judith Chazin-Bennahum. Dubuque, Iowa: Kendall-Hunt, 2007.

Takanori, Nagai. "Picasso and the Minotaur." *Picasso: The Love and the Anguish, the Road to Guernica.* Kyoto: The National Museum of Modern Art, 1995.

Taymanova, Marianna. "Alexandre Dumas in Egypt: Mystification or Truth." In *Travellers in Egypt*, ed. Paul and Janet Starkey.

Teneuille, Marie-Dominique de, ed. "Manet/Velázquez. La manière espagnole au XIXe siècle." Paris: Musée d'Orsay, 16 Sept. 2002–5 Jan. 2003.

Tiersot, Julien. "Bizet and Spanish Music." *Musical Quarterly* 2, no. 4 (Oct. 1925).

Tzara, Tristan. "Picasso et la Poésie." *Commentari* 4, no. 3 (July–Sept. 1953): 181–203.

————. *Surréalisme au service de la révolution* 4 (1932): 20.

Van Loo, Esther. "La Veritable Carmen." *Musica fur* (1960). "*Carmen 1875–1969*: Dossier d'Oeuvre," Bibliothèque Nationale de l'Opéra collection, Paris.

Westermann, W. L. "The Castanet Dancers of Arsinoe." *Journal of Egyptian Archaeology* (1924): 135.

Wilder, Victor. "Georges Bizet." *Le Ménestral*, 4–18 July, 1875.

Secondary Journals, Encyclopedias, and Materials

"Bizet, Georges." *Encyclopaedia Britannica*. 11th ed. 1911.

"Bizet, Georges." *New Encyclopaedia Britannica*, vol. 2. 1092–93.

"Bizet, Georges." *The New Grove Dictionary of Music and Musicians*. Washington, DC: Grove's Dictionaries of Music, 1980.

Chronique du Toreo Illustré. 1800s.

Clément, Felix, and Pièrre Larousse. "*Carmen and Bizet*." *Dictionnaire Lyrique*.

David, Félicien. "*Le Désert*. Dossier d'Oeuvre." Bibliothèque Nationale de l'Opéra, Paris.

L'Echo Taurin. 1930s.

Encyclopedia Judaica.

Encyclopedie de l'Histoire.

Encyclopedia of Islam.

Flamenco.

Le Furet Nîmois. 1870s.

Gazette de Nîmes. 1870s.

Jaleo.

Journal of the Gypsy Lore Society. London, 1888.

"Mithraism." *Encyclopaedia Britannica*, 11th ed. 1911.

La Muleta. 1890s.

Musée Picasso. Billets d'entrée à la corrida (42 pieces), 1926–1963; Écrits de Picasso, 1905–1962, B/1 a B/4; Classeur 6, Guillaume Apollinaire (50 letters), 1905–1916; Classeur 6, Louis Aragon (25 letters), 1919–1953; Classeur 10, Georges Bataille (1 letter), 1961; Classeur 13, José Bergamín (3 letters), 1952; Classeur 14, Madame Bizet (1 letter), 1948; Classeur 84, Michel Leiris (80 letters), 1927–1958; Classeur 14, Mañuel Ortíz (14 letters), 1918–1944; Classeur 165, Igor Stravinsky (12 letters), 1917–1962; Dossier de Provence, 1923–1969, E.14; Lettres reçue et documentation sur la corrida, 1917–1963, A.18.

Nîmes Musée des Cultures Taurines. 1957. E.14.

Nîmes-Taurin. 1900s.

The New Grove Dictionary of Music. Washington, DC: Grove's Dictionaries of Music, 1980.

Revue Encyclopedique. London: Treuttel and Wurtz, 1819.

Revue de Musicologie. 1976.

Revue Tauromarchique Illustré. Nîmes. 1899. Microfiche.

Scott, M. C. Rochfort. *Voyage en Egypt*.

Shaler, W. *Sketches of Algiers*.

Sol y Sombra. (Southern French bullfighting reviews.)

Le Toréador. 1800s.

Le Toreo. Franco-Espagnol. 1900s.

Toros. 1900s.

Toros et Toreros. 1900s.

Toros-Revue. 1890s.

Trollope, Anthony. *Autobiography*. 1858.

Published and Recorded Orchestral Scores

Bizet, Georges. *L'Arlésienne Suite*. 1872. London: Decca, 1959.

————. *Carmen*. 1875. Paris: Éditions Choudens, 1875.

————. *Carmen* (Vocal score). Libretto by Henri Meilhac and Ludovic Halévy. Choudens, 1875.

————. *Carmen* (Orchestral score). 1875. Choudens, 1880.

———. *Carmen.* Perf. Stevens, Peerce, Merrill, Reiner. 1951. Naxos Digital Recording, 2009. CD.

———. *Carmen* (1875 Opéra-Comique version). Hollywood: Angel, 1970.

———. *Carmen*, Libretto (Chester, New York: G. Schirmer, 1959).

———. *Carmen*, suites 1 & 2. La Crosse, Wisconsin: Platinum Disc Co., 1971. CD.

———. *Carmen Suites.* Cond. Leopold Stowkowski. New York: Columbia Records, 1977.

———. *Carmen: Opéra en quatres actes.* 1875. Paris: Choudens, 1904.

———. *Carmen* (Opéra-Comique version). Perf. Orchestre National de Bordeaux-Aquitaine. Naxos Digital Recording, 2009. CD.

———. "*Carmen.* Dossier d'Oeuvre: 1875–1969." Bibliothèque Nationale de l'Opéra, Paris.

———. *Carmen.* "Partition Chant et Piano arranged by the author." n.d. Paris: Choudens.

———. *Djamileh.* Libretto by Louis Gallet. 1871.

———. *La Jolie Fille de Perth.* Libretto by J. H. Vernoy de Saint-Georges and Jules Adenis. 1866. Choudens, 1868.

———. "Partition Chant et Piano de Carmen Opéra-Comique." *Carmen.* 1875. Paris: Choudens, March 1875.

———. *Les Pecheurs de Pearles.* Perf. Fenice Theatre Orch. Naxos Digital Recording, 2008. CD.

———. *Symphony in C major.* 1855, 1871. Choudens, 1880.

Daudet, Alphonse. *L'Arlésienne.* Composed by Georges Bizet. Choudens, 1872.

Guiraud, Ernest. *Carmen.* Composed by Georges Bizet. 1871. Paris: Editions Choudens, 1871.

Meilhac, Henri, and Ludovic Halévy. *Carmen.* Composed by Georges Bizet. 1875. Librairie Théâtrale, Gerard Billaudot, ed., 1981.

———. *Carmen.* Composed by Georges Bizet. 1875. New York: Dover Publications, 1989.

Sarasate, Pablo. *Carmen: fantasie de concert pour violin et piano op. 25.* New York: C. Fisher, 1922.

Carmen Films and Stage Productions

Carmen. Dir. Cecil B. DeMille, 1915.

Blood and Sand. Dir. Fred Niblo, 1922.

The Loves of Carmen. Dir. Charles Vidor, 1948.

Carmen and Don José. Chor. Ruth Page, 1974.

Cante Gitano. Dir. Tony Gatlif, 1981.

Carmen. Dir. Carlos Saura. Chor. Antonio Gades, 1983.

Carmen Suite. Chor. Alberto Alonso, 1983.

Sevillanas, Dir. Carlos Saura. 1992.

Latcho Drom. Dir. Tony Gatlif. 1993.

Mondo. Dir. Tony Gatlif, 1995.

Flamenco. Dir. Carlos Saura. Chor. Gypsy dancers. 1995.

Gadjo Dilo. Dir. Tony Gatlif, 1997.

Carmen. Dir. Francesco Rosi, 1999.

Vengo. Dir. Tony Gatlif, 2000.

Carmen. Chor. Salvador Tavora, stage production, 2001.

Carmen. Chor. Mats Ek. Cullberg Ballet, 2002.

Carmen. Chor. Roland Petit. Paris Opera Ballet, 2003.

The Car Man. Chor. Matthew Bourne. London: Adventures in Motion Pictures, 2003. Film.

Karmen Gei. Dir. Joseph Ramaka, 2005.

Exils. Dir. Tony Gatlif, 2004.

Carmen. Dir. Rafael Aguilar, stage production and film, 2005.

Carmen Hip Hopera. Dir. Robert Townsend, 2001.

Carmen Jones. Dir. Otto Preminger, 2001.

U-Carmen. Dir. Mark Dornford-May, 2007.

Index

Bizet, Georges, xii, xvi, 30, 31, 40–43, 32–67, 68, 135, 152, 154, 193, 194–195, 197–198, 213n15, 216n66; biographies of, 212n5; Jacques (son), 41; Jean (son), 38

body, 84–87; language of, 182; as moving archive, 178–193; Carmen's, 192

Bolero, 45, 59

Bonaparte, Napoleon, 132, 142, 146, 152, 210n34, 238n17

Borrows, George, xiv, 19–21, 25

braceo (flowering of arms in flamenco), 190–192

Braudel, Ferdinand, xvi, 74

Breton, André, 234n24

Bull, image of in art and bullfight, 54, 68, 70, 153, 160, 163, 164, 165, 166, 171, 172, 173, 174, 175, 177, 198

bullfighters (matadors): Cara Ancha, 172; Conchita Citron, 160; El Lagartijo, 172

bullfighting, xviii, 196; Picasso's interest in, 160, 161, 169

bullring, 155, 159, 160, 163, 164, 166, 167, 169, 171, 172, 173, 174, 177, 185. See also *corrida*

Butler, Judith, 199–201, 240n13

café cantante (singing café), 59, 137, 147, 171

Café d'Algiers, 141, 144

Café du Fleuve, 143, 147

Café sin Nombre, 147

café, flamenco, xvii; Middle Eastern, 133–151

Caliph, 237n2

Caló (Gypsy language), 15, 19

Calvé, Emma, 39, 215n44

Camara, Petra, 147

Cambrubi, Mariano, 148

Camp, Maxine du, 146, 152

Campbell, Joseph, 79

cantaor, 3, 176, 182, 184–185, 187, 192, 199–200

cante jondo (deep song), 59, 69, 92, 157, 167, 176, 187–188

cante, 5, 198–199

cantiga, 188

Carlos III, 139

Carmen (character), 2–8, 9–28, 68–70, 81–87,

135–137, 142, 151, 234n35; body of, xiv, 14, 83, 135, 192, 200–201, 202; as clairvoyant, 197; costume of, 197–198; as dancer of flamenco, 197; envisioned by Picasso, 153, 154, 155; as fantasy, 132–152; as femme fatale, 198; geography, 198, 202; as Gypsy, 136, 202; as healer, 197; Indian figure, 136; as Middle Eastern dancer, 198; as mythic being, 202; as nomad, 204; way of being, 202

Carmen (novella), xvi, 9–31, 20–21, 210n35

Carmen (opera): xii, 35–36, 40–44, 47–55, 57–65, 78–81, 142, 152, 206, 208n3; Carmen, representations of, 194–195, 205–206, 239n29–67; premiere cast of, 205–206; score of, 32–67, 212–213n6

Carmen Suite, 196

Carmen, choreography of: Alonso, 196, 239n5; Gades/Hoyos, 197; *Karmen Gei*, 195; Rosi, 198; Tavora, xii, 197

Carr, Raymond, 1

Caruso, Enrico, 39

Carvalho, Léon, 215–216n54

castanets, 51, 58–59, 72, 144, 158

Castro, Americo, xiii, xvi, 32, 72, 210n33

Catal Huyuk, 72, 74, 75

cave art, 69–92

ceremonial culture, 72

Charnon-Deutsch, Lou, xiv, 207

cigarettes, as theme in *Carmen*, 22–24, 44, 48–49, 148, 163, 170, 217n68

Cintron, Conchita (*toreadora*), 160

city, as urban space of performance, 138

Clébert, Jean-Paul, 138, 140

Clément, Catherine, xiv, 207

collage, Surrealist concept of, 168

compás (Flamenco rhythms), 58, 187–188, 199–200

corrida (bullring/arena/bullfight), 27, 29, 49, 51, 54–55, 78, 155, 159–160, 163–164, 166–167, 169, 171–174, 177, 196

Cortuja, La (tobacco factory), 48–49, 148, 217n72

Creation stories: Bible, 76–78, 84–87; *Enuma Elish*, 75–76; Genesis, 76–68, 86–87

153–155; masculine identity, 155, 165, 166, 170, 175, 176; Spanish exile of, 18, 155, 156, 158, 159

Pirenne, Henri, xiii, xvi, 181

portal/gateway, 181

Pragmaticas (laws against Spanish Gypsies), 103–118

Prix de Rome, 214n17

prophecy (fortune-telling), 75

prostitution, 72, 82–83

Proust, Marcel, 5–8, 215n50

Pyrénées, 17, 150

Quatre Gats (café), El, 166

Qu'ran, 84, 187, 190, 227n72

Rajasthan, India, 139, 151

Ramaka, Joseph, 195

raqs sharqi (dance of the Almehs), 145

rawi (reciter of poems), 192

religious ritual, 73

Revue des Deux Mondes, La, xiv, 13, 16, 20

Rives du Barada (café), 146

Rom, Gypsy people as, 140

Romanticism, 9–10, 20, 29, 35, 39, 42, 44, 58, 64, 68, 132–152

Rosi, Francesco, 198

sacred spaces: Garden of Eden, 77–78; Huluppu Tree, 76, 85–87; Inanna's garden, 85; Tree of life/creation, 85

sacrifice, 174

Sacromonte, 203

Saete, 187

Saïd, Edward, on Orientalism, 132–152

Saintes-Maries de la Mer (Gypsy pilgrimage site), 155, 180

Sara the Black, 226n55

Sarabande, 145

Sargent, John Singer, 155

Schéhérazade, 151

Schlegel, Frederich, 142

seclusion, architectural, 192

Seguidillas, xi, 45, 51, 58–60, 65

Seguidillas Boleras, xi, 147, 218n81, 220n5

Seguidillas Manchegas, xi

Sephardi Jews, xvii, 1, 2, 4–5, 178, 187, 188, 192, 238n22

Serpent, biblical, 86–87

Serral, Dolores, 147, 148

Sevillanas, 59–60

sexuality, female, 68–92

Siguiríya, xviii, 6, 59, 178–193, 197

slavery, 81–82, 127–131

Soleá, 2, 4, 6, 69, 198

space: feminine, 192; Islamic, 178–193; sacred, 192; secluded, 81–82; vital, 188

Spanish Civil War (1936–1939), xii, 175–177

Spanish culture, 153–177

Spivak, Gaytri, 132, 135, 137, 198

Steingrass, Gerhard, 147, 187

Stendhal, Henry Beyle, 10, 31, 209n11

Sufi musical influence, 184

Sumer, 73

Surrealism, 160, 162, 164, 166, 167, 168, 176, 234n24

Surrealist Manifesto (Breton), 162, 166

tambourine, 73, 146

Tariq, 'al, 211n37

Tavora, Salvador, xii, 197

Tobacco factory (La Cortuja), 48–49, 148, 217n72

Torah, 87

toreador, 49

totems, 85, 87, 170, 177

tourism, Middle Eastern, 132–152

trance (*duende*), 73

travel writers, romantic, 132–152, 238n17

Triana (Gypsy barrio), 17, 25–26, 217n78

Triana, Antonio el de, 147

Tricorne, Le (1919), 164

Tuareg tribe, 136, 144

Tzara, Tristan, 168

Tzigane (Gypsy), 140

Umayyad dynasty, 182, 184

umma (Muslim community), 182

Una illamada, 202, 240n10

Uruk, 85

veiling, 81–83, 144

Venus figures, 68–92

Wagner, Richard, 37, 40, 57, 61–62, 64–65,
   214n29, 214n34

Women: Neolithic, 73; labor of, 48–49

World's Fair (Paris, 1937), 175

Xino *barrio* (Gypsy quarter, Barcelona), 156, 157

Yahweh (God of the Kingdoms of Israel and
   Judah), 78

Zahra, Madinat 'al- (Cordoba), 179

Zambra (flamenco dance of Moorish origin), 59,
   187–188, 193

Zambra Mora, 231–232n44

zapata (shoe), 148

zapateado (footwork), xi, 200

zarzuela, 45

Ziryab, 184

Zuniga, 49–52

About the Author

Ninotchka Devorah Bennahum, choreographer, cultural historian, and native of New Mexico, is an Associate Professor of Theater and Dance at the University of California, Santa Barbara, and the author of *Antonia Merce*. In 1986, she received her doctorate in Performance Studies from New York University's Tisch School of the Arts. In 1991, she founded The Route 66 Dance Company to bring flamenco, modern, and ballet dancers and musicians together. She is a contributing editor for *Dance Magazine*. She writes on ballet and flamenco dance for *The Village Voice*, *The New York Times*, the *Albuquerque Journal*, and elsewhere and teaches dance history for American Ballet Theater's summer intensive program for pre-professional dancers in New York City. She lives in SoHo, New York.